THE
CELTIC BOOK
OF DAYS

*Ancient Wisdom for Each Day of the Year
from the Celtic Followers of Christ*

Also by Ray Simpson
Available from Anamchara Books

Celtic Christianity:
Deep Roots for a Modern Faith

Facing Death Now:
Practical Strategies for a Good Death

The Celtic Book of Days

*Ancient Wisdom for Each Day of the Year
from the Celtic Followers of Christ*

RAY SIMPSON

ANAMCHARA BOOKS

Copyright © 2017 by Anamchara Books, a Division of Harding House Publishing, Inc. All rights reserved. No part of this publication may be reproduced or transmitted in any form or by any means, electronic or mechanical, including photocopying, recording, taping, or any information storage and retrieval system, without permission from the publisher.

Anamchara Books
Vestal, NY 13850

Printed in the United States of America.

IngramSpark 2020 paperback ISBN: 978-1-62524-813-8
ebook ISBN: 978-1-937211-13-4

Another version of this book is published in the UK as Celtic Daily Light*. This is a revised and edited version of that book.*

Unless otherwise indicated, scripture quotations are from either the author's or the editor's own versions of the Bible verses.

Scripture quotations labeled cjb are taken from the Complete Jewish Bible, copyright 1998 by David H. Stern. Published by Jewish New Testament Publications, Inc. www.messianicjewish.net/jntp. Distributed by Messianic Jewish Resources Int'l. www.messianicjewish.net.
Scripture quotations labeled erv are from the Easy-to-Read Version, copyright ©2006 World Bible Translation Center.
Scripture quotations labeled esv are from the English Standard Version® Bible, copyright © 2001 by Crossway Bibles, a publishing ministry of Good News Publishers. The ESV® text has been reproduced in cooperation with and by permission of Good News Publishers. Unauthorized reproduction of this publication is prohibited. All rights reserved. The ESV® Bible (The Holy Bible, English Standard Version®) is adapted from the Revised Standard Version of the Bible, copyright Division of Christian Education of the National Council of the Churches of Christ in the U.S.A. All rights reserved.
Scripture quotations labeled gnb are from Good News Bible® (Today's English Version Second Edition, UK/British Edition). Copyright © 1992 British & Foreign Bible Society. Used by permission.
Scripture quotations labeled gnt are from the Good News Translation® (Today's English Version, Second Edition), copyright © 1992 American Bible Society. American Bible Society, 1865 Broadway, New York, NY 10023 (www.americanbible.org). Used by permission. All rights reserved.
Scripture quotations labeled gwt are from GOD'S WORD®, a copyrighted work of God's Word to the Nations. Quotations are used by permission. Copyright © 1995 by God's Word to the Nations. All rights reserved.
Scripture quotations labeled isv are from The Holy Bible: International Standard Version® Release 2.1. Copyright © 1996–2012, The ISV Foundation. All rights reserved internationally. Used by permission.
Scripture quotations labeled jb are from the Jerusalem Bible,
Scripture quotations labeled jbp are from J. B. Phillips, "The New Testament in Modern English," 1962 edition, published by HarperCollins. Used by permission.
Scripture quotations labeled nab are from the New American Bible, copyright © 1991, 1986, 1970. Confraternity of Christian Doctrine, Inc., Washington, DC. Used with permission. All rights reserved.
Scripture quotations labeled nasb are from the New American Standard Bible®, copyright © 1960, 1962, 1963, 1968, 1971, 1972, 1973,1975, 1977, 1995 by The Lockman Foundation (www.Lockman.org). Used by permission.
Scripture quotations labeled niv are from the Holy Bible, New International Version®, NIV®, copyright © 1973, 1978, 1984, 2011 by Biblica, Inc.® Used by permission. All rights reserved worldwide.
Scripture quotations labeled nlt are from the Holy Bible, New Living Translation, copyright © 1996, 2004, 2007 by Tyndale House Foundation. Used by permission of Tyndale House Publishers Inc., Carol Stream, Illinois 60188. All rights reserved.
Scripture quotations labeled nkjv are from the Holy Bible, New King James Version, copyright © 1982 by Thomas Nelson, Inc. Used with permission. All rights reserved.
Scripture quotations labeled nrsv are from the New Revised Standard Version Bible, copyright 1989, Division of Christian Education of the National Council of the Churches of Christ in the United States of America. Used by permission. All rights reserved.
Scripture quotations labeled rsv are from the Revised Standard Version of the Bible, copyright 1952 (2nd edition, 1971) by the Division of Christian Education of the National Council of the Churches of Christ in the United States of America. Used by permission. All rights reserved.

CONTENTS

Introduction	7
Daily Readings Throughout the Year	10
Who's Who in the Celtic World	380
Index of People	388
Index of Subjects	391
Index of Bible Texts	394
Sources and Acknowledgements	400

INTRODUCTION

The readings in this book are taken from the words of Celtic pilgrims, poets, or saints. In addition, however, I have included the sayings of people from many lands who are natural soul friends to the Celtic saints. Throughout the year, interweaving with the cycles of the church year and natural seasons, you'll find themes like these:

- God's guidance
- spiritual disciplines
- wisdom from the Desert Christians
- stories of saints and angels

Scripture Readings
Every book in the Bible is covered during the year. If you read the scripture readings for each date, by the end of the year, you will have worked your way through the entire Bible.

Easter Readings
Readers who wish to synchronize readings with Easter should start the Easter readings on April 1 if Easter Day falls after April 1. Count the number of days after April 1 that Easter falls. Choose the same number of days' readings from the period July 1 through 27, and use these from March 21 to April 1. (If Easter Day falls before April 1 transfer the right number of days' readings from March 21.) Readings about the Cross will then synchronize with Holy Week. This will allow you to synchronize the readings with all the church seasons without losing any readings chosen for a particular saint's anniversary, except for the anniversary of John Wesley on May 24. When you reach July, omit those readings you used in April; the *Book of Days* date will again correlate with the date in your diary.

Helpful Resources
At the back of the book, you'll find:

- **Who's Who in the Celtic World:** to help you keep track of the many individuals who inhabited the world of both the ancient and modern Celts.

- **Index of People:** so that you can find material on a favorite Celtic saint, particular author, or specific source.

- **Index of Subjects:** to help you find readings particularly linked to areas of interest or need, such as anger, healing, depression, evangelism.

- **Index of Bible Texts:** identifying the particular Bible passages used on each date.

- **Map:** showing key places mentioned in the book and the historical geographic location of the Celtic saints (for example, St. Petroch in the southwest and St. Mungo in Scotland).

Please note: The term "Celtic church" is used as shorthand for "churches in Celtic lands" within the one, universal Christian Church during the fifth to tenth centuries after Christ.

—*Ray Simpson*

WINTER

REACHING OUT

*Following God is a pilgrimage of faith.
The road ahead is only revealed as we step out in trust,
with God the Creator, the Son, and the Spirit before us.*

JANUARY 1 ✛ LET US GO FORWARD

Psalm 105:1–22; Joshua 1; Philippians 3:12–4:1

*Forgetting what lies behind,
and reaching forward to what lies ahead,
I press on toward the goal of God's upward call,
my high vocation in Christ.*
PHILIPPIANS 3:13–14

A new year. New resolutions. Yet, if we just go forward into this year with nothing but our own flimsy resolutions, they are likely to come to nothing. We can carry so much more forward with us into the new year if we respond to this Celtic call:

Let us go forth
in the goodness of our merciful Father,
in the gentleness of our brother Jesus,
in the radiance of the Holy Spirit,
in the faith of the apostles,
in the joyful praise of the angels,
in the holiness of the saints,

in the courage of the martyrs.
Let us go forth
in the wisdom of our all-seeing Father,
in the patience of our all-loving Brother,
in the truth of the all-knowing Spirit,
in the learning of the apostles,
in the gracious guidance of the angels,
in the patience of the saints,
in the self-control of the martyrs.
Such is the path of all servants of Christ,
the path from death to life eternal.
(FROM CELTIC FIRE, ROBERT VAN DER WEYER)

Whatever our regrets from last year, now we must put them behind us. We can release them into the hands of Christ, placing everything that lies ahead into his sure hands.

*Go before us in our pilgrimage of life.
Anticipate our needs, prevent our falling,
and lead us to our destiny.*

JANUARY 2 ✢ GOD'S WAY FOR A NEW YEAR

Psalm 105:23–45; Isaiah 31; Acts 19

Turn back to him whom you have utterly betrayed....
Everyone will throw away their self-made idols.
ISAIAH 31:6–7

A Church of Scotland minister has suggested that the Reformers of the fifteenth century made a mistake when they abolished the Christmas festival in Scotland. This created a vacuum, he suggests, which the pagan New Year's celebration of Hogmanay—now dominant in Scotland—could fill.

Whatever the truth of that, we can all glean something from the wisdom of Samson, the Celtic saint who did not see Christians and pagans as enemies. In doing so, we can celebrate the pagan festivals with a wider appreciation.

Samson arrived in Guernsey in the fifth century at the time of the New Year, which, his anonymous sixth-century biographer tells us, the islanders celebrated "according to a vile custom of their forbears." Samson made friends with these pagans. He included everyone, and he exuded a spirit of love, not judgment.

"Prudent in spirit," his biographer tells us, "to soften their hardness, he called them all together in one place and, God showing the way, a discussion took place for the removal of so great evils. Then all these folk, truly loving him, forswore these evils for his sake and truly promised to unreservedly follow his guidance." The children tended to run wild at this season, so Samson called them together also, gave each a little present, and told them in Jesus' name to change their ways.

His method was one of meeting, not denunciation. Confronted by his dedicated love, the people's hardness melted away. They threw away all that was empty, and the customs of generations were enriched.

May our celebration of the turning year's ancient festivals have that same richness!

Lord of the years, may we celebrate the good life past
and not forget the Giver of that life.
God of the call, may we contemplate the good road ahead
and walk along it, with love in our hearts, hand in hand with you.

JANUARY 3 ✤ INTO THE UNKNOWN WITH GOD

Psalm 106:1-23; Genesis 12; Acts 20

*The Lord said to Abram, "Leave your country, your people,
and your family's home, and go to the land I will show you."*
GENESIS 12:1

Home is not a place, it's a road to be traveled, we say,
our only defense is the armor of God,
with the Gospel of Peace our feet are shod;
so alone, alone,
we walk into the great unknown.
Mightier than fear is the Shield of Faith we bear;
our task is to lighten another's load,
and home for us is the great high road,
so alone, alone,
we walk into the great unknown.
Righteousness our Breastplate, the Belt of Truth we wear;
we go where conquering armies have trod,
but we carry the Sword of the Word of God;
so alone, alone,
we walk into the great unknown.
The seed of God's love in the hearts of folk we sow;
and stronger and taller that seed will grow,
that all creation the truth may know;
then alone, alone,
it will conquer the great unknown.
(FROM COLUMBA, THE PLAY WITH MUSIC)

*Lord, be within me to give me strength,
over me to protect me, beneath me to support me,
in front of me to be my guide,
behind me to prevent me falling away,
surrounding me to give me courage,
so that alone, alone,
naked of culture, family, and home,
I may walk into the great unknown.*

JANUARY 4 ❖ ON THE MOVE FOR GOD

Psalm 107:1–16; Joshua 2; Acts 21

*Some wandered in trackless wastes,
finding no path to a city where they could stay.
Hungry and thirsty, their soul fainted within them.
Then they cried to the Lord in their trouble,
and the Lord delivered them from their distress,
and led them by a straight way.*
PSALM 107:4–7

Therefore let us live by this principle, that we live as travelers on the road, as pilgrims, as guests of the world . . . singing with grace and power, "When shall I come and appear before the face of my God?"
COLUMBANUS

In the nineteenth century, Alexander Carmichael collected many journey prayers, some of which went back to the times when Celtic Christians such as Brendan traveled the seas in coracles. At the time when Carmichael was writing, travelers spent time before and after their voyages in small prayer places.

This spirituality continues in the different circumstances of modern life. It is reflected, for example, in this prayer, written and displayed in an airport chapel:

Home!
Relaxed, warm-welcomed,
full of ease, embraced and nourished.
Newly arrived from far away, yet home.
The words that sped me on my way
still echo in this foreign place.
The hands that held me there
now greet me here and I am home
with that same God who knew and loved me then.
This end of journey too is but a staging post
on another journey from this,
on to another home.
ANONYMOUS

*May Father aid me, may Son aid me,
may Spirit aid me, on sea and land
in the shielding of the City everlasting.*
CARMINA GADELICA

JANUARY 5 ✣ THE AIDAN WAY AHEAD

Psalm 107:17-43; Joshua 3; Luke 10:1-24

I am sending you out like lambs among wolves.
LUKE 10:3

The famous sculpture of Saint Aidan on Holy Island has four features that have much to say to us as we begin another year. His face, his torch, his staff, and his Celtic cross all tell us something different.

Aidan's face looks with faith-filled vision to the future and to the south, to the regions that had never heard the Good News.

Where does Christ want us to direct our attention this year?

Aidan takes with him from the past the torch of the Faith to hand on to others as a living flame.

To whom does God want us to hand on the flame of faith in the coming year?

Aidan carries everywhere with him his pastoral staff, a sign of gentle love and compassion for all.

Where do we need to grow in gentleness and compassion?

There is something else in this sculpture we must never forget: behind and above Aidan, as a shield wherever he goes, is a cross with a circle. Aidan had a sacrificial mission—to plant a cross in the soil of a new land and in the soul of its people. The circle meant that the message of the cross was to encompass all. It was not to be only a message of words, however, but an *experience* of the cross to be lived and applied in every area of life, every moment of every day.

No gain without pain. No false triumph. No words divorced from humble service. This is the only way our dreams and resolutions will survive the rocks of human nature. Only so will setbacks be surmounted and the serene strength of Christ be ours as we journey on in faith.

> God be with you at every leap;
> Christ be with you on every steep;
> Spirit be with you in every deep;
> each step of the journey you go.

> *All that I do, all whom I'll meet,*
> *all that I'll ever be I offer now to you God.*

JANUARY 6 ❖ WISE KINGS OF THE LONG JOURNEY

Psalm 106:24-48; Joshua 4; Matthew 2:1-11

The three magi were overwhelmed with joy when they saw the star.
They entered the house and saw the child with Mary his mother,
and they knelt and worshipped him. Then, opening their treasure chests,
they offered him gifts of gold, frankincense, and myrrh.
MATTHEW 2:10–11

At a new year, we step out afresh on virgin ground. Let us learn from the Wise Kings of the Long Journey how our journey should be.

The first magi stands for gold, something we all want, something good in itself. It stands for prosperity, and all the things money can buy. Hopefully, many of us will have times of prosperity. But gold cannot buy love, truth, eternity; it cannot fill the heart. This king's wisdom was that he knew this, and he had journeyed to find that which would fill his heart, that for which he could give his life. In this wise person, money was put in perspective, and he was willing to kneel and offer it as a gift.

The second king brings incense, signifying that he is at home with the routines of religion and of scholarship. These things, too, can be good. But, just as the pocket cannot satisfy the heart, neither can the brain. Perhaps this man had come to realize that. He was drawn onward by a sense of mystery. As he knelt, he was filled with a sense of wonder that no amount of theory could have produced. When the heart is right, we have a sense of wonder at the smallest things, and all life becomes a sign of God's Presence.

The third king is a sad person. Myrrh was an herb used in burial, and adults don't usually talk about death in front of a newborn baby—and yet the magi offers it as a gift to the Baby Jesus. This wise man had an intuitive understanding of the suffering and early death that was to mark Jesus' life. He shows us how to accept and be dignified in the times of loss, disappointment, or failure.

High King of the universe,
we offer you our possessions, make them all your own.
We offer you our mindsets and we place them at your feet.
May we be filled with your Presence as incense fills a holy place.
We offer you the shadows of our lives, the things that are crushed;
our little deaths and our final death.
May these be like the straw in the stable.
May something beautiful for you be born in all this straw.

JANUARY 7 ✢ ANOTHER WAY

Psalm 2; Numbers 22:1-35; Matthew 2:12-23

Being warned in a dream
not to return to King Herod,
the visitors who studied the stars
returned home by another road.
MATTHEW 2:12

After the star, the dim day.
After the gifts, the empty hands.
And now we take our secret way
back to far lands.

After the cave, the bleak plain.
After the joy, the weary ride.
But journey we, three new-made men,
side by side.

Came we by old paths by the sands.
Go we by new ones this new day,
homewards to rule our lives and lands
by another way.
AUTHOR UNKNOWN

I beg assistance, God of my journey,
to accept that all of life is only on loan to me,
to believe beyond this moment,
to accept your courage when mine fails,
to recognize the pilgrim of my heart,
to hold all of life in open hands.
JOYCE RUPP, OSM (A PILGRIM AT GLENDALOUGH)

Be a smooth way before me, be a guiding star above me,
be a keen eye behind me, this day, this year, forever.

JANUARY 8 ❖ STRONG LEADERSHIP

Psalm 72; Genesis 12; Luke 4:14-22

The Lord said to Abram...,
"I will make you and your children into a great nation,
and I will bless you... so that you will be a blessing."
GENESIS 12:1, 2

One frosty night, I meditated under the stars on the hill overlooking Edinburgh, a place known as Arthur's Seat. Our world seemed to me to be sinking under a sea of troubles, and those who were meant to lead us seemed to be blighted by small-mindedness. I sensed that God was wanting to release the potential for great leadership that lies untapped in so many people. The spirit that animated that great leader Arthur can animate us, too.

Unlike the well-known Celtic saints, the life of the great Celtic war hero Arthur is shrouded in the mists of legend. And yet, wherever he may have lived and whatever the actual details of his life, we can be grateful that here was a man who dared to lead, to stand up to the tyrant, to rally the forces of good, and to live out Christ's values.

The legends give a sense of Arthur's Christ-centered strategy for the nation during the period after the Roman troops left, when brutal Saxon invaders were taking over. Arthur built a chain of defended towns to protect the Britons from the invaders, and so secured, for a period, what is known as "Arthur's Peace." He was thwarted by quarrelling Celtic kings, yet, according to Stephen Lawhead in *Arthur,* he was given a vision for Britain: "A land shining with goodness where each man protects his brother's dignity, where war and want has ceased, and all races live under the same law of love and honor ... a land bright with truth, where a man's word is his pledge ... where the True God is worshipped and his ways acclaimed by all."

> Some nation must produce a new leadership, free from the bondage of fear, rising above ambition, flexible to the direction of God's Holy Spirit. ... Some nation must give a lead. Some nation must find God's will as her destiny, and God-guided people as her representatives at home and abroad.
> Will it be your nation?
> FRANK BUCHMAN

Lord, give us that inner dynamic that calls out and combines
the moral and spiritual responsibility of individuals
for their immediate sphere of action.

JANUARY 9 ❖ CONTEMPLATIVE LEADERSHIP

Psalm 23; Genesis 13; Luke 11:1-13

This is what the Lord God, the Holy One, says to you, . . .
"Quietness and trust shall be your strength."
ISAIAH 30:15

Arthur may have looked out from that hill named Arthur's Seat toward the defended cities he had established at Dunedin, Dundonald, Dunbarton, Stirling, and Dunpelder. These cities stood there as a result of the hard work he had led; his leadership caused action and concrete results.

We need that kind of leadership today—and yet if the kingdom of God is to be established in the heart of a people, the leadership of action needs to be complemented by leadership of a different kind, one that cultivates the inner life. A fine example of such leadership, working hand in glove with Arthur, is Moninna. (Moninna's real name was Edana, to which was added the affectionate prefix "Mo.") Saint Brigid had inspired Monenna to found a monastery in her native Ireland, and such was its quality that crowds flocked to her. When they encroached too much upon her calling to the inner life, she moved away to Scotland, where she had space for a daily discipline of contemplation. At the summit of the high rock where Edinburgh castle now stands, she built herself a prayer cell. The hill became known as Edana's Hill, later as Dunedin, and much later as Edinburgh. Through the vehicle of her quiet contemplation, God led her to match Arthur's strategy by founding a community of prayer in each of his five defended towns. These two types of leadership ensured that both the outer and the inner life of society were looked after.

Moninna's type of leadership is still as needed as Arthur's. We need a brain drain in reverse, a constant stream of people who are ready to leave behind the whirlpool of business and concentrate on the contemplative life. In fact, we need both kinds of leadership—the active and the contemplative—as never before.

In which direction is God calling you?

Holy Three,
help me to live at the still center of the world's whirring wheels
where everything is led by you.

JANUARY 10 ❖ NEW BEGINNINGS, NEW BIRTHS

Psalm 139; Genesis 15; Luke 1:57-80

You, my little child, will be called an interpreter of the Most High God;
you will go ahead of the Lord to get the road ready for him,
to tell his people they will be delivered, set free of their failures.
LUKE 1:76-77

A new year is a time for new beginnings and new births. The above prophecy, given by John the Baptist's father over his baby son, is echoed in the lives of many of the Celtic saints. Such prophecies were signs that God was doing something new from the very beginning of their lives.

Take, for example, the parents of Saint Samson—Anna and Amon. They were court officials in neighboring kingdoms of fifth-century Wales. Anna had no children, and she took to fasting, to charitable giving, and to church-going in order to persuade God to give her a child. One day when she and her husband were in church, they overheard an animated discussion about a man in North Wales who could foretell with uncanny accuracy what would happen to people. So Amon and Anna undertook a three-day journey to see this man, Librarius, who gave them overnight accommodation. The next day, Librarius surprised them twice. First, he told them, before they had spoken of it, that he knew they had come because Anna was barren and they wanted him to prophesy that they would have a baby. Second, he asked Amon not to give him payment, but instead to have made a silver rod the same length as his wife and to give this to God. This rod was a symbol of a ruler's control. Apparently, God wanted both Amon and Anna to put God first, before power, before one another, and even before the baby for which they longed. Amon was so eager to respond that he made not one but three rods—one for him, one for his wife, and one for their child—and handed them all over.

That night, an angel told Anna in her dreams that she would indeed have a baby who would be holy, profitable to many, seven times brighter than the silver her husband had given to God—and that "of the British race there has not been or will be anyone like him." The angel encouraged Anna to trust God and to name the baby Samson, after the biblical Samson, who was so strong for God. Today, anyone who has read the *Life of St. Samson* cannot doubt that all that was prophesied indeed came to pass! The promise of new birth was fulfilled.

Holy God, holy and mighty,
you can bring a holy child to birth in a barren womb;
you can bring a new thing to birth in a barren land.
Bring to birth in me that new thing that is your will.

JANUARY 11 ✣ A NURSERY OF SAINTS

Psalm 1; Genesis 17; Romans 4

*Abraham is the spiritual father of us all. As the Scripture says:
"I have made you a father of many peoples."*
ROMANS 4:16–17

Is the faith community to which you belong like a museum—or a nursery? Museums are orderly . . . but also lifeless. Nurseries are messy . . . but they foster life. Ever since Abraham, God has been in the business of nurturing people of faith. It's often a messy and unpredictable business! Here is the story of how a nursery of saints began in Ireland.

The day before Saint Comgall was born, Mac Nisse of Connor heard a horse and carriage passing by. He said to the people around him, "That carriage carries a king."

However, when everyone went outside to have a look, they could see only two occupants—Sedna and his pregnant wife Birga—neither of whom were royal. Had Mac Nisse got it wrong?

He insisted that his first "seeing" had not been mistaken. "It is the baby that woman is carrying who shall be a king," he said. "He will be adorned with all sorts of virtues and the luster of his miracles will light up the world."

And all this proved to be true. Comgall, the child Birga was carrying, would grow up to establish the famous community at Bangor, at which, it was said, some four thousand monks were under the grace of God. Among the famous missionaries who trained there and went on to win countless disciples on the continent were Columbanus and Gall. The service book of the monastery, *The Antiphonary of Bangor*, survives in the Ambrosian Library in Milan. Bangor became known as "The Vale of Angels," and later Bernard of Clairvaux described it as being "truly sacred, the nursery of saints."

Sometimes individuals develop their own little nurseries. Saint Ita, who died in January 570, was originally named Deidre. She adopted her new name—the Latin word for "likewise, thus"—to signify her hunger for God; she longed to be like a mirror that simply reflected Divine love. As a result of her great love and her powers of healing and prophecy, she became known as "the foster mother of the saints of Ireland." When Comghan was dying in a monastery, he felt God tell him that if Ita laid hands upon him in prayer he would go straight to heaven. She complied . . . and one day in heaven we will learn what happened next!

*Lord, I would like to be part of a nursery of saints.
Show me what needs to happen for this to be.
May my life be a seedbed of prayer and friendship
lived out in fellowship with others.*

JANUARY 12 ∴ THE DIVINE PLAN

Psalm 9; Genesis 18; Colossians 1:1–23

*For this is God's plan: to make known his secret,
the abundant, glorious secret he has for all peoples.*
COLOSSIANS 1:27

Glimpses of God's plan were given when Columba's birth was foretold to elders of Ireland in visions and dreams. Columba's mother Eithne dreamed she was given a great cloak that stretched from Ireland to Scotland and contained every color of the rainbow. A young man took this radiant cloak from her, which made her extremely sad. Then the young man returned to Eithne and said, "You have no need of grief but rather of joy and delight. The meaning of this dream is that you will bear a son, and Ireland and Scotland will be full of his teaching."

The Life of St. Samson of Dol tells us that God also used a dream to protect Samson's God-given destiny; lest it should be contaminated in any way during his childhood, "divine providence wrapped him round and preserved him uninjured." Samson's father had turned against the plan to send his son to a Christian school, but, after a powerful dream, Amon said to his wife, "Let us lose no time in sending our son, rather God's son, to school, for God is with him and we ought to do nothing against God."

> I believe that God has a Divine Plan for me. I believe that this plan is wrapped in the folds of my being, even as the oak is wrapped in the acorn and the rose is wrapped in the bud. I believe that this Plan is permanent, indestructible and perfect, free from all that is essentially bad. Whatever comes into my life that is negative is not a part of this God-created Plan, but is a distortion caused by my failure to harmonize myself with the Plan as God has made it. I believe that this Plan is Divine, and when I relax myself completely to it, it will manifest completely and perfectly through me. I can always tell when I am completely relaxed to the Divine Plan by the inner peace that comes to me. This inner peace brings a joyous, creative urge that leads me into activities that unfold the Plan, or it brings a patience and a stillness that allow others to unfold the Plan to me.
> GLENN CLARK

*Lord, help me to relax into your plan for me.
Unfold it for me as the acorn unfolds into the oak.*

JANUARY 13 ⁘ UNWANTED BABY

Psalm 12; Genesis 16; Colossians 1:24-29

Before you were born, I chose you.
JEREMIAH 1:4

King Loth of Dunpelder, in Lothian, was a small pagan ruler who sent his daughter Tannoc to a convent founded by Moninna. There his daughter gave her life to God. She thrived in the atmosphere of spiritual and intellectual learning. One day her father offered her in marriage to the Prince of Rheged in the hope of forging an alliance. The fifteen-year-old Tannoc, however, informed Rheged's Prince Owen, "I am already promised to a King far greater than you will ever be." A furor ensued, and Tannoc was exiled to live among some peasants. Owen tracked her down and raped her before returning to his home at Carlisle. Alone in the woods, Tannoc must have felt all the rage and humiliation that every raped woman feels. Abandoned by her father, scorned by her own privileged class, she was friendless. Was this the end of the bright hopes she had had at the convent? With all her heart she had tried to choose God's way . . . but what would become of her now? Had God abandoned her?

The peasants at the farm were followers of Christ, and they offered her support, especially when she realized she was pregnant. Did Tannoc rebel at first against the uninvited life inside her? It would have been natural for her to do so, but perhaps she realized that the baby was as much a victim as she was herself, with no one to turn to for help. In the end, she cherished it with the full passion of her love. In so doing she found her own destiny.

With a touch of courage and wry humor, Tannoc named her baby Kentigem, which in her tongue meant "Big Chief." Her friends fetched the village priest from nearby Culross; he christened the child "Mungo," which meant "my beloved," and he adopted them both. Tannoc now belonged to a family—and Mungo became a shepherd of souls, the founder of Glasgow, an inspiration to millions, and a saint.

Are you carrying unwanted life within you? A literal baby perhaps . . . or perhaps some other result of violence, the living scars of rejection and loss of identity. If so, you will be in anguish, caught in a cycle of anger and denial.

But it need not end there. God calls to this life within you. God has purpose for you and for that which you carry within you. Whenever you doubt this, think of Mungo. Believe that something beloved, something (or someone) with authority and sainthood will come into being through you. The God of creation can use even our deepest wounds to bring good into the world.

King of the universe, you are present even in our pain.

JANUARY 14 ❖ DIVINE WATER

Psalm 46; Habakkuk 2:1-14; Luke 3:1-22

After all the people had been baptized, Jesus was baptized too.
LUKE 3:21

Christ is baptized and the whole world is made holy.
He wipes out the debt of our sins;
we will all be purified by water and the Holy Spirit.
AN ORTHODOX ANTIPHON

For as the rain and the snow come down from heaven,
and do not return there, but water the earth
and make it blossom, . . . so shall my word be, says the Lord.
ISAIAH 55:10, 11

Although he was without sin, Jesus Christ came in a body as physical as any other human body. Then, at his baptism in the River Jordan, Jesus received a vision as he came out of the water. He saw the Spirit in the form of a gentle dove and heard his Father declare from on high, "You are my dearly loved Son with whom I am deeply pleased."

Christians understand that Christ is the Word of God made flesh; through the power of his Incarnation, he is present in all creation. Yet at the same time, creation is disordered. Just as humankind is infected with a broken relationship with the Creator, the whole creation also shares the same fate of being unfulfilled without the Redeemer. So how can Christ be everywhere present in the Earth?

Jesus' baptism had a cosmic significance: the sinless Savior entered the streams of the Jordan, cleansing the waters and imparting Divine redemption to the entire material creation. As he came up out of the water, he carried the created world up with him. He saw heaven open, which the first human beings, Adam and Eve, had closed against themselves and posterity, when the angel's flaming sword shut the gates of paradise. But now the gates were opened, the waters of the sea were made sweet, and the Earth was glad. At the same time that water fell over Christ's human body, the love of the Creator cascaded over him, covering him with glory. God and matter become one in Christ. (*Adopted from Brendan O'Malley's* Pilgrim's Manual: St. David's.)

In the words of poet Gerard Manley Hopkins, "The world is charged with the grandeur of God."

Lord, water the world. Revive our dryness.
Soak our soreness. Refresh our tiredness.
Wash away our dirt. Cool our wounds.
Immerse us in your love.

JANUARY 15 ❖ GROWING UP

Psalm 15; Genesis 21:1-21; Luke 2:41-52

The child Jesus grew and became strong;
he was full of wisdom and God blessed him.
LUKE 2:40

As Mungo grew up, he learned some invaluable lessons from his mother Tannoc. She belonged to the generation that still cherished the healthy and pleasant Roman practice of a daily hot bath, and she taught her son to enjoy this cleanliness. He practiced it to the end of his long life. Another lesson he learned from Tannoc was a sensitivity to the wild creatures of nature. Long walks with his mother by the river and in the forests were his school. He learned the names of flowers and their seasons, the feeding and mating habits of birds and beasts, and how to win the confidence of the furred and feathered creatures.

This love of animals was common to all the Celtic Christians. Anyone who has loved a family dog is familiar with an animal's ability to love, understand, and communicate with humans in wordless language. Domestic animals are not the only ones with this gift, but people rarely allow a relationship of trust to develop with wild creatures. Mungo, however, learned to understand animals, fish, and birds with his heart. All through his life, this gift revealed itself, as it does in this first story of his boyhood.

At Culross one day, some robins were pecking on the ground for scraps. Village boys, as boys sometimes will, started throwing stones at them. One bird was hit and fell to the ground, and the boys ran away. But Mungo ran to the fallen bird, smoothed and stroked its feathers, and prayed, "Lord Jesus Christ, in whose hands is the breath of every creature, tame or wild, give back to this bird the breath of life, that your name may be glorified." After a little while, the bird revived and flew away. The villagers said it was a miracle. (And according to tradition, the robin flew straight into Glasgow City's coat of arms, where it now proudly perches on the top of the oak tree!) (*Based on* The Beloved St Mungo *by Reginald B. Hale.*)

Many of us have missed out, in one way or another, on some aspect of the "developmental process." As a result, areas of our lives may have not grown in wisdom, strength, or sensitivity as they were meant to. It's never too late to grow in new ways, however—and from Mungo, we can learn the wisdom of long walks; we can open ourselves today to observe the breath of God in the little things we encounter. And as we learn from them, we shall grow.

Help me to grow today in understanding and sensitivity,
in patience and prayerfulness.

JANUARY 16 ❖ FURSEY, A VALIANT PILGRIM

Psalm 84; Genesis 22; Colossians 2:1-5

The God of gods will be seen in Zion.
PSALM 84:7 NRSV

A boat landed on the East Anglian shore near Burgh Castle, the site of the last fort the Romans built before they left Britain. From the boat stepped three brothers, two priests, and other Christians, all of whom had come from Ireland to share the faith with the Anglo-Saxons. Perhaps they had heard that East Anglia's king had found faith in Christ while in exile in Gaul, and that he had recently brought Bishop Felix over from Burgundy to spread this faith from the south of his kingdom. Whatever the reason, the wind of the Spirit was surely what had blown them to this place.

The leader of this faith-sharing team was Fursey. As a boy in Ireland he had devoted all his energy to the study of the Bible and to the disciplines taught by the monasteries. He had preached the Word of God to such effect that he had become renowned for the power of his words, deeds, and life. Now, however, he could no longer endure the crowds who flocked to hear him. His life passion was to do whatever God gave him to do—and that is why he had come as a pilgrim for the Lord's sake in a strange land.

The king welcomed him; Fursey's persuasive teaching and way of life won many to Christ, and it confirmed believers in their faith. Soon the king gave Fursey and his companions land at Burgh Castle on which to establish a Christian community.

After some years at Burgh Castle, Fursey felt God call him to hermit life in the Fens. There he spent his time in daily prayer, study, and manual work. Once he became ill and had an out-of-the-body experience; he heard angels singing these words: "The saints shall go from strength to strength," and, "The God of gods shall be seen in Zion."

Eventually, Fursey sensed that pagans from a neighboring kingdom would soon invade, so our intrepid pilgrim next sailed for Gaul. There he was welcomed by Clovis II, the Christian king of the Franks. Fursey established a monastery at Lagny, where he died on January 16, 649.

God of gods, establish your presence among us.
May your people advance from one virtue to another
and may the kingdoms of this world become the kingdom of our God.

JANUARY 17 ✢ THE CALL TO THE DESERT

Psalm 26; Genesis 23; Colossians 2:6–23

*The Lord says, "You must leave them
and separate yourselves from them.
Have nothing to do with what is unclean."*
2 CORINTHIANS 6:17 GNB

Celtic Christians drew inspiration from the examples of the fourth- and fifth-century believers who fled the false, comfortable ways of the cities to live for God alone in the Egyptian and Syrian deserts. These ancient believers became known as the Desert Mothers and Fathers. The movement began with Paul the Hermit and Antony, who founded desert communities. They are depicted together on many high crosses that still stand in Ireland.

When the Roman Emperor Constantine made Christianity the official religion of the Roman Empire in the fourth century, churches were built with public money. People who put career before calling became clergy, and there were no more martyrs to inspire faith. The church became respectable, part of a culture that talked about Christian things but overlaid the Gospel simplicities with politics, power, and wealth. Some people began to ask whether it was possible any longer to live a truly Christ-like life while tied to the structures and possessions of such a greedy society. Many, inspired by the example of Antony and Paul, went out to the deserts to live out the Gospel.

By the time Antony died at age 105, on January 17, 356, monastic communities were in many parts of the Roman Empire, each touched in some way by his example. It is sometimes said that Antony went into the desert with nothing but a cloak . . . and he left behind a desert full of Christians.

Shortly after Antony's death, Pachomius established more organized monasteries in the south of Egypt, but with similar goals. Pachomius had first met Christ's followers when he was a miserable conscript in the army at Thebes. Some Christians had brought him food as an act of love, and when he asked who these people were, he was told that Christians "are people who bear the name of Christ, the only Son of God, and who do all manner of good things for everyone." This so struck Pachomius that he vowed that when he was released from the army he too would follow Christ. His call to the desert came through a voice that told him three times: "The Lord's will is to minister to the human race in order to reconcile them."

*Lord, if possible,
take me from environments that hide your face.
Wherever I am, take from me all that is false.
Use me as a reconciler in your name.*

JANUARY 18 ✥ UNITY

Psalm 122; Genesis 24:1-53; Colossians 3:16-4:1

Be of the same mind. Have the same love.
Focus together on a single purpose.
PHILIPPIANS 2:2

The spread of Christianity to diverse cultures posed this question: How do Christians remain united? Cyprian, a second-century church leader, urged Christians to think of themselves as members of a choir, whose conductor was the bishop. Antony too was sought out for advice by Christians of very different backgrounds—peasants and politicians, army officers and teachers—and his secret of unity was to live the simplicity of the Beatitudes, the beautiful attitudes Jesus described in Matthew 5.

We learn that so many people followed Antony's way of life in the desert that their cells in the hills were like tents filled with divine choirs—people chanting, studying, fasting, praying, rejoicing, distributing alms, and maintaining love and harmony among themselves. It was as if one truly looked on a land all its own, a land of devotion and righteousness, "for neither perpetrator nor victim of injustice was there, nor complaint" (The Life of Antony, *Athanasius*).

The secret of the Celtic Christians' unity was that they made themselves one with the Trinity—Father, Son, and Holy Spirit—and they also made themselves one with the people among whom they lived. In this way they experienced unity in diversity, unity without uniformity.

When we are united, we want what is good for the other. In order to make ourselves one, however, we must empty ourselves, as Jesus emptied himself. This brings about a universal love. The attitude of making ourselves one in all things except sin should be the basis of our relationship with everyone, with those in authority and with those who have nothing.

Sometimes it may seem easier to be united with those who follow another faith, or no faith at all, than with those who follow Christ differently from ourselves. Have you sometimes caught yourself speaking disparagingly of other Christians? Remember, you do not have to agree with them to be of the same love. Whenever you find yourself doing this, decide to make yourself one, intent on a single purpose—spreading Christ's message of love.

Father, I make myself one with you.
Jesus, I make myself one with you.
Spirit, I make myself one with you.
True Christ-followers of every kind,
I make myself one with you.

JANUARY 19 ❖ LOOK FOR THE ANCIENT WAY

Psalm 82; Genesis 26:1-25; Hebrews 11:1-16

"Stand at the crossroads," says the Lord,
"and look for the ancient way; ask which way the good road takes,
and take it; so shall you be safe and prosper."
JEREMIAH 6:16

Picture Branwalader sailing into the sweeping, golden bay. He and his monks beach the boat, climb up the slope, and there kneel in prayer. As they settle into their new home, they meet local Jersey fishermen, who also become believers, and together they build a place of prayer on the hill beside what is now called St. Brelade's Bay. (Branwalader, whose name in Welsh means "Raven Lord," is known in French as *Brelade*.)

Branwalader was said to be the son of Kenen, a Cornish king. Renowned in his land, he forsook his fame and fortune for the life of a wandering missionary monk. He most likely trained at the Welsh monastery at Llantwit Major, where Samson was a fellow pupil.

These two would eventually work together in Ireland, Cornwall, the Channel Isles, and Brittany. To this day, a Church of St. Samson stands in Guernsey and a Church of St. Brelade in Jersey. When the North Men laid waste the Breton church where the earthly remains of these two saints were kept, King Athelstan brought them for safekeeping, still together, to his monastery at Milton Abbas, on January 19 in 935.

Many pilgrims come to the Fisherman's Chapel where Branwalader first prayed, and they sense there a call to return to ancient ways. Within the Celtic heritage the different strands of the church—biblical, Catholic, charismatic, mystical, socially concerned, ecumenical—are woven together into a common pattern of prayer. We too can become part of this weaving.

God's love is around us like the sea round an island
and we stand secure on the rocks of our faith.
He has given his word like a beacon to guide us.
His love is a harbor in which we are safe.
All glory to God our leader and captain.
All praise to the Son, our guide and our light.
All praise to the Spirit—the wind and the power.
All honor and praise and glory and might.
SUSAN HALLIWELL AND JENNY CORNWALL OF ST. BRELADE

JANUARY 20 ✢ ONE CHOIR

Psalm 125; Ezekiel 37:15-28; John 17:1-23

I pray that they all may be one, Father!
May they be in us, just as you are in me and I am in you.
JOHN 17:21

In 613, at a time when two power-hungry rivals claimed the "Chair of Peter," Columbanus wrote this letter to Pope Boniface IV:

> For all we Irish, inhabitants of the world's edge, are disciples of Saints Peter and Paul and of all the disciples who wrote the sacred canon [of the New Testament] by the Holy Spirit. We accept nothing outside the evangelical and apostolic teaching. None of us was a heretic . . . no one a schismatic; but the Catholic Faith, as it was first transmitted by you, successors of the holy apostles, is maintained unbroken. . . . For among us it is not who you are but how you make your case that counts. Love for the peace of the Gospel forces me to tell all in order to shame both of you who ought to have been one choir. Another reason is my great concern for your harmony and peace. "For if one member suffers all the members suffer with it."
>
> Therefore, my dearest friends, come to an agreement quickly. . . . I can't understand how a Christian can quarrel with a Christian about the Faith. Whatever an Orthodox Christian who rightly glorifies the Lord will say, the other will answer Amen, because he also loves and believes alike. "Let you all therefore say and think the one thing," so that both sides "may be one"—all Christians.
>
> Jesus has gathered us, is gathering us, and will gather us out of all regions, till he should make resurrection of our hearts from the earth, and teach us that we are all of one substance, and members of one another.

Thrice Holy God, eternal Three-in-One,
make your people holy, make your people one.
Stir up in us the flame that burns out pride and power.
Restore in us the love that brings the servant-heart to flower.
Thrice holy God, come as the morning dew;
inflame in us your love, which draws all lesser loves to you.

JANUARY 21 ✣ THE PLEASURE OF UNITY

Psalm 133; Genesis 27:1-29; 1 Corinthians 12:12-31

> *How wonderful it is, how pleasing,*
> *when a family lives together in unity.*
> PSALM 133:1

Barinthus, grandson of Ireland's famed King Niall, loved to share his experience of how unity between a father and son can be restored. When Barinthus's son Mernoc rebelled and ran away from home, Mernoc backpacked until he found an island on which some monks had settled. Here he put things right with God, with himself, and with his fellows. In his heart, he forgave and grew to love his father. This released in him prophetic and healing gifts, which God used with great effectiveness.

Barinthus heard about this and set out to visit his son. Although there was no physical communication between them, God's Spirit revealed to Mernoc in his prayers that his father was on his way to visit him. Mernoc did not just sit back and wait; he took action to restore unity with his father. While Barinthus was still three days' journey away, Mernoc set out to meet him halfway. When at last they saw each other, they warmly embraced, and Mernoc introduced his father to his island friends, the monks.

These monks lived separate lives in cells that were some distance from each other; from Night Prayer until dawn they neither saw nor spoke to one another. Yet, as he was later to recount to Brendan, Barinthus was greatly struck by their togetherness. "The brothers came to greet us out of their cells like a swarm of bees," he recounted. "Though their dwellings were divided from one another, there was no division in their conversation, their counsel, or their affection."

Barinthus and Mernoc left for a fortnight's boating trip together, and the monks could see that they too were no longer divided in any way. Father and son were one. And their unity gave them such pleasure!

> *Dear Father God, what pleasure it gives you*
> *when our relationships reflect the love*
> *you and Jesus and the Spirit have for one another and for us.*
> *I know that I am only as near to you, Father,*
> *as I am to the person from whom I am most divided.*
> *I pray for those persons I am furthest from.*
> *In my heart I reach out to them.*
> *And you are pleased,*
> *and I am pleased.*

JANUARY 22 ✤ CALLS FOR UNITY

Psalm 127; Genesis 33; Romans 12

*Though we are many ... we are joined to each other
like different parts of one body.*
ROMANS 12:5

The founders of the churches were all bishops, three hundred and fifty in number, famed and holy and full of the Holy Spirit. They had one head, Christ. They had one leader, Patrick. They maintained one Eucharist, one liturgy . . . one Easter. . . . What was excommunicated by one church was excommunicated by all.
CATALOGUE OF THE SAINTS OF IRELAND, SIXTH TO NINTH CENTURY

Always be of one mind.
DAVID'S FINAL MESSAGE TO HIS FOLLOWERS IN WALES

Always keep God's peace and love among you, and when you have to seek guidance about your affairs, take great care to be of one mind. Live in mutual goodwill also with Christ's other servants, and do not despise Christians who come to you for hospitality, but see that you welcome them, give them accommodation, and send them on their way with friendship and kindness. Never think you are superior to other people who share your faith and way of life.
CUTHBERT'S LAST WORDS AS NOTED BY BEDE

Keep the peace of the Gospel with one another, and indeed with all the world.
THE LAST WORDS OF HILDA TO HER SISTERS AT THE WHITBY MONASTERY

There is only one true flight from the world . . .
the flight from disunity and separation,
to unity and peace in the love of other people.
THOMAS MERTON

The walls of separation do not reach heaven.
CORNERSTONE COMMUNITY, BELFAST

*Peace between believers, peace between neighbors,
peace between lovers in love of the King of Life.
Peace between person and person,
peace between wife and husband,
peace between parents and children.
The peace of Christ above all peace.*

JANUARY 23 ❖ SAYINGS OF ANTONY

Psalm 39; Proverbs 12; Luke 13:22-30

*In your sight my lifetime seems nothing...
I am only your guest for a little while.*
PSALM 39:5, 12 GNT

Once Antony was talking with some brothers when a hunter came upon them. He saw Antony and the brothers enjoying themselves and disapproved. So Antony said to him, "Put an arrow in your bow and shoot it." The hunter did this. "Now shoot another," said Antony, "and another, and another."

Then the hunter said, "If I bend my bow all the time it will break."

Abba Antony replied, "It is like that in the work of God. If we push ourselves beyond measure, the brothers will soon collapse. It is right therefore, from time to time, to relax."

Someone once asked Antony, "What shall I do?"

Antony replied, "Do not presume your own righteousness; do not grieve over something that is past; control your tongue and your belly."

Here are two other sayings of Antony:

> The spaces of our human life
> set over against eternity
> are most brief and poor.

> The time is coming when people will be insane,
> and when they see someone who is not insane,
> they will attack that person, saying,
> "You are insane, because you are not like us."

Finally, we recall the occasion when someone asked Antony, "What shall I keep in order that I may please God?"

Antony answered, "Always keep God before your eyes; always keep the example of the holy Scriptures; and wherever you stay, keep yourself there long enough not to move on in a rush."

*Keeper of eternity, help me keep you ever before me.
Help me keep the example of your saints ever before me.
Help me keep sufficient sense of proportion to relax when needed,
to savor the blessings of hospitality with ever-grateful poise.*

JANUARY 24 ✢ MORE DESERT SAYINGS

Psalm 69:19-36; Proverbs 14; Luke 13:31-35

An honest answer is a sign of true friendship.
PROVERBS 24:26 GNT

If you have a chest full of clothing, and leave it for a long time, the clothing will rot inside it. It is the same with thoughts in our heart. If we do not carry them out by physical action, after a long while they will spoil and turn bad.
ABBA PASTOR

When someone wants to return evil for evil, they are able to hurt their neighbor's conscience even by a single nod.
ABBA ISAIAH

Unless a person says in their heart, "I alone and God are in this world," they shall not find quiet.
ABBA ALLOIS

Abba Arsenius was taking counsel with an old Egyptian man when someone said to him, "Abba Arsenius, how is it that you, such a great scholar of Latin and Greek, should take counsel from this countryman?"

Arsenius answered, "It is true I have acquired the learning of the Greeks and the Latins, as this world goes; but the alphabet of this countryman I have not yet been able to learn."

> We do not go in to the desert to escape people
> but to learn how to find them.
> THOMAS MERTON

Infinite One of the wise heart,
Saving One of the clear sight,
Knowing One of the hidden deeps,
may I learn from you as an eager pupil;
may I learn from life as a humble child;
may I learn from night, may I learn from day,
may I learn from soul friends, may I learn from the stillness.

JANUARY 25 ❖ KNOWING THE WILL OF GOD

Psalm 3; Genesis 17:1-14; Acts 22:1-16

The God of our ancestors has chosen you to know his will.
ACTS 22:14 NLT

So often we miss God's will for us because we spend our lives like actors, acting out a script that others have written for us. We need to learn to follow not our conditioning or our compulsions, but what our deepest souls desire.

Someone asked Abba Nisteros, a friend of Antony, "What good work shall I do?"

He replied, "Not all works are alike. For Scripture says that Abraham was hospitable, and God was with him. Elijah loved solitary prayer, and God was with him. And David was humble before God, and God was with him. Therefore, whatever you see your soul desire according to God, do that thing and you shall keep your heart safe."

Sometimes God uses circumstances to draw out our true calling, as happened in the life of Saint Mungo. Mungo had grown to manhood and was ordained a priest in the area around where he was born. No doubt he had dreams of being called to some glorious, sacrificial task. Instead, he was called to visit an ailing old priest, Fergus, who lived seven miles upstream.

When he arrived, Mungo was dismayed to find how the old man was failing; he stayed with him, cooked him supper, and listened to the old man's memories of his home on the river Clyde, where the great missionary Ninian had established a church. About midnight, Fergus had a seizure and died in Mungo's arms. His last words were, "Promise you will bury me at the old church hallowed by Ninian."

So Mungo put Fergus's body in the wagon, hitched up the oxen, and went a day's journey to the little church by the Clyde. He found that the folks who lived there had gathered at the church, looking forlorn, for they had not seen a priest for several years. The next day, at the funeral, as Mungo looked at these sad faces, he knew he could not return home as he had planned.

God's plan, he realized, was that he build up a community of faith there. Soon his mother joined him. She called the community "Eglais Cu" (the loved church), meaning the people there lived as a family. Today, her name for the community is pronounced "Glasgow."

Lord, teach me that your plan unfolds
as I follow the desire you put in my soul,
as I follow the way of unselfish service
and as I let one thing lead to another.

JANUARY 26 ✢ SAVED BY THE KING

Psalm 62; Genesis 17:15-27; Acts 22:17-29

*They kept on stoning Stephen as he called out to the Lord,
"Lord Jesus, receive my spirit!"*
ACTS 7:59 GNT

Long-ago Celtic Christians heard of the martyr's death of Polycarp, the disciple of the Apostle John, who had become a bishop in the eastern Roman Empire. When Polycarp was a very old man, he was led before the Roman proconsul, who urged him to abandon his faith. "Have respect for your age," they told him. "Swear by the genius of Caesar and say, 'Away with the atheists.'" (The proconsul considered atheists to be people who would not worship the Roman gods, which included the Emperor.)

But Polycarp looked sternly at the noisy mob in the stadium. Waving his hand at them, he said, "Away with the atheists."

The proconsul did not give up, however. "Swear, and then we will release you. Curse the Christ."

Polycarp said, "Eighty-six years have I served Christ, and he has done me no wrong. How then can I blaspheme my King who saved me?"

Centuries later, Mungo's generation had their own turn to face persecution. Mungo had developed a close friendship with King Rhydderch of Strathclyde, but in the 540s, Morcant, a pagan ruler, raided the farms of Christians in Rhydderch's territory; then pagans threw out the Christian ruler and church leaders in the Carlisle area. A violent mob swept through the town of Falkirk, and its bishop, Nevydd (who may have ordained Mungo) died a martyr's death; his place of worship was burned over him. Mungo, deeply grieved, next suffered the death of his beloved mother. Then he learned that the priceless library at Whithorn had gone up in flames, while the members of its Christian community had fled to Gaul. Worse, there was now no Christian bishop in the entire north, and no one to ordain new priests.

Rhydderch conferred with Mungo, and they agreed together to ask an Irish bishop to come over and consecrate a bishop of the north. But Rhydderch had a better idea; he insisted that, although the minimum age for becoming a bishop was thirty, the twenty-five-year-old Mungo was the man to be consecrated. "Be to the flock of Christ a shepherd," Rhydderch told him. "Hold up the weak, bind up the broken, bring again the outcast, seek the lost."

With all Mungo's soul, he answered, "I will, with the help of God."

King of the universe, in all my trials you save me.

JANUARY 27 ❖ GOOD FROM THE BAD

Psalm 38; Genesis 18:16-33; Mark 13:3-13

*Make good use of every opportunity you have,
because these are evil days.*
EPHESIANS 5:16 GNT

We should never delude ourselves that following Christ is all roses. The world holds much that is bad and ugly, and Christ's followers have no guarantee they will be immune. We can, however, learn to discover God in the ugliest of situations—and we can use evil days as an opportunity to do good, just as Saint Mungo did.

Not long after his consecration as a bishop, an angry crowd, headed by Morcant, arrived on Mungo's doorstep. "Your royal friend Rhydderch," Morcant crowed, "has sailed away into exile, and now I am king of Strathclyde."

Riding with Morcant was a young man, a distant relative of Mungo, who was decidedly unfriendly. He lashed out with his stirrupped foot and kicked Mungo in the chest, knocking him down. "You bastard bishop!" he shouted as he rode away.

Mungo had no choice but to move. He set out to join David in Wales, so that a new mission might move north from a sound base in the south. But in order to get to Wales, he had to go on a difficult journey. As Mungo and his companions trudged through the dales, they found not only a strange and craggy landscape but also a hostile population.

Finally, however, they reached the headquarters of the Christian Prince Urien, who conducted his government in exile near Penrith. The prince was the most statesmanlike of the Christian leaders of that generation, and Mungo and his friends discussed with him the region's sad situation.

Perhaps Mungo had intended to pass quickly through on his way to Wales, but instead, he turned aside, and with God helping him, he persuaded many to follow Christ. As he journeyed, crowds gathered. Some jeered, but others were healed and some decided to give themselves to Christ. The Christian faith revived there. At Crosthwaite in 533, a crowd worshipped God as a large cross was erected.

It had looked like an ugly situation. But God can bring good out of the bad.

*Lord, help me to face the ugly things in my situation today.
Use me to bring good out of the bad.*

JANUARY 28 ✣ A GOOD AND FAITHFUL SERVANT

Psalm 13; Genesis 19:1-29; Matthew 24:45-51

"Well done, you good and faithful servant," said his master. . . .
"Come on in and share my happiness."
MATTHEW 25:21 GNT

In Wales, Mungo was known by his formal name, Kentigern. He created teams of spiritual leaders in Wales and worked with them, and one of these leaders was Asaph. Together, Asaph and Mungo established the large Christian community at Llanelwy.

Six hundred years later, Joceline of Furness wrote the story of Llanelwy's founding. Kentigern, Joceline wrote, had set his heart on building a monastery to which the scattered children of God might come together like bees from East and West, from North and South. Young men, scattered throughout a hostile countryside, heard the news of the founding of the monastery. Many slipped quietly away from home to wend their way through the forests. Like the early Christians, they were an underground movement. But they came by the hundreds, every sort of Briton, from farm laborers to men of noble rank.

After prayer, Joceline wrote, they manfully set to work. Some cleared and leveled land; others built foundations, carried timber, and erected a church of planed woodwork after the British fashion, enclosing it all in a *llan* or rampart. When it was done, they named it Llanelwy, and 965 people moved in. One-third labored on the land; one-third looked after the buildings, cooking, and workshops; and one-third were responsible for worship, teaching, and scribing.

In 573, the pagans in the north suffered a mighty defeat, and Rhydderch regained his throne, though by this time, the Christian religion had been virtually wiped out. The prince asked his friend Mungo to lead a mission to his kingdom. Mungo spent eight years working from a halfway base at Hoddam, and then he moved back to Glasgow. There, Mungo had heart-to-heart meetings with Columba from Iona and with Bishop Gregory in Rome. These men may have discussed their plan for the conversion of the English people.

At the end of his life, Mungo's dying words were, "My children, love one another . . . be hospitable . . . keep the laws of the church. . . . She is the Mother of us all."

Help me to be faithful
in things both great or small, in setback or success,
faithful to the true church, faithful to my call.

JANUARY 29 ✢ BE VULNERABLE

Psalm 6; Genesis 20; Luke 9:43-62

*Foxes have holes; birds have nests,
but Humanity's Child has nowhere to lay his head.*
LUKE 9:58

Young mothers often find themselves crying. They feel so weak, needy, small, so overwhelmed by the demands of motherhood. But then they think of their babies. These tiny human being are all those things, too—weak, needy, and small. Babies are so dependent upon others, so vulnerable, and yet that is precisely why their mothers love them so fiercely.

When people are hard, prickly, proud, defensive, no feeling can flow. They cannot reach out and touch others. Others find it equally difficult to touch them. When people are vulnerable, however, they draw out our love for them. Is this why God made us with a capacity to be hurt, so that we can love and be loved more deeply? God needs us and wants us to be lovable. By being vulnerable, we are being open to God and to others. We are being human.

Celtic Christians were vulnerable. They had no riches stored up, no protected stone mansions; instead, they were vulnerable to the elements, to predators, to visitors. And how they were loved—loved by the people around them and by God. When they died, those around them often saw special guards of honor sent from heaven to welcome them. How lovely to be vulnerable!

Yet it is all too easy to adopt an I-don't-need-anyone attitude. How can we overcome this? Perhaps we can join with the members of the Northumbria Community, the modern-day Celtic Christian group, and follow this call:

> We are called to intentional, deliberate VULNERABILITY. We embrace the vulnerability of being teachable expressed in a discipline of prayer, in exposure to Scripture, in a willingness to be accountable to others, in ordering our ways and our heart in order to effect change . . . by making relationships the priority and not reputation . . . living openly amongst unbelievers and other believers in a way that the life of God in ours can be seen, challenged or questioned.
> RULE OF LIFE OF THE NORTHUMBRIA COMMUNITY

*Take from me, O Lord: pride and prejudice,
hardness and hypocrisy, selfishness and self-sufficiency
that I may be vulnerable, like you.*

JANUARY 30 ❖ ENDLESS ADVENTURE

Psalm 18; Genesis 21:1-21; 2 Corinthians 4:16–5:10

God makes me strong ... sure-footed as a deer ...
keeps me safe on the mountains ... trains me for battle.
PSALM 18:32–34 GNT

Paulinus of Nola described the endless adventure of the Desert Christians like this:

> Not that they beggared be in mind, or brutes, that they have chosen a dwelling place afar in lonely places: but their eyes are turned to the high stars, the very deep of Truth. Freedom they seek, an emptiness apart from worthless hopes: din of the market place and all the noisy crowding up of things, and whatever wars on the Divine, at Christ's command, and for his love, they hate. By faith and hope they follow after God, and know their quest shall not be desperate, if but the Present conquer not their souls with hollow things: that which they see they spurn, that they may come at what they don't see, their senses kindled like a torch that may blaze through the secrets of eternity.
>
> Life is meant to be an adventure; change is a gift that we have to learn to use aright. In Celtic folktales a curse that could happen to a person was to enter a field and not to be able to get back out of it. To be stuck in that place forever. It was seen as a definite curse to be unable to venture or change. ... The open gate is the opposite to this. It is the invitation to venture and to grow, the call to be among the living and vital elements in the world. The open gate is the call to explore new areas of yourself and the world around you.
> DAVID ADAM, THE OPEN GATE

You who are heroic Love have built adventure
into each day and into every life.
Help me to explore, to overcome, and to step out
towards this day's horizons
in the spirit of Christ the Endless Adventurer.

JANUARY 31 ❖ EASTERN LIGHT

Psalm 56: Proverbs 8:22–36; John 1:1–14

In the beginning was the Life Force....
The Life Force was the source of life,
and this life brought light to humanity.
JOHN 1:2, 4

The New Testament—as well as other Greek writings of the time—uses the Greek word *logos* to describe the life force that people believed lay behind the material things of the universe. Science fiction films sometimes reflect a similar belief; for example, "The Force be with you" was a saying in *Star Wars*.

This concept of the Life Force, which was strong in the Eastern world, was taken up by the Apostle John, who led many people in Eastern parts to faith in Christ. John, who had personally experienced the "flow" of this Life Force, helped people understand that it was channeled in an almost unbelievable way in one human being, Jesus Christ. When you feel this Life Force, your hopes and your horizons are transformed.

I muse on the eternal Logos of God, and all creation is lit up.
I muse on the eternal Light, and every person is lit up.
I muse on the eternal Life, and God's heaven is lit up.
I muse on the beloved disciple at the Last Supper,
and God's sacrament is lit up.
I muse on the beloved mother and apostle at the cross,
and Christ's church is lit up.
I muse on the risen Christ at Lake Galilee,
and all our Easters are lit up.
I muse on the eternal Lamb of God,
and eternity's tenderness is lit up.
I muse on the radiance of the Eastern light,
and pray that it becomes the transforming glory of the West.

Grant to me, O Lord, that tender love, that deathless vision,
that flowing life of John the loved disciple
until the Logos, the Lamb, and I, your little loved one,
flow together as one.

FEBRUARY 1 ✥ BRIGID'S DAY BLESSINGS

Psalm 66; Leviticus 25:1-7; John 12:20-26

Never forget these commands that I am giving you today . . .
write them on the doorposts of your house and on your gates.
DEUTERONOMY 6:6, 9 GNT

St. Brigid's Day falls on Imbolc, the day of the old Celtic season that marks the coming of light after the dark days of winter, the time of the suckling of the ewes. On St. Brigid's Day each year a cross is blessed and placed in homes as an extended prayer to repel the dark powers of evil and hunger that may have taken hold during the winter, and to invite in the light and provision of God.

This custom stems from an account of how Brigid cared for a pagan chief. To help make the Gospel clear to him, she made a cross from the floor's rush matting, and he subsequently became a follower of Christ. Those who still observe this custom hang rush crosses in their homes, as well as in outbuildings and other places that are not used much in winter but which will be needed in the warmer days of the growing season.

Perhaps you have a greenhouse or shed, a summer cottage or boat, a business or sporting location that will come back into use once winter is over. Why not bless these places? Why not look ahead and make sure you have no "off-limit" areas in your life where God is not welcome?

Dear Lord, may all that is here
reflect the harmony and wholeness you want for your creation.
Bless the moon that is above us, the earth that is beneath us.
May the animals in this place be happy and healthy.
Bless the hard work to be done here:
the seedlings that shall grow here,
the neighbors we shall greet here
and all whose gaze comes here.
Circle this place by day and by night.
Keep far from it all that harms, bring to it all that is good.
May this place be fragrant with the presence of the Lord,
God's peace be always here and in those who dwell here.

FEBRUARY 2 ❖ LIGHTS

Psalm 43; Exodus 13:1–16; Luke 2:22–35

God is light and in him there is no darkness at all.
1 JOHN 1:5 NIV

Forty days after Jesus' birth, Mary and Joseph presented him to God in the Temple, as Jewish law dictated. This was known as "the Meeting," to mark the meeting in the Temple between the infant Jesus and Simeon, who recognized that Jesus was the true Light of the world. In the sixth-century, Eastern churches began to celebrate this occasion on February 2 as a thanksgiving for the ending of the plague. Later, this day became popular in the Western Church as Candlemas. The blessing of the candles to symbolize Christ, the true Light of the world, has become the day's distinctive feature, a fitting thing to do near the start of Imbolc, the Celtic season of light.

Candlemas is a bittersweet celebration, however. It is a feast day, and the revelation of the child Jesus in the Temple calls for rejoicing. Nevertheless, the prophetic words of Simeon speak of the falling and rising of many, and the sword that will pierce. The old man's words point forward to Good Friday and Easter. It is as if we say, on February 2, "One last look back at Christmas—and now, we turn toward the Cross." (*Adapted from the Church of England's* The Promise of His Glory.)

> Christ as a light illumine and guide me,
> Christ as a shield overshadow me,
> Christ under me, Christ over me,
> Christ beside me on my left and my right.
> This day be within and without me,
> lonely and meek yet all-powerful.
> Be in the mouth of each to whom I speak,
> in the mouth of each who speaks to me.
> Christ as a light illumine and guide me.
> JOHN MICHAEL TALBOT, BASED ON ST. PATRICK'S BREASTPLATE

Your Holy Spirit rested on Simeon and he recognized your coming.
May we recognize you in our lives.
Simeon recognized in you the true light that brings light to the world.
Help us to receive and radiate that light.
Simeon foresaw that your mother would be pierced to the heart.
Give us the faithful love she showed at the Cross.

FEBRUARY 3 ❖ THE EVER-FRUITFUL WOMAN

Psalm 68:1-16; Leviticus 25:8-22; John 2:1-12

The kingdom of God is like a woman
who takes some yeast and mixes it with flour
until the whole batch of dough rises.
LUKE 13:20-21

Brigid was the spiritual midwife who helped bring to birth Christian Ireland, and she is a potent symbol of womanhood. Compassion, energy, and healing powers flowed through her; everything she set her hand to increased. Her large monastery at Kildare, in the central plain of Ireland, had a powerful influence.

> Her heart contained no poison, no snake lurked within her breast.
> She nursed no grudges, harbored no resentments.
> In the spiritual field where she sowed, the weather was always right.
> When she sowed the seeds of the Gospel in people's hearts, the soft rain would fall so the seeds would sprout.
> When she taught Christians how to grow in the image of Christ, the sun shone in the day, and the rain fell at night, so the fruits of good works would swell.
> When she welcomed the sick and the dying, the weather was warm and dry to prepare their souls for God's harvest.
> Now in heaven she intercedes for us, sending upon us the gentle dew of God's grace.
> A MEDIEVAL IRISH HYMN TO BRIGID

You who put beam in moon and sun,
you who put fish in stream and sea,
you who put food in earth and herd,
send your blessing up to me.
Bring forth the warmth, the tears, the laughter
from our repressed and frozen ground;
bring forth loving, healing, forgiving,
to our fretting, festering wound.
Bring in light and truth and singing
after dark and frigid years.

FEBRUARY 4 ✢ FULLNESS

Psalm 68: 17–35; Leviticus 25:23–38; John 5:43–54

> *Put me to the test and you will see*
> *that I will open the windows of heaven*
> *and pour out on you in abundance all kinds of good things.*
> MALACHI 3:10 GNT

Brigid was born about 455 CE, the daughter of Leinster's pagan King Dubtach and his slave woman, Broicsech, who was a Christian. After Brigid was conceived, two bishops from Scotland prophesied over her mother great things for her unborn child. Dubtach's infertile, jealous wife forced him to sell Broicsecil as a slave to a druid priest. The food the priest gave Broicsecil made her vomit, so a good kind woman was allowed to feed her from her own stock. When Brigid was born, even as a child, she wanted to be holy, and so she rejected anything that was not wholesome.

She grew strong and bold and generous. She loved to liberally feed the sheep, the birds, and the poor. Eventually, she returned to her father's house, where she exasperated Dubtach with her habit of giving away his food and goods.

Brigid constantly took the initiative, finding creative and surprising ways to help others. Once when she was traveling with her father, her attendant fell ill. Brigid fetched water from a well, prayed over it, and gave it to her servant to drink. It tasted like ale, he discovered. He drank it—and he recovered.

Brigid's mother was still a hardworking slave, and Brigid often returned to help her. *Lives of the Saints* from the Book of Lismore records a song she sang as she churned the butter for her mother and their many visitors: "Mary's Son, my friend, come and bless the kitchen. May we have fullness through you." Through Brigid, God multiplied the butter as Christ once multiplied loaves and fishes.

Eventually, Brigid's faith-filled way of life won the heart of the druid. He too decided to follow Christ, and he gave Brigid's mother her freedom. Brigid's generosity truly flowed out from her in all directions.

> *Mary's Son, my friend, come and bless the kitchen.*
> *May we have fullness through you.*
> *Mary's Son, my friend, come and bless the school.*
> *May we have fullness through you.*
> *Mary's Son, my friend, come and bless the soil.*
> *May we have fullness through you.*
> *Mary's Son, my friend, come and bless the work.*
> *May we have fullness through you.*

FEBRUARY 5 ❖ FULL BARRELS

Psalm 37:1-20; Leviticus 25:39-55; John 15:1-18

Give to others, and God will give to you.
Indeed, you will receive a full measure, a generous helping,
poured into you—all that you can hold.
The measure you use for others is the one that God will use for you.
LUKE 6:38

Dubtach, frustrated with Brigid's generosity with his goods, arranged a marriage between his beautiful daughter and a member of a noble family. Brigid refused. Eventually, Dubtach allowed her to become a nun and gave her a dowry.

When Brigid took the veil, an old bishop was so awe-struck by the holy fire he saw above her, that he unintentionally read the words of the consecration of a bishop over her, a privilege normally reserved for men in Brigid's day. He told a colleague who objected, "I have no power in this matter. This dignity has been given by God to Brigid."

Brigid resolved to establish a community where women could work and pray together. The king in Kildare refused her request for a grant of land, but finally, he relented when she said she would accept a plot of land as small as the size of her cloak. Once Brigid had a foothold, however, the area of land never seemed to stop growing! The church was built in a place that had been set aside for pagan worship, where a sacred flame was always kept alight. The nuns, too, kept a fire burning outside the church, night and day—an undying fire, to represent the resurrection, that was not extinguished for a thousand years.

According to the church's rules, Brigid needed priests to perform the sacraments, so she chose Bishop Conleath to govern with her . . . but no one can doubt who was really in charge! Conleath brought with him monks and many skilled craftsmen; a double monastery of men and women grew under Brigid's leadership. Sick people came to the monastery and were healed; lepers were given barrels full of apples; bishops, kings, and saints—such as Finnian—came for advice.

God wants to prosper our work, too. The prayer that follows is an ancient Celtic churning prayer. As you pray it, think of the lumps as standing for something you contribute to the world through your work.

Come, you rich lumps, come!
Come, you rich lumps, come!
Come, you rich lumps, masses large,
come, you rich lumps, come!
CARMINA GADELICA

FEBRUARY 6 ❖ TRUE WEALTH

Psalm 37:21-40; Leviticus 26:1-13; John 5:19-29

Do not store up riches for yourselves here upon earth,
where moths and rust destroy,
and robbers break in and steal.
Instead, store up riches for yourselves in heaven,
where moths and rust cannot destroy,
and robbers cannot break in and steal.
MATTHEW 6:19-20 GNT

"Her heart and mind were a throne of rest for the Holy Spirit," wrote Brigid's unknown biographer. "She was simple towards God; compassionate towards the wretched; she was splendid in miracles and marvels." Brigid's monastery brewed ale for the churches round about, and her representatives went out far and wide. Easter was an opportunity for her to minister to even larger numbers of people: a blind person, a person with tuberculosis, another with leprosy, and yet another with a mental illness were all healed through Brigid. Once, when Brigid visited a place where people feared to preach God's Word because of a person there who was raving and violent, she challenged the man to preach the Word of God himself—and he did! When her nuns reported to her that they had seen the Devil, she told them calmly, "Make Christ's Cross on your face and on your eyes."

Someone in the ninth century composed a famous poem entitled "Hail Brigid." Its theme is the triumph of Christianity, symbolized by the abandonment of the ancient hill-fort of Allen as the seat of the once-powerful kings of Leinster, and its replacement by Brigid and her Kildare monastic network. Kildare became the main source of blessing and protection for the people who lived in the region.

Later Celts imagined Brigid as a midwife or a wet nurse, present at Christ's birth, and she also became a symbol of the Bride of Christ. She was known as the guardian of the poor who work the land, and the patron of those who study. Beautiful prayers have come down to us that reflect these traditions, such as the one that follows:

May the fruits God gave Brigid lie on me.
May the delights God gave Brigid lie on me.
May the healings God gave Brigid lie on me.
May the virtues God gave Brigid lie on me
and on my loved ones.

FEBRUARY 7 ❖ VIGILS

Psalm 28; Genesis 32; Matthew 4:1-11

*The Spirit led Jesus into the desert,
where he stayed for forty days, and was tested by Satan.*
MARK 1:12

Even the busiest Celtic Christians made time to get away for prayer vigils, especially during the weeks before Easter. Samson, for example, kept Lent by taking just three small loaves and withdrawing to a remote spot for the forty days of Lent. Sometimes he would eat nothing for six days, but refresh himself with food on Sundays, the day that celebrates Jesus' resurrection. Often, Samson would stand throughout the night, letting his staff drop from his hands while he prayed.

What do ordinary mortals do on a vigil? Some of us may emulate these aspirations of an unknown Celtic hermit:

*A remote, hidden little cabin for forgiveness of my sins,
a conscience upright and spotless before Heaven.
Making good the body with good habits,
treading it boldly down.
Feeble tearful eyes for forgiveness of my passions.
Eager wailings to cloudy Heaven,
sincere and truly devout confession,
fervent showers of tears. . . .
Dry bread weighed out, well we bow the head;
water of the fair colored hillside,
that is the draught I would drink.
Stepping along the paths of the Gospel,
singing psalms every hour.
An end of talking and long stories,
constant bending of the knee.*

FEBRUARY 8 ✢ JESUS, FORGIVE MY SINS

Psalm 41; Genesis 35:1–15; Luke 18:9–14

Jesus, Son of David, have mercy on me.
MARK 20:48 NLT

Celtic Christians had checklists of common faults; these were incorporated in what were known as "Penitentials." The prayer of confession below is a useful checklist.

> Jesus, forgive my sins.
> Forgive the sins that I can remember
> and also the sins I have forgotten.
> Forgive the wrong actions I have committed
> and the right actions I have omitted.
> Forgive the times I have been weak in the face of temptation
> and those when I have been stubborn in the face of correction.
> Forgive the times I have been proud of my own achievements
> and those when I have failed to boast of your works.
> Forgive the harsh judgments I have made of others
> and the leniency I have shown myself.
> Forgive the lies I have told to others
> and the truths I have avoided.
> Forgive the pain I have caused others
> and the indulgence I have shown myself.
> Jesus have pity on me, and make me whole.
> (FROM CELTIC FIRE, ROBERT VAN DER WEYER, UNATTRIBUTED)

Remember that Celtic Christians believed God made our hearts horizontal, not just vertical; in other words, we are designed to share our secrets with another trusted human being as well as with God. The Celts called this person an "anamchara," a spiritual companion along the way, someone who can be trusted with our intimate confessions.

I apologize, Lord . . . for the shabbiness of my living,
for the shoddiness of my working, for the shallowness of my praying,
for the selfishness of my giving, for the fickleness of my feeling,
for the faithlessness of my speaking, for the dullness of my hearing,
for the stinginess of my sharing, for the slothfulness of my thinking,
for the slowness of my serving, for the coldness of my loving.

FEBRUARY 9 ✢ The Golden Rule

Psalm 10; Leviticus 19:1-18; 1 John 3:11-18

Love your neighbor the same way you love yourself.
LEVITICUS 19:18

Teilo is celebrated in *The Welsh Triads* as one of the three blessed "Visitors of the Isle of Britain." (The other two were David and Padarn.) Teilo was the one who spread the Gospel through Wales and Brittany in the sixth century; when I read about him, I get a sense of warm fellowship being generated throughout the many Christian communities he helped to establish.

He was born opposite Caldey Island and trained under Paulinus. During his studies, he met another pupil who also did much to spread the Gospel: David. When David started his main establishment at what is today the city of St. David's, Teilo went with him; he was good at cooperative teamwork.

Teilo obtained grants of land and established many Christian communities. Notable among these was his own, which was probably at Great Llandeilo. Entries in the margin of the Gospels of St. Chad (written about 700) refer to him as the founder of a monastery known as "The Family of Teilo." This was a prototype of the kind of community led by a monk who was also a bishop of his people. Such a monastery was the hearth or hub of a large extended family of Christ-followers.

When the plague decimated the population in 547, Teilo led a mass exodus of Christians to Brittany; there he linked up with Samson, who had settled at Dol. According to the story, the two of them planted a great orchard of fruit trees, three miles long, reaching from Dol to Cai. Teilo stayed in Dol seven years and established other communities in the surrounding region.

The hermit Cadoc is said to have once asked Teilo, "What is the greatest wisdom in a person?"

Teilo answered, "To refrain from injuring another person when one has the power to do so."

Teilo did not abuse his power. Instead, he followed the Golden Rule: "Do to others what you would like them to do to you."

Teach me, Gentle Jesus of the cradle and the cross,
to forego vengeance at all times
and to reach out my hands in love to all.

FEBRUARY 10 ✢ MARTYRDOM

Psalm 17; Daniel 3; Hebrews 11:17-38

They were stoned, they were sawn in two,
they were killed by the sword.
They went round clothed in skins of sheep or goats—
poor, persecuted, ill-treated. . . .
They wandered like refugees in the deserts and hills,
living in caves and holes in the ground.
What a record all these have won by their faith!
HEBREWS 11:37–39 GNT

The long-ago Christian Celts had an instinct for going all-out. The stories of Christ's earliest followers who had been killed for their faith inspired them. The Celts' eagerness to take extreme measures led them to not only admire these martyrs but, since the Celts themselves faced no physical persecution, to find nonphysical ways to become martyrs. They may have read what Saint Jerome wrote to a young woman whose widowed mother had given away all her possessions and entered a convent: "Your mother has been crowned because of her long martyrdom. It is not only the shedding of blood which is the mark of a true witness, but the service of a dedicated heart is a daily martyrdom. The first is wreathed with a crown of roses and violets, the second of lilies." They also read in *The Life of St. Martin* (who was the first official saint *not* killed for his faith): "He achieved martyrdom without blood. For of what human sorrows did he not, for the hope of eternity, endure the pain—in hunger, in night watchings, in nakedness, in fasting, in the insults of the envious, in the persecutions of the wicked, in care for the sick, in anxiety for those in peril."

The Celts called those who had lost actual blood for the sake of their faith "red martyrs," while they referred to those who gave up home and possessions as "white martyrs." The Irish came up with the idea of "glas martyrs" (the Gaelic word *glas* can be translated as either "green" or "blue"), people who endured an extended penance or pilgrimage, going into exile from either home or comfort because of their love of God. The word *glas*—which can refer to weather that is cold and bracing, but can also be used to describe the wan, blue color of a corpse—carries implications of both life and death. Green martyrs live a quiet, daily struggle for goodness and purity, shedding the bad habits and routines that separate them from God.

The Celtic concept of martyrdom means we put aside everything that comes between us and God . . . and that we are willing to lay down our lives for our neighbor.

Take my life. I lay it down.

FEBRUARY 11 ✣ CAEDMON, THE SONG MAKER

Psalm 45; Exodus 15:1-21; Matthew 25:14-30

Let them tell of God's works with songs of joy.
PSALM 107:22

The first of English poets he
who, nurtured by the Whitby sea,
a poor and simple cowherd seemed.
Yet here the gold of poetry gleamed
though hidden deep within his soul,
for from the company he stole,
fearful to be found afraid
when they their entertainment made;
the very least among the throng
with little speech nor any song.
Then in the stillness of one night
his soul was filled with heavenly light.
A vision of the world being made
of God's creation all displayed
as in the stable stall he lay.
Dreaming he heard an angel pray
and speak to him of God's great world
and how its majesty unfurled.
Then day by day to his inspired mind
that had seemed deaf and dumb and blind
there came sweet words so bright and clear.
Then Mother Hilda came to hear
and stayed with all her Abbey folk
while Caedmon, poet of Whitby spoke....
Then folk would learn the poems by heart
or memorize a favorite part
making them one with Christian praise
in those remote, unlettered days.
TOM STAMP

Praise you, Wisdom and Founder of all.

FEBRUARY 12 ✣ STAND UP

Psalm 11; Jeremiah 20; 2 Timothy 1

Do not be ashamed, then, of witnessing for our Lord;
and don't be ashamed of me, a prisoner for Christ's sake.
2 TIMOTHY 1:8

When we are teenagers, peer pressure is a powerful force. We have lost the security we once found as children who belonged to our parents, and so many things seem uncertain; we seek temporary safety by going along with the crowd. Even as adults, we often still need exceptional courage to stand up to peer pressure. Whatever our age, Cuthbert's example can encourage and inspire us.

When Cuthbert was a teenager, he saw a crowd gather by the River Tyne to watch an unusual sight. Curious, he joined the crowd to find out what was happening.

Some monks who had recently built a monastery were trying to get timbers to it along the river estuary, but a contrary wind was driving their rafts out to sea. Their five rafts looked like birds bobbing up and down on the waves. Meanwhile, on shore, the other monks had seen what was happening, but their efforts to help came to nothing. So they gathered round a rock and prayed for their brothers. The people from the outside community did not like strangers, especially these strange men who had brought with them new beliefs—and now, a crowd had gathered around the praying monks to jeer. They shouted, "Good riddance!" to the men on the rafts, who were in danger of drowning.

When Cuthbert realized what was going on, he did not remain silent. "Do you realize what you are doing?" he asked them. "Would it not be more humane to pray for their safety rather than to gloat over their misfortune?"

Now the crowd turned their verbal abuse at Cuthbert. "Nobody here is going to pray for them," they shouted.

Cuthbert responded by dropping to his knees and praying. The wind at once completely changed direction and brought the monks to a perfect landing beside the monastery.

The crowd fell silent, hushed by a sense of shame and awe. Many of them felt a genuine respect for Cuthbert, and they thought well of him from that time on.

Lord, I crave the approval of others
and I don't like standing out in a crowd—
yet you want me to be true and loving.
Give me grace to pray, and courage to stand up
beside anyone who is rejected and in danger.

FEBRUARY 13 ❖ MODOMNOC'S BLESSING

Psalm 128; Numbers 7:22-27; 1 Peter 3:8-12

I promise I will give you a land flowing with milk and honey.
EXODUS 3:8

In the Hebrew scripture, God frequently promised to bring the people of Israel to a land full of honey, which meant a land full of blessing. Thousands of years later, Celtic Christ-followers often invited God to give blessings to the land—and some of these blessings included honey. What happened to Modomnoc, whom we celebrate today, was the ultimate in generous blessing.

Modomnoc—who was said to have been born into Ireland's great O'Neill family—had come to study under Saint David at his Pembrokeshire monastery. One of Modomnoc's duties during his many years there was beekeeping, an essential part of the monastery's provision, which he had greatly developed.

When the time came for him to return to Ireland, the whole monastery prayed with him and sent him on his way with God's blessings—but unfortunately, the monastery's entire swarm of bees followed him and settled on his boat! Beekeepers know the effort required to get a swarm of bees back into their hive, but Modomnoc finally succeeded in doing this. A day or two later, he repeated his farewells and set out again for the boat. The same thing happened all over again, and Modomnoc once again painstakingly returned the bees.

Modomnoc suggested that this time he would linger until the bees were tired and sleepy, and then he would quietly slip away. This gave the brothers yet another opportunity to pray over him and invite God's blessings on him and his new work in Ireland. This time, as David prayed, he realized that God intended the bees to be part of the blessing David was to give to Ireland.

So David prayed for the bees, using the words of the blessing below. David's twelfth-century biographer observed that the blessing was fulfilled completely, for any bees sent back from Ireland dwindled to nothing in Wales, while the bees in Ireland, a land that previously had no reputation for bees, flourished beyond measure.

We are each called to release God's blessing on the people and creatures around us. Remember, however, that in order to bless another you may need to let go of something that is precious to you!

May the land to which you are journeying
abound with your offspring.
May you forever leave our land
and your offspring never increase here.
But may they never fail to increase
in the land to which you go.

FEBRUARY 14 ✢ LOVER'S CONTEMPLATION

Psalm 63; Exodus 24:1–11; Revelation 1:9–20

My whole being desires you....
Your constant love is better than life itself, and so I will praise you....
I will give you thanks as long as I live....
My soul will feast and be satisfied....
All night long I think of you.... I cling to you.
SELECTED FROM PSALM 63:1–8 GNT

Love reaches out beyond all human feelings. It is greater than voices can express; neither the movements of the human tongue nor articulated words can contain it. The soul, bathed in light from on high, no longer uses human speech, which is always inadequate. Like an overabundant spring, all feelings overflow and spring forth toward God at the same time. In this short moment, it says so many things that the soul, once it has recovered itself, could neither express nor go over them in its memory.
JOHN CASSIAN

Columba went to seek a place remote from men and fitting for prayer.
ADAMNAN

Cuthbert dwelt (at Lindisfarne) also according to Holy Scripture, following the contemplative amid the active life.
LIFE OF CUTHBERT BY AN ANONYMOUS MONK OF LINDISFARNE

Cuthbert finally entered into the remoter solitude he had so long sought, thirsted after, and prayed for. He was delighted that after a long and spotless active life he should be thought worthy to ascend to the stillness of Divine contemplation.
BEDE

There is a contemplative in all of us, almost strangled but still alive, who craves quiet enjoyment of the Now and longs to touch the seamless garment of silence which makes us whole.
ALAN P. TOREY

Lord, you are my island; in your bosom I rest.
You are the calm of the sea; in that peace I lie.
You are the deep waves of the ocean; in their depths I stay.
You are the smooth white strand of the shore; in its swell I sing.
You are the ocean of life that laps my being; in you is my eternal joy.
ATTRIBUTED TO COLUMBA

FEBRUARY 15 ✢ SOLITUDE

Psalm 27; Exodus 24:12-18; Mark 1:35-39

*Very early the next morning, long before daylight,
Jesus got up and left the house.
He went out of the town to a solitary place, where he prayed.*
MARK 1:35 GNT

The one who abides in solitude and is quiet, is delivered from fighting three battles—those of hearing, speech, and sight. Then that person will have but one battle to fight—the battle of the heart.
ANTONY OF EGYPT

Cuthbert served as prior at Lindisfarne, but "finally fled from worldly glory and sailed away privately and secretly. . . . After some years, desiring a solitary life, he went to the island called Farne, which is in the midst of the sea and surrounded on every side by water, a place where, before this, almost no one could remain alone for any amount of time on account of the many illusions caused by devils. But he fearlessly put them to flight, and, digging down almost a cubit of a man [the length of a man's arm from his fingertips to his elbow, about a foot and a half] into the earth, through very hard and stony rock, he made a space to dwell in. He also built a marvelous wall another cubit above it by placing together and compacting with earth, stones of such great size as none would believe except those who knew that so much of the power of God was in him; therein he made some little dwelling places from which he could see nothing except the heavens above."
LIFE OF CUTHBERT BY AN ANONYMOUS MONK OF LINDISFARNE

In Wales and Ireland as many as five hundred place names (for example Dysart or Disserth) still recall a place where some believer, inspired by the Desert Christians, made the desert of the heart their own. And a place in the Channel Isles is still named, simply, Egypt.

Today people create desert places of their own, and "desert days" in their homes. Solitude is an essential part of our spiritual well-being.

*Still is the earth; make still my body.
Still is the night; make still my mind.
Still are the spheres; make still my soul.*

FEBRUARY 16 ✣ BROKENNESS

Psalm 51; Jeremiah 4:19-31; Luke 23:26-43

A broken and a contrite heart, O God, you will not reject.
PSALM 51:17

The soul, harassed with sin and toil, finds repose only in humility. Humility is its sole refreshment amid so many evils. . . . Mortification is indeed intolerable to the proud and hard of heart, but a consolation to the one who loves only what is meek and lowly.
RULE OF COLUMBANUS

I read and write. I worship my God every day and every night.

I study the Scriptures, puzzling over their meaning, I write books for the guidance of others.

I eat little, and sleep little. When I eat I continue praying, and when I sleep my snores are songs of praise.

Yet I weep for my sins, because I cannot forget them. O Mary, O Christ, have mercy on this wretched soul.
A SCRIBE IN A CELTIC MONASTERY

I asked God for strength, that I might achieve;
I was made weak, that I might learn to humbly obey.
I asked for health, that I might do great things;
I was given infirmity, that I might do better things.
I asked for power, that I might have the praise of people;
I was given weakness, that I might feel the need of God.
AN UNKNOWN AMERICAN SOLDIER

Spirit of the living God, fall afresh on me.
Break me, melt me, mould me, fill me.
Spirit of the living God, fall afresh on me.
DANIEL IVERSON

FEBRUARY 17 ❖ TRIALS

Psalm 40:1-11; Jeremiah 4:1-18; 2 Thessalonians 1

Consider yourselves fortunate when all kinds of trials come your way.
JAMES 1:2 GNT

Cuthbert, Bede tells us, was prepared by the fires of temporal pain for the joys of eternal bliss. Herefrith, the abbot of Lindisfarne, told Bede exactly what happened.

When Herefrith and some monks came to visit Cuthbert on Farne Island, they discovered that Cuthbert was terminally ill. Cuthbert declined Herefrith's offer to leave some brothers on the island to care for him. Instead, he told Herefrith, "Come back when God directs you."

Five days of violent weather followed Herefrith's return to Lindisfarne, and the storms kept any brothers from returning to Cuthbert. Herefrith reported, "As events proved, this was a divine dispensation. For in order that Almighty God might, by chastisement, purify his servant from all blemish of worldly weakness and in order that he might show his adversaries that they could avail nothing against the strength of his faith, he wished to test him by bodily pain and by a still fiercer contest with the ancient foe, cutting him off from human beings for that length of time."

When Herefrith and his companions did return at last, Cuthbert assured him, "It happened through the providence of God that destitute of human company and care I should suffer some trials." He went on to tell Herefrith that once he was alone, his illness immediately became worse. He crawled to the guest hut by the shore and lay there without moving for five days, his only food a few nibbles of onions. "My adversaries have never persecuted me so frequently, during all the time I have been living on this island, as over the last five days," he told his friend. And yet clearly Cuthbert valued this experience.

After that, some brothers stayed with Cuthbert until he died. One of them, Beda, was one of Cuthbert's oldest friends, who surely comforted Cuthbert in the time he had left after his days of trial.

Lord, if this day you have to correct us,
put us right, not out of anger
but with a mother's and a father's heart.
So may we, your children, be kept free of all falseness and foolishness.
FROM MEXICO

FEBRUARY 18 ✢ ANGER

Psalm 40:12-17; Jeremiah 12:1-6; Ephesians 4

Be angry, but do not sin. Do not let the sun go down on your anger.
EPHESIANS 4:6 NIV

Anger is the most fierce passion. It is a boiling and a stirring up of wrath against one who has caused injury—or is thought to have done so. It constantly irritates the soul and above all at the time of prayer it seizes the mind and flashes the picture of the offensive person before one's eyes.
EVAGRIUS

A restless brother in a desert community frequently became angry with his brothers. So he thought to himself: "I'll go and live in a place of solitude; once I won't have to speak to or listen to anyone I shall be at peace and the anger will disappear." So he went to live alone in a cave. One day he filled a jug with water for himself, and placed it on the floor. It suddenly overturned. He filled it a second time and the same thing happened, as it did a third time. His anger flared up and he smashed the jug in rage.

Later, when he came to himself, he realized he had been subverted by the spirit of anger, and that he had no one to blame. "Here am I alone," he said to himself, "and despite this the spirit of anger has conquered me. I shall return to the community, for in every place there is need for struggle, for patient perseverance, and above all, for the help of God." So he returned to his community.
SAYINGS OF THE DESERT FATHERS

A love that cannot find an outlet turns inward, and not being able to reach out and touch the thing it loves, be it a place or a people in that place, turns to anger and becomes confused.
BRIAN KEENAN, AN EVIL CRADLING

The Desert Fathers and Mothers did not focus on who is to blame for the passions that bind us. They knew that the wounds within us all destroy our own and others' lives. Our task, they thought, was to fight against the passions, and to seek healing with the help of God and each other in order to love as we were made to love.

Help me conquer anger by gentleness,
greed by generosity, apathy by fervor.

FEBRUARY 19 ✢ TEARS

Psalm 42; Jeremiah 8:18–9:10; 2 Corinthians 2

Return to the Lord with fasting, weeping, and mourning. . .
for your God is gracious and merciful.
JOEL 2:12–13

When we die, we will not be criticized for having failed to work miracles. We will not be accused of having failed to be theologians or contemplatives. But we will certainly have some explanation to offer to God for not having mourned unceasingly. . . . When the soul grows tearful, weeps, and is filled with tenderness, and all this without having striven for it, then let us run, for the Lord has arrived uninvited and is holding out to us the sponge of loving sorrow, the cool waters of blessed sadness with which to wipe away the record of our sins. Guard these tears like the apple of your eye until they go away, for they have a power greater than anything that comes from our own thoughts and our own meditation.
JOHN CLIMACUS, ABBOT OF SINAI, SEVENTH CENTURY

David of Wales, we are told by his biographer Rhigyfarch, was "overflowing with daily fountains of tears." This is how David comforted the mother of a dead boy: "Filled with compassion for human weakness, he approached the body of the dead boy, whose face he watered with his tears and restored him to his mother."

When Cuthbert offered up the saving Victim [that is, when he celebrated Holy Communion] as a sacrifice to God, he offered his prayer to the Lord not by raising his voice but by shedding tears which sprang from the depths of his heart.
BEDE

Grant me tears when rising,
grant me tears when resting,
beyond your every gift altogether for love of you, Mary's Son.
Grant me tears in bed to moisten my pillow
so that his dear ones may help to cure the soul.
Grant me contrition of heart so that I may not be in disgrace.
O Lord, protect me, and grant me tears. . . .
O Creator, flowing in streams from my eyes.
For my anger and my jealousy
and my pride, a foolish deed,
in pools from my inmost parts bring forth tears.
OLD IRISH (TRANSLATED BY DAVIES)

FEBRUARY 20 ⁘ ATHLETES OF THE SPIRIT

Psalm 18:30-50; Jeremiah 15:10-21; 1 Timothy 4

*Physical exercise has value in this life,
but spiritual exercise makes us stronger
in both this life and the next.*
1 TIMOTHY 4:8

Most of us enjoy sports—or at least watching them. A strong, supple body brings joy; the sense of being pitted against the odds gives a thrill; and the sweat, the brawn, the skill, the brain, the pounding heart, and the pulsing muscles are all part of sports' attraction.

Cuthbert, who was agile and acrobatic as a youth, went on to become, in Bede's words "our athlete of God." The Fathers and Mothers of the Deserts, as well as the Celtic saints, were known as "athletes of the Spirit." Built into their lives was disciplined training and daily exercise of body, mind, and spirit. This spiritual athleticism was part of the monastic ideal. The old saints strove for a prize, an eternal prize. Their chosen way of life involved pitting themselves against opponents, though their opponents were spiritual forces within and without. Their life was a race—a race against encroaching apathy, unbelief, or arrogance—and it took all they had, both physically and spiritually.

Wondrous the warriors who lived in Iona,
thrice fifty in monastic rule
with their boats along the main sea,
three score men a-rowing.
FROM THE BOOK OF LISMORE

*Bless to me my body,
bless to me my brain,
bless to me my training,
bless to me my game.*

FEBRUARY 21 ✢ TAMING THE TONGUE

Psalm 39; Jeremiah 1; James 3

Does anyone think they are religious?
If they do not control their tongue, their religion is worthless....
The tongue is like a forest fire.
JAMES 1:26; 3:6

A group of desert monks traveled by boat to visit Antony. Another old monk whom they did not know was also on the boat, and it turned out that he, too, was visiting Antony. Antony said to the old monk, "Did you find good brothers to accompany you?"

"Indeed they are good," said the monk, "but their house has no door. Whoever wishes may enter the stable door and set the ass loose." He said this because whatever came into their minds they spoke about with their mouths.
SAYINGS OF THE DESERT FATHERS

The elders at Iona agreed that Aidan "was worthy to be made a bishop and that he was the man to send to instruct those ignorant unbelievers, since he had proved himself to be preeminently endowed with the grace of discretion, which is the mother of all virtues."
BEDE

Three sisters of lying: perhaps, maybe, guess.

Three elegant things that are best ignored: elegant manners in someone whose heart is false; elegant words from someone who is foolish; elegant prayers from a priest wanting money.

Three signs of rudeness: a visit that lasts longer than the welcome; sharp questions that cut a person's soul; effusive gratitude when none is meant.
CELTIC TRIADS

Could you sell your parrot to the town gossip with an easy mind?
WILL ROGERS

Teach me
when to be silent and when to speak,
when to listen and when to leave,
when to praise and when to refrain,
when to laugh and when to weigh,
when to tell and when to wait.

FEBRUARY 22 ✢ ANOINTINGS

Psalm 89:19–37; Jeremiah 16; 2 Peter 1

*Jesus said, "You are Peter
and on this rock I will build my Church.
And the gates of the underworld can never hold out against it.
I will give you the keys of the kingdom of heaven:
Whatever you bind on earth shall be bound in heaven;
whatever you loose on earth shall be loosed in heaven."*
MATTHEW 16:18–19 JB

In the Celtic church, earthly appointments followed spiritual anointings.

Celtic church leaders in the west of Britain were accustomed to come together for a synod during the forty-day period of prayer before Easter. Samson was not among them, however, for he had made up his mind to be free of all worldly involvements, and he had gone to a cave to be alone and pray during this time. Such was the attraction of his holiness, though, that the church leaders sent a letter urging him not to work for himself alone, since his ministry would be profitable to many, and instead, to come to the synod. Samson did as they asked, and on the day of his arrival at the synod, they appointed him abbot of a monastery that Bishop Germanus had founded.

At that same synod, Samson had a dream of himself surrounded by crowds of "delightful beings" and by the apostles Peter, John, and James, dressed in silk vestments with golden crowns (the garb of Eastern bishops). In his dream, the men went into the church in order to pray (as Samson thought), but in fact, they ordained Samson deacon.

Samson did not tell anyone his dream but on February 22, the day when bishops ordained new priests, Bishop Dubricius also had a dream: he dreamed Samson was one of them. Since it was the custom to ordain three new priests, and only two candidates had so far been agreed upon, Dubricius and his fellow bishops decided the dream was a message from God that Samson should become the third ordinand. When they informed Samson, he confided to them the dream God had given him.

What a confirmation this was! As Samson sat in the special chair for the ordination, those who stood by saw a dove hover over him throughout the ceremony. And when Samson celebrated Holy Communion, they saw what looked like fire coming out of his mouth and nostrils. Samson later said that from that day onward, whenever he celebrated Holy Communion, he could see angels assisting him.

Lord, may all the roles I fill today be divine appointments.

FEBRUARY 23 ✢ DO NOT JUDGE

Psalm 112; Jeremiah 18:1-12; Matthew 7:1-6

Do not judge others, or you, too, will be judged.
For in the same way that you judge others, you too will be judged.
MATTHEW 7:1

A Desert Christian, coming into Scete, asked a local brother to lead him to two desert fathers he had long desired to meet. His first choice was Arsenius. Arsenius received him, prayed, and then sat with him in silence. The brother who acted as guide said, "I must take my leave," and the confused visitor did likewise. Then they went to Abba Moses, a former thief who had been converted. Moses gave them a meal and entertained them both royally.

The guide asked his visiting friend, "Which of the two is more to your liking?"

"To my mind the one who gave us a good welcome and meal," the visitor replied.

This came to the ears of one of the fathers, who prayed, "Lord, reveal to me how it is that one man serves you by withdrawing from sight and speech, and another serves you by being a good fellow with everyone." He was shown the answer in a dream: Two ships sailed down the river. In one he saw the Holy Spirit sailing with Father Arsenius in silence and peace. In the other boat he saw Father Moses, and the angels of God were feeding him with lashings of honey.
SAYINGS OF THE DESERT FATHERS

> The camel never sees its own hump,
> but its neighbor's hump is ever before it.
> *ARAB PROVERB*

> Whenever I say "they,"
> I should hear an alarm bell.
> D. PRESCOTT

> *Christ be in heart of foe and stranger,*
> *Christ be in those who drive me to anger,*
> *Christ be in me to welcome and "manger."*

FEBRUARY 24 ⁘ AMBITION

Psalm 145; Jeremiah 13:15-27; 1 John 2

*"Do you think you are going to be a king
and rule over us?" Joseph's brothers asked him.
So they hated him even more because of his dreams. . . .
They plotted against him and decided to kill him.*
GENESIS 37:8, 18 GNT

Joseph's brothers thought they would not reach their own potential if their brother fulfilled his. This fear was the opposite of the truth. In reality, Joseph's brothers reached their own historic leadership roles *through* Joseph, not in spite of him.

> Of all the emotions and desires within the human breast, the one that is most often misunderstood and misused is ambition. This emotion distinguishes us from all the other creatures that inhabit the world. An animal, bird, fish, or insect has no ambition; it simply looks for food in order to sustain itself for another day. But the human being can look ahead, anticipating the consequences of present actions far into the future.
> Ambition itself is neither good nor bad; what matters is how it is directed. Ambition may be directed towards the accumulation of power and wealth, towards material superiority over others. Such ambition is evil, because power and wealth can only be gained at the expense of others. Or ambition may be directed towards holiness and moral perfection, towards becoming like Christ himself. The emotion which lusts after power and wealth is the same emotion which yearns for holiness and perfection; the difference lies in the way in which the emotion is directed.
> PELAGIUS

> The approach of the Celtic missionaries was essentially gentle and sensitive. They sought to live alongside the people with whom they wanted to share the good news of Christ, to understand and respect their beliefs and not to dominate or culturally condition them.
> IAN BRADLEY

*Give me the ambition
to use everything I have for the highest purposes,
to abuse no person, to misuse no powers,
to harness skills to service,
and to bring great things to flower.*

FEBRUARY 25 ✢ LORD, HAVE MERCY

Psalm 31:1-10; Jeremiah 14; 1 John 1

God, have mercy on me, a sinner.
LUKE 18:13

In the story told in Luke 18, Jesus contrasts the wordy smugness in the prayers of the religious person with the simple heart-cry of the man who knew how sinful and needy he was: "Have mercy on me, a sinner."

His one sentence laid the foundation for a long heritage of prayer. Saint Patrick urged his followers to make these words their own, which he had learned was the constant prayer of the universal church: "Lord, have mercy; Christ, have mercy." The Desert Christians began this prayer with the words, "Lord Jesus Christ," to make sure that God's own Son—not just any old lord—was being addressed. Some groups repeated the prayer constantly, hundreds and thousands of times, until in the end it became "a conditioned reflex." This custom has been continued among some Eastern Orthodox Christians and is now reviving also in the West. It is known as the "Jesus Prayer."

Repeating this prayer is not "vain repetition," as some Christians have alleged, not if the prayer comes from the heart and not just from the head. Some Christians reserve the Jesus Prayer for Saturday evenings, when they say it repeatedly as a preparation for Sunday. Others shorten the prayer to just the name "Jesus."

For myself, I find this prayer most powerful when I am desperate, despondent, physically weak, or pressed by competing demands. In these circumstances, I lack the energy to form my own prayers, I lack the purity to be sure that my prayers are not really ego demands, and I lack the wisdom to know how to sort out competing demands. So I give up trying to be in charge of my life; instead, I merely carry on doing whatever I have to do, praying the Jesus Prayer in my weakness.

Isn't that all that God requires of any of us?

Lord Jesus Christ, have mercy on me, a sinner.

FEBRUARY 26 ⁘ DETACHMENT

Psalm 31:11-24; Jeremiah 13:1-11; 1 John 3:1-10

We seem to have nothing, but we really possess everything.
2 CORINTHIANS 6:10 GNT

Unless a person says in his heart,
"I alone and God are in this world," he shall not find quiet.
ABBA ALLOIS

I adore not the voice of birds,
nor snuff, nor gambling in this world,
nor a boy, nor gambling, nor women.
My Druid is Christ, the Son of God,
Christ, Son of Mary, the Great Abbot,
the Father, the Son and the Holy Spirit.
ATTRIBUTED TO COLUMBA

Let us be careful that no image
except that of God take shape in the soul.
COLUMBANUS

I wear life like a loose robe.
ANONYMOUS WOMAN

Let nothing disturb you, nothing dismay you,
all things pass, God never changes.
Peace attains all that it strives for.
They who live in God find they lack nothing.
God alone suffices.
ST. TERESA OF AVILA

*Wean me from false anxieties,
wean me from false addictions,
lead me to desire nothing but you,
till my soul is at peace.*

FEBRUARY 27 ✢ WAR AGAINST EVIL

Psalm 58; Jeremiah 18:4-17; 1 John 4

*So put on God's armor now! Then when the evil day comes
you will be able to resist the enemy's attacks
and after fighting to the end, you will still hold your ground.*
EPHESIANS 6:13 GNT

It is not for quiet or security that we have formed a community in the monastery, but for a struggle and a conflict. We have met here for a contest, we have embarked upon a war against our sins. . . . The struggle upon which we are engaged is full of hardships, full of dangers, for it is the struggle of a person against himself. . . .

For this purpose we have gathered together in this tranquil retreat, this spiritual camp, that we may day after day wage an unwearying war against our passions.
FAUSTUS OF RIEZ

While Cuthbert sang his psalms, he worked with his hands, and so by toil he drove away the heaviness of sleep, or else indeed he went round the island finding out how everything was getting on. . . . He used to blame the faintheartedness of brothers who were upset if aroused during the night. "No one annoys me by rousing me from sleep," he used to say, "rather, the person who wakens me gladdens me. . . ." In his zeal for right living he was keen to reprove sinners, yet he was kind and forbearing in pardoning those who were penitent, so that sometimes, when someone was confessing their sins to him, he would burst into tears, and so, by his own example, show the penitent what he should do. . . .

Not until he first gained victory over our invisible enemy by solitary prayer and fasting did he take it upon himself to seek out a remote battlefield further away from his fellows [the Inner Fame Island]. . . . At the entry of our soldier of Christ armed with "the helmet of salvation, the shield of faith and the sword of the spirit which is the word of God" the devil fled and his host of allies with him.
BEDE, LIFE OF ST CUTHBERT

*Teach us, good Lord, to serve you as you deserve,
to give and not to count the cost,
to fight and not to heed the wounds,
to labor and not to ask for any reward
except that of knowing that we do your will.*
IGNATIUS LOYOLA

FEBRUARY 28 ❖ MASTERING THE SPIRITS

Psalm 59; Jeremiah 3:1-8; 1 John 5

*We know that the whole world lies under the power of the evil one.
But we know that the Son of God has come
and given us understanding
so we may know the One who is real and true.*
1 JOHN 5:19-20

Thirty years before Saint David was born, God spoke to his father in a dream. In the dream, he was hunting and came upon a stag, a fish, and a hive of bees. A voice told him to send the hive, portions of the stag's meat, and the fish to a local monastery, where they would be preserved for a son who would be born to him.

The three gifts, he was told in the dream, were symbols of three features of his future son. The honeycomb symbolized wisdom, for as the honey lies embedded in the wax, so his son would perceive the spiritual meaning embedded in the Bible's words. The fish symbolized his lifestyle, for as fish live in water, so this son would live in God and say no to addictive food and drink, eating only basics such as bread and water. The stag represented the power he would have over Satan, the ancient serpent. In stories told in medieval bestiaries, stags that are ill or old use their breath to draw snakes from their holes and then swallow them; the stags then find water and drink large amounts to overcome the poison—and they "shed all their old age." In a similar way, the son who would be born would overcome humanity's ancient enemy, and he would renew his life in flowing springs of tears. In this way, the future son, in the power of the Trinity, would acquire a healing knowledge of the way to overcome evil spirits.

All this was fulfilled in David's life. And we too, in our turn, can gradually learn mastery of self and evil.

*Lord, as fish live in water, may I live in you.
Grant me the strength to do without things.
Grant me the wisdom to see the "within" of things.
Grant me the knowledge to take the measure of evil spirits.
Grant me understanding to know you, who alone are true.*

FEBRUARY 29 ❖ TAKE A LEAP

Psalm 61; The Song of Songs 1; 2 John

There is a fragrance about you. . . .
No woman could help loving you.
Take me with you, and we'll run away;
be my king and take me to your room.
We will be happy together, drink deep, and lose ourselves in love.
THE SONG OF SONGS 1:3–4 GNT

Once every four years, in a Leap Year, according to an old tradition, women can "take a leap" and ask young men to marry them on February 29. Although we no longer observe this custom, today is a day when all of us may take a leap into the Spring that will soon be here . . . and into the love that is in the air.

I praise two who is one and two
who is really three
who made. . .
love in our senses. . . .
EARLY MIDDLE WELSH

The month of February, a feast is rare.
The spade and the wheel are hard at work.
The ox has no voice to complain.
The evenings grow longer, the mornings earlier.
The sun grows brighter, but the clouds are darker.
A rainbow is seen after storms.
The greatest pleasure is friendship.
FROM WELSH GNOMIC POEMS

Lord, may we leap into your love today,
and may these graces be born in us:
the grace of form, the grace of voice,
the grace of provision, the grace of goodness,
the grace of wisdom, the grace of caring,
the grace of godly speech.
INSPIRED BY THE CARMINA GADELICA

MARCH 1 ∴ DAVID OF WALES, THE WATERMAN

Psalm 60; 1 Samuel 17:31-54; 1 Peter 5

*In the same way that the oceans overflow with water,
the earth shall be filled with the certainty of God's abundance,.*
HABAKKUK 2:14

David the faithful witness of Christ's new Law, like a bright star from heaven shines forth in Britain. His illustrious life and teaching adorn Wales. Like the birth of the Forerunner, the Baptist, his birth was divinely foretold. The future greatness of Christ's servant is declared by heavenly signs: honey, water and mystic deer. This is the champion of the British, the leader and teacher of the Welsh, supporting the citizens of God. Single-hearted, he condemns luxury. Spurning the city, he seeks the valley as befits the lowly. At his birth, the people name him "Dewi ddyfryr," which means "Water-life David." He cures the blind, he expels diseases and he drives away the devil. A doctor of Christ's law, he writes a book which God completes. May David, our leader and strong champion, overcome by his prayers the Goliaths, the giant enemies, of our time.
ADAPTED FROM THE ANCIENT WELSH MISSAL TEXT, ABOUT 1440

David and his monks were known as the Watermen:

As fish live in water so these folk live in God.
As birds fly high and carefree so these folk move in God.
As deer run straight and graceful so these folk run with God.
As waters flow so clearly so these folk flow with God.
As fire burns bright and fiercely so these folk blaze for God.

*Lord, inspired by David and the Watermen,
help us to live in you as fish live in water,
help us to move in you as birds fly in air,
help us to run to you as deer run through the forest,
help us to flow with you as water flows,
help us to burn brightly for you as fire burns.
and may the fire of faith blaze afresh in us.*

March 2 ✥ The Answer to the Rat Race

Psalm 64; 1 Samuel 16:1-13; Luke 14:7-14

Jesus said, "When you are invited to a celebration
do not sit down in the best place . . . sit in the lowest place,
so that your host will come to you and say,
'Come on up, my friend, to a better place.'"
Luke 14:8, 10

Chad was probably the youngest of four brothers who trained under Aidan at Lindisfarne, but he was also the brightest. This never went to his head, and he was always a model of humility. He went over to Ireland for his "further education," but when his brother Cedd, who was Abbot of Lastingham, died, Chad was sent back to Northumbria to take his place as abbot. There he became known as an admirable teacher, though he also encouraged a recruit who wanted to do only manual labor rather than book work.

Meanwhile, the king of the Northumbrians, Oswy, had gone along with the appointment of a monk named Wilfred as Bishop of the Northumbrians. Wilfred was so mesmerized by the practices and pomp of the Roman style of church life that he went to the continent to be "properly" consecrated—and then stayed on and on, leaving the post back home vacant. Oswy became restive, and eventually, he asked Chad to fill the empty position.

Chad was Bishop of the Northumbrians for three years until 669. Then the Bishop of Rome sent the powerful Theodore of Tarsus to be Archbishop of Canterbury and to bring the English church into line with standard Roman organization. When Theodore explained to Chad that his consecration as bishop had not met these norms, Chad replied that he had never considered himself worthy to be a bishop in the first place. He was willing to resign, which he did in favor of Wilfred. His genuine humility and holiness made such an impression on Theodore, however, that he re-consecrated Chad as a bishop, and, when the Bishop of Mercia died, Theodore asked Chad to take his place.

On one point, though, Theodore was firm. Chad, like Aidan, loved to evangelize by walking everywhere, and he refused to ride on a horse. Mercia, however, was a huge diocese, so Theodore not only ordered Chad to use a horse, but he physically lifted him onto a horse with his own hands! Humility is a wonderful quality—but we must be careful not to be so humble that we squander our own health and well-being.

Servant King, be king of my hearth and king of my heart,
be king of my hands and king of my head,
be king of my thoughts and king of my habits.

MARCH 3 ✧ WIN ALL PEOPLE BY ALL MEANS

Psalm 65; 1 Samuel 17:55–18:5; Ephesians 3

*The people tried to keep Jesus from leaving, but he said to them,
"I must preach the Good News about the Kingdom of God
in other towns also. This is what God sent me to do."*
LUKE 4:42–43

David's ministry in Wales started with a literal splash. The priest who baptized him was assisted by a blind man named Movi, who was the one to immerse David under the water. The water splashed up over Movi's eyes—and he regained his sight. David's ability to heal people's vision is revealed in another story as well, this one about Paulinus, who had a reputation as "a fosterer of righteousness" somewhere in Carmarthenshire. During the years that Paulinus taught David, the older man's eyesight deteriorated badly. One day, he invited each of his pupils to come up in turn and pray for his eyes, making the sign of the cross over them. The young David, held back, too bashful to even look at the teacher he respected so much. But Paulinus said to him, "Touch my eyes, and, even without you looking at me, I shall be healed." The old man's sight did indeed return—and David's reputation grew.

After several years, Paulinus felt God saying to him, "Dewi [the Welsh name for David] has used the talents I have given him as fully as he can while he is here. Now I want to send him out so that he can use different approaches to win as many people as possible, from different walks of life, to my way. He must be free to give strong food to strong people, and milk to weak people." Paulinus commissioned David to go out and "win bundles of souls."

David did just that. He gathered a team of followers and built monastic centers in twelve key places, some as far from Wales as Glastonbury, Bath, and Crowland. He also helped families and people in ordinary jobs to follow Christ. David and his companions became "all things to all people." He and his followers are said to have given four rules to the people they met: pray, watch, work, and abstain from strong drink.

*Great God, who called your servant David
to be an apostle and father in God to the people of Wales,
grant that, inspired by the fire of his faith
and the flexibility of his approach,
we too may see divine fruit in our land.*

MARCH 4 ✣ GOD-INSPIRED LOCATIONS

Psalm 78:52-72; 1 Samuel 24; 2 Corinthians 1

> *The Lord rejected the descendants of Joseph,*
> *he did not select the tribe of Ephraim;*
> *instead he chose the tribe of Judah, and Mount Zion,*
> *which he dearly loves. There he built his temple*
> *like his home in heaven. . . . He chose his servant David.*
> PSALM 78:67–70 GNT

Before David of Wales embarked on his great apostolic mission, he and some close friends had waited on God in the shadow of the Black Mountains. There they built a chapel and a cell, where Llanthony Abbey now stands. They took it for granted that on their return, they would establish their permanent headquarters there.

However, the mission itself opened David's eyes in a new way and changed his mind. During a conversation back at the home base with his uncle, Bishop Giuisdianus, David said: "My angel companion told me that in this place which I intend to make my base scarcely one person in a hundred will gain their eternal reward, but there is another place not far away, where hardly any of those buried in the Christian cemetery will be cut off from God."

That is how God guided David and his friends to change their plans, and to build a large, permanent center in the valley where David was born, near the site of today's St. David's Cathedral.

Are you willing to change your plans? Are you allowing God to show you larger horizons, different approaches to your mission? God wants to give you a feel for the spirit of people and places, so that you move in inspired ways, to inspired places, with inspired timing . . . and so that you experience inspired outcomes.

Ask God to lay on your heart a special place to which you can apply this prayer:

> *O God, although you do not live in manmade temples*
> *you choose to work through them.*
> *Pour down your blessing upon this place and all who minister here*
> *that it may be a strength to those who have oversight,*
> *a joy and inspiration to all faithful Christians,*
> *a home of prayer and devotion*
> *setting forth to the world a pattern of true holiness and worship.*
> FROM THE PRAYER OF ST. DAVID'S CATHEDRAL (ADAPTED)

MARCH 5 ✜ WORKING FOR GOOD

Psalm 80; 1 Samuel 25:1-3; 1 Peter 2:1-10

*You will earn the trust and respect of others if you work for good;
if you work for evil, you are making a mistake.*
PROVERBS 14:22 GNT

Buried beneath the sands near Perran-Zabulo in Cornwall lie the remains of a prayer cell built by Piran, a monk who landed there in the fifth century. A tall Celtic cross now stands beside it. Although little else is now known about Piran, his life has inspired many working people throughout the centuries in the West Country of Britain and in Brittany. The Cornish tin miners made him their patron and celebrated his festival on March 5.

And we too can be encouraged, in our everyday work, by the example of Christians who treated their work as prayer in action; to be aware as well of the presence of heavenly persons, inspiring us to link our work with the relationships we have with others on Earth and in heaven.

I will build the hearth
as Mary would build it.

Who are they on the lawn outside?
Michael the sun-radiant of my trust.
Who are they on the middle of the floor?
John and Peter and Paul.
Who are they on the front of my bed?
Sun-bright Mary and her Son.

I am smooring the fire as the Son of Mary would smoor.
[To smoor is to damp all overnight fire with the day's ashes.]
CARMINA GADELICA

*I see to the fridge in the presence of the angel of the loveliest delights.
I see to the washer in the presence of Mary of the pure-white demeanor.
I see to the garage in the presence of Joseph of the fire.
I see to the office in the presence of the Creator of order.
I see to the people I meet in the presence of the all-friendly Christ.
I see to the things that will batter my mind
in the presence of the Spirit who brings calm.*

MARCH 6 ⁘ OVERCOME EVIL

Psalm 88; 1 Samuel 26:1-21; Titus 2

Do not let evil defeat you; instead, conquer evil with good.
ROMANS 12:21 GNT

Once David and his friends built their headquarters, they then had to learn a hard lesson: being in the place of God's choosing does not make us immune to opposition. Once God's kingdom gets a foothold, things that are not of God in that place can feel threatened—and they may react ferociously.

First came the honeymoon period for David, however. Many Christ-followers gathered to celebrate his new center's opening in the place then known as Rosina Vallis. They lit a bonfire that seemed to encircle the whole area with the presence of God, and even to light up Ireland as well.

And then came the reaction. The local bigwig, a man named Baia, saw the crowds and the engulfing smoke. To him, the dark clouds seemed to symbolize what would happen to the region if it were under David's influence. Baia's wife persuaded him to retaliate. Together, they armed their slaves with knives and sent them out to kill the monks. On their way, however, the slaves came down with a sudden fever, and by the time they reached the celebration, they had only enough strength left to hurl four-letter words at the monks. They had to return with their mission unaccomplished.

Before they reached the gates, Baia's wife rushed toward them with new instructions. While they had been gone, the cattle had also been mysteriously infected, and many had died. "Go back to the servant of God," she told the slaves now, "and ask him to pray God to have mercy on the cattle."

The slaves did as she instructed. They told David, "The land where you have settled shall be yours forever."

"Your cattle shall come to life again," he responded.

And both things came true. Baia's wife soon reverted to spite, however. She forced her female servants to undress every day where the monks couldn't help but see them. The monks became distracted. How could they be single-minded with all that naked female flesh constantly on parade? They became so demoralized that a delegation urged David to relocate the monastery elsewhere—somewhere with fewer temptations.

But this was David's reply: "You know that the world hates Christ's followers. You know that God's people Israel faced innumerable setbacks on their desert trek to the Promised Land. They were beaten to their knees, but not overthrown. Learn from them not to let evil overcome us but to overcome evil with good."

Director, Savior, Strengthener, help me to stand firm.

March 7 ❖ To Work is to Pray

Psalm 85; 2 Samuel 7:18-29; 2 Thessalonians 3

*St. Paul wrote: When we were with you we used to say,
"Anyone who is unwilling to work doesn't deserve to eat."*
2 THESSALONIANS 3:10

David's monastery became known for it hard, manual work. The monks did not hire oxen to do the plowing; they did it themselves, placing the wooden beams that drew the ploughs on their own sweating shoulders. They tirelessly dug the ground with picks, spades, and hoes; and they cut wood with saws. Each person meditated while he worked; they only spoke when they needed to.

At the end of a hard day's work, when they returned to the cloisters for a period of study, prayer, and writing, no one complained. Then, the instant the church bell rang, they would leave whatever they were doing, however absorbed in it they may have been, and go silently to the church to chant psalms; visitors noticed that both their voices and their hearts were in tune. Finally, for three hours before retiring to bed, the monks kept a silent prayer vigil in the church (and all the while, we are told, they avoided the common pitfalls of sneezing, yawning, and spitting!) When the brothers had gone back to their cells at last, David would stay alone in the church, pouring out his prayers. At cock-crow the next morning, the monks would rise for still more prayers. On Saturday nights, imitating the women who went to Jesus' tomb the night before his resurrection, the monks kept vigil until the early hours of Sunday.

The monks wore simple clothes, mainly leather. Their suppers were sparing but creative. Special dishes were cooked for the frail, and for visitors who were weary after a long journey.

None of the monks had any personal possessions, not even a psalm book. The "this is mine" mentality did not mar the monastery. When someone joined the monastery, he had to dispose of his wealth before entering, but David would not accept a penny of it for the monastery; he also declined donations from people who wanted to control them. Like the Taize Community of today, the entire income of the monastery came through the work of the monks, and they each had an equal share. The monks also shared their hearts and their failings openly with David, who was a real father to them. And they accepted his authority, willingly carrying out practical requests without question.

*Teach me, good Lord, to work with all my heart
until it can be said of me, as it was of David and his monks,
"To work is to pray."*

March 8 ✣ Rapport

Psalm 133; 1 Samuel 20:1-23; Hebrews 10:1-25

Friends always show their love.
What are families for if not to share their troubles?
PROVERBS 17:17

I have visited several Christian communities where brothers or sisters seem to flow together in mutual love. They have esteem in their hearts for one another and trust in their eyes, and they help each other in practical ways. That same spirit of rapport marked David and his brothers, as the stories about Brother Aidan reveal. From the beginning, Aidan was one of David's inner circle of three, good friends whom the biographer describes as "being alike of one mind and desire."

Once, when Aidan was outdoors studying one of the monastery's books, which had no doubt been painstakingly transcribed, David asked him to go on an errand that involved taking two oxen and a wagon to fetch some timber from a distance away. Aidan was, as always, so ready to carry out errands in a good spirit that he left immediately, leaving his precious book still open on the ground.

Having loaded the wagon with the timber and begun his return journey, the wagon and oxen careened over a cliff. Aidan calmly made the sign of the Cross over them and then was able to retrieve them safely from the sea. Further along, such a downpour burst from the sky that the ditches overflowed . . . and Aidan suddenly remembered that precious book!

He arrived back at the monastery and unloaded the timber first before he went to get the book. All the while, he must have been worrying about the damage the downpour had done to it—but to his surprise, he found it in exactly the same condition as it was when he left it. When the other brothers heard the story, they decided that Aidan's humility and faith had been a shield for the oxen, just as David's fatherly faith on behalf of his dear brother had provided a shield for the book.

Aidan's deep spiritual rapport with David continued even after he moved far away to Ireland, where he founded a monastery. One day before Easter Eve, Aidan was praying in the monastery, when he suddenly knew that someone would poison David's food at his Easter Day supper. He immediately sent one of his monks, who managed, with divine guidance, to cross the sea and reach David in time to warn him.

May the great God be between your two shoulders
to protect you in your going and your coming.
May the Son of Virgin Mary be near your heart
and the perfect Spirit be upon you pouring.
CARMINA GADELICA

MARCH 9 ✢ AUTHORITY

Psalm 101; 2 Samuel 5; Matthew 7:13–29

*The crowd was amazed by the way Jesus taught.
He wasn't like the teachers they were used to hearing;
instead, he taught with authority.*
MATTHEW 7:28–29

There are two kinds of authority: outer and inner. Christ's inner authority drew people to him, and it still draws them. David had this kind of authority too.

In David's day, one hundred and eighteen British church leaders, worried people might no longer follow their leadership, called a synod at a place named Brevi. David, who was not interested in church politics, stayed away. Meanwhile, so many people came to the synod that they had to pile up clothing to create a mound from which the speakers could be seen and heard. But speaker after speaker failed to get the ear of the people, and the leaders panicked, terrified that the people would go home disillusioned with the organized church. Then Paulinus, under whom David had studied, urged the others to bring David to the synod, for he "conversed with angels, was a man to be loved." Three times David refused the invitation, until his holy old friend Bishop Dubricius personally went to him. David told him, "I can't preach but I will give what little help I can with my prayers."

As they reached the outskirts of the crowd, David heard the wailing of mourners. Dubricius wanted to hurry him up to the top of the piled-up clothes, but David insisted on going first to the bereaved person, a mother whose son lay dead. He comforted the mother, who begged him to restore her son. While Dubricius must have waited impatiently, David spent still more time praying over the son, who then revived. The mother instantly dedicated her son to serve God under David. David gave the young man the Gospel Book to carry ahead of him as he finally made his way to the front of the crowd. All eyes followed them, and the crowd buzzed as the news of the young man's healing spread from person to person. Now the people clamored for David to speak.

For years afterward, people swore that mound of clothes grew taller as David talked to them. He spoke with authority and not as others had done. His authority was built on his decision to be with the people in all their needs.

Where does God want you to grow in authority? True authority makes its mark through prayer and service.

*God take from me delusions of grandeur.
May my authority grow through prayer and service.*

MARCH 10 ❖ SIMPLICITY

Psalm 86; 2 Samuel 7:1-17; Hebrews 8

God made us simple, but we have made ourselves very complicated.
ECCLESIASTES 7:29 GNT

David gave the Welsh people rules to help them live simply for God. Today, a growing number of Christ's followers also claim a Rule of Life. Some do so for the good of their souls; others do it for the good of the poor who receive unjust payment for what they produce; and still others do so for the good of Nature, to prevent natural resources from being squandered. All who follow a Rule of Life seek to find simplicity in a complicated world.

Life so easily drives us hither and yon, in many directions at once. This is nothing new; spiritual leaders have always recommended that we resist our human tendency to a divided mind. William Penn the Quaker observed, "People must follow the ten commandments of God or they condemn themselves to the ten thousand commandments of men." Jesus' comment about the pure in heart (Matthew 5:8) basically means, "Blessed is the person whose motives are unmixed."

Whether or not we follow a formal Rule, we all need this purity of heart. Otherwise, we use up the energy and time that should be directed to one purpose only: being Jesus for others. It's that simple!

> We wish to "live simply that others may simply live," to avoid any sense of judging one another; and God will make different demands of each of us. . . . A simple lifestyle means setting everything in the simple beauty of creation. Our belongings, activities and relationships are ordered in a way that liberates the spirit; we cut out those things that overload or clutter the spirit.
> FROM THE WAY OF LIFE OF THE COMMUNITY OF AIDAN AND HILDA

Too long have I worried about so many things.
And yet, my Lord, so few are needed.
May I today live more simply—like the bread.
May I today see more clearly—like the water.
May I today be more selfless—like the Christ.
FROM RUSSIA

MARCH 11 ♦ GOD SPEAKS THROUGH CHILDREN

Psalm 8; 2 Samuel 9; Mathew 21:12-17

*With the words of babies you have laid the foundation for strength,
in order to stop anyone who opposes you.*
PSALM 8:2

Sometimes small children blurt out something that communicates God's heart in a way an adult cannot. After all, children often pick up the spirit of a person or a place more quickly than do adults, who have protected themselves with layers of sophistication. A child having a Spirit-led tantrum was the one who caused the boy Cuthbert to think again about his life.

For the first eight years of his life, Cuthbert thought about nothing except games, pranks, and running here and there. He boasted that he had beaten all the other boys his own age—as well as many older boys—at wrestling, jumping, running, and other exercises. When the others were tired out, he looked around in triumph, as though he were ready to start afresh.

One day, as a crowd of children, including Cuthbert, were playing together in a field, dashing back and forth, tumbling around, and contorting their bodies, a three-year-old rushed up to Cuthbert and scolded him the way an adult would. The younger child told Cuthbert he should stop spending all his time running around; instead, he should begin to use his mind to exercise some control over his body. Cuthbert pooh-poohed the idea—at which the little boy promptly burst into tears. Between his sobs, he told Cuthbert that God wanted him to be a holy priest and a leader in the church—so how could he waste his life doing things that were against his nature and his calling?

Cuthbert soothed the child in a friendly way. Then he went home at once to think about what the little boy had said. From that time on, people noticed he behaved in a more mature way; they concluded that the Spirit who spoke to him through the words of a young child also spoke to him in the secret recesses of his heart.

*I pray, Lord, for the children whom I know.
Help me to encourage them,
to listen to the thoughts and pictures you put into their minds.
Help me to receive humbly what they tell me,
and to keep at least half an ear cocked
for your voice coming to me through them.*

MARCH 12 ✢ TEMPTATION

Psalm 109:1-15; 2 Samuel 11; Hebrews 2

*Now Jesus can help those who are tempted
because he himself was tempted in all the ways we are.*
HEBREWS 2:18

If you fall into temptation in the place where you live, do not desert the place when the temptation comes; for if you do, you will find that, wherever you go, the temptation you are running away from will be there ahead of you.
SAYINGS OF THE DESERT FATHERS

God's will would I do,
my own will bridle.
God's due would I give,
my own due yield.
God's path would I follow,
my own path refuse.
Christ's death would I ponder,
my own death remember.
Christ's agony would I meditate,
my love to God make warmer.
Christ's cross would I carry,
my own cross forget.
Repentance of sin would I make,
early repentance choose.
The love of Christ would I feel,
my own love know.
CARMINA GADELICA

O Christ, Champion of all tests,
when the first thought strikes, help me to resist.
When the first look overwhelms, help me to resist.
When the first fascination takes hold, help me to resist.
If I fall, save me.

MARCH 13 ✢ A KIDNAPPED YOUTH FINDS GOD

Psalm 109:16-31; 2 Samuel 15:13-37; Hebrews 5

How can a young man keep his life pure?
By doing what you tell him to do.
With all my heart I try to serve you.
PSALM 119:9–10

I, Patrick, am a sinner, the most awkward of country bumpkins, the least of all the faithful, and the most contemptible amongst very many. My father was Calpornius, a deacon, son of a certain Potitus, a priest of the village of Bannavem Taburniae, and there I was captured by slave traders.

At the time I was about sixteen years old, and I did not know the true God. Along with thousands of other people, I was taken in captivity to Ireland. It was no more than we deserved, for we had turned our backs on God and did not keep his laws. Neither did we obey our priests who reminded us of our salvation. So the Lord scattered us among many nations, even to the utmost part of the earth, where my insignificance might be seen by strangers.

In Ireland the Lord opened my eyes to my unbelief, so that I might at last face up to my wickedness and be converted with all my heart to the Lord my God. He respected my humbling and had mercy on my youth and ignorance. Even before I knew him, he watched over me. Before I was able to tell good from evil, he protected me and comforted me as a father would his son.

So I cannot keep quiet—nor should I—about the tremendous blessings and the grace that the Lord poured out on me in the land of my captivity.
THE CONFESSION OF PATRICK

I arise today in vast might,
inviting the Trinity,
entrusting myself to the Three,
honoring the One,
meeting in the Creator.
SAINT PATRICK'S BREASTPLATE

March 14 ✢ The Fervent Spirit

Psalm 110; 2 Samuel 24; Luke 18:1–8

*The Spirit comes to help us, weak as we are.
For we don't know how we ought to pray,
but the Spirit pleads with God for us
in groans words cannot express.*
ROMANS 8:26

As a beardless adolescent I was captured before I knew what to look for and what to avoid. I was like a stone lying deep in the mud; but he that is mighty came and lifted me up in his mercy, and raised me to the top of the wall. That is why I ought to shout in a loud voice, and return something to the Lord for all his benefits here and in eternity, which the human mind cannot even begin to comprehend.

After coming to Ireland I was put to work tending cattle, sheep and hogs, and many times during the day I would pray. More and more the love of God and the fear of God came to me, so that my faith was strengthened and my spirit was moved. In a single day I would pray as often as a hundred times, and nearly as often at night, when I was staying in the woods and in the mountains. I would rouse myself before daylight to pray, whether in snow, frost or rain; it made no difference, and I felt no bad effects. Because the Spirit in me was fervent, I knew no sluggishness.
THE CONFESSION OF PATRICK

*Christ beside me, Christ before me,
Christ behind me, Christ within me,
Christ beneath me, Christ above me.
Christ to right of me, Christ to left of me,
Christ in my lying, my sitting, my rising.
Christ in heart of all who know me,
Christ on tongue of all who meet me,
Christ in eye of all who see me,
Christ in ear of all who hear me.*
SAINT PATRICK'S BREASTPLATE

MARCH 15 ✢ PRAYER CHANGES THINGS

Psalm 111; 2 Samuel 23:1-7; Acts 12:11-19

A voice said to him, "Elijah, what are you doing here?
Return to the desert near Damascus, then enter the city."
1 KINGS 19:13, 15 GNT

One night in my sleep I heard a voice saying to me, "Fast well, for soon you will be back to your own country." And in a little while the same voice said to me, "See, your ship is ready." But it wasn't close by, it was perhaps two hundred miles away, at a place I had never been to, nor did I know a single person there. But I made up my mind to run away, and so I left the man with whom I had spent the last six years. I went in the strength of the Lord who guided me well, and I feared nothing up to the time I came to that ship.

On the day I arrived, the ship was scheduled to depart, and I told them I had the wherewithal to sail with them. But the ship's captain was displeased, and his answer was sharp and indignant, "You are wasting your time trying to book a passage with us." When I heard this I left them to return to the little shack where I was staying. On the way I began to pray, and before I had finished praying I heard one of the sailors shouting at me from behind. "Come quickly," he called out, "the men are asking for you." Immediately I reversed my direction and headed back. "We are taking you on faith," the crew explained. "Make friends with us in any way you like." But I did not become intimate with them through fear of God; and yet I hoped that an opportunity would open up when I could say to them, "Come to faith in Jesus Christ," for they were pagans. So I came aboard and we sailed immediately.
THE CONFESSION OF PATRICK

This day I call to me
God's strength to direct me, God's power to sustain me,
God's wisdom to guide me, God's vision to light me,
God's ear to my hearing, God's word to my speaking,
God's hand to uphold me, God's pathway before me,
God's shield to protect me.
SAINT PATRICK'S BREASTPLATE

MARCH 16 ✤ WITH GOD NOTHING IS IMPOSSIBLE

Psalm 53; 2 Samuel 22:1-25; Luke 9:10-20

*In your goodness you fed your people with manna
and gave them water to drink.
Through forty years in the desert
you provided all they needed.*
NEHEMIAH 9:20-21

After three days we reached land [probably modern France], and for the next four weeks we traveled through a deserted countryside. We ran out of food and became famished. One day the captain spoke to me, "What do you say, Christian? Your God is supposed to be great and all-powerful, why can't you pray for us? We are starving to death. It's hard to believe we will ever see another person alive." I then said plainly to them all, "Turn in faith and with all your hearts to the Lord my God, for whom nothing is impossible. He will send you food on your way until you have all that you can eat, for he has abundance of it everywhere." And with God's help it happened. Suddenly a herd of pigs appeared on the road right before our eyes. The men killed a number of them and spent two nights there until they regained their strength. Their hounds were also fed, and from that day they had plenty of food.
THE CONFESSION OF PATRICK

*I arise today in the might of Heaven,
brightness of sun, whiteness of snow,
splendor of fire, speed of lightning,
swiftness of wind, depth of sea,
stability of earth, firmness of rock.
God's legions to save me, to protect me
from snares of the demons, from evil enticements,
from failings of nature, from one man or many
that seek to destroy me nearby or afar.*
SAINT PATRICK'S BREASTPLATE

MARCH 17 ✧ IRELAND TURNS TO CHRIST

Psalm 115; 1 Chronicles 29:10-25; Acts 11:1-18

Happy are those whose God is the Lord.
PSALM 144:15

After a few years I was back with my parents in Britain. They received me as a son, and begged me never to go away from them again after all the trials I had been through. But then I saw in a vision of the night a man who seemed to be coming from Ireland, carrying many letters. His name was Victoricus. He gave one of them to me and I read the opening lines, which were, "The voice of the Irish." While I was reading I thought I heard the voices of the people who live by the wood of Voclut, which is by the western sea. They cried as with one voice, "We ask you, son, to come and walk once more among us." I was heartbroken at this, and could read no further, and so I woke up. Years later, thanks be to God, the Lord granted them what they had asked.

I owe an immense debt to God, who granted me so much grace that many people in Ireland were reborn in God through me. Clergy were ordained everywhere to look after these people, who had come to trust the Lord who called them from the ends of the earth. It was essential that we spread our nets so that a great multitude should be taken for God, and that there were plenty of clergy to baptize and counsel the people, as the Lord tells us to do in the Gospel.

So it came about that Ireland, a land filled with people who never had the knowledge of God . . . now has a people of the Lord who are called the children of God. It was not my grace, but God, victorious in me, who resisted all opposition when I came to the people of Ireland to preach the Gospel and to suffer insults from unbelievers. If I should be worthy, I am ready to give even my life most willingly and unhesitatingly for his Name. I am bound by the Spirit who witnesses to me. Christ the Lord told me to come here and stay with the people for the rest of my life, if he so wills, and he will guard me from every evil that I might not sin before him.
THE CONFESSION OF PATRICK

Christ for my policing today:
against poison and burning, against drowning and wounding
that there may come to me a multitude of rewards.
SAINT PATRICK'S BREASTPLATE

March 18 ✢ Come with Boldness

Psalm 52; 1 Chronicles 22; Hebrews 4:12-16

In union with Christ ... we have boldness
to go into God's presence with every confidence.
EPHESIANS 3:12 GNT

The month of March, great is the pride of the birds.
The wind is bitter blowing over the ploughed field.
The crops are short while the days grow longer.
Every creature knows its enemy,
every bird knows its mate,
every plant springs out of the earth.
"The bold person succeeds while the reckless person fails."
WELSH GNOMES

Around me I gather
these forces to save my soul and my body
from dark powers that assail me;
against false prophesyings
and false gods all around me,
against spells, against knowledge unlawful
that injures the body, that injures the spirit.
SAINT PATRICK'S BREASTPLATE

As surely as the seasons unfold
and spring follows winter
so sure is your steadfast love,
O God.
As burns
released from winter's bondage
leap joyously in the sea,
melt our frozen hearts
that we may worship you.
As buds uncurl
and flowers open their faces to the sun,
turn us to the light and warmth
of your presence.
KATE MELLHAGGA

MARCH 19 ❖ WHEN YOUNG AND STRONG

Psalm 103; 1 Chronicles 28: 1–10; Luke 5:1–11

Love the Lord your God with all your ... strength.
DEUTERONOMY 6:5 NLT

Better late then never, the saying goes. But why waste the energy that comes with youth on things that are contrary to the true nature God gave us? God wants the flower of our lives, and, in fact, we may not reach our full flower if we do not give youth's physical powers, passions, and purposes to God. Our physical powers cannot be kept separate from our spiritual destination. They need to be harnessed (though not handcuffed!) to God.

God has a use for both physical weakness and physical strength. We can be a fragile reed for God—or a body builder for God. Patrick is said to have used the strong man Mac Carton as his bodyguard. The muscular young Cuthbert, too, was strong for God.

> In accordance with the example of Samson the strong, who was once a Nazirite, Cuthbert sedulously abstained from all intoxicants; but he could not submit to such abstinence in food, lest he became unfit for the work he needed to do. For he was robust of body and sound in strength, and fit for whatever labor he cared to undertake.
> BEDE'S *LIFE OF CUTHBERT*

> I pass over the many other great things Cuthbert did in the flower of his youth, because I am keen to describe how as a mature adult he showed peaceable qualities and the power of Christ in serving God. So I omit how Cuthbert, when based at an army camp, face to face with the enemy, and with the most meager of food rations, yet lived in abundance throughout that time. He was strengthened by divine aid, just as Daniel and the three young men, though they refused the royal food that their religion did not allow, grew greatly in physical stature on the meager food allowance of slaves.
> *LIFE OF CUTHBERT*, ANONYMOUS

> *God who created me nimble and light of limb ...*
> *not when the sense is dim*
> *but now from the heart of joy*
> *I would remember him.*
> H. C. BEECHING

MARCH 20 ✧ SPRING CROSSROADS

Psalm 108; 2 Chronicles 1:1-12: Matthew 26:1-25

*Listen! Wisdom is calling out. Reason is making herself heard.
... At the crossroads she stands.*
PROVERBS 8:1, 2 GNT

The Spring equinox—one of the two days in the year when day and night are equal lengths because the sun is crossing the equator—is also St. Cuthbert's Day.

As the heralds of Spring
golden trumpet
the arrival of Easter,
as the dark night of Lent passes
and the days lengthen,
so, like Cuthbert,
bright star of the North,
we would become
your Easter people, O Christ,
shepherds of your sheep,
peacemakers and hospitality givers,
open to change and partnership,
Spirit led, in solitude and costly service.
KATE MCLLHAGGA, CUTHBERT'S FOLK

I also omit how Cuthbert saw the soul of a farm manager carried up to the sky at his death; how he wonderfully sent demons packing; or how he healed people of disturbed mind through his prayers.
LIFE OF CUTHBERT, *ANONYMOUS*

*God of Springtime,
while the sun is crossing over the equator,
may I be crossing over from dark to light,
from complaining to appreciation,
from dithering to boldness,
from stagnation to creativity,
from coldness to love,
from me to you.*

March 21 ⁜ O Bless the Lord!

Psalm 150; Isaiah 12; Matthew 21:1-17

May everything that breathes praise the Lord!
PSALM 150:6 GWT

The eighth-century Celi De (Friends of God) community at Tallaght, Ireland, sang the Benedicite every day between the evening meal and vespers:

> O all you works of the Lord, O bless the Lord.
> To the Lord be highest praise and glory forever!
> And you angels of the Lord, O bless the Lord.
> To the Lord be highest praise and glory forever!
> And you, the heavens of the Lord, O bless the Lord,
> and you clouds of the sky, O bless the Lord,
> and you, all armies of the Lord, O bless the Lord.
> To the Lord be highest glory and praise forever.
> And you, sun and moon, O bless the Lord,
> and you, the stars of heaven, bless the Lord,
> and you, showers and rain, O bless the Lord.
> To the Lord be highest glory and praise forever.
> And you, all breezes and winds, O bless the Lord,
> and you, cold and heat, O bless the Lord.
> To the Lord be highest glory and praise forever.
> And you, all that grows in the ground, O bless the Lord,
> and you, all that swims in the waters, O bless the Lord,
> and you, all birds that fly in the air, O bless the Lord.
> To the Lord be highest glory and praise forever.
> And you, all people on earth, O bless the Lord,
> and you, holy ones and humble in heart, O bless the Lord.
> To the Lord be highest glory and praise forever.
> SELECTED FROM THE SEPTUAGINT VERSION OF THE BOOK OF DANIEL

And may all that is within me,
and all things I touch
and all people I meet this day
give highest glory and praise to you!

MARCH 22 ✢ FASTING

Psalm 33; Leviticus 16:29-34; Matthew 27:1-10

The Lord watches over those who obey him,
those who trust in his constant love. He saves them from death;
he keeps them alive in times of famine.
PSALM 33:18-19 GNT

One day, the young monk Cuthbert was traveling by horse on a Friday. He stopped at a house to ask for food for the horse, but when the housewife there urged him to have something to eat also, because it was winter and there was a long road ahead without any stopping places for food, Cuthbert resolutely declined. On Fridays, many Christians of the day refrained from eating until afternoon because they wanted to make an act of solidarity with their Lord who was nailed to the cross on a Friday.

As the journey wore on, however, Cuthbert realized he would not get to his destination by nightfall. Since he was now weak from hunger, he sought shelter in a shepherd's hut that was not used in winter, where he tethered the horse. As he did so, some straw fell from the roof, along with a folded cloth.

He picked up the cloth—and found to his amazement that half a warm loaf and some meat were wrapped inside it. "Praise God," he said, "who has deigned to provide a supper for me who am fasting out of love for him." He divided the bread with the horse, who was also hungry—and from that day on, Cuthbert became more ready than ever to fast, for he realized that the same God who had fed the fasting prophet Elijah in a deserted place had provided for him also.

God always delights to do this for those who follow the path of denial. We, too, can follow this path, by taking up our cross (whatever it may be) each day.

Christ's Cross over this face and thus over this ear,
Christ's Cross over these eyes, this mouth, this throat,
the back of this head, this side,
to accompany before me, to accompany behind me.
Christ's Cross to meet every difficulty
both on hollow and on hill. . . .
Christ's Cross over my community,
Christ's Cross over my church,
Christ's Cross in the next world,
Christ's Cross in this world.
EARLY IRISH LYRICS

MARCH 23 ✣ CREATION

Psalm 22:1-15; Leviticus 17; Revelation 13:1-14:1

> *... the Lamb that was slain from the creation of the world.*
> REVELATION 13:8 NIV

As the flare of a volcano's eruption briefly reveals the fires at the Earth's center, so the light on Calvary was the bursting forth of the very nature of the Everlasting—the great love that burns always in the heart of God. Celtic Christ-followers profoundly understood the truth that a cross was always in God's heart even before a cross stood on the hill outside Jerusalem. God foresaw that evil would enter creation—and God prepared for it before the foundation of time by building a cross.

But why did God go ahead with a universe in which evil was a possibility? Well, consider what kind of a world it would have been if sin was an impossibility, a world in which we were not free to choose: a world in which creatures would have been like robots and would have responded to God's commands in the way a computer responds to our touch. By creating beings with the dangerous gift of free will, God brought into existence the conditions in which evil became a possibility.

But God made sure that the possibility of separation from God was met with the possibility of that separation being healed. Thus the broad beams on which the universe is built are in the shape of a cross. The cross, the ultimate expression of the law of self-sacrifice, runs like a scarlet thread through the Bible, through human experience, and through all creation.

> *I see his blood upon the rose*
> *and in the stars the glory of his eyes.*
> *His body gleams amid eternal snows,*
> *his tears fall from the skies.*
> *I see his face in every flower,*
> *the thunder and the singing of the birds*
> *are but his voice—and carven by his power*
> *rocks are his written words.*
> *All pathways by his feet are worn,*
> *his strong heart stirs the ever beating sea.*
> *His crown of thorns is twined with every thorn,*
> *his cross is every tree.*

JOSEPH MARY PLUNKETT, IRELAND (DIED IN THE 1916 REBELLION)

MARCH 24 ✢ THE WOUNDS OF CHRIST

Psalm 22:16-31; Isaiah 50; Matthew 27:11-26

But the Lord made the punishment fall on him,
the punishment all of us deserved.
        ISAIAH 53:6 GNT

Himself to himself offering,
the dying God becomes
brother to reed and thorn.
The lash unmakes him,
bearer of the tree; he bears also
the inner wounds of scorn.
He learns death's lore.
To unlock this dark chamber:
five potent wounds in the flesh,
on hand, foot, flank.
Himself, himself abandoning,
he sings, dry as stone—
a desolate cry, sweeter than lark-song.
Last fires consume him.
And the surge from below the oceans' floor
carries him, vessel of sorrow, Father-ward.
        DAVID ALSTON, DEAN AND CHAPTER OF DURHAM CATHEDRAL

How different our lives would be
if we could see that sin is not just a collision with the divine will,
but a wound in the divine heart
        SELWYN HUGHES

Nothing in my hand I bring,
simply to your Cross I cling.
Naked, come to you for dress,
helpless, look to you for grace.
Foul I to the fountain fly,
wash me Savior or I die.
        A. M. TOPLADY

March 25 ✣ Mary

Psalm 113; Isaiah 7:10-16; Luke 1:26-45

The angel said to Mary, "God has shown favor to you.
You will become pregnant, and you will have a son. . . .
The holy wind of God will come upon you
and God's power will cast its shadow over you."
Luke 1:30, 35

Since there was no record of the precise day of the year on which Christ was born, the church gave him an official birthday on December 25 to coincide with the winter solstice celebrations. Once this date was fixed in the fifth century, it was a natural progression to celebrate the conception of Jesus on a date exactly nine months earlier, March 25. This is also a day to dwell on the woman who made her womb and every fiber of her being so wholly available to the Son of God.

Smooth her hand, fair her foot,
graceful her form, winsome her voice, gentle her speech.
Stately her mien, warm the look of her eye,
mild the expression of her face
while her lovely white breast heaves on her bosom
like the black-headed sea-gull on the gently heaving wave.
The shield of the Son of God covers her face.
The inspiration of the Son of God guides her.
The word of the Son of God is food to her.
His star is a bright revealing light to her.
The darkness of night is to her as the brightness of day.
The day to her gaze is always a joy
while the Mary of grace is in every place
with the seven beatitudes encompassing her.
Carmina Gadelica

Glory be to you
for the anointing of joy you gave
to Mother Mary,
Glory be to you
for this queen among the angels
causing such delight in heaven, such Life on earth.

March 26 ❖ The Dream of the Tree

Psalm 130; Lamentations 2:1–13; John 19:1–24

*Jesus went out, carrying his cross,
and came to "The Place of the Skull." . . . There they crucified him. . . .
Pilate wrote a notice and had it put on the cross.
"Jesus of Nazareth the king of the Jews," is what he wrote.*
JOHN 19:17, 19 GNT

The wooden cross-beam on to which Christ was nailed was often called a tree; another Old English term for this was "rood," a word that meant literally, "a rod, a pole, or a scaffold." Celtic Christians understood that this tree, like all creation, was affected by the crucifixion of Christ, which had cosmic significance.

In the ninth century, the imagination of the Saxon Northumbrians who had accepted Christ through Aidan's Irish mission produced deeply moving poetry that expresses this idea. The eighteen-foot-high cross that stands inside the church at Ruthwell, Dumfriesshire, has carved on its sides words spoken by the cross. Someone took those few words and expanded them into one of the great Christian poems in English literature, known as *The Dream of the Rood*.

Wondrous was the tree of victory
and I was stained by sin, stricken by guilt.
I saw this glorious tree joyfully gleaming, adorned with garments,
decked in gold; the tree of the Ruler
was rightly adorned with rich stones;
yet through that gold I could see the agony
once suffered by wretches, for it had bled
down the right hand side. Then I was afflicted,
frightened at this sight; I saw that sign often change
its clothing and its hue, at times dewy with moisture,
yet I lay there for a long while
and gazed sadly at the Savior's cross;
until I heard it utter words; the finest of trees began to speak.
THE DREAM OF THE ROOD, TRANS. KEVIN CROSSLEY-HOLLAND

*I come to rest in the name of the Father.
Lying on my bed in your name, a noble King. . . .
I place the tree upon which Christ was crucified
between me and the heavy-lying nightmare, between me and each evil thing.*
FROM COUNTY CORK, COLLECTED BY DOUGLAS HYDE

MARCH 27 ⁂ THE YOUNG WARRIOR ON THE CROSS

Psalm 54; Isaiah 42:10-13; Matthew 27:27-44

*Christ himself carried our failures in his own body to the tree,
so that we might be finished with sin and alive to all that is good.*
1 PETER 2:24

In the poem *The Dream of the Rood* the tree now speaks:

> I remember the morning a long time ago
> that I was felled at the edge of the forest
> and severed from my roots. Strong enemies seized me,
> bade me hold up their felons on high,
> and made me a spectacle. Men shifted me
> on their shoulders and set me on a hill.
> Many enemies fastened me there.
> I saw the Lord of humankind
> hasten with such courage to climb upon me.
> I dared not bow or break there
> against my Lord's wish, when I saw the surface
> of the earth tremble.
> I could have felled
> all my foes, yet I stood firm.
> Then the young warrior, God Almighty,
> stripped himself, firm and unflinching.
> He climbed upon the cross, brave before many, to redeem humankind. . . .
> They drove dark nails into me; dire wounds are there to see,
> the gaping gashes of malice; I dared not injure them.
> They insulted us both together; I was drenched in the blood
> that streamed from the Man's side after he set his spirit free.
> THE DREAM OF THE ROOD, TRANS. KEVIN CROSSLEY-HOLLAND

*I wrap my soul and my body of fears
under your guarding, O Christ.
O Christ of the tears, of the wounds, of the piercings,
may your cross this night be our eternal shield,
your cross between us and all enemies without;
your cross between us and all enemies within;
your cross our sure way from earth to heaven.*

MARCH 28 ✢ HIS WOUNDS MAKE US WHOLE

Psalm 55; Isaiah 52:13-53; Matthew 27:45-56

We despised and rejected him; he endured suffering and pain.
No one would even look at him—we ignored him as if he were nothing.
ISAIAH 53:3 GNT

At the cry of the first bird
they began to crucify you,
O cheek like a swan;
it was not right ever to cease lamenting,
it was like the parting of day from night.
Ah! though sore the suffering
put upon the body of Mary's Son,
sorer to him was the grief,
that was upon her for his sake.
EARLY IRISH POEM

We are guilty and polluted, O God,
in spirit, in heart, and in flesh,
in thought, in words, in act
in your sight we are hardened in sin.
Put forth to us the power of your love,
come leaping over the mountains of our transgressions;
wash us in the blood of conciliation
like coming down the mountainside, like the lily of the lake.
CARMINA GADELICA

Father everlasting and God of Life
give us your forgiveness.
In my wild thought, in my foolish deed,
in my rough talk, in my empty speech.
Father everlasting and God of life
give us your forgiveness.
In my false desire,
in my hateful acts, in my destructive courses,
in my worthless tastes.
O Father everlasting and God of life
crown me with the crown of your love.
CARMINA GADELICA

MARCH 29 ✣ A VIEW OF CHRIST IN THE TOMB

Psalm 16; Lamentations 1:1–10; John 19:38–42

*Joseph took the body down, wrapped it in a linen sheet,
and placed it in a tomb which had been dug out of solid rock. . . .
The women who had followed Jesus
from Galilee went with Joseph
and saw the tomb . . . and went back home
and prepared spices and perfumes for the body.*
LUKE 23:53, 55–56 GNT

There they lifted him from his heavy torment;
they took Almighty God away.
The warriors left me standing there, stained with blood;
sorely was I wounded by the sharpness of spear-shafts.
They laid him down, limb-weary;
they stood at the corpse's head,
they beheld there the Lord of Heaven;
and there he rested for a while, worn out after battle.
And then they began to build a sepulcher;
under his slayer's eyes, they carved it from the gleaming stone,
and laid therein the Lord of Victories.
Then, sorrowful at dusk
they sang a dirge before they went away, weary
from their glorious Prince;
he rested in the grave alone.
But we still stood there, weeping blood,
long after the song of the warriors
had soared to heaven.
The corpse grew cold, the fair human house of the soul.
THE DREAM OF THE ROOD, *TRANS. KEVIN CROSSLEY-HOLLAND*

*Lord, we mourn
for a life of such goodness, cut down in its flower,
for a people who forfeited the flowering of their destiny,
for a city that turned away from its Savior,
for a planet that rejected its Maker,
for ourselves, who languish, alone and lost.
Lord, we offer you, like the women who came to your tomb,
our tears, our memories, the spices of our faith, the ointment of our tenderness,
the flowers of our personality.*

MARCH 30 ✣ CHANGE OUR SADNESS INTO JOY

Psalm 142; Isaiah 63; Matthew 27:57-66

*Mary Magdalene and Mary the mother of Jesus
were watching and saw where the body of Jesus was placed.*
MARK 15:47

Today a grave holds him who holds creation in the palm of his hand.
A stone covers him who covers with glory the heavens.
Life is asleep and hell trembles
and Adam is freed from his chains.
Glory to your saving work
by which you have done all things!
You have given us eternal rest,
your holy resurrection from the dead.
With a mother's sorrow Mary wept and cried
"What Simeon foretold in the temple
has happened today: a sword pierces my soul.
But change my sadness into joy by your resurrection."
FROM AN ORTHODOX LITURGY FOR HOLY SATURDAY

You may be a scholar, able to speak Greek and Hebrew
but in death only the language of God matters.
You may be a craftsman, able to fashion fine furniture
but in death only God's spiritual handiwork survives.
You may be a musician, able to play the harp and lyre
but in death only the Spirit's music persists.
You may be a priest, able to recite long prayers
but in death only prayers of the heart are heard.

Death is only a breath away.
So listen for God's word.
Be transformed by his hand.
Move to his rhythm, and pray to him with all your heart.
IRISH, FROM CELTIC PARABLES, ROBERT VAN DER WEYER

Change my sadness into joy by your resurrection.

MARCH 31 ❖ FLOODING RESURRECTION

Psalm 23; Lamentations 3:1-2; Matthew 14:22-32

New every morning, fresh as the sunrise, are the Lord's faithful mercies.
LAMENTATIONS 3:23

When last the raging spring storm had abated
and the night's dark banners from the East had fled,
he swiftly rose, and donned his simple raiment
and barefoot left behind his narrow bed.

Heedless of thorn and stone, he sought the seashore
and on a rock he sat and watched the sun
rise in the East flooding resurrection.
A gull called out, a new day had begun.

Across the calming waters sang the sea-hounds,
mothers calling for their snowy young.
A shoal of fish swam near the rock he sat on
spinning, spinning silver in the sun.

And one by one he watched the world renewing—
a cricket chirped, a bee sought out a flower.
He picked a shell strewn careless on the shoreline
and marveled at the Architect's great power.

The sand, each grain, lay perfect in arrangement
to leave the imprint of his searching feet;
refreshed and calm he retraced his journey
and oh! the upward climb seemed hard yet sweet.

Who knows this man, what words he used in praying
or what his soul had seen beyond the sea—
perhaps he was out fishing with his Master
or busy storing sweetness like the bee?
L. SMITH, DEAN AND CHAPTER OF DURHAM CATHEDRAL

*Deep peace of the green-blue sea,
deep peace of the rising sun,
deep peace of the shore-side Christ,
deep peace of the Risen One be ours today.*

SPRING

RISING UP

*Fire, water and the tree of life
(formed in the shape of a resurrection cross)
illustrate our new life in Christ,*

APRIL 1 ✜ I RISE UP IN CHRIST'S STRENGTH

Psalm 114; Isaiah 35; Matthew 28:1–10

You have died with Christ...
you have been raised to life in Christ...
you have stripped off the old self with its habits
and have clothed yourself with the new self.
COLOSSIANS 2:20; 3:1,9–10

The people say that the sun dances on Easter day in joy for a risen Savior.
ALEXANDER CARMICHAEL

The glorious gold-bright sun was after rising on the crests of the great hills, and it was changing color—green, purple, red, blood-red, intense white, and gold-white, like the glory of the God of the elements to the children of men. It was dancing up and down in exultation at the joyous resurrection of the beloved Savior of victory.
OLD BARBARA MACPHIE TOLD THIS TO ALEXANDER CARMICHAEL

Risen Christ, we welcome you.
You are the flowering bough of creation;
from you cascades music like a million stars,
truth to cleanse a myriad souls.
From you flee demons, omens and all ill will;
around you rejoice the angels of light...

I rise up clothed in the strength of Christ.
I shall not be imprisoned, I shall not be harmed,
I shall not be down-trodden, I shall not be left alone,
I shall not be tainted, I shall not be overwhelmed.
I go clothed in Christ's white garments,
I go freed to weave Christ's patterns,
I go loved to serve Christ's weak ones,
I go armed to rout out Christ's foes.
A CELTIC EUCHARIST, THE COMMUNITY OF AIDAN AND HILDA

Christ of the Easter morning,
hope is one of your best gifts to us
so teach us to give it to others.
A PRAYER FROM BRAZIL

APRIL 2 ✤ NEW LIFE

Psalm 1; Amos 9:11-16; Mark 8:14-21

Jesus asked his disciples, "Why are you talking about having no bread? Do you still not see or understand? Are your hearts hardened? . . . Don't you remember? When I broke the five loaves for the five thousand, how many baskets of pieces did you pick up?"

"Twelve," they replied.

"And when I broke the seven loaves for the four thousand, how many baskets of pieces did you pick up?"

They answered, "Seven."

He said to them, "Do you still not understand?"

MARK 8:17-21 NIV

When Ninian sat down for dinner one night with his brothers, he realized there were no green vegetables on the table. "Run down to the garden and pick some of the vegetables that are springing up," he asked someone.

The chief gardener spoke up. "There won't be any growth yet. I was still planting seeds this morning."

"In that case," said Ninian, "go in the faith of the Lord to search for vegetables, for God Almighty can accomplish anything."

The gardener quickly made his way to the heart of the garden—and to his surprise found all sorts of vegetables already growing. He returned to the brothers with enough to share with them all.

Ninian was given a gift of faith for a particular occasion. This was possible because he constantly cultivated an attitude of faith. We, too, can cultivate an attitude of faith, by frequently meditating on Scriptures and stories from the Celtic saints. As we do this, we will be given promptings that are in fact a gift of faith for a particular need.

Be alert for such an occasion today.

May the blessing of the five loaves and the two fishes,
which God shared out among the five thousand, be ours.
May the King who did the sharing bless our sharing.
May the food we eat restore our strength,
give new energy to tired limbs, new thoughts to weary minds.
May our drink restore our souls,
give new vision to dry spirits,
and new warmth to cold hearts.
And once refreshed, may we give new pleasure to you, who gives us all.
CELTIC GRACES

APRIL 3 ❖ A FEAST FOR EVERYONE

Psalm 45; Nehemiah 5:14-19; Luke 24:13-35

Those who God approves will ask, "When, Lord,
did we see you hungry and feed you?..."
The King will reply, "I tell you,
whenever you did this for one of the least important of these
my brothers and sisters, you did it for me."
MATTHEW 25:37, 40

The story is told that one Easter Day, when King Oswald had sat down with Bishop Aidan, a silver dish full of rich foods was placed on the table before him. Oswald and Aidan had just raised their hands to ask a blessing on the bread when there came in an officer of the king, whose duty it was to relieve the needy. The messenger told Oswald that a very great multitude of poor people from every district were sitting in the precincts and asking alms of the king. He at once ordered the dainties which had been set in front of him to be carried to the poor, the dish to be broken up, and the pieces divided among them.

The bishop, who was sitting by, was delighted with this devoted action, grasped Oswald by the right hand, and said, "May this hand never decay." His blessing and his prayer were fulfilled in this way: when Oswald was killed in battle, his hand and arm were cut off from the rest of his body, and they have remained uncorrupt until this present time; they are in fact preserved in a silver shrine in St Peter's church, in the royal city (later named Barnburgh).
FROM BEDE'S THE ECCLESIASTICAL HISTORY OF THE ENGLISH PEOPLE

O beloved Father who has redeemed us
and who reigns serenely as sun and sea,
may you forgive us our sins both past and present.
Remedy in heaven our faults
and may we today welcome with joy our Lord.
AN TIMIRE, COLLECTED BY SEAN O FLAIN
MOUNT MELLERAY MONASTERY, IRELAND

APRIL 4 ❖ RISEN FROM THE DEAD

Psalm 116; Isaiah 25:1-11; John 20:1-11

Women received back their dead, raised to life again.
HEBREWS 11:35 NIV

A number of Irish Christians gained a remarkable reputation for bringing dead people back to life. Among these was Tighernach, who went to heaven on April 4, 549. When Eithne, the daughter of the king of Munster, committed suicide rather than be forced to marry a British prince, Tighernach prayed over her and brought her back to life. Kieran the Elder also had a unique ministry to the victims of group casualties. When seven harpers of Aengus were waylaid and killed by brigands while on a journey, Kieran prayed over them, and they were all restored. Then, according to legend, a local ruler wanted to arrange decent funerals for a group of his soldiers who had been killed in battle, but he did not have enough vehicles to arrange the funerals. Kieran once again came to the rescue, prayed over the soldiers, and they, too, were restored to life.

This victory over death was also seen in the accurate historical accounts we have of Cuthbert's visits to the plague-ridden Northumbrian people. He trudged through the devastated villages to minister to the few poor people who remained. As he was about to leave one village, he asked the priest, "Are you sure there is no one left whom I have not seen?" The priest looked around, and found one tear-stained woman standing at a distance. She had lost one son in the plague, and now seemed about to lose the other son she was holding in her arms. Cuthbert made his way to her, blessed her, kissed the boy, and said to his mother, "There is no need to be sad any more. Your infant will be healed and will live, and no one else in your family will die from this plague." Mother and son both lived long, bearing witness to Cuthbert's life-giving ministry.

Lead us from death to life,
from the death of disease to the life of wholeness,
from the death of despair to the life of hope,
from the death of the body to the life of resurrection.

APRIL 5 ❖ RESTORED RELATIONSHIPS

Psalm 49; Hosea 1:1–2:1; John 21:1–14

Eutychus... fell to the ground from the third story and was picked up dead. Paul went down, threw himself on the young man and put his arms around him. "Don't be alarmed," he said. "He's alive!" The people took the young man home and were greatly comforted.
ACTS 20:9–10, 12 NIV

In the middle of the night, thieves planned to carry off some bullocks that belonged to Ninian's community. That same day, however, Ninian had prayed for God's blessing on his herds. Then he left to spend the night with a neighbor.

Ninian's prayer had a powerful effect on the thieves. First, they were overcome with dizziness and stumbled around, upsetting the bull. The bull then attacked them and gored the leader.

The next morning, when Ninian returned, he found the panic-stricken men huddled around their leader, who was now dead. "Tell me," asked Ninian, "why did you wish to harm a person who never wished to harm or cheat you in even the smallest way?" Then, in the name of God, he released them from sin and from all ill effects from what they had done.

But that is not the end of the story. Next, Ninian knelt beside the dead man and prayed, "O Christ, throned on high, I beg you to give life to this corpse. Impart warmth to his whole body; let the spirit enter into his frozen limbs and restore the functions of life."

And the dead man came back to life. The terror-struck men poured out heartfelt words to the Lord.

Raise us from greed to generosity,
raise us from falseness to friendship,
raise us from death to life.

APRIL 6 ❖ A NEW PAGE

Psalm 124; Ezekiel 17:22-24; Colossians 3:1-15

*You have been raised to life with Christ,
so set your hearts on the things that are of heaven.*
COLOSSIANS 3:1 GNT

The resurrection of Christ turned the page of human history. It can also bring a new page into our own tattered lives.

In the Book of Kells there is no picture of the resurrection but only the word "Una" in the center of the page, denoting the first day of the week, the day of resurrection. In *Exploring the Book of Kells,* George Otto Simms describes the resurrection page:

> Angels are guarding the capital letter U, one at each of its four corners. It looks at first like a dark, dull page, but out of the dim gloom the feet, the hands and the faces of the four angels, painted with white lead, shine out gleaming and bright. These angels are looking up and out from the page. . . . They are alive and alert, not asleep, nor downcast. Their message is "Christ is risen, he is not here. Why look for the living among the dead?"
>
> We also observe, in the top right-hand corner, that the fierce monster is speeding away out of the picture. The power of this enemy has been overcome. The beast is on his way out, defeated. . . . The capital U, with a tangle of graceful birds in the heart of the letter, and surrounded by guardian angels, helps us to have a picture in our minds of the empty tomb on the first Easter Day.

*Last night Christ the Sun rose from the dark.
The mystic harvest of the fields of God
and now the little wandering tribes of bees
are brawling in the scarlet flowers abroad.
The winds are soft with bird song all night long.
Darkling the nightingale her descant told
and now inside church doors the happy folk
the Alleluia chant a hundredfold.
O Father of your folk, be yours by right
the Easter joy, the threshold of the light.*
SEDULIUS SCOTTUS

APRIL 7 ✢ A ROUGH ROAD TO RESURRECTION

Psalm 126; Exodus 13:17-22; John 20:19-31

*All people die; it's human nature.
And in the same way, Christ makes everyone alive.*
1 CORINTHIANS 15:22

A pious and formidable woman named Canair had a vision while praying in her hermit's hut. She saw a tower of fire rise from each church in Ireland, but the tallest and straightest of these towers arose from an island called Inis Cathaig. "I must leave here, and go and live there," Canair decided, "for that will be the place of my resurrection."

Unfortunately for her, the hermit Senan who already lived there was as formidable as he was pious. He had made the island his own, and the presence of a woman there was not part of what he wanted for his life. So when Canair arrived on the island, after following the vision of the tower of fire that had lead her there, Senan welcomed her at the harbor . . . and then suggested she travel on to her sister who lived some miles away.

"I have not come here in order to do that," Canair retorted. "I have come here to stay with you on this island."

"Women cannot enter this island," declared Senan.

Canair was not to be outdone. "How can you say that? Christ came to redeem women no less than men. He suffered for women just as much as he suffered for men. Women have always tended and served Christ and his apostles. Women just as much as men enter the kingdom of heaven. So why can't you receive women on your island?"

"You are stubborn!" Senan told her.

Canair smiled. "In that case shall I get what I ask for—a place for myself on this island—and can I receive the Sacrament from you?"

"You will be given your place of resurrection," said Senan, "but it will be here on the sea's edge. And I fear the sea will carry off your remains."

"The spot of earth where my dead body shall lie will not be the first spot of earth that this sea will carry away," Canair replied calmly.

While they were arguing, the sea had come up to Canair's waist without her noticing. Eventually, they had to move a little up the shore—and there, Senan did give her Holy Communion. And then Canair went straight to heaven. So who had the last word?

ADAPTED FROM THE "BOOK OF LISMORE" RECORDED IN THE LIVES OF THE SAINTS

*Thank you, Lord, that even if we are difficult or blinkered,
you can put holy desires into our hearts
so that we will come through obstacles to our eternal resurrection.*

APRIL 8 ⁜ LIGHT THE RESURRECTION FIRE

Psalm 148; Hosea 4; 2 Corinthians 4:1–15

Throughout our lives we are always in danger of death for Jesus' sake, in order that his life may be seen in this mortal body of ours. This means that death is at work in us but life is at work in you. . . . For we know that God who raised the Lord Jesus to life, will also raise us up with Jesus and bring us, together with you, into his presence.
2 CORINTHIANS 4:10–11, 14 GNT

Once a year at the spring solstice, the King of Tara, High King of all Ireland, gathered together at the high Hill of Tara the regional kings, their druids, shamans, bards, and advisors. There, at a giant celebration, they lit a bonfire to invoke the Sun to shower blessings upon them and their crops in the coming season. On that day, it was forbidden for anyone else to light a fire.

Patrick, knowing of this celebration but unaware of the ban on the lighting of other fires, ascended the Hill of Slane, which could be seen from Tara. There, he and his fellow Christ-followers lit a large fire to celebrate the resurrection of their Lord Jesus Christ, true God, Sun of Suns.

High King Loegaire was extremely upset when he heard what Patrick had done, and he ordered his men to arrest the Christians and bring them to him. His shamans intuited immediately what this was all about. "If the fire of this new religion is not put out this night," they told the king, "it will not be put out until Doomsday. Moreover, the person who kindles it will supersede the kings and rulers of Ireland unless he is banned."

When they came with their chariots to arrest Patrick, he, according to the medieval *Life of Saint Patrick*, quoted Scriptures such as "Some trust in chariots and some in horses but we will trust in the name of our mighty God" (Psalm 20:7) and "Let God arise and scatter his enemies" (Psalm 68:1). As he spoke, a storm burst so violently over their heads that the horses and their riders fled. Although the king's men lay in wait to catch Patrick and his men as they left, all they saw passing them was a herd of deer.

And that is how the tradition grew that as these Christ-followers prayed the prayer today known as "Patrick's Breastplate," God shielded them from their enemies' eyes—and this why the prayer is also known as "The Deer's Cry."

*I arise today
through the strength of Christ's birth and baptism.
I arise today through the strength of Christ's crucifixion and burial.
I arise today through the strength of his resurrection and ascension.*
FROM ST PATRICK'S BREASTPLATE

April 9 ✢ Get Ye Up!

Psalm 149; Ezekiel 37:1-14; Luke 8:40-56

A messenger arrived from Jairus's home with the message,
"Your little girl is dead. There's no use troubling the Teacher now."
Luke 8:49 NLT

The Traveling People have a special place in Irish life, and they can offer fresh perspectives on old truths. Travelers assume that anyone who has a house big enough to have stairs must be very important, so they call such a person "one of them." Although some Travelers cannot read, they can still tell a Bible story like no one else, as the following Traveler's story illustrates:

> 'Twas like this. Jesus Christ was going along the road, and the sun was blazing, and he was all sweating, and the crowds were all there after him; and they were shouting and roaring and belting each other. Then all of a sudden up comes a big man, important and "one of them," and he drops down and looks up at Jesus Christ, and says to him: "Jesus Christ, would ye ever help me? Me daughter's back home and she's dead or near it. Would ye ever make her better?"
>
> Says Jesus, "I will, of course. Come on back and show me where ye live." Then back they go, the two of 'em, till they come to the big man's house and in they go. And ye know what? 'Twas a house with stairs. Stairs all the way up, and didn't Jesus go up them stairs, and he was nearly deaf, 'cause there was loads of women and they were bawling and shouting, and he's never heard anything like them. And he stops there on the stairs with his hands shutting off the noise from his ears, and says he, "Will ye shut up and get out, the lot of ye!" And didn't they do so, and there was just Jesus Christ there with the daddy and the mammy and the corpse. And says he to the corpse, "Get ye up out of that!" And she, she opened her eyes and looks at him, and she's able to get straight up there and look at him again. And she wasn't sick any more. And Jesus Christ, he looks at her too. And he sees she's well, and says he to the mammy, "Give her a cut o' bread."

Living Christ, you can do anything, anything, anything!
You can come to my house, to the most out-of-reach house!
I name the person I have lost faith for: _____.
Come to his house, to the place where she is.
Come today.

APRIL 10 ❖ CHRIST'S BODY IS GOD'S

Psalm 34; Hosea 5:4-15; John 20:11-18

Mary Magdalene stood crying outside the tomb of Jesus....
Jesus came to her and said, "Mary." She turned towards him....
"Do not hold on to me," Jesus told her.
JOHN 20:11, 16–17 NIV

How many people are put off by Christianity because the members of the church—Christ's Body—treat it in a possessive way, as though it were their own rather than God's? We need to remember the lesson Mary Magdalene had to learn from the risen Christ—and hand his Body back to God.

One of Ireland's most poignant spots is the island hermitage at Gougane Barra, founded by Finbarr. Finbarr was instructed by Bishop MacCuirb, a fellow pupil of David of Wales. He went to live at Loch Iree and started a school there where students could study the scriptures. Five of these students, as well as some others, established churches and offered them to the oversight of Finbarr. Finbarr himself built a church in his home area, but God told him that would not be his place of resurrection. So Finbarr crossed the river to Gougane Barra and built a place of worship there, where he stayed for a considerable time.

However, two of his former pupils received a prophecy: "Gougane Barra will be your place of resurrection." They dared not believe this, since it seemed obvious that this was Finbarr's place. Finbarr welcomed them for a visit, however, and they talked and prayed things through. "Don't be depressed," Finbarr told them. "I give this church and all its treasures to you and to God."

In fact, Finbarr built a total of twelve churches, and gave them all away. God led him further along the river and told him, "This will be your place of resurrection." Today that place is Cork City—and the spires of its St. Finbarr's Cathedral glitter like jewels above the city.

Lord of the church, Servant King,
take from us attitudes and practices
that put barriers between the church and the people:
cultural elitism in worship, clerical status,
arrogance, smugness, treating the church as our property,
rather than God's.
Make us a pilgrim people,
a church without walls.

APRIL 11 ✢ FEELINGS OF FAILURE

Psalm 3; Jonah 1; John 21:15–25

I trust you will know that we are not failures. We pray to God that you will do no wrong—not in order to show that we are a success, but so that you may do what is right, even though we may seem to be failures. For we cannot do a thing against the truth, only for it.
2 CORINTHIANS 13:7–8 GNT

The man who wrote a biography of David of Wales five hundred years after David's death was so eager to promote his own diocese that he recorded any bit of folklore, however far-fetched, that served to make his diocese seem more important. Although we cannot take all that is written at face value, we can still reflect upon those episodes, which, when the embroidery is removed, were clearly believed to have taken place.

One such is the belief that Patrick, when he returned to his parents on the northwest coast of Britain, went on a mission to Dyfed, intending to settle at a pleasant place there named Rosina Vallis. However, an angel spoke to him in a vision: "God has not planned this place for you, but for a child who will not be born until the next generation." Patrick probably felt rejected, disappointed, and rather a failure, until God gave him the call to be the leader of a mission to Ireland, affirming him with these words: "You will be radiant with signs and virtues, bringing the whole nation under my rule. I will be with you." The place where this vision was given came to be known as Patrick's Seat.

Patrick made his preparations to leave. And then before he boarded the boat for Ireland, God used him to raise someone from the dead. Clearly, even though the angel had pushed him on his way, God had a purpose for Patrick!

When we feel like failures, when we cannot grasp the goals on which we have set our hearts, we need to remember Patrick's Seat. Patrick felt a failure—but went on to raise someone from the dead and to win a nation to Christ! Find a seat of your own, somewhere you can contemplate, not what is not to be, but what, with God, is yet to be.

There is always a "yet to be" with God. The darkest moment of night comes just before the dawn.

You pour your grace on those in distress
without stop or stint.
Son of Mary, Son of the disappointments,
who was, who shall be, with ebb and flow,
with me wherever I go.

APRIL 12 ❖ TUNING IN

Psalm 50; Jonah 2; John 8:12-30

I do nothing on my own initiative, but only what the Father teaches.
JOHN 8:28

We need to tune in to the deeper, unseen currents that shape our lives and civilization. More and more people who are in touch with the intuitive or feminine sides of their natures are coming to understand this. When these folks run into Christians who fear or denounce this way of looking at the world, they end up being put off by Christianity.

But why should Christians assume that devils have all the best ears? The pre-Christian Celtic people, especially the shamans, had finely developed powers for seeing into people and the future. The Celtic saints' experience reassures us that Christ's followers can also develop intuitive powers—as did Jesus—in a way that attunes them to the Divine wavelength. Cuthbert was someone with this sort of deep intuition.

One day, when Cuthbert was having lunch with the Abbess Aelfflaed, he seemed to have a seizure, and his dinner knife fell from his hands. At first he made light of it, but eventually, his companions drew out of him what he had "seen": the soul of a man from Aelfflaed's estate being suddenly snatched from this earth. Aelfflaed only thought to ask about the well-being of her monks, and they were all well. The next day, however, they discovered that a shepherd named Hadwald had fallen from a tree and died at the very hour Cuthbert had dropped his knife.

The point of this story is not obvious. I wonder, though, if it could have been God's way of pointing out that the least should be treated as the greatest in the kingdom of heaven? If the Divine eye is on the sparrow, then we too must appreciate that all life is precious. No death is unimportant to the Kingdom.

Cuthbert had many other "seeings," many of which affected the future of political powers, the course of the church's mission, and his own future. I like to think, however, that these "tunings" to invisible things come for the same purpose that Christ came—to seek and to save those who are most needy and lost.

Make me attentive to the lap of the waves.
Make me attentive to the movements of the sky.
Make me attentive to the grasses that grow.
Make me attentive to the soul's every sigh.
Make me aware of the landscape that must pass away.
Make me aware of the new landscape coming to be.
Make me aware of the universe within.
Make me aware of the beatings of your heart.

APRIL 13 ✥ WAITING

Psalm 46; Hosea 3; Acts 1:1–11

Be still and know that I am God.
PSALM 46:10 NIV

In the ground of your being I have my home
so do not seek me in the world apart.
Within your spirit true communion lies.
You are no homeless stranger in a land afar
no alien in a foreign shore, for I am with you.
Do but be still and know that I am God.
I look upon the world with your dark eyes;
I feel the flowing air on your cool cheek;
I hear the twittering in the moving trees,
for with your senses I perceive.
I am with you, I am within you.
So do not turn away but come to rest in me.
Within you is our meeting place.
But be still, and I will speak in silence
to your loving, wayward heart.
DAME PAULA FAIRLIE

God with me lying down,
God with me rising up,
God with me in each ray of light,
nor I a ray of joy without hint.
Christ with me sleeping,
Christ with me waking,
Christ with me watching
every day and night.
God with me protecting,
God with me directing,
The Spirit with me strengthening
forever and forevermore.
Chief of Chiefs. Amen.
CARMINA GADELICA

APRIL 14 ✣ LISTENING

Psalm 95; Hosea 9:10-17; Acts 1:12-26

If you have ears to hear with, then listen!
MATTHEW 11:15

Go to your cell; it will teach you all things.
SAYINGS OF THE DESERT FATHERS

Be slow to anger, quick to learn, also slow to speak,
as Saint James says, and equally quick to listen.
COLUMBANUS

By quietly listening to the description of the stages, transitions and miraculous deeds of a saint's life, we can begin to discern and appreciate our life patterns as well as our own kinship with Jesus.
EDWARD C. SELLNER, WISDOM OF THE CELTIC SAINTS

God gave us two ears and one mouth.
Why don't we listen twice as much as we talk?
CHINESE PROVERB

Listen . . .
to the fragile feelings, not to the clashing fury;
to the quiet sounds, not to the loud clamor;
to the steady heartbeat, not to the noisy confusion;
to the hidden voices, not to the obvious chatter;
to the deep harmonies, not to the surface discord.
ANONYMOUS

You be my wisdom, you my true Word,
I ever with you, and you with me, Lord.
You my great Father and I your true son,
You in me dwelling and I with you one.
IRISH, EIGHTH CENTURY

Lord, a thousand voices shout at me this day,
sound-bites and slogans, images and screens,
conversations and traffic, newspapers and Internet. . . .
Help me to filter out and turn away
all that is not of you, and to see and hold tight to all that is of you.

April 15 ✥ Silence

Psalm 106:24-38; Jonah 3; Revelation 7:13-8:1

Let a person dwell alone in silence, for the Lord has laid this upon them.
LAMENTATIONS 3:28

God calls most, if not all, of us to sometimes draw apart and be silent. And God calls some people to make this the main call upon their lives. Solitaries who are following such a call (as distinct from people who are running away from something) should be encouraged. In the Catalogue of the Saints of Ireland there was an entire order of such people—anchorites.

An old Celtic word for prayer meant literally "the quiet of Christ." The Celtic Christians learned the value of silence from the Desert Fathers and Mothers. It was said that Abba Agatha carried a pebble in his mouth for three years until he learned to be silent!

> Allow me with your peace and charity to remain in silence in these woods.
> COLUMBANUS IN A LETTER TO THE FRENCH BISHOPS

> Silence is the element in which great things fashion themselves together.
> THOMAS CARLYSLE

> Souls of prayer are souls of deep silence. That is why we must accustom ourselves to deep stillness of the soul. God is the friend of silence. See how nature, the trees, the flowers, the grass grow in deep silence. See how the stars, the moon and the sun move in silence. The more we receive in our silent prayer, the more we can give in our active life. Silence gives us a new way of looking at everything. We need this silence in order to touch souls. Jesus is waiting for us in the silence. It is there that he speaks to our souls. Interior silence is very difficult but we must make the effort to pray. A soul of prayer can make progress without recourse to words by learning to be present to Christ. In silence we find a new energy and a real unity.
> MOTHER TERESA OF CALCUTTA

In silence I become aware of you, O Lord.
In the silence I adore you, O Lord.
In the silence my sins stand out and are washed away.
In the silence my problems fall into their rightful place.
In the silence I become a grateful person,
and in the silence, O Lord, we become one.

APRIL 16 ✢ DIVINE GUIDANCE

Psalm 32; Jonah 4; Acts 16:1–10

I will instruct you and teach you in the way you should go.
PSALM 32:8 NIV

Toward the end of the ninth century, the monks of Lindisfarne set sail for Ireland to escape a renewed Viking invasion. The monks took with them their priceless book, now known as the Lindisfarne Gospels. Tragically, they hit bad weather, the boat heeled over to one side, and the copy of the Gospels, adorned with gold figures, fell overboard and sank to the bottom of the sea.

The monks postponed their voyage and returned to dry land. There they were given a vision, in which God directed them to go to the shore at Whithorn, the Christian community on the western coast of Scotland, founded by Ninian. When they arrived there, they found that, due to an unusually low tide, the sea had receded much further than usual. The monks walked a mile or two out from the shore—and there, to their amazement and joy, they found their precious volume, still with the covers clasped together. The gold was unspoiled, and the colors had not run. Nobody could have guessed that the book had ever had contact with water.
(RECORDED IN SYMEON'S HISTORY OF THE CHURCH OF DURHAM, TWELFTH CENTURY)

Men and women guided by God are the greatest forces in shaping history.
DUTCH ATOMIC SCIENTIST

The Holy Spirit is the most intelligent source of information in the world.
FRANK BUCHMAN

*Lord, you have a plan for every person
and for every situation in the world.
But our eyes are so dim. We are so deaf.
Help us to become wholly God-guided instruments.
Help us always be in just the place you wish us to be.*

APRIL 17 ❖ COME, CREATOR SPIRIT

Psalm 13; Hosea 11:1-11; Acts 2:1-13

Master and Creator of heaven, earth, and sea,
and all that is in them! Stretch out your hand to heal.
ACTS 4:24, 30 GNT

Come, O Creator Spirit, come
enter our minds and fill our hearts,
implant in us grace from above.
May your creatures show forth your love.
Past ages called you Paraclete,
Gift to humanity of God Most High,
Well-spring of life, fire, charity,
and anointing Spirit of peace.
You bring to us your seven gifts,
you are the power of God's right hand,
the Promise of God to the church,
words of life upon human lips.
Illumine our hearts anew
and pour your love into our souls.
Refresh our weak frame with new strength,
fortitude and grace to endure.
Cast away our deadly foe.
Grant us your peace forevermore.
With you as our Guide on the way
evil shall no more harm our souls.
Teach us the Trinity to know
in Father, Son, and Spirit, One:
the Three in One and One in Three
now and ever, eternally.
A MODERN ADAPTATION OF VENI CREATOR,
ASCRIBED TO RABANUS MAURUS, A NINTH-CENTURY SOLITARY IN GAUL

Come, O Holy Spirit, come.

APRIL 18 ✢ WIND

Psalm 11; Job 27; Acts 2:14–36

The wind blows wherever it wishes;
you hear the sound it makes
but you do not know where it comes from or where it is going.
It is like that with everyone who is born from Spirit-wind.
JOHN 3:8

Breathe in Christ with every breath.
ANTONY OF EGYPT

Long years ago across the western water
winds brought to this our shore
one glorious within, a king's own daughter
to teach our land Christ's law.
CORNISH HYMN FOR ST. BURYAN (WHO LANDED NEAR ST. IVES WITH PIRAN)

Blessed be the wind.
Without wind most of the earth would be uninhabitable.
LYALL WATSON

Once when Columba was at sea a great storm, with gusts of wind blowing from all sides, arose and his boat was buffeted by great waves. Columba tried to help the sailors bail out the water that came into the boat, but they said to him, "Your doing this does little to help us in this danger. You would do better to pray for us as we perish." Columba stopped bailing water and began to pour out prayers aloud to God. Marvelous to relate, as soon as he stood up in the prow and raised his hands to God, the wind ceased and the sea stilled. The crew were amazed and gave glory to God.
ADAMNAN

Wind, wind, blow on me.
Blow away the cobwebs that clog my spirit,
dispel the suffocating air of unbelief,
blow near the things that are pure and good,
blow through me the breath of God
and blow me along the path of your choice.

APRIL 19 ❖ WATER

Psalm 4; Job 26; Acts 2:37-47

"Anyone who trusts me
will have life stream from her innermost being."
Jesus said this about the Spirit,
which those who trusted their lives to him would receive.
JOHN 7:38-39

The author of life is the fountain of life. . . . Let us seek the fountain of life, the fountain of living water, like intelligent and most wise fish, that there we may drink the living water that springs up to eternal life.
COLUMBANUS

Slake your thirst from the streams of the divine fountain. The fountain of life calls to us, "Let whoever is thirsty come to me and drink." Take note what you are to drink; remember what God spoke through Jeremiah, "They have forsaken me, the fountain of living water, and drunk from leaking cisterns." The person who thus drinks is the person who loves, who draws satisfaction from the Word of God, who adores, who yearns, who burns with the love of wisdom.
ADAPTED FROM THE GAELIC

Fechin had a God-given ability to cause water to flow in dry places. Saint Fechin's well, in County Sligo, Ireland, marks the place where he prayed for a source of water for a parched region. At Fore, life was so hard for the monks that Fechin hewed out rock with his own hands until water burst through. At Omly, he immersed the entire population in the waters of baptism. At his death in 665, a friend saw a light so bright that all Ireland's demons fled for a time.

What would the world be
once bereft of wet and of wildness?
Let them be left, O let them be left wetness and wildness.
GERARD MANLEY HOPKINS

Bathe us in your cleansing rivers.
Soak us in your healing waters.
Drench us in your powerful downfalls.
Cool us in your bracing baths.
Refresh us in your sparkling streams.
Master us in your mighty seas.
Calm us by your quiet pools.

APRIL 20 ✢ FIRE

Psalm 21; Ezekiel 15; Acts 3

Jesus said: I came to set the earth on fire.
Luke 12:49

From the age of eight until he entered a monastery, Cuthbert was brought up by a Christian nanny named Kenswith, a widow who had become a nun. Cuthbert always called her "Mother" and often visited her in her old age. Once when he was lodging in Kenswith's village, a house on the eastern edge of town caught fire and a fierce wind blew the flames toward the other houses. The village seemed about to be immersed in a conflagration.

Panic-stricken, Kenswith ran to the house where Cuthbert was staying and begged him to ask God to save their homes. Cuthbert calmly turned to her and said, "Don't worry, the flames will do no harm." Then he lay prostrate on the earth outside the house and prayed silently. As he was praying, a strong, fresh wind arose from the west and drove the flames away from the houses, so that no further harm was caused. The people were grateful, and they took time to give thanks to the Lord.

Fire is a powerful force and, as this story illustrates, it can destroy—but it can also be a positive force, and it is a biblical symbol of God's Spirit. Destruction and growth are often the two sides of the same coin, and the term "Celtic fire" is used to describe the living, glowing faith at the heart of the Celtic peoples. This was symbolized by the fire that, in monasteries as in homes, was kept alight night and day. The fire at Brigid's monastery at Kildare was said to be kept lit for a thousand years.

Thank you, Father, for your free gift of fire
because it is through fire that you draw near to us every day;
it is with fire that you constantly bless us.
Our Father, bless this fire today.
With your power enter into it. Make this fire a worthy thing.
A thing that carries your blessing.
Let it become a reminder of your love. A reminder of life without end.
Make the life of this people be baptized like this fire.
A thing that shines for the sake of people.
A thing that shines for your sake.
Father, heed this sweet-smelling smoke.
Make our lives also sweet smelling, holy things, fitting for you.
A Masai prayer

APRIL 21 ❖ EARTH

Psalm 103; Job 28; Acts 4:1-22

The Lord knows what we are made of, that we are but dust.
Our days are as fleeting as grass.
PSALM 103:14–15

Earth to earth, ashes to ashes.
FUNERAL SERVICE, BOOK OF COMMON PRAYER

To be of the earth is to know the restlessness of being a seed:
the darkness of being planted,
the struggle towards the light,
the pain of growth into the light,
the joy of bursting and bearing fruit,
the love of being food for someone,
the scattering of your seeds,
the decay of the seasons,
the mystery of death
and the miracle of birth.
JOHN SOOS

Earth, teach me stillness as the grasses are stilled with light.
Earth, teach me suffering as old stones suffer with memory.
Earth, teach me humility as blossoms are humble with beginning.
Earth, teach me caring as the mother who secures her young.
Earth, teach me courage as the tree that stands all alone.
Earth, teach me limitation as the ant that crawls on the ground.
Earth, teach me freedom as the eagle that soars in the sky.
Earth, teach me resignation as the leaves that die in the fall.
Earth, teach me regeneration as the seed that rises in the spring.
Earth, teach me to forget myself as melted snow forgets its life.
Earth, teach me to remember kindness as dry fields weep for rain.
UTE PRAYER

Creator, make me malleable, like your earth.
Savior, make me humble, like your earth.
Spirit, make me receptive, like your earth.

APRIL 22 ✧ "ACQUIRE" THE HOLY SPIRIT

Psalm 25; 1 Samuel 10:7-73; Acts 4:23-37

"Give us some of your oil for our lamps."
They replied, "We may not have enough for ourselves;
go and buy your own."
MATTHEW 25:8–9

The Celtic tradition of hermits living close to God and nature was lost or overlaid in the West, but in the East, this tradition continued. In Russia, it flowered in the tradition of the *staretz*—the holy hermit who lived alone but in deep solidarity with the people of his neighborhood. Seraphim was a notable Russian staretz of the nineteenth century whom I consider to be a soul friend for followers of Celtic spirituality. Once, sitting on a stool by his cell in the forest, he had this conversation about the Holy Spirit with young Nicholas Motovilov, whom he called a friend of God:

> "When you were a child you wanted to know the purpose of the Christian life but none of the ecclesiastics told you. I will try to tell you. Prayer and good works are good, but they are only means to an end. The true end of the Christian life is to acquire the Holy Spirit."
>
> "What do you mean by acquisition?" Nicholas asked.
>
> "You know what it means to earn money; don't you? Well, the Holy Spirit is also capital, but eternal capital. Our Lord compares our life to trading and says, 'Buy gold from me' [Revelation 3:18]. Good works, if they are done for the love of Christ, bring us the fruits of the Holy Spirit. In the parable of the virgins at a wedding [Matthew 25:9–15], the foolish virgins were told to buy oil for their lamps. What they were lacking was the grace of the Holy Spirit. So you see that the one essential thing is not just to do good, but to acquire the Holy Spirit as the one eternal treasure which will never pass away. . . .
>
> "This Holy Spirit, the All-Powerful, takes up his dwelling in us and prepares in our souls and bodies a dwelling place for the Father."

Come Holy Ghost, our souls inspire
and lighten with celestial fire.
Thou the anointing Spirit art,
who dost thy sevenfold gifts impart.
VENI CREATOR, NINTH CENTURY

APRIL 23 ❖ The Glow of the Spirit

Psalm 30; Exodus 33:7-23; Acts 5:1-16

Be aglow with the Spirit.
ROMANS 12:11 RSV

If you would get the center of your soul right, you should first of all get ready the needed materials, so that the heavenly Architect can begin to make the building. The house must be light and airy, with windows, which are the five senses, so that the light of heaven, the Sun of righteousness, can penetrate to our inner dwelling. The door of the house is Christ in person, for he said "I am the door."

When mind and heart are united in prayer, without any distraction, you feel that spiritual warmth which comes from Christ and fills the whole inner being with joy and peace. We have to withdraw from the visible world so that the light of Christ can come down into our heart. Closing our eyes, concentrating our attention on Christ, we must try to unite the mind with the heart, and, from the depths of our whole being, we must call on the Name of our Lord, saying, "Lord Jesus Christ, have mercy on me a sinner."

To the degree that love for the Lord Jesus warms the human heart, one finds in the Name of Jesus a sweetness that is the source of abiding peace.
SERAPHIM OF ZAROV

The love and fear of God increased more and more in me and my faith began to grow, and my spirit to be stirred up, so that in one day I would say as many as a hundred prayers and nearly as many at night, even when I was staying out in the woods or on the mountain. And I used to rise before dawn for prayer, in snow and frost and rain, and I used to feel no ill effect and there was no slackness in me. I now realize it was because the Spirit was glowing in me.
SAINT PATRICK

Eternal Creator of day and night
cleanse us by your refining fire,
kindle in us the Pentecostal flame,
and make our hearts burn with heavenly desires.

APRIL 24 ✥ THE JOY OF THE SPIRIT

Psalm 9; Isaiah 61:1-9; Acts 5:17-42

The fruit of the Spirit is joy.
GALATIANS 5:22

> The expression on his face seemed so extraordinary. A light shone from within, illuminating his features. His whole being seemed enfolded in the grace of the Holy Spirit and raised above the earth. He spoke to me about the heavenly joys of those who have a share in God's glory. It was as though he himself was actually living all this at that very moment, partaking of this bliss and enabling me to live it with him. He seemed unable to find words to express what he was experiencing, so he ended: "O my joy, such bliss, such beatitude, I cannot describe it all!"
> ANNE EROPKINE, DESCRIBING HER VISIT TO FATHER SERAPHIM IN 1830

The Celtic saints knew that the spiritual life is one of great joy. These joys come to us in different forms, in the various circumstances of our lives. When Cuthbert, for example, returned to Fame Isle to lead the life of a hermit, "he spent almost two months greatly rejoicing in his newfound quiet."

Once he sent some visitors on their way with the injunction to cook the goose that was hanging in the visitors' hut. Since they had plenty of food, they left it there instead—but then they found the weather turned against them and they could not sail for day after day. Eventually, Cuthbert went over to their hut and explained "with unruffled mien and even with joyful words" that their problems were caused by their failure to eat the goose as he had advised. They immediately cooked the goose, and the weather immediately became fair. They returned home with some feelings of shame because they had not taken Cuthbert's words seriously, but with even greater feelings of joy because they realized God took such good care of his servant Cuthbert that the Spirit even used the elements to give a gentle rebuke to those who took his words too lightly. They rejoiced because the Creator took such good care of themselves that God corrected them by means of a miracle.

Grant me the grace to appreciate your providence,
to contemplate your glory
and to become part of creation's song of joy.

APRIL 25 ❖ The Peace of the Spirit

Psalm 37:23-40; Micah 4:1-5; Acts 6

The fruit of the Spirit is peace.
GALATIANS 5:22

Learn to be peaceful, and thousands around you will find salvation. . . . There is nothing better than peace in Christ, for it brings victory over all the evil spirits on earth and in the air. When peace dwells in a person's heart it enables them to contemplate the grace of the Holy Spirit from within. The person who lives in peace collects spiritual gifts as it were with a scoop, and sheds the light of knowledge on others. All our thoughts, all our desires, all our efforts, and all our actions should make us say constantly with the Church, "O Lord, give us peace!" When a person lives in peace, God reveals mysteries to them.
SERAPHIM OF ZAROV

Live in peace.
COLUMBANUS

Peace of all felicity,
peace of shining clarity,
peace of joys consolatory.
Peace of souls in surety,
peace of heaven's futurity,
peace of virgin's purity.

Peace of the enchanted bowers,
peace of calm reposing hours,
peace of everlasting, ours.
GEORGE MCLEAN (TRANS.), POEMS OF THE WESTERN HIGHLANDERS

Deep peace of the quiet earth,
deep peace of the still waters,
deep peace of the setting sun,
deep peace of the forgiving heart,
deep peace of the true call,
deep peace of the Son of Peace,
be ours, today, forever.

APRIL 26 ✢ BAPTIZED IN THE SPIRIT

Psalm 40; Jeremiah 31:23-34; Acts 7

He will baptize you with holy wind and with fire.
LUKE 3:16

As Seraphim enthused about people in the Bible whose lives overflowed with the Holy Spirit, his young friend Nicholas Motovilov interjected, "But how can I know that I myself have this grace of the Holy Spirit?"

Seraphim gripped him firmly by the shoulders and said, "My friend, both of us this moment are in the Holy Spirit, you and I. Why don't you look at me?"

"I can't look at you, because the light flashing from your eyes and face is brighter than the sun and I am dazzled!" Nicholas replied.

"Don't be afraid, friend of God, you yourself are shining just like I am; you, too, are now in the fullness of the Holy Spirit, otherwise you wouldn't be able to see me as you do."

Nicholas later wrote about what he saw: "You can see only the blinding light which spreads everywhere, lighting up the layers of snow covering the glade, and igniting the flakes that are falling on us both like white power."

Then Seraphim drew out of him, step by step, what he was feeling: "An amazing well-being . . . a great calm in my soul . . . a peace no words can express . . . a strange unknown delight . . . an amazing happiness. . . ." Seraphim related each of these to experiences recounted in the Bible.
SERAPHIM OF ZAROV

In whom does the Holy Spirit dwell? In the one who is pure without sin. It is then that a person is a vessel of the Holy Spirit, when the virtues have come in place of the vices.
COLMÁN MAC BÉOGNAE, THE ALPHABET OF DEVOTION

O Thou who camest from above
the pure, celestial fire to impart,
kindle a flame of sacred love
on the mean altar of my heart.
CHARLES WESLEY

APRIL 27 ✢ The Fullness of the Holy Spirit

Psalm 57; Joel 2:23-32; Acts 8

Be filled with the Spirit.
EPHESIANS 5:18

In 1931, Seraphim asked his young God-seeker, Motovilov, "What are you feeling, friend of God?"

"I'm amazingly warm," his friend replied.

"Warm? what are you saying my friend? We are in the depths of the forest, in mid-winter, the snow lies under our feet and is settling on our clothes. How can you be warm?"

"It's the warmth one feels in a hot bath."

"Does it smell like that?"

"Oh no! Nothing on earth can compare to this. There's no scent in all the world like this one!"

"I know," said Father Seraphim, "for it is the same with me. I'm only questioning you to find out what you are discovering. It is indeed true, friend of God, that no scent on earth can compare to this fragrance, because it comes from the Holy Spirit. . . . The warmth isn't in the air, it is within us. This is what the Holy Spirit causes us to ask God for when we cry to him, 'Kindle in us the fire of the Holy Spirit.' Warmed by it, hermits are not afraid of winter hardship, protected as they are by the mantle of grace which the Holy Spirit has woven for them. . . . Now you know, my friend, what it is like to be in the fullness of the Holy Spirit."
SERAPHIM OF ZAROV

The fifteen strengths of the soul: the strength of faith, the strength of gentleness, the strength of humility, the strength of patience, the strength of mortification, the strength of obedience, the strength of charity, the strength of justice, the strength of mercy, the strength of generosity, the strength of forgiveness, the strength of serenity, the strength of moderation, the strength of holiness, the strength of divine love.
COLMÁN MAC BÉOGNAE, THE ALPHABET OF DEVOTION

Spirit of God, the breath of creation is yours.
Spirit of God, the groans of the world are yours.
Spirit of God, the wonder of communion is yours.
Spirit of God, the fire of love is yours.
And we are filled.

APRIL 28 ❖ SEEK THE SUPREME ILLUMINATION

Psalm 14; Ezekiel 36:22-32; Acts 9:1-31

> *I pray that you may have the power to understand*
> *how broad and long, how high and deep, is Christ's love.*
> *Yes, may you ... be completely filled with the very nature of God.*
> EPHESIANS 3:17–19

To receive and be aware of the light of Christ within one, it is necessary to withdraw from outward things, as far as this can be done. After purifying one's soul by contrition and good works and proclaiming one's faith in Christ crucified, people should shut their eyes and concentrate on bringing their mind down into the depths of their heart, ardently calling on the name of our Lord Jesus Christ. Then according to the ardor of their heart for the Beloved, they will find a sweetness, through inviting the Name, that evokes a longing to seek the supreme illumination. When the mind is concentrated in the heart through this exercise, then the light of Christ begins to shine, lighting up the temple of the soul with its radiance.

Lost in contemplation of the uncreated Beauty, people forget the things of the senses, even themselves, and prefer to be buried in the earth rather than lose their unique treasure—God.
SERAPHIM OF ZAROV

Faith with action, desire with constancy, calmness with devotion, chastity with humility, fasting with moderation, poverty with generosity, silence with discussion, distribution with equality, endurance without grievance, abstinence with exposure, zeal without severity, gentleness with justice, confidence without neglect, fear without despair, poverty without pride, confession without excuse, teaching with practice, progress without slipping, lowliness towards the haughty, smoothness towards the rough, work without grumbling, simpleness with wisdom, humility without favoritism, the Christian life without pretence—all these are contained in holiness. It is then that a person is holy, when he or she is full of divine love.
COLMÁN MAC BÉOGNAE, THE ALPHABET OF DEVOTION

May I be lost in wonder, love, and praise.

APRIL 29 ✣ FIRE OR ICICLES?

Psalm 43; Malachi 3:1-5; Acts 9:32-43

I will put my law within them,
and I will write it on their hearts.
JEREMIAH 31:33 ESV

God warms the heart and inward parts. When we feel a chill in our hearts coming from the devil (for the devil is cold), let us call on the Lord. God will come and warm us with perfect love, not only love for himself but for our neighbor as well; and at the touch of this fire Satan's chill will vanish.

Nothing so much as idle words has power to extinguish that fire brought by Christ and enkindled in our heart by the Holy Spirit. When mind and heart are united in prayer and the soul is wholly concentrated in a single desire for God, then the heart grows warm and the light of Christ begins to shine and fills the inward being with peace and joy.

One must constantly watch over the heart. The heart cannot live unless it is full of that water which boils in the heat of the divine fire. Without that water the heart grows cold and becomes like an icicle.
SERAPHIM OF ZAROV

The person who will not have fear of God will not have love of God. The person who will not have love of God will not have fulfillment of God's commandment. The person who will not have fulfillment of God's commandment will not have eternal life in heaven. For fear underlies love. Love underlies holy work. Holy work underlies eternal life in heaven.

Love of the living God cleanses the soul. It satisfies the mind. It increases rewards. It drives out vices. It despises the world. It cleanses, it concentrates thoughts.
COLMÁN MAC BÉOGNAE, THE ALPHABET OF DEVOTION

Kindle in our hearts, O God,
the flame of that love which never ceases,
that it may burn in us, giving light to others.
May we shine forever in your temple,
set on fire with your eternal light,
even your Son Jesus Christ,
our Savior and our Redeemer.
COLUMBA

APRIL 30 ✛ THE WILD SPIRIT

Psalm 18:30–50; Ezekiel 11:1–13; Acts 10

*In the beginning, when God created the universe,
the earth was empty and formless...
and the Spirit of God moved over the face of the waters.*
GENESIS 1:1–2

The Hebrew word for "spirit" used in this passage also means "power," or "awesome wind." Jesus said that God's Spirit is like the wind that blows where it wills: it may be a gale or it may be a breeze, and there is no point in us trying to control it.

Non-religious people over the millennia have tried to ignore the Spirit of God; religious people have tried to tame the Spirit. Some of the Celtic Christians knew better than to do either. That is no doubt why Celts have used the Wild Goose as a symbol for the Holy Spirit.

> The Holy Spirit is not a tame bird, kept in a clean cage, to be released for short bursts at charismatic meetings. . . . The Holy Spirit makes his habitation in some of the wildest and darkest places this world has to offer. . . . The Holy Spirit is wonderfully free, able to go to the dark places of our own lives, for healing, to the dark unvisited places of our churches, and to the dark and demon-infested places of our society.
> MICHAEL MITTON

*Spirit of God, be wild and free in me.
Batter my proud and stubborn will.
Blow me where you choose. Break me down if you must.
Refashion me as you will.
Move me powerfully away from the games I play
in order to try and tame you.
Lead me into the wild places, the places of dream or scream,
the new frontiers or the total quiet, the long dark tunnels
or the wide, sunny vistas, to speak to lions,
to move mountains, to bear tragedy,
to mirror you.*

MAY 1 ❖ WORK THAT FULFILLS

Psalm 67; Deuteronomy 28:1-14; Matthew 21:28-31

*In every work he set his hand to,
he did it with all his heart and prospered.*
2 CHRONICLES 31:21

The first day of May marks Beltane, the season of growth. We look back and thank God for preserving the Earth and its produce through winter and spring. We look forward to the cattle going out to the higher summer pastures . . . and to people everywhere going out to experience the fullest potentialities of work and enterprise.

May Day is also a celebration for the workers of the world. The word *agriculture*, which means "cultivation of the land," retains the Celtic understanding of the intimate relation between human work and Earth's work. Only when that relationship—in high-tech industry and commerce, as well as in agriculture—is one of care and prayer, does either Earth or human society experience the fullness of blessing that is inherent in them both.

In a true understanding of work, the owners of capital, managers, and employees work together like fingers on a hand to serve the needs of the world, all aware that the hand is an instrument of God. A curse will come upon us if our motive is to treat the world as a cake, from which we hope to get a bigger slice for ourselves. Blessing, which selfishness denies us, is the true birthright of the world of work.

This means that our involvement in work has to go beyond mere good management into heartfelt participation, in a way that the Celtic farmers understood when they blessed the May-time shearing of the sheep:

Go shorn and come woolly, bear the female Beltane lamb;
the lovely Brigid endow you and the fair Mary sustain you.
CARMINA GADELICA

Be up and doing to make progress, slack to take revenge,
careful in word, eager in work.
COLUMBANUS

*May the wealth and work of the world be
available to all and for the exploitation of none.
May I do no work that I cannot pray over.
May this May Day be a holy day,
when rest from work makes us blest in work.*

MAY 2 ✥ TO WORK IS TO PRAY

Psalm 76; Nehemiah 13; Ephesians 6:5-9

Work as if you were serving the Lord rather than human beings.
EPHESIANS 6:7

When Noel Dermot O'Donoghue was a child in rural southwest Ireland, every step in the workday had a prayer to go with it. He wrote, "The seedsman is his own priest. The work is equally labor and liturgy."

The language of this chicken farmer's prayer song may be quaint, but we need the sentiment behind it in our work today, whatever it is we count up or multiply in the course of our labor:

> I will rise early on Monday morning. I will sing my rhyme.
> I will go sunwise with my egg bowl to the nest of my hen.
> I will place my left hand to my breast, my right hand to my heart,
> I will seek the loving wisdom of God
> abundant in grace, in broods, and in flocks.
> I will close my two eyes quickly
> as in blind man's buff, moving slowly
> I will stretch my left hand over there
> to the nest of my hen on the other side.
> The first egg I shall bring near me;
> I will whisk it round behind me and place it in my bowl.
> The next time I shall lift my left hand and place two eggs in the bowl.
> Then I will lift my right hand, and seek the ruling of heaven's King
> and there shall be three more eggs in the bowl.
> I will raise my left hand a second time
> in the name of Christ, King of power,
> and there shall be ten eggs in the bowl.
> Thus when I have ceased, my brood will be complete
> beneath the breast of speckled hen.
> In the name of the most holy Trinity
> I will set the eggs on Thursday
> and the glad brood will come on Friday.
> CARMINA GADELICA

Lord, show me how to pray like this over my work...
and teach me not to count my chickens until they are hatched.

MAY 3 ✣ EXCELLENCE IN WORK

Psalm 104:1-23; Exodus 31; Matthew 21:33-46

Whatever your hand finds to do, do it with all your might.
ECCLESIASTES 9:10 NIV

May is the time of rising sap, business ventures, creative enterprise, new productivity targets, and fresh fashions. All these things are like seeds; we are like priests; and each of these labors can become a liturgy.

> During the winter months, the women of Highland households are up late and early at Calonas—the whole process of wool working from the raw material to the finished cloth. The industry of these women is wonderful, performed lovingly, uncomplainingly, day after day, year after year, till the sands of life run down. The life in a Highland home of the crofter class is well described in the following lines:
>
> In the long winter night all are engaged.
> Teaching the young is the grey-haired sage;
> the daughter at her carding, the mother at her wheel,
> while the fisher mends his net with his needle and his reel.
> ALEXANDER CARMICHAEL

If Jesus built a ship, she would travel trim.
If Jesus roofed a house, no leaks would be left by him.
If Jesus planted a garden, he would make it like paradise.
If Jesus did my day's work, it would delight his Father's eyes.

Lord, give me love and common sense
and standards that are high.
Give me calm and confidence
and—please—a twinkle in the eye.
CHRISTIAN WORKERS' PRAYER

May 4 ✢ May in Bloom

Psalm 139; Ezekiel 34:20-31; Luke 8:4-15

Where could I get away from your spirit?
If I traveled beyond the east
or lived in the furthest place in the west, you would be there.
Psalm 39:7, 9-10

When I do see the May in bloom,
I ain't afeard to ask the Almighty for Eternal Life.
AN OLD WILTSHIRE COUNTRYMAN

Look at the animals roaming the forest: God's spirit dwells within them. Look at the birds flying across the sky: God's spirit dwells within them. Look at the tiny insects crawling upon the grass: God's spirit dwells within them. Look at the fish in the river and sea: God's spirit dwells within them. There is no creature on earth in whom God is absent. Travel across the ocean to the most distant land, and you will find God's spirit in all the creatures there. Climb up the highest mountain, and you will find God's spirit among the creatures who live at the summit. When God pronounced that his creation was good, it was not only that his hand had fashioned every creature; it was that his breath had brought every creature to life.

Look, too, at the great trees of the forest; look at the wild flowers and the grass in the field; look even at your crops. God's spirit is present within all plants as well. The presence of God's spirit in all living beings is what makes them beautiful; and if we look with God's eyes, nothing on the earth is ugly.
PELAGIUS TO AN ELDERLY FRIEND

I program my computer with the love of God.
God be with me now as I call words into being.
May they make real my work of love.
May they join the work of creation.
Called from nothing, uttered over chaos,
bringing order.
ESTHER DE WAAL

MAY 5 ✣ THE NUT TREE FLOWERING

Psalm 104:24–35; Ezekiel 36:1–12; Matthew 13:24–30

Look at the way flowers grow.
MATTHEW 6:28

The face of nature laughs in the springtime,
her breath fresh and her eyes clearest blue.
Horses gather at the river's edge to drink its fresh clean water;
the sparkling waterfall cries with joy as its torrent hits the rocks.
The blackbird's call is wild and free, rejoicing at the new abundance of food;
the cuckoo, that lover of warmth, begins its happy chorus.
Sheep and cattle gobble the crisp, juicy grass;
the meadows are alight with colors of flowers in bloom.
The sun glints through the fresh green leaves,
the wind rustling through the branches
is the harp of nature, playing a song of love.
Men are vigorous and strong, women pretty and gay;
the whole world is in love with its Creator.
IN CELTIC FIRE, ROBERT VAN DE WEYER (UNATTRIBUTED)

O Son of God, do a miracle for me and change my heart,
You, dear child of Mary, are the refined molten metal of our forge.
It is you who makes the sun bright, together with the ice.
It is you who creates the rivers and the salmon all along the river.
That the nut tree should be flowering, O Christ, it is a rare craft.
Through your skill too comes the kernel, you fair ear of our wheat,
Though the children of Eve ill deserve the bird flocks and the salmon,
it was the Immortal One on the cross who made both salmon and birds,
It is he who makes the flower of the sloes grow
through the surface of the blackthorn,
and the nut flower on other trees.
Besides this, what miracle is greater?
TADHG OG OHUIGINN (DIED 1448, TRANS. BY K. H. JACKSON, ADAPTED)

MAY 6 ✤ BLESSINGS

Psalm 29; Genesis 49:1-26; Luke 6:27-36

*Almighty God who blesses you with blessings of corn and flowers,
blessings of ancient mountains,
delightful things from everlasting hills.*
GENESIS 49:25–26 GNT

In the Old Testament blessing is life, health, and fertility for the people, their cattle, their fields . . . blessing is the basic power of life itself.
CLAUS WESTERMANN

Celtic Christ-followers never lost sight of the fact that God delights to have a world that overflows with blessing. Since Augustine, however, too many Christians have looked at the world only to see what is wrong with it. A jaundiced outlook has overtaken many of us—and yet blessing is an essential part of our biblical and our Celtic birthright, a birthright we need to recover.

Abraham, whom we call our father in the faith, had his entire vocation carved out for him in terms of blessing: "All the communities of the earth shall find blessing in you" (Genesis 12:4). When Jacob gave his final blessings to the twelve tribes that grew from of his twelve sons, he gave each one a blessing that was appropriate to their character and circumstances (Genesis 49). Blessings of a whole tribe were passed on through a father and sons. Then, in the Christian New Testament, Christ's final act before his ascension was to bless his assembled apostles. And through the hands of the apostles and their successors, the Lord continues to bless his people even now.

*O, King of the Tree of Life,
the blossoms on the branches are your people,
the singing birds are your angels, the whispering breeze is your Spirit.
O, King of the Tree of Life,
may the blossoms bring forth the sweetest fruit,
may the birds sing out the highest praise,
may your Spirit cover all with his gentle breath.
The blessing of God and the Lord be yours,
the blessing of the perfect Spirit be yours,
the blessing of the Three be pouring for you
mildly and generously, mildly and generously.*
CARMINA GADELICA

MAY 7 ✢ MAY TIME'S FAIREST GIFT

Psalm 117; Song of Songs 2; Acts 10

*In the trees... the birds make their nests and sing.
From the sky you send rain on the hills,
and the earth is filled with your blessings.*
PSALM 104:12–13 GNT

May time is the fairest season
with its loud bird song and green trees,
when the plough is in the furrow
and the oxen under the yoke,
when the sea is green and the land many colors.
On the hill and in the valley, on the islands of the sea,
whichever path you take
you shall not hide from blessed Christ.
It was our wish, our Brother, our way,
to go to the land of your exile.
Seven saints and seven score and seven hundred
went to the one court with blessed Christ
and were without fear.
The gift I ask, may it not be denied me,
is peace between myself and God.
May I find the way to the gate of glory.
May I not be sad, O Christ, in your court.
EARLY MIDDLE WELSH

*May the road rise to meet you,
may the wind be always at your back,
may the sun shine warm upon your face,
the rain fall soft upon your fields,
and until we meet again, may God hold you
in the hollow of his hand.*
TRADITIONAL IRISH BLESSING

MAY 8 ✢ THE EARTH IS PRECIOUS

Psalm 24; Job 38:1-30; Acts 11:19-30

The earth is the Lord's and everything in it.
PSALM 24:1 NIV

In 1854, the U.S. Government offered to buy a large area of Native-owned land, and promised in return a "reservation" for the Indian people. Chief Seattle's reply has been described as the most beautiful and profound statement ever made about the Earth.

> We are part of the earth and it is part of us. The perfumed flowers are our sisters; the deer, the horse, the great eagle, these are our brothers. The rocky crests, the juices in the meadows, the body heat of the pony, and human beings—all belong to the same family. The rivers are our brothers—they quench our thirst. The rivers carry our canoes, and feed our children. If we sell you our land, you must remember, and teach your children, that the rivers are our brothers, and yours, and you must henceforth give the rivers the kindness you would give any brother.
>
> The white man treats his mother, the earth, and his brother, the sky, as things to be bought, plundered, sold like sheep or bright beads. His appetite will devour the earth and leave behind only a desert. There is no quiet place in the white man's cities, no place to hear the unfurling of leaves in the spring, or the rustle of an insect's wings. This we know: all things are connected. Man did not weave their web of life; he is merely a strand in it. Whatever he does to the web, he does to himself.
>
> You may think that you own God as you wish to own our land; but you cannot. He is the God of all humanity, and his compassion is equal for the red and the white people. This earth is precious to him, and to harm the earth is to heap contempt on its Creator.
>
> CHIEF SEATTLE

In the name of the One who gives the growth,
may we tend the seedbed earth.
In dependence on the God of life,
may we cherish the precious Earth,
the Earth of the God of life,
the Earth of the Christ of love,
the Earth of the Spirit Holy.

MAY 9 ⁂ IMMERSION

Psalm 119:1-24; Jeremiah 2:1-13; Acts 16:11-34

As they traveled down the road, they came to a place where there was some water, and the official said, "Here is some water. What is to keep me from being baptized?" The official ordered the carriage to stop, and both Philip and the official went down into the water, and Philip baptized him.
ACTS 8:36–38 GNT

Celtic Christians usually did not perform their baptisms in a font of collected water. Instead, they went to the source of water—a spring, well, or river—and were baptized there. Throughout their lives, they would then frequently sprinkle water on themselves or stand in water to remind them that baptism is a way of life, a way of being immersed in God. The Orthodox Christians of the East have a similar understanding:

> The voice of the Lord cries out across the waters saying:
> "Come, all of you, and receive the spirit of wisdom,
> the spirit of understanding, the spirit of reverence of God,
> who is shown to us in Jesus Christ,
> as he wades into the waters of the river Jordan,
> the river which rolls back its currents
> as it looks upon the Lord coming to be immersed."
> You came as a man, O Christ our King,
> to receive the immersion of a servant
> from the hands of the Forerunner;
> this was because of our sins, O you, Lover of humankind.
> The Forerunner, John the Baptizer,
> became all trembling as he looked upon you coming toward him.
> "How can the candlestick illumine the light?" he cried out.
> "How can a slave lay hands upon his Lord?
> Make me and these waters holy, O Savior,
> who takes away the sins of the world."
> Make this a fountain of immortality:
> A gift of cleansing. A remission of sins.
> A healing of compulsive habits. A destroying of demons.
> A renewing of our God-given nature.
> ADAPTED FROM THE ORTHODOX RITE OF THE BLESSING OF THE WATERS

Immerse us in your pure water and your gift of tenderness.
Immerse us in your healing water and your gift of wisdom.
Immerse us in your renewing water and your gift of reverence.

MAY 10 ❖ THE FIVE-STRINGED HARP

Psalm 119:17-40; Song of Songs 4; 1 Corinthians 6:12-20

*You know that your bodies are parts of the body of Christ,
... so use your bodies for God's glory.*
1 CORINTHIANS 6:15, 20 GNT

Celtic Christians rely on all their bodily senses, which they call "the five-stringed harp," as vehicles for the presence of God.

*Bless my hands, Lord.
May they be put to good use and not wasted idly.
May they work hard and honestly,
yet still grasp every opportunity to stroke and caress.
May they never be raised in violence.
Bless my feet, Lord.
May they always walk on hallowed ground,
may they not run away in fear but plod courageously on.
May they never wander off your courageous path.
Bless my eyes, Lord.
May they see beyond the masks so often worn and look deeply into the soul.
Help them to drink in the beauty of the sunrise and sunset,
the shimmering sun dancing through the waves.
May they marvel at the brilliance of tiny jewel-like snow crystals,
glistening in the moonlight.
May they see into the hunger, suffering, and injustices of the world.
Help me to know when to open them and when to look away.
Bless my ears, Lord,
that I may always hear the real message of what is being said.
Grant my ears the wisdom of knowing what to cherish and what to reject.
Thank you for the gift of hearing— the communication it enables—
the music that inspires my soul and the pain that moves me to compassion.
Thank you for the gift of silence, a calm to my soul.
Bless my mind, Lord.
May it always feed and grow on your holy word
and consider all things from your godly perspective.*
ADAPTED FROM SUE BLOOMFIELD, THE COMMUNITY OF AIDAN AND HILDA

MAY 11 ⁖ PRESENCE

Psalm 119:41-56; Genesis 4:1-16; Acts 13:1-12

So the one who came down is the same one who went up,
above and beyond the heavens,
to fill the whole universe with his presence.
EPHESIANS 4:10 GNT

Everything spoke of a Presence, vibrated with God's love. They saw a universe ablaze with his glory, suffused with a presence that calls, nods and beckons—a creation personally united with its Creator in every atom and fiber.
DAVID ADAM

The material is shot through with the spiritual; there is a "within-ness" of God in all life. The whole earth is sacramental: everything is truly every blessed thing.
RON FERGUSON, CHASING THE WILD GOOSE

Earth's crammed with heaven
and every common bush afire with God.
ELIZABETH BARRETT BROWNING

There's no plant in the ground
but is full of his blessing.
There's no thing in the sea but is full of his life.
There is naught in the sky but proclaims his goodness.
Jesu! O Jesu! it's good to praise thee!
There's no bird on the wing but is full of his blessing.
There's no star in the sky but is full of his life.
There is naught 'neath the sun but proclaims his goodness.
Jesu! O Jesu! it's good to praise thee!
CARMINA GADELICA

MAY 12 ❖ ART

Psalm 119:57-64; Exodus 35; Acts 13:13-43

*God has filled him with his spirit and given him skill, ability
and understanding of every kind of artistic work.*
EXODUS 35:31

According to the Book of Armagh, the company that accompanied Patrick on his mission to Ireland included artists. Patrick himself taught young people who were training for the ministry to write the alphabet in a beautiful, graceful style. Before Patrick's arrival, the people of Ireland had been all but destitute of literature, but in the centuries following Patrick, art and calligraphy flowered in Ireland. The flower of that flowering was the Book of Kells.

This book is believed to be have been created at Iona in the eighth century, and taken to the monastery at Kells for safekeeping during a Viking invasion. Bright natural pigments were used to draw its images, spirals, knot work, and key-patterns. The ornament is profuse and varied, sometimes drawing on both Pictish and Byzantine art. The twelfth- and thirteenth-century Welsh historian, Geraldus Cambrensis, concluded that the Book of Kells was "the work of an angel, not of a man." A more modern author, Nicolete Gray, wrote in *A History of Lettering* that the three Greek letters that form the monogram of Christ on the Chi Rho page are "more presences than letters." Shining through the brilliance of the artistic skills is the splendor of spiritual understanding.

We all have something of the artist in us, and we can learn much from these Irish artists—for example, that an artist does not have to be conventional. An artist may go in directions that seem unconventional or bizarre to others, but that may in fact be a form of humility and openness to Divine creativity, a willingness to be "foolish" for Christ. An artist must at the same time attain to an inner purity, honesty, and integrity of spirit, understanding the inner, God-given nature of each element of creation the artist wishes to portray, and how that reflects an aspect of the ultimate nature of the Creator.

> The Irish sense of balance in imbalance, of riotous complexity moving swiftly within a basic unity, would now find its most extravagant expression in Irish Christian art—in the monumental high crosses, in miraculous liturgical vessels such as the Ardagh Chalice, and, most delicately, of all, in the art of the Irish codex.
> THOMAS CAHILL, HOW THE IRISH SAVED CIVILIZATION

*God, fill your people with your Spirit
and give us skill, ability, and understanding
for every kind of artistic work.*

May 13 ✛ The Importance of Little Things

Psalm 119:65-80; Exodus 37; Acts 13:44-52

*Jesus said: If you're faithful with little things
you will be faithful in larger ones too.*
Luke 16:10

Do the little things that you have seen and heard through me.
THE LAST WORDS OF DAVID OF WALES

Faithfulness in little things is a big thing.
JOHN CHRYSOSTOM

I come in the little things, says the Lord.
ANONYMOUS

We can do little things for God. I turn the cake that is frying on the pan, for love of God. That done, if there is nothing else to call me, I prostrate myself in worship before the One who has given me grace to work. Afterwards I rise happier than a king.
BROTHER LAWRENCE

When we read the lives of the saints, we are struck by a certain large leisure, which went hand in hand with a remarkable effectiveness. They were never hurried; they did comparatively few things, and these not necessarily striking or important; and they troubled very little about their influence. Yet they always seemed to hit the mark; every bit of their life told; their simplest actions had a distinction, an exquisiteness that suggested the artist. The reason is not far to seek. Their sainthood lay in their referring the smallest actions to God.
E. HERMON

*God in my rising and lying down,
God in my dressing and undressing,
God in my cleaning and cooking,
God in my locking and unlocking,
God in my greeting and speaking,
God in my counting and viewing,
God in the little things,
God in this thing,
God in that thing,
God in all things.*

MAY 14 ✢ BEING FULLY PRESENT

Psalm 119:129-144; Exodus 40; Acts 14

*If your gift is practical service,
give yourself to your work with all your heart.*
ROMANS 12:7

How often do we think, "How boring!" about someone we are with, or something that we do, or even about our life as a whole? We can respond to this problem in two ways. The first way is to rush into the pursuit of trifles—into anything so long as it is new and catches our fancy. Some people spend their lives doing this. It is not, of course, an answer at all; it is merely a temporary distraction. The second way to respond to the problem of boredom is to develop an attitude of "being fully present," so that the meaning, energy, color, and adventure—with which, all unseen, the present moment is crammed—become available to us.

This is sometimes called "the sacrament of the present moment." By giving ourselves with all our hearts to whatever this moment holds, we can "be fully present" in all sorts of ways. Perhaps the words of someone speaking to us are like water off a duck's back. Then we decide to become fully present to that person, and we become aware of his unique history, future, and present, of the wonder of a life. Or perhaps we are mindlessly reciting a familiar psalm, or Mary's Song (the Magnificat)—but then, we imagine that we are the psalmist or Mary, and we feel their feelings soar through us. Boredom flees; emotions flow; encounters, tears, healings come.

> It is this ability to fuse together the unique time and place of Christ's birth in Bethlehem with our own specific present . . . which is part of the genius of Celtic spirituality; a realization that the eternal moments of the Incarnation or the Crucifixion or the Resurrection can transcend time and space, enabling us to relocate Bethlehem or Calvary or the Garden of the Third Day in our own back yard.
> PATRICK THOMAS

*Fill this moment, Lord.
Open my eyes to your presence. Open my ears to your call.
Open my heart to your glory, now, in me, in all.*

MAY 15 ✤ GOD'S PLAN

Psalm 132; Jeremiah 32; Acts 13

I chose you to go and bear bountiful fruit, the kind of fruit that never spoils.
JOHN 15:16

From the time he was a young man, Cuthbert had a strong sense of God's plan for his life. He knew he had to give his life to God, and that God planned for his training to be at Melrose. When he arrived at Melrose, the prior there, Boisil, knew that God would one day use Cuthbert as a leader in the church simply from the way Cuthbert dismounted from his horse and treated his servant.

Cuthbert was a natural leader of people, yet he also had a strong inner inclination toward the solitary life. How could he know which of these was God's will for him? One day he was talking with Abbess Aelfflaed on Coquet Island about what God's plan might be for the Northumbrian kingdom and its ruler, as well as for its church. His conversation with her revealed that because he had heeded Boisil's prophetic words for him, he had become willing to accept a call to be a bishop for a time in life . . . yet at the same time, he had also made plans to have a period as a contemplative. He was open to further direction from the abbess's insights; he was open to better understanding God's will for his life, no matter where it led him.

> I cannot invent new things like the airship which sails on silver wings
> but today a wonderful thought in the dawn was given
> and the stripes on my robe,
> shining from wear, were suddenly fair
> bright with light falling from heaven—
> Gold and silver and bronze light from the windows of heaven.
> And the thought was this:
> that a sacred plan is hid in my hand;
> that my hand is big, big, because of this plan;
> that God, who dwells in my hand, knows this sacred plan
> of the things God will do for the world, using my hand.
> TOYOHIKO KAGAWA

> As tools come to be sharpened by the blacksmith, so may we come, Lord.
> As sharpened tools go back to their owner,
> so may we go back to our everyday life to be used by you.
> A PRAYER FROM AFRICA

MAY 16 ❖ SET SAIL

Psalm 107:1-16; Zechariah 10; Acts 15:36-16:5

*When they pass through their sea of trouble,
I, the Lord, will strike the waves.*
ZECHARIAH 10:11 GNT

Shall I abandon, O King of Mysteries, the soft comforts of home?
Shall I turn my back on my native land,
and my face towards the sea?
Shall I put myself wholly at the mercy of God,
without silver, without a horse, without fame and honor?
Shall I throw myself wholly on the King of kings,
without a sword and shield, without food and drink,
without a bed to lie on?
Shall I say farewell to my beautiful land,
placing myself under Christ's yoke?
Shall I pour out my heart to him,
confessing my manifold sins and begging forgiveness,
tears running down my cheeks?
Shall I leave the prints of my knees on the sandy beach,
a record of my final prayer in my native land?
Shall I then suffer every kind of wound that the sea can inflict?
Shall I take my tiny coracle across the wide, sparkling ocean?
O King of the Glorious heaven,
shall I go of my own choice upon the sea?
O Christ, will you help me on the wild waves?
EARLY IRISH, SOMETIMES ATTRIBUTED TO VOYAGERS SUCH AS ST. BRENDAN

*Jesus who stopped the wind and stilled the waves
grant you calm in the storm times;
Jesus Victor over death and destruction
bring safety on your voyage;
Jesus of the purest love, perfect companion
bring guarding ones around you;
Jesus of the miraculous catching of fish
and the perfect lakeside meal
guide you finally ashore.*
FROM *THE FIRST VOYAGE OF THE CORACLE*,
THE COMMUNITY OF AIDAN AND HILDA

MAY 17 ✢ LET GOD BLOW US

Psalm 107:17-43; Ezekiel 12:1-16; Acts 16:6-40

*Some went down to the sea in ships,
doing business on the great waters;
they saw the deeds of the Lord, his wondrous works in the deep.*
PSALM 107:23-24 ESV

Brendan chose fourteen monks from his community, took them to the chapel, and made this proposal to them, "My dear fellow soldiers in the spiritual war, I beg your help because my heart is set upon a single desire. If it be God's will, I want to seek out the Island of Promise of which our forefathers spoke. Will you come with me? What are your feelings?" As soon as he had finished speaking, the monks replied with one voice, "Father, your desire is ours also. . . ." When all was ready, Brendan ordered his monks aboard, the sail was hoisted, and the coracle was swept out to sea. For the next two weeks the wind was fair, so that they did no more than steady the sail. But then the wind fell, and they had to row, day after day. . . . When their strength eventually failed, Brendan comforted them: "Have no fear, brothers, for God is our captain and our pilot; so take in the oars, and set the sail, letting him blow us where he wills."
FROM THE LIFE OF BRENDAN THE NAVIGATOR

Brothers and sisters, God is calling you to leave behind everything that stops you setting sail in the ocean of God's love. You have heard the call of the Wild Goose, the untamable Spirit of God: be ready for him to lead you into wild, windy or well-worn places in the knowledge that he will make them places of wonder and welcome.

He is giving you the vision of a spoiled creation being restored to harmony with its Creator, of a fragmented world becoming whole, of a weakened church being restored to its mission, of healed lands being lit up by the radiance of the glorious Trinity.

In stillness or storm, be always vigilant, waiting, sharing, praising, blessing, telling. Sail forth across the ocean of God's world knowing both the frailty of your craft and the infinite riches of your God.
FROM THE FIRST VOYAGE OF THE CORACLE, THE COMMUNITY OF AIDAN AND HILDA

*Dear God, be good to us;
your sea is so wide, and our boats are so small.
prayer of the Breton fishermen*

MAY 18 ❖ PENTECOST ON AN ISLAND

Psalm 97; Exodus 19:1-19; Acts 18:1-17

The Lord is king! Earth, be glad! Rejoice, you islands of the seas!
PSALM 97:1 GNT

Brendan and his crew at last sailed in to an island. Streams of water gushed down from the hills and there was an abundance of fish and sheep. It was Good Friday, the day of Jesus' death, so they sacrificed the finest sheep in celebration of Jesus, whom Christians know as the Lamb of God. However, the hermit who lived on the island, and who had welcomed them lovingly, felt God wanted them to go to a second island nearby to celebrate the resurrection of Jesus on Easter Day.

So off they sailed. One of the birds welcomed them, landing on Brendan's shoulders and flapping its wings with joy. Then at dusk, as they sang God's praises, the birds joined in, chirping in perfect harmony. The hermit brought over food from his island which was to last the monks forty days, for they were told to stay for the Pentecost celebration and then sail on. The day after Pentecost the hermit brought them another forty days' supplies and they again embarked on the wide sea.
FROM THE LIFE OF BRENDAN THE NAVIGATOR

I am bending my knee
in the eye of my Father who made me,
in the eye of the Savior who redeemed me,
in the eye of the Spirit who cleansed me,
in friendship and affection,
I am bending my knee.
O Mighty One, O Holy Three,
I am bending the knee.
Bestow on us fullness in our need.
The smile of God, the trust of God in our need
that we may do on the world you made
as angels and saints do in heaven.
Each day and night in bloom and in blight
we'll be bending the knee.
CARMINA GADELICA (ADAPTED)

MAY 19 ✣ WELLS OF LIFE

Psalm 74; Numbers 21:10-20; John 4:1-30

Jesus, tired out, sat down by Jacob's Well.
When a Samaritan woman came to draw up some water, . . .
Jesus said to her, "The water I give
will be a well of everlasting life."
JOHN 4:6–7, 14

May 19 is the English day for dressing wells. This tradition is rooted in the time, both before and after the arrival of Christianity, when wells were community focal points, not only as places to draw water but also for meetings and worship. The Celtic Christian church met at the sites of wells, using water as a powerful expression of God's power to sustain, cleanse, and renew.

The Celtic lands already had parallels in their own traditions with scriptural stories of wells. Although formal church councils forbade the worship of wells, we learn of Celtic Christ-followers being divinely guided to discover a well when a water supply was needed. Celtic Christians used well water for baptism and to bless pilgrims. They bathed in wells and were healed, they used wells as waymarks of God's deeds, and they established churches beside wells. Adamnan's *Life of Columba* describes a poisonous well that the Picts "worshipped as a god," which "was converted by the saint into a blessed well." David is said to have done something similar at Glastonbury, where he came to a well full of poison, blessed it, and caused it to become warm; it was called the Hot Baths. The well at Ffynnon Enddwyn in Wales became famous when Saint Enddwyn was cured after bathing in it. Ffynnon Ddyfnog Well in Wales is said to owe its healing properties to the action of Saint Ddyfnog who did penance there by standing under the cold water. John of Tynemouth wrote in 1350 that the waters from the well on Ramsey Island "when drunk by sick folk, convey health of body to all"; a man suffering from a swelling in his stomach drank from it, vomited out a frog, and was cured immediately! According to the stories told about Saint David and Teilo, God caused wells to appear for their needs, and this well water tasted as pleasant as wine.

Today, water companies' advertisements often emphasize truths such as "every drop is precious; we should never take water for granted." And we hear prophet voices calling us to "dig up the ancient wells"—that is, God-given sources of renewal in our heritage.

Help me to drink deeply,
and rediscover the ancient sources of renewal.

May 20 ❖ Evangelism of the Heart

Psalm 145; Zechariah 8; Acts 14

Whoever is not against us is on our side.
MARK 9:40

A young Desert Christian met a pagan priest and immediately went on the attack: "Demon, where are you running away to?"

Furious at being addressed in this manner, the man beat the Christian with a stick, left him half dead, and went on his way.

A little further on, the same priest met an old Desert Christian who greeted him and spoke to him warmly. Astonished, the man asked, "What good do you see in me that you greet me in this way?"

The old monk replied, "I am sorry for you, for I see you wearing yourself out without realizing that this is all in vain,"

The other man responded, "I was touched by the way you greeted me. Your kindness made me realize that you come from God." After that, the man joined the Christian monastic life. Moreover, he persuaded others to do the same.

The lesson of this story is that we should seek to welcome those of another faith as persons in their own right; we should establish a relationship before seeking to share our faith. Moreover, as Christ's representatives we should never put down another person, be rude, or assume the worst.

So often, however, Christians demonize people of another faith, just as the young Desert Christian did. We cling to false stereotypes of others by referring to the worst aberrations of their religion, all the while disregarding the aberrations of Christianity. The truth is that we all have similar needs and feelings. We are always more alike than we are different.

The pagan priest clearly had feelings of self-doubt, or he would not have asked, "What good do you see in me?" The last thing he needed was for someone else to put him down. He needed to be cherished. And when the old monk showed him loving acceptance, the man was freed to meet Christ. He went on to introduce others to Christ, because he knew that they also wanted to be cherished—and Jesus loves and cherishes each of us.

O Christ, you had compassion on the crowds.
You drew people to yourself;
you rejected none who knew they were needy.
Grant us hearts like yours,
hearts that go out in genuine greeting,
in humble welcome, till, in the fellowship of sharing,
souls are drawn to you.

MAY 21 ❖ REINCARNATION OR RESURRECTION?

Psalm 41; Ecclesiastes 12:1-8; 1 Corinthians 15:35-58

> *When the body is buried, it is mortal;*
> *when raised, it will be immortal.*
> *When buried, it is ugly and weak;*
> *when raised, it will be beautiful and strong.*
> *When buried, it is a physical body;*
> *when raised it will be a spiritual body.*
> 1 CORINTHIANS 15:42–44 GNT

Most people believe in some kind of afterlife. For a human life to be snuffed out does not fit with our awareness that each person has so much unfulfilled potential. Out-of-the-body experiences also tell us that this life is not all there is.

Today, many people believe in reincarnation. This is not a new idea, of course. Many cultures down through the centuries have also shared this belief. Its great appeal is that it keeps alive hopes for future development. Death is not the end if we can hope to be reincarnated in another form.

Some believe that we are each reincarnated as either a higher or a lower being. In the West, this belief is often egocentric: we assume that other people will be reincarnated as lower beings, while we ourselves will be reincarnated as higher beings! To feed our own egos, we may claim we were royal personages in previous lives. These are selfish views of reincarnation. There is another, self-negating view of reincarnation: that my essence will be absorbed into the cosmic stream of life. I will surrender my ego and become one with the Universe.

The pre-Christian people of Britain also believed in a type of reincarnation. However, they believed that we will each be the same person in the next life, with the same tastes and interests, but the environment in the Other World will be immeasurably better. A warrior will have superb horses and endless victories there; a king will rule with absolute power.

Celtic Christ-followers said to these old beliefs: Yes, we, too, believe we will still be the same persons in the next life; we will not lose our individuality and be absorbed by the cosmos. However, we are all so selfish that our ego as well as our body has to die first. Then, and only then, will there be a resurrection of our true personality. If we were fighters on earth, our fighting in the next life will be transformed into a non-destructive plane. If we are rulers, we will be become humble servant-kings like Christ was.

Death is not a full stop. It is only the end of the first page of our story.

> *May you be as free as the wind,*
> *as soft as sheep's wool, as straight as an arrow,*
> *so that you may journey ever nearer to the heart of God.*

MAY 22 ✣ STORM AND SUNSHINE

Psalm 6; Job 37; Acts 19:21–20:6

The storm makes my heart beat wildly...
at God's command wonderful things happen....
And now the light in the sky is dazzling, too bright for us to look at;
and the sky has been swept clean by the wind.
JOB 37:1, 5, 21 GNT

Glowering clouds that produce sudden squalls remind me of human nature's unpredictable outbursts. We can never assume, just because life goes smoothly now, that we will always be immune from these sudden outbreaks! If we build our lives on such a false assumption, we will not be able to handle the squalls when they do come. Instead, we will try to run away, or we will collapse; panic or fear will control our hearts. But if we accept now that these things are part—though only part—of life's scenery, we will maintain perspective in the storm.

Clouds teach us that the threats and squalls of life soon pass; they are never permanent. They swirl in and out of the clear sky. When the sun breaks out again, we are reminded that the Lord delights to restore the goodness of life. As the wind dries the rain, so the damp evaporates from our lives. The sun warms the Earth, and we too can bask in God's rays. Yet the smoke rising from chimneys teaches us that we have a part to play; we do not need to be totally at the mercy of Nature's vagaries. Instead, we can say, "Lord, I will do what I can to stoke the fires of the Faith."

> King, you ordained the movements of every object: the sun to cross the sky each day... the clouds to carry rain from the sea, and rivers to carry waters back to the sea.
> THE CELTIC PSALTER

Through his creation God encircles and strengthens us.
HILDEGAARD OF BINGEN

Lord, may the swirling storm clouds remind me that I am a creature, not Creator,
that I am liable to suffer from the changes and chances of this mortal life.
May the clouds teach me to look always to you,
the Creator of both storm and sunshine.
May they teach me to maintain joy when life is frowning
and to maintain perspective in and out of season.

MAY 23 ❖ DREAMS

Psalm 77; Joel 2:28-32; Acts 16:1-10

I will pour out my spirit on everyone;
your sons and daughters will proclaim my message,
your old folk will have dreams,
and your young folk will see visions;
I will pour out my spirit on ... both men and women.
JOEL 2:28–29

The Bible records dreams through which God spoke to individuals and sometimes to nations. Today, psychologists tell us that our dreams are nearly always about ourselves, with each person and event in our dream worlds actually a symbol for some aspect of our own psyches. Even from this purely psychological perspective, dreams can carry powerful messages to us.

For several centuries in the West, most people lost touch with the world of imagination, spirit, and dreams. Toward the turn of the second millennium, however, that changed. "Dream guidance" became popular, but the modern glut of material on this topic is often confused and simplistic, encouraging our egos to collide with each other in ways that leave inquirers more confused and self-centered than when they started. In contrast, Celtic saints, like the biblical characters, sometimes had God-given clarity in their dreams. They were open to the Divine voice reaching them through many channels, including dreams. Deeply meaningful dreams came to people whose lives and psyches were pure. Dreams accompanied the births of some of the most holy Celtic Christians.

Saint Ita, for example, was given dreams from God throughout her life. Once she dreamed that an angel gave her three precious stones. The angel explained that these represented the Father, the Son, and the Holy Spirit, and said to her, "Always in your sleep and vigils, the angels of God and holy visions will come to you, for you are a temple of God, in body and soul."

O Christ, Son of the living God,
may your holy angels guard our sleep.
May they watch over us as we rest
and hover around our beds.
Let them reveal to us in our dreams
visions of your glorious truth,
O High Prince of the universe,
O High Priest of the mysteries.

MAY 24 ❖ A UNIVERSAL SPIRIT

Psalm 105; Job 31; Acts 15:1–21

*Christ ... has made a unity
of the conflicting elements of Jew and Gentile
by breaking down the barrier which lay between us ...
So you are ... fellow citizens with every other Christian—
you belong now to the household of God.*
EPHESIANS 2:14, 19 JBP

The churches in Celtic Britain were part of the "one catholic and apostolic church" throughout the world, yet at the same time they responded to direct promptings of the Holy Spirit in their unique mission. Today, however, some Christians maintain that it is no longer possible to be both Catholic and "Spirit-led"; we cannot be true to our own call from God and still be part of the larger church body.

These words from a famous sermon by John Wesley can inspire us that we can still be both different and unified:

> Though we cannot think alike, may we not love alike? May we not be of one heart, though we are not of one opinion? ... Every wise person will allow others the same liberty of thinking which they desire they should allow themselves.... And how shall we choose among so much variety? No one can choose for, or prescribe to, another. But everyone must follow the dictates of their own conscience, in simplicity and godly sincerity. They must be fully persuaded in their own mind; and then act according to the best light they have.
>
> My only question at present is this, "Is your heart right, as mine is with yours?" ... Learn the first elements of the Gospel of Christ and then you shall learn to be of a truly catholic spirit.
>
> While the person of a truly catholic spirit is united by the tenderest and closest ties to one particular congregation, their heart is enlarged towards all humanity, those they know and those they do not; they embrace with strong and cordial affection neighbors and strangers, friends and enemies. This is catholic or universal love.
>
> A person of catholic spirit is one who gives their hand to all ... who is ready to "spend and be spent for them," yes, to lay down their life for their sake.

*Give me a heart that is open to all,
a heart that embraces everyone as a brother or sister in Christ,
a heart that wills their wholeness as one family.*

May 25 ✣ Three Ways to Spell Faith

Psalm 106:1-24; Joshua 1:1-9; Acts 16:35-40

The chains fell off Peter's hands. . . . Peter and the angel passed by the first and second guard posts. . . . Then Peter knocked at the door where many people were praying for him. The servant girl recognized his voice—and was so happy she ran back to tell the others and forgot to open the door!
ACTS 12:7, 10, 12, 14

Irish jokes are known for their distinctive and delightful sense of humor. Here is an Irish faith story that shows some of that same humor.

Samthann, Abbess of Clonbroney, once sent a message to her local king to release a prisoner named Fallamain. The haughty king refused. So Samthann sent messengers to whom she gave these instructions: "If the king will not release him, say to the prisoner, 'In the name of the Holy Trinity you will be freed from your chains and come safely to Samthann, the Servant of the Trinity.'"

When the king heard this, he doubled the prisoner's chains and put eight guards on duty at the prison and another eight at the town gate. At midnight, however, the prisoner's chains fell away from his legs, and he walked away free.

As he passed the first set of guards, they said "Who are you, going about like this?"

He replied, "I am Fallamain who was in chains."

The guards laughed and said to him, "If you were that man you would not be appearing in public like this."

So Fallamain went on his way and climbed over the wall. The second set of guards by the gate never even saw him. And on the third day, he reached Samthann.

From this story, we can learn three ways to spell faith:

For	Forsaking	R
All	All	I
I	I	S
Trust	Take	K
Him	Him	

Lord, I do believe a little bit.
Today, help me to exercise that little bit of faith,
so that it grows a little bit more.

May 26 ✢ The Faces of Love

Psalm 111; Joshua 1:10-18; Acts 15:22-41

*It sparks like lightning, it spreads like the plague,
it burns like the fire, inside the fire, inside the fire.
It radiates like the inside of the first moment of the cosmos.*
INSPIRED BY SONG OF SONGS 8:6

What does the love of God do to a person? It kills their desires. It purifies their heart. It protects them. It banishes vices. It incurs rewards. It lengthens life. It cleanses the soul.

The four redemptions of the soul: fear and repentance, love and hope. Two of them protect it on earth, the other two waft it to heaven. Fear shuts out the sins that lie ahead. Repentance wipes out the sins which come before. Love of the Creator and hope of the Creator's kingdom: that is what wafts it to heaven. Any person, then, who will fear and love, and who will fulfill God's desire and commandment, will have respect in the sight of people in this world, and will be blessed with God in the next.
COLMÁN MAC BÉOGNAE, THE ALPHABET OF DEVOTION

Whoever loves allows herself willingly to be corrected.
Whoever loves suffers blows willingly for her formation.
Whoever loves is willingly cast out in order to be wholly free.
Whoever loves is willing to be alone in order to love Love
and to possess her.
HADEWIJCH OF BRABANT

You keep us loving.
You, the God whose name is Jove,
want us to be like you—
to love the loveless and the unlovely and the unlovable,
to love without jealousy or design or threat
and, most difficult of all, to love ourselves.
EVENING LITURGY, IONA COMMUNITY

*Thrice holy God, come as the morning dew,
hold up in us your love, which draws all lesser loves to you.*

MAY 27 ✢ A HEART FOR EVERYONE

Psalm 112; Joshua 2; Acts 17:1-15

When the day of Pentecost came ... a large crowd gathered ... and they exclaimed: "Some of us are from Rome, both Jews and Gentiles converted to Judaism, and some of us are from Crete and Arabia—yet all of us hear them speaking in our own languages about the great things that God has done!"
ACTS 2:1, 6, 7, 11 GNT

When we speak of "Celtic Christianity," we are not describing a religion that is ethnic in an exclusive sense. The essence of Celtic spirituality is a heart wide open to God in every person, in all the world. It is inclusive, crossing frontiers, not erecting barriers. It goes so deep that, without losing what is distinctive, it becomes universal.

Bede, the great historian of Jarrow Monastery who is honored on this day, understood this most clearly. Despite the fact that he disliked some of the rustic habits of the Irish, he marveled at their hospitality to foreigners:

> Many in England, both nobles and commoners, went to Ireland to do religious studies or to live an ascetic life. The Irish welcomed them all gladly, gave them their daily food, and also provided them with books to read and with instruction, without asking for any payment. . . . The Picts now have a treaty of peace with the English and rejoice to share in the catholic peace and truth of the church universal.
>
> Under the influence of these Irish teachers the spirit of racial bitterness was checked and a new intercourse sprang up between English, Picts, Britons, and Irish...the peace of Columba, the fellowship of learning and piety, rested on the peoples.
> VIDA D. SCUTTA, INTRODUCTION TO BEDE'S ECCLESIASTICAL HISTORY OF THE ENGLISH PEOPLE, EVERYMAN EDITION

Set us free, O God, to cross barriers for you,
as you crossed barriers for us.
Spirit of God, make us open to others in listening,
generous to others in giving,
and sensitive to others in praying,
through Jesus Christ our Lord.
BROTHER BARNABUS, SSF

MAY 28 ✢ I AM

Psalm 102; Joshua 4; Acts 26:1-18

God said to Moses
"I am [I act, I become, I remain] who I am.
Tell the people: 'I AM has sent me to you.'"
EXODUS 3:14

Celtic Christ-followers have a vivid awareness of God's Presence—the same eternal being-ness that spoke to Moses—in all creation. At the same time, they know that the creation itself is not God.

I am all around you, in every single thing you experience.
I am so rich, I am everywhere at any given moment.
I am so pure, I am translucent.
Since before the dawn of all that is,
I was speaking all creation into being.
I am not creation. I spoke creation into being.
I am not a stone, I am not the wind, I am not the earth.
I am a still small voice wooing you to my way of truth.
Do not be surprised:
I am more than man, I am more than woman.
I speak to my creation in ways that are fitting to those who listen.
I am so much more
than the highest imagined sum of all humankind.
But my love for each one is greater than all the thoughts of humankind.
I will meet you in the place it is hardest for you to look. . . .
In your feeling, in your thoughts, in the Truth of myself.
I will meet you in your essence, the very stuff that makes you, you.
I will never impose myself on you. . . .
Invite me into your life moment by moment
and I will be your guide, keeper, teacher, friend, counselor, confidant.
I will make you a new creature
and sanctify your ways until my thoughts are your thoughts
and your thoughts are mine. . . .
TED CARR

Great I AM, I come to you.
I bring to you everything, even my chains and darkness.
Jesus of Nazareth, you always were, always are, always will be.
Spirit, may your love be my healing, my shield, and my fulfilling.

MAY 29 ✢ REFLECTING THE TRINITY

Psalm 100; Joshua 5; Acts 18:1-17

A rope made of three cords is hard to break.
ECCLESIASTES 4:12 GNT

The God whom the Celtic peoples came to know and love is the God whose very essence is a loving relationship. God is one, but the Divine personality has three permanent elements, just as ours does (mind, body, spirit). We suffer if we ignore any of these aspects of our own personalities, and our spiritual lives will experience a similar damage if we do not recognize all three aspects of God's nature.

In the Divine Being, these three elements are so distinctive that they are more truly called persons than elements, for each of them personally manifests love. As we go deeper into this understanding, God becomes close and accessible; and something of this unity of loves is reflected in human life, which is made in God's image.

Marriage, for example, reflects the Trinity. The verse above from the Book of Ecclesiastes, which refers to "the threefold cord," is sometimes used at weddings, reminding the bride and groom, as well as their guests, that it takes three to make a true marriage: the two human individuals plus God.

We can also see a reflection of the Trinity in:

> a tender kiss,
> a warm embrace,
> the comradeship of sports,
> an adult's affirmation of a child, a meal shared,
> two people listening to each other,
> a group making music, hospitality,
> love turned outward to the world,
> young people serving the old,
> people from different cultures or religions celebrating,
> people playing.

> *Father, eternal Love Maker,*
> *Savior, eternal Love Mate,*
> *Spirit, eternal Love Messenger,*
> *Three of limitless love—*
> *I come to you, I abandon myself to you,*
> *I lose myself in you, I find myself in you.*
> *To you be all glory forever.*

MAY 30 ⁘ THREE YET ONE

Psalm 78:52-72; Judges 6:1-24; Luke 24:36-49

As Jesus came up out of the water he saw heaven opening
and the Spirit coming down on him like a dove.
And a voice came from heaven,
"You are my dearly loved Son. I am so pleased with you."
MARK 1:10-11

These verses show us the Trinity: The Father in the form of a voice. The Son in the form of Jesus. The Spirit in the form of a dove.

The concept of the Trinity made sense to the Celts. Celtic Christ-followers saw the Trinity less as a lofty spiritual concept and more as a practical principle reflected in the ordinary world. When Irenaeus was asked to explain the Trinity, for example, he simply pointed to a person's hands. There is more than one hand, but only one person; on a single hand there are several fingers, but still only the one hand. The Celtic Christians saw other pointers to God's nature in creation around them, as is illustrated by the legend of Patrick picking up a three-leafed shamrock to explain the Trinity.

> Three joints in the finger, but only one finger fair.
> Three leaves of the shamrock, yet only one shamrock to wear,
> Frost, snowflakes, and ice, yet all in water their origin share.
> Three Persons in God; to one God alone we make prayer.
> TRADITIONAL IRISH

The sun serves as another illustration of the Trinity: there is the sun itself, which the human eye cannot look at directly; there is a single ray that we can see at a particular time and place; and there is the sun's warmth that radiates the entire Earth.

> God is at once infinite solitude (one nature)
> and perfect society (three persons);
> one infinite love in three subsistent relations.
> THOMAS MERTON

> *The Three who are over my head,*
> *the Three who are under my tread,*
> *the Three who are over me here, the Three who are over me there,*
> *the Three who in heaven do dwell, the Three in the great ocean swell,*
> *pervading Three, O be with me, pervading Three, O be with me.*
> CARMINA GADELICA

MAY 31 ✥ THE LOVE OF THE THREE

Psalm 79; Judges 6:25-40; Acts 18:18-28

God said, "Let us make human beings in our image."
GENESIS 1:26 NLT

May we sense God's playfulness when we see children playing.
May we feel God's intimacy when we nestle close to another.
May we surmise the risks that God takes
in the chances and opportunities that are ours.
May we savor the flow of God's friendship
when we see the embraces of friends or lovers.

Deep within all of us dwells the Blessed Trinity. At the depth of our being, the Father continually loves the Son, while the Son responds to the Father in love and prayer through the Holy Spirit. In our prayer of meditation we desire to be part of the love and prayer of Jesus to the Father. Rather than think up words or aspirations or images of our own, we wish to unite ourselves with the loving prayer going on continually within us. In this prayer, we also seek to open ourselves completely to the Holy Spirit, that the Holy Spirit may bring about in us conversion, repentance and faith in the Good News of Jesus Christ.
MGR TOM FEHEILY, THE CHRISTIAN MEDITATION CENTRE, DUNLAOGUIRE, IRELAND

O Father who sought me,
O Son who bought me,
O Holy Spirit who taught me.
IRISH, COLLECTED BY DOUGLAS HYDE

May the love of the Three give birth to a new community.
May the yielding of the Three give birth to a new humanity.
May the life of the Three give birth to a new creativity.
May the togetherness of the Three give birth to a new unity.
May the glory of the Three give birth to a new society.

JUNE 1 ✧ LITTLE TRINITIES

Psalm 73; Judges 7; Acts 19:1-10

*May the grace of the Lord Jesus Christ,
the love of God and the fellowship of the Holy Spirit be with you all.*
2 CORINTHIANS 13:14 NIV

The Celtic peoples, with their love of significant numbers, have always given special significance to the Triad, an arrangement of three statements that sum up a person, a thing, or a situation, often with a blend of humor, deep meaning, and paradox.

> Three sisters of lying:
> perhaps, maybe, guess.
> Three sources of new life:
> a woman's belly, a hen's egg, a wrong forgiven.
> WELSH TRIADS

> Three things are pleasant in a home:
> good food upon the table;
> a man who lovingly kisses his wife;
> children who refrain from quarrelling.

> Three attitudes are godly in the Church:
> true love of the Lord;
> kindness amongst the pews;
> a fair dealing with self.

> Three ideas enlarge a person's mind:
> a humble heart; a generous soul;
> honesty in business.

A mother whispers this prayer into the ear of her infant:
The blessing of the Holy Three, little love, be the gift to you—
wisdom, peace, and purity.
CARMINA GADELICA

Three things I wish for myself:
true spiritual beauty;
a heart of giving;
eyes with pools of meaning.
JANET DONALDSON, A POCKET BOOK OF CELTIC PRAYERS

JUNE 2 ✢ PRAISE OF THE TRINITY

Psalm 75; Isaiah 6:1–8; Acts 19:11–20

*Immerse people everywhere in the Father,
the Son, and the Holy Spirit.*
MATTHEW 28:19

By the singing of hymns eagerly ringing out,
by thousands of angels rejoicing in holy dances
and by the four living creatures full of eyes,
with the twenty-four joyful elders
casting their crowns under the feet of the Lamb of God,
the Trinity is praised in eternal threefold exchanges.
ALTUS PROSATOR, ATTRIBUTED TO COLUMBA

Clear and high in the perfect assembly
let us praise above the nine grades of angels
the sublime and blessed Trinity.
Purely, humbly, in skillful verse
I should love to give praise to the Trinity
according to the greatness of his power.
God has required of the host in this world
who are his, that they should at all times,
all together, fear the Trinity.
EARLY WELSH

*Power of all powers, we worship you.
Light of all lights, we worship you.
Life of all lives, we worship you.
Maker of all creatures, we honor you.
Friend of all creatures, we honor you.
Force of all creatures, we honor you.
Love before time, we adore you.
Love in dark time, we adore you.
Love in present time, we adore you.*

JUNE 3 ✢ DEEPEST STRENGTH

Psalm 71; Joshua 6; Acts 19:21-41

*Jesus went away to a hill to pray.
When evening came, the boat with the disciples in it
was in the middle of the lake, while Jesus was alone on the land.*
MARK 6:46-47

Glendalough, in the shadows of the Wicklow mountains, became a place of grace through the obedience to God of one man—Kevin. He lived as a hermit beside the lower lake for seven years, clad only in animal skins, with stone for his bed. He spent long hours up to his waist in the lake praising God. His great strength and endurance sprang from his extraordinary faith and his commitment to monastic celibacy and the teachings of the Desert spiritual tradition. As well as being a hermit and a founder of monasteries, he wrote poetry and prose, and a Rule for monks in Irish verse. He was attractive, gentle, loving, with an unusual affinity with animals and birds.

He was deeply attracted to the poetic experience of the hermit life; courageous in his desire to draw out to the edge to test his strength and endurance. He chose hardship quite deliberately; his cell was on the dark side of the lake which remained in shadow for six months of the year. Why was this so? Perhaps it was a desire to feel very exposed; to test himself to the limit, and through that test to find his own deepest strength, but perhaps most of all it was through an ascetic way of life that he found the poetry of his own soul.
MICHAEL RODGERS OF GLENDALOUGH

The tenth-century *Life of Kevin* suggests that "the branches and leaves of the trees sometimes sang sweet songs to him, and heavenly music alleviated the severity of his life." Eventually, many people joined Kevin, and he built a community beside the lower lake.

*Let me not spoil one leaf, nor break one branch,
let me not plunder, blunder, pollute, exploit
but rather see and hear and touch and taste and smell,
and in my sensing, know you well.*
MARIE CONNOLLY, A GLENDALOUGH PILGRIM

JUNE 4 ✢ PETROC'S VIEW

Psalm 70; Isaiah 43:14-21; Acts 20:17-30

*No god is like your God, riding in splendor across the sky,
riding through the clouds to come to your aid.*
DEUTERONOMY 33:26 GNT

Petroc sailed from Ireland, where he had trained in a monastery, to Cornwall, where he founded his own monastery at Padstow (Petroc's Stowe). A Celtic wheel cross can still be seen outside the door of the church, and in the churchyard are faint markings said to be of the cross that once stood at Petroc's monastic gateway.

In his old age, Petroc set out with twelve companions to live as a hermit on Bodmin Moor, settling himself in a beehive hut by the river. Dom Julian Stonor identifies this as the stone beehive hut by the stream that runs out of Rough Tor Marsh and claims, "It is one of the oldest Christian holy places in England." Perhaps it was here that Petroc enjoyed that close affinity with nature that shows in many of the stories about him—such as his rescuing a stag from a hunter—and perhaps it was here that he looked out and meditated on Nature's changing sounds and sights.

> Though I am silent there is singing around me.
> Though I am dark there is vision around me.
> Though I am heavy there is flight around me.
> WENDELL BERRY

Creation is full of amazing variety. Sometimes the morning sky is filled with pink streaks, sometimes a golden glow. Without these daily surprises, the marvelous could otherwise become mundane. Flowers, human temperaments, and the very nature of God all come to us to in infinite varieties of expression.

*Thank you,
Creator of the world,
for the music and medicine of flowers
which give us a scent of heaven upon earth.
May those who look at them see your glory.*

JUNE 5 ✣ THIS IS MY BODY

Psalm 62; Joshua 8:30-35; Acts 20:1-12

the Lord Jesus, on the night he was betrayed, took a loaf of bread,
gave thanks for it, and broke it in pieces, saying,
"This is my body that is for you. Keep doing this in memory of me."
1 CORINTHIANS 11:24 ISV

Draw near, and take the body of the Lord.
THE ANTIPHONARY OR BANGOR, *(THE IRISH MONASTERY FOUNDED BY COMGALL)*

When Cuthbert offered up the Saving Victim
as a sacrifice to God, he offered his prayer to the Lord
not by raising his voice but by shedding tears
which sprang from the depth of his heart.
BEDE

The table of bread and wine is now to be made ready.
It is the table of company with Jesus and with all those who love him.
It is the table of sharing with the poor of the world,
with whom Jesus identified himself.
It is the table of communion with the earth
in which Christ became incarnate.
So, come to this table, you who have much faith
and you who would like to have more;
you who have been to this sacrament often,
and you who have not been for a long time;
you who have tried to follow Jesus, and you who have failed.
Come. It is Christ who invites us to meet him here.
IONA COMMUNITY, AN INVITATION TO COMMUNION

You are very welcome, O body of Christ.
It was by your death on the cross,
you who were born of the fair and gentle virgin,
that the human race was redeemed, that evil was conquered.
Please do not hide your faithfulness from me,
a poor sinner who approaches you.
Though I have deserved your anger
please return and help me, Lord Jesus.
COLLECTED IN INIS MEAN, FROM MOUNT MELLERAY MONASTERY, IRELAND

JUNE 6 ✢ ALL THIS GOD GIVES US

Psalm 61; Joshua 10:1-15; Matthew 11:1-19

The blind can see, the lame can walk, and the Good News is preached.
MATTHEW 11:5

He who so calmly rode
the little ass fair of form,
who healed each hurt and bloody wound
that clave to the people of every age:
He made glad the sad and the outcast,
he gave rest to the restless and the tired.
He made free the bond and the unruly,
each old and young in the land.
He stemmed the fierce-rushing blood,
he took the keen prickle from the eyes,
he drank the draught that was bitter,
trusting to the High Father of heaven.
He gave strength to Peter and Paul,
he gave strength to the Mother of tears,
he gave strength to Brigid of the flocks,
each joint and bone and sinew.
CARMINA GADELICA

O Lord, charity without limit and mercy without measure,
of your love you have today come to me
and on my part it was hope which enabled me to receive you.
I give you my body as a temple
my heart as your altar, and my soul as your chalice.
O Lord, holy sinless lamb, O merciful redeemer,
O gentle infant Jesus, cover me with your cloak.
Grant me sanctuary with your heart,
draw me into your kingdom, heal me by your sweetness and charity.
Revive me by your death, hide me within your wounds,
wash me with your blood, fill me with your love
and make me in every way agreeable to your heart, O Lord.
AN TIMIRE, COLLECTED BY SEAN O FLOW,
MOUNT MELLERAY MONASTERY, IRELAND

June 7 ✣ A Visit of the Holy Spirit

Psalm 48: Judges 5:1-10; Acts 21:1-16

While Peter was still speaking, the Holy Spirit came down on all those who were listening to his message. The Jewish believers who had come from Joppa with Peter were amazed that God had poured out the gift of the Holy Spirit on foreigners also.
Acts 10:44–45

One day some founders of Christian communities came to visit Columba when he was on the island of Hinba. As they shared Holy Communion, one of them saw a tongue of fire, flaming and bright, all ablaze from Columba's head as he stood before the altar. It rose up like a steady pillar until the end of their worship.

On another occasion when Columba was staying on the island of Hinba, the Holy Spirit poured onto him in matchless abundance for a period of three days and nights. He remained alone inside a bolted house throughout this time, neither eating nor drinking. Yet rays of light of immeasurable brilliance could be seen flooding out by night through the chinks of the doors and the keyholes, and those who came near could hear Columba singing songs that had never been heard before. Afterward, he confided to a few people that many mysteries that had been hidden from the beginning of the world had been revealed to him, and obscure, difficult passages in the Bible had been made more plain to him than the light of day.

> Your son Christ, it is clear,
> is one of the three persons of the deity
> and all things have indeed been created by him.
> He is in union with the Father, with the Holy Spirit,
> he is their peer, it is from them, with the permission of all,
> that the Holy Spirit proceeds.
> Blathmac, sixth century

> O Christ, our dearest Savior, kindle our lamps,
> that they may evermore shine in your temple
> and receive unquenchable light from you
> that will lighten our darkness
> and lessen the darkness of the world.
> Attributed to Columba

JUNE 8 ❖ WORDS FROM COLUMBA

Psalm 47; Joshua 23; Acts 21:17-26

Let us not become tired of doing good;
for if we do not give up, the time will come when we will reap the harvest.
So then, whenever we have the chance,
we should do good to everyone.
GALATIANS 6:9-10

One day Columba was working in his study at Iona when he heard a man shouting on the other side of the ferry crossing at Mull. Columba's servant Diarmait overheard Columba say to himself, "The man who is shouting is too careless to watch what he is doing. Today he will tip over my ink." And sure enough, the ink was spilled later that day! A person's voice can reveal a restless, insensitive spirit. This is likely to result in clumsy actions as well.

One night, one of Columba's monks came to the door of the church when everyone was asleep and stood there in prayer for a time. Suddenly, he saw the entire church filled with light. He was unaware that Columba was praying inside, and the sudden flash of light frightened him. He returned to his cell, but the next day Columba rebuked him for "trying to see surreptitiously a light from heaven that is not given to you." The lesson here? Perhaps that we must each learn to accept grace from God in the measure given to us, and not to grasp after what is given to others.

> These my children are my last words to you. That you have heartfelt love amongst yourselves. If you thus follow the example of the holy fathers, God, the comforter of the good, will be your helper. And I, abiding with him, will intercede for you, and he will not only give you sufficient to supply the needs of this present life, but will also give you the good and eternal rewards which are laid up for those who keep his commandments.
> COLUMBA

Inspire us with your love, O Lord,
that our loving quest for you may occupy our thoughts;
that your love may take complete possession of our being.
COLUMBA

June 9 ❖ They That Seek the Lord

Psalm 134; Joshua 24:1-28; Acts 21:27-40

They who seek the Lord will not lack any good thing.
PSALM 134:10

Delightful it is to stand on the peak of a rock,
in the bosom of the isle, gazing on the face of the sea.
I hear the heaving waves chanting a tune to God in heaven;
I see their glittering surf.
I see the golden beaches, their sands sparkling;
I hear the joyous shrieks of the swooping gulls.
I hear the waves breaking, crashing on rocks,
like thunder in heaven. I see the mighty whales.
I watch the ebb and flow of the ocean tide;
it holds my secret, my mournful flight from Eire.
Contrition fills my heart as I hear the sea; it chants my sins,
sins too numerous to confess.
Let me bless almighty God,
whose power extends over sea and land,
whose angels watch over all.
Let me study sacred books to calm my soul;
I pray for peace, kneeling at heaven's gates.
Let me do my daily work, gathering seaweed,
catching fish, giving food to the poor.
Let me say my daily prayers, sometimes chanting,
sometimes quiet, always thanking God.
Delightful it is to live on a peaceful isle, in a quiet cell,
serving the King of kings.
ATTRIBUTED TO COLUMBA

Thank you for sleep.
Thank you for warmth.
Thank you for your rest in my soul.
Thank you for your touch within me.

JUNE 10 ✢ THREE GIFTS OF GOD

Psalm 32; Genesis 37:1–11; Acts 23:1–11

The eye is the lamp of the body.
If your eye is healthy, your whole body will be full of light.
MATTHEW 6:22

Since boyhood, Columba had devoted himself to training and studying wisdom; with God's help, he had kept his body chaste and his mind pure and shown himself, though placed on earth, fit for the life of heaven. . . . He was brilliant in intellect and great in counsel. He spent thirty-four years as an island soldier, and could not let even an hour pass without giving himself to praying or reading or writing or some other task. Fasts and vigils he performed day and night with tireless labor and no rest. At the same time he was loving to all people, and his face showed a holy gladness because his heart was full of the joy of the Holy Spirit.
ADAMNAN

Purity, wisdom, and prophecy, these are the gifts I would ask of thee,
O High King of Heaven, grant them to me.
The lamp of the body is purity,
and those that have it their God shall see,
for the pure in heart know how to love,
and I have longed my love to prove.
This is the gift I would ask of thee,
O Lord of my manhood, bestow it on me,
your wisdom I pray for, a light for the mind,
and those that seek it shall surely find
the way in which to serve and lead;
my people are lost and a shepherd need.
The gift of the soul is prophecy;
enlarge my vision that I may see
the past and the present and future as one
that here on this earth thy will be done.
Purity, wisdom, and prophecy,
these are the gifts I would ask of thee;
O High King of Heaven, grant them to me.
COLUMBA'S PRAYER
FROM COLUMBA, THE PLAY WITH MUSIC

JUNE 11 ✢ HEALING TRANSFORMATION

Psalm 37:23-40; Genesis 37:12-36; Acts 23:12-22

My dear friends, do not believe all who claim to have the Spirit, but test them to find out if the spirit they have comes from God.
1 JOHN 4:1 GNT

Columba's connection with God poured out from him in healing for those around him. This healing took various forms, transforming greed into generosity and sickness into health.

During Columba's journey back from a meeting of rulers near Limavady, Ireland, the bishop of Coleraine arranged for him to lodge at the local monastery. Folks from all around brought offerings and laid them out in front of the monastic buildings. As Columba looked at them and blessed them, he pointed to one gift and said, "The man who gave this enjoys the mercy of God on account of his generosity and his mercies to the poor." However, he pointed to another gift of food with these words: "This is the gift of a man who is both wise and greedy. I cannot so much as taste it unless he first makes penance for his greed."

Columba's words spread through the crowd. When they reached Columb mac Aedo, the man who had given the food to which Columba had pointed, he walked forward and knelt in front of Columba, confessed, and promised to renounce greed, mend his ways, and practice generosity. Columba told him to stand up, and then Columba announced that Columb was a changed man. He was no longer grasping, and he walked away tall. Though he had been chastened, he had also been affirmed, and now he was free to be truly generous.

On another occasion, Columba saw from Iona a threatening rain cloud moving toward Ireland. He knew that it would bring a life-threatening sickness to a particular district there, so he sent one of his monks—a man named Silnan—to sail over to Ireland with these directions: "Take this bread I have blessed in the name of God, dip it in water, and then sprinkle that water over both the people and their livestock in that place, and they will soon recover their health." When Silnan landed, he found six men in one house who were already near to death. He sprinkled them as Columba had directed, and they were all restored to health. News of this spread throughout the region, and many people came to Silnan with their livestock. He sprinkled them all and saved them from disease.

Step by step you lead us. Feed and remake us
till we are glad to be givers, till we joy in being brothers,
till we delight in being sisters, till heaven laughs in delight
at our pleasure in each other.

JUNE 12 ✢ THE THREE CROSSES OF IONA

Psalm 35; Genesis 39; Acts 23:23-35

*People who refuse to pick up their crosses
and follow in my steps are not fit to be my disciples.*
MATTHEW 10:38

The restoration of Iona and the founding of the Iona Community in the twentieth century seem to be a fulfillment of Columba's prophecy: "Iona of my love, instead of monks' voices shall be lowing of cattle; but ere the world shall come to an end, Iona shall be as it was."

The founder of the modern Iona Community, Lord MacLeod, wrote about the three ancient crosses on Iona:

> *St John's Cross* is the first to get you back to the Truth. The opening chapter of his Gospel reads, "The world was made by Christ and without him was not anything made that was made." This means that Christ is CREATOR and not just Redeemer. Jesus, here and now, is as much involved in politics as he is in prayer. He is to be obeyed in material problems.
>
> *St Martin's Cross.* Martin was horrified that all the monks in Gaul were interested in was their salvation. He persuaded them to get back to comforting people in the towns, in the matters of their housing, their education, and their employment. One of his fellow monks was an uncle of Columba, and he went to Iona and showed Columba the kind of "all-in" Christianity that so rapidly converted the West of Scotland.
>
> *St Matthew's Cross.* Matthew was a tax collector. The love of money was the curse of Gospel times, as it is of ours today.

*Lord God, in the dawn of creation
and in the presence of your Son,
your light shattered the force and lure of darkness.
We ask your help today
for those who, in public and personal life,
are in the grip of that which is wicked;
for those who deal in rumors and perpetrate cheap gossip,
for those who are slaves to a vice they fear to name,
for those who have traded openness for secrecy,
morality for money, love for lust.
We ask for a light—not to blind them
but to show them the way out of their darkness.*
IONA COMMUNITY, THE WEE WORSHIP BOOK

JUNE 13 ❖ COMRADES

Psalm 44; Genesis 40; Acts 24:1-23

Righteousness lifts up a nation.
Proverbs 14:34

Fellowship replaced hostility between brothers in many a monastery, and this spirit overflowed into the people among whom they lived. This story, handed down by word of mouth, illustrates this.

When Columba visited the monastery on the Isle of Eigg, he discovered that two monks were preaching in a spirit of rivalry. Columba asked them both to stretch out their right hands toward the sky. "One of you is slightly taller than the other, but neither of you are remotely within reach of that cloud up there," he said. "So fall to your knees. Pray for one another and for the people of your kingdom whom you serve." Both monks dropped to their knees and their prayers, which used to stick in the thatch, now reached to heaven. They were now comrades, helping to forge a community of peace.

> The Celtic people in the west of Britain called themselves Cymru which means "the land of comrades" (this is how we have the name Cumbria today). The invading Anglo-Saxons renamed the southern part Wales, which means "land of foreigners." This is a typical example of the suspicions, caricatures and prejudices that developed with the emergence of the separate nations of Wales, England, Scotland, and Ireland and one cannot but help feel that the community God intended for this group of islands was continuously damaged by the darkness of evil and human sin. Interestingly, many are now looking to the Celtic church as a resource for healing the hurts and divisions between our nations.
> MICHAEL MITTON

We pray for an uprising of people who give leadership
free from the bondage of fear, repenting the blindness of the past,
rising above ambition, flexible to the direction of your Holy Spirit,
reaching out with generous hearts to neighboring peoples.

JUNE 14 ⁘ BRINGING OUT THE BEST IN OTHERS

Psalm 40:12–17; Genesis 41; Acts 24:24–25:12

Do not use harmful words, but only helpful words,
the kind that build up and provide what is needed,
so that what you say will do good to those who hear you.
EPHESIANS 4:29 GNT

Columba had a way of seeing what was good in others—and then calling it forward. By affirming goodness in others, he allowed them to grow into their God-given natures.

This happened when he paid a visit to the large and important Clonmacnoise Monastery, in Ireland. There, while the brothers crowded around Columba, a boy crept in behind Columba. The brothers tended to look down on the boy because of his negative attitudes and unpleasant speech, but the boy had heard the Bible story of the woman in a crowd who was healed after she touched just the edge of Jesus' cloak, so the boy wanted to touch the edge of Columba's cloak without being noticed. Columba, like Jesus, sensed in his spirit that someone was there. He turned around, grabbed the boy, and pulled him forward. Some of the brothers tried to shoo the boy away, but Columba hushed them. "Open your mouth and put out your tongue," he told the boy, and then he reached out and blessed the boy's tongue. He said to the brothers, "Do not let this boy's present disposition make you despise him. From now on he will cease to displease you. Indeed, he will please you greatly, and grow, little by little, day by day, in goodness and greatness of spirit. Wisdom and discernment will increase in him, and he will become an outstanding figure in your community. God will give him eloquence to teach the way of salvation." This boy was Ernene mac Craseni. He became famous throughout the churches of Ireland and was highly regarded, just as Columba had promised.

On another occasion, the foster parents of Domnell mac Aedo brought their boy to Columba. Columba looked at him for a while and then gave this prophetic blessing: "This boy will outlive all his brothers and be a famous king. He will never be handed over to his enemies but will die at home in his bed, in peaceful old age, in the friendly presence of his household." All this came true.

May Father, Son, and Spirit replenish and renew you
so that an island shall you be in the sea,
a hill shall you be on the land, a well shall you be in the desert,
health shall you be to the ailing.
ATTRIBUTED TO COLUMBA

JUNE 15 ❖ FATHERS

Psalm 38; Proverbs 4; Ephesians 5:21-6:4

Fathers, do not exasperate your children;
Instead, bring them up in the training and instruction of the Lord.
EPHESIANS 6:2-4 NIV

Although Samson's father and mother gave him a nanny when he was small, they made sure they gave their child plenty of their own attention as well. They made little plays about the Christian festivals together, and they read together.

At the age of five, Samson proudly announced to his parents that he wanted to go to school—to the School for Christ, made famous by Illtyd, for boys who would go on to be ordained into the Christian ministry. At first, Samson's father, Amon, opposed this. He wanted his son to follow a career that would bring in money, one that would strengthen the family's links to high society. The issue became an almost daily battle with his wife. Finally, God spoke powerfully to Amon in a dream. The dream showed Amon that his wife and his son's desire was not a mere whim, but truly the will of God. Amon's wife was pregnant again, but the two of them now worked together, united in purpose, and introduced Samson to his new school.

> When you face God in prayer, become in your thoughts like a speechless babe. Do not utter before God anything which comes from knowledge, but approach God with childlike thoughts, and so walk before God as to be granted that fatherly care which fathers give their children in their infancy.
> ISAAC OF NINEVEH, SEVENTH CENTURY

Father, may we know fatherly love in our lives.
Help all fathers to reflect you.

JUNE 16 ✧ ISLAND SOLDIERS

Psalm 97; Exodus 3; Acts 25:13-27

So then, my dear friends, stand firm and steady.
Keep busy always in your work for the Lord,
since you know that nothing you do in the Lord's service is ever useless.
1 CORINTHIANS 15:58 GNT

A mind prepared for red martyrdom.
A mind fortified and steadfast for white martyrdom.
Forgiveness from the heart for everyone.
Constant prayers for those who trouble you.
Fervor in singing.
Three labors in the day—prayers, work, and reading.
FROM THE RULE OF COLUMBA
(NOW IN THE BURGUNDIAN LIBRARY, BRUSSELS)

Iona, Iona, Iona,
the seagulls crying,
wheeling, flying
o'er the rain-washed bay;
Iona, Iona,
The soft breeze sighing,
the waves replying
on a clear, blue day, Iona.
Iona, Iona,
the waters glisten,
the wild winds listen
to the voice of our Lord;
Iona.

Iona's blessing strengthens and firmly it will hold you;
then from this rocky fortress goes forth our island soldier;
may Christ who calmed the tempest with safety now enfold you.
COLUMBA'S PRAYER
FROM COLUMBA, THE PLAY WITH MUSIC

Lord, may these graces flower as never before—
the grace of authenticity and trust,
the grace of forgiving love and laughter,
the maturity of pity for those who manipulate.

JUNE 17 ✣ GOD'S GLORY IN US

Psalm 8; Isaiah 28:1-6; 2 Corinthians 3

All of us reflect the essence of God;
and that same essence, coming from the Lord who is the Spirit,
transforms us into his essence, in an ever greater degree of glory.
2 CORINTHIANS 3:18

The glory of God is seen in a human life lived to the full.
IRENAEUS

Plunge yourself into humility and you will see the glory of God.
ST. ISAAC OF SYRIA

He is a bird round which a trap is closed;
a leaking ship unfit for a wild sea,
an empty vessel and a withered tree—
who lays aside God's wishes unimposed.
He is the sun's bright rays, pure gold and fine,
a silver chalice overfilled with wine,
holy and happy, beautiful in love—
who does the will of God in heaven above.
ANCIENT IRISH LYRIC TRANSLATED BY MOLLOY CARSON

People are my scenery.
A LONDON LANDLADY

Holy Spirit, Enlivener:
breathe on us, fill us with life anew.
In your new creation, already upon us,
already breaking through,
groaning and travailing,
but already breaking through, breathe on us.
Till that day when night and autumn vanish:
and lambs grown sheep are no more slaughtered:
and even the thorn shall fade and the whole earth shall cry
Glory at the marriage feast of the Lamb.
In this new creation, already upon us, fill us with life anew.
GEORGE MACLEOD

JUNE 18 ❖ GENTLENESS

Psalm 56; Isaiah 40:1-11; Matthew 11:25-30

Jesus said, "Learn from me because I am gentle and humble."
MATTHEW 11:29

Aidan, the apostle of the English, was a gentle man.

> When Oswald came to the throne of Northumbria he sent to the Irish leaders at Iona and asked them to send him a leader, by whose teaching his people might learn the lessons of faith in the Lord and receive the sacraments. He obtained his request without delay, and was sent Bishop Aidan, a man of great gentleness.
> BEDE

When Paul listed gentleness as one of the nine fruits of the Spirit (Galatians 5:23), he used the Greek word *praotes*. This word overflows with meanings; it is far removed from some current images of gentleness as sweetness, powerless passivity, or timidity. Plato considered gentleness to be "the cement of society." Aristotle defined it as the midpoint between being too angry and never becoming angry at all; the gentle person expresses anger for the right reason and duration and in the right way. It is the characteristic needed when exercising discipline (Galatians 6:1), facing opposition (2 Timothy 2:25), and opening ourselves to hearing God's Word without pride (James 1:21).

> This is the most important part of the rule;
> love Christ, hate wealth;
> devotion to the King of the sun
> and kindness to people.
> If anybody enters the path of repentance
> it is sufficient to advance step by step.
> Do not wish to be like a charioteer.
> FROM THE RULE OF ST. COMGALL

Gentle Christ,
may I see you more clearly love you more dearly
and follow you more nearly, day by day.
BASED ON THE WORDS OF RICHARD OF CHICHESTER

JUNE 19 ✢ WHEN THE GOING GETS TOUGH

Psalm 57; Joshua 71; Acts 26

*Make sure that your endurance carries you all the way
without failing, so that you may be perfect and complete.*
JAMES 1:4 GNT

The tempests howl, the storms dismay,
but strength can win the day.
Heave, lads, and let the echoes ring.
For clouds and squalls will soon pass on,
and victory lie with work well done.
Heave, lads , and let the echoes ring.
Hold fast! Survive! And all is well,
God sent you worse, he'll calm this swell.
Heave, lads, and let the echoes ring.
So Satan acts to tire the brain,
and by temptation souls are slain.
Think lads of Christ, and echo him.
The king of virtues vowed a prize,
for him who wins, for him who tries.
Think lads, of Christ, and echo him.
ATTRIBUTED TO COLUMBANUS'S MONKS
ROWING UP THE RHINE AGAINST THE TIDE

*In the steep common path of our calling,
whether it be easy or uneasy to our flesh,
whether it be bright or dark for us to follow,
may your own perfect guidance be given us.
Be a shield to us from the ploys of the deceiver
and in each hidden thought our minds start to weave
be our director and our canvas.
Even though dogs and thieves try to wrench us away from the fold
be our Shepherd of glory near us. Whatever matter, issue or problem
that threatens to bring us to grief, hide it from our eyes
and drive it from our hearts forever.*
CARMINA GADELICA

JUNE 20 ✣ Like the Leaves of Summer

Psalm 1; Proverbs 11:1-31; Matthew 25:31-46

*Those who depend on their wealth will fall like the leaves of the autumn,
but the righteous will prosper like the leaves of summer.*
PROVERBS 11:28 GNT

The beauty of summer, its days long and slow,
beautiful too visiting the ones we love.
The beauty of flowers on the tops of fruit trees,
beautiful too the covenant with the Creator.
The beauty in the wilderness of doe and fawn,
beautiful too the foam-mouthed and slender steed.
The beauty of the garden when the leeks grow well,
beautiful too the charlock in blossom.
The beauty of the horse in its leather halter,
beautiful too keeping company with a king.
The beauty of the heather when it turns purple,
beautiful too moorland for cattle.
The beauty of the season when calves suckle,
beautiful too riding a foam-mouthed horse.
The beauty of the fish in his bright lake,
beautiful too its surface shimmering.
The beauty of the word with which the Trinity speaks,
beautiful too doing penance for sin.
But the loveliest of all is the covenant,
with God on the Day of Judgment.
THE LOVES OF TALIESIN

*God of the long day, you who are eternally awake,
I offer you my eternal "yes"—
the flower of my humanity,
the energy and awareness of my days,
the creativity of my life, the beauty of form
and the hope of future potential.
Amen and Amen. Praise be to you. Amen.*

JUNE 21 ❖ THE LONGEST DAY

Psalm 19:1-6; Genesis 49:1-12: John 10

I came so you could have life—life in all its fullness.
JOHN 10:10

Today is the summer solstice of the northern hemisphere.
    Sap rises.
    Lambs frolic.
    Buds burst.
    Children play.
    Hedgerows drip.
    Bodies surge
    Brains storm.
    God's days are long.
    Christ's athletes race.
    Spirit's energies are strong and true.

> Life be in my speech,
> sense in what I say,
> the bloom of cherries on my lips
> till I come back again.
> The love Jesus Christ gave
> be filling every heart for me,
> the love Jesus Christ gave
> filling me for everyone.
> Traversing forests, traversing valleys long and wild—
> the fair white Mary still uphold me,
> the Shepherd Jesus be my shield.
>   *TRADITIONAL GAELIC*

*God, eternally awake,
may your energies flow through me.
God of the rising sap,
may I be your sap today.
God of the longest day,
may my life be a long day for you,
always reflecting your light,
open, awake.*

JUNE 22 ✣ GROWING GREEN

Psalm 59; Exodus 15:1-21; Matthew 21:33-43

I will sing about your strength.
Morning by morning, I will sing about your love.
PSALM 59:16

In the morning, my Lord, I offer you praise
as I water my plants set out in their trays,
as I think of their roots, to make the plant strong
and I feed on your word, which never is wrong;
as I look at the leaves, turned face to the sun
may I look towards you until this day is done,
as I admire the bright flowers giving glory to you
may I bring pleasure in the things that I do.
As I look at the fruit, tasty and sweet,
may I taste of you to the people I meet.
As I think of the seed, hidden away,
may I plant one seed for you on this day.
In the morning, my Lord, I offer you praise
as I water my plants set out in my trays.
CRAIG ROBERTS, POCKET CELTIC PRAYERS

O Son of my God, what a pride, what a pleasure
to plough the blue sea!
... The sounds of the winds in the elms
like the strings of a harp being played,
the note of the blackbird that claps
with the wings of delight in the glade.
ATTRIBUTED TO COLUMBA

God of the rising green,
God of the sweeping blue,
God of the long bright day,
may I sweep glory to you.

JUNE 23 ❖ THE ALL-TEEMING SEA

Psalm 61; Isaiah 63:7–64:5; Acts 27

*You welcome those who find joy in doing what is right,
those who remember how you want them to live.*
ISAIAH 64:5 GNT

About 580, Columba's friend Cormac-of-the-Sea (who became Bishop of Durrow) was becalmed on the sea after visiting the Orkney and Shetland isles, which he had evangelized. Meanwhile, on Iona, Columba became aware while he was praying that dangerous sea creatures had attacked Cormac's ship. Columba called the Iona brothers to intercede for a change of wind, and Cormac was blown safely on his way. A long dialogue in Old Irish was passed down through the generations, telling what passed between the two friends when Cormac finally arrived in Iona.

COLUMBA:
you are welcome, O comely Cormac,
from over the all-teeming sea.
What sent you forth, where have you been
since the time we were on the same path?
Two years and a month to this night
is the time you have been wandering from port to port,
from wave to wave. Resolute the energy
to traverse the wide ocean!
Since the sea has sent you here
you shall have friendship and counsel.
Were it not for Christ's sake, Lord of the fair world.
You had merited satire and reproach!
You are welcome, since you have come
from the waves of the mighty sea
though you travel the world over...
it is in Durrow your resurrection shall be.

CORMAC:
O Columcille of a hundred graces...
we shall abide in the West if you desire it.
Christ will unfold his mysterious intentions!

*Unfold your mystery in my life, Lord of the fair world,
and may I see your welcome everywhere.*

JUNE 24 ✢ A NEW JOHN THE BAPTIST

Psalm 60; Exodus 4; Luke 7:18–35

Jesus began to talk about John the Baptist to the crowds....
You saw much more than a prophet, he told them....
John is greater than anyone who has ever lived.
But the person who is smallest in the Kingdom of God
is greater than John.
Luke 7:24, 26, 28

Every generation needs people like John the Baptist who make a radical break with comfort and convention, who prepare the way for new Divine action. In some ways, Columba was a John the Baptist figure for his time, as these verses suggest.

He broke passions, brought to ruin secure prisons;
Colum Cille overcame them with bright action.
Connacht's candle, Britain's candle, splendid ruler;
in scores of curraghs with an army of wretches
he crossed the long-haired sea.
He crossed the wave-strewn wild region, foam-flecked,
seal-filled, savage, bounding, seething, white-tipped, pleasing, doleful.
Wisdom's champion all round Ireland, he was exalted;
excellent name: Brittany's nursed, Britain's sated.
He left chariots, he loved ships, foe to falsehood;
sun-like exile, sailing, he left fame's steel bindings.
Triumphant plea; adoring God, nightly, daily,
with hands outstretched, with splendid alms, with right actions.
Fine his body, Colum Cille, heaven's cleric—
a widowed crowd—well-spoken just-one, tongue triumphant.
The Last Verses of Beccan

Give us, O God,
something of the spirit of your servant John the Baptist:
his moral courage, his contentment with simplicity,
his refusal to be fettered by this world,
his faithfulness in witness to the end.
From A Pilgrim's Manual: St. David's, Brendan O'Malley

JUNE 25 ✥ CHOICES

Psalm 62; 1 Kings 18:1-46; Acts 28

Elijah went up to the people and said,
"How much longer will you hesitate between two opinions?
If the Lord is God, worship him."
1 KINGS 18:21

A poor man named Nesan once had the privilege of giving accommodation to Columba, and he stretched his meager means to give generous hospitality. Before he departed, Columba asked him how many cows he had.

"Five," Nesan informed him.

"Bring them to me that I may bless them," said Columba. As he raised his hand in blessing, he added, "From today on, your little herd of five cows will increase until you have one hundred and five cows. Also, your seed will be blessed in your children and grandchildren." And all these things were fulfilled.

On another occasion, however, a rich man named Vigen declined to offer hospitality to Columba—and Columba made quite the opposite prophecy about him. "The riches of this miser, who has rejected Christ in the pilgrim visitors, will from this moment diminish little by little until there is nothing left. He will end up a beggar and his son will run from house to house with a half-empty bag. A rival will strike him with an axe and he will die in the trench of a threshing floor." Unfortunately, all this came true, also.

May the yoke of the Law of God be on this shoulder.
May the coming of the Holy Spirit be on this head.
May the sign of Christ be on this forehead.
May the hearing of the Holy Spirit be in these ears.
May the smelling of the Holy Spirit be in this nose.
May the vision that the People of Heaven have be in these eyes.
May the speech of the People of Heaven be in this mouth.
May the work of the Church of God be in these hands.
May the good of God and of the neighbor be in these feet.
May God be dwelling in this heart.
May this person belong entirely to God the Father.
TRADITIONAL IRISH

JUNE 26 ✢ RAINBOW PEOPLE

Psalm 67; Genesis 9:1–17; Revelation 21

When the rainbow appears in the clouds I will see it
and remember the everlasting covenant
between me and all living beings on earth.
That is the sign of the promise I am making to all living beings.
GENESIS 9:16–17 GNT

My heart leaps up when I see a rainbow in the sky. The wonder of a rainbow lies in its ethereal beauty, the harmony of its colors, its arching providence, its hidden depths. A rainbow is a sign of God's blessing, a prism of unity, and a mirror of the many-colored human personality made in God's image. This natural phenomenon is full of spiritual significance, its colors a challenge to us to follow Christ more closely.

> Red is the color of sacrificial love. As Christ spilt his blood for us, so we are to "spill" what we own and share it with our sisters and brothers.
>
> Orange is the signal of our love. It is our witness to Christ in word and action.
>
> Yellow is the root of our love—prayer. It may seem weak or pale. Some people will overlook it or laugh at it. We must not be paralyzed by this dismissive attitude, for it has a glory all its own; without it, the other colors would be nothing.
>
> Green is the off-shoot of our love—the nurture of life in our bodies and in the eternal things we steward. When something gets out of order in any organism it loses its health. Foster and guard vitality.
>
> Blue is the setting of love—it is the creating of a beautiful stable environment. Our dress should enhance the features of our God-given personality. Our homes should reflect the artistry of our souls, and so draw others towards the author of our soul.
>
> Indigo is the thinking of love—it is our study, our wisdom, our spiritual discipline.
>
> Violet is the communion of love. It is good communication. It is like the electric current that can link the world.
> INSPIRED BY CHIARA LUBICH AND THE FOCOLARE SPIRITUALITY

Be thou my vision, O Lord of my heart.
NINTH CENTURY, IRISH

JUNE 27 ✤ PENANCE

Psalm 32; 2 Samuel 21:1-14; Matthew 5:21-26

So David summoned the people of Gibeon and said to them,
"What can I do for you?
I want to make up for the wrong that was done to you,
so that you will bless the Lord's people."
2 SAMUEL 21:3 GNT

Restitution was the hallmark of the Penitentials that Celtic church leaders popularized throughout Europe. Unlike the continental church, where confession was made to a priest and absolution received without restitution having to be made to the wronged person, the Celts based penitence upon restitution. Sin had to be dealt with. Wrongs had to be put right. The relationship with the wronged person needed to be restored.

When Columba corrupted Christianity with violence, his great act of penance was to go into exile from his beloved homeland for the rest of his life, in order to take Christ's love to another land. More recently, Christ-followers have made penance for the way the Crusades associated Jesus with the mindless killing of Muslims, going on prayer walks along routes where innocent people were killed. One of these penitents told me of local Muslims coming to the walkers in tears and in love. The walkers' goal was not to convert Muslims; it was to make penance and to ask forgiveness. If Muslims could be convinced that following Christ is a path of unconditional love, a whole new set of dynamics might come into play in the Middle East and around the world!

What wrongs have others suffered because of Christianity? And what can we do to make acts of atoning service? How can we set down the old baggage of hate, hurt, fear, and mistrust, so that we need not carry it into the third millennium?

We weep for Christian buildings that speak of domination,
for Christian communities that became places of greed,
for churches that became distant from the poor.
Forgive us, Lord, for the sins committed by Christians
during the Age of Pisces,
for being corrupted by power, for not listening to you
or to the cries of the people,
for not honoring your presence in creation
in the simple things all around.

JUNE 28 ❖ GRATITUDE

Psalm 63; 1 Chronicles 16:8-36; Philippians 4

> *Be filled with gratitude.*
> COLOSSIANS 2:7

Our most deadly sickness is the national epidemic of whining. Our cry-baby culture is influencing the world and cultivates a great and overwhelming sense of self-pity. There are two causes for this. First, an over-indulgence in the electronic media; second, the inability to express gratitude.
MICHAEL MEDVED, U.S. FILM CRITIC AND AUTHOR

> My dear King, my own King, without pride, without sin,
> you created the whole world, eternal, victorious King. . . .
> And you created men and women to be your stewards of the earth,
> always praising you for your boundless love.
> THE CELTIC PSALTER

Hilda was attacked by a fever which tortured her with its burning heat, and for six years the sickness afflicted her continually; yet during all this time she never ceased to give thanks to her Maker and to instruct the flock committed to her charge both in public and in private. Taught by her own experience she warned them all, when health of body was granted to them, to serve the Lord dutifully and, when in adversity or sickness, always to return thanks to the Lord faithfully.
BEDE

> Gratitude is the root of all virtue.
> A PAGAN SAYING

> My speech—may it praise you without flaw;
> may my heart love you,
> King of heaven and earth.
> My speech—may it praise you without flaw;
> make it easy for me, great Lord,
> to do you all service and to adore you.
> My speech—may it praise you without flaw;
> Father of all affection,
> hear my poems and my speech.
> EARLY IRISH LYRICS

JUNE 29 ❖ GIVING

Psalm 15; Malachi 3:6-12; 2 Corinthians 9

Giving makes you happier than receiving does.
ACTS 20:35

Aidan neither sought nor cared for this world's possessions,
and he loved to give away to poor people whom he met
all the gifts he received from kings and rich men of the world.
BEDE

There are three causes for the inordinate love of money:
desire for pleasure, vainglory and lack of trust.
And the last is stronger than the other two.
MAXIMUS THE CONFESSOR, C. 580–662

Never be greedy, always be generous, if not in money, then in spirit.
COLUMBANUS

Columba tells us, that
the generous shall never go to hell.
But those who steal and those who swear
shall lose their right to God.
CARMINA GADELICA

God's work done in God's way will not lack supplies.
HUDSON TAYLOR

*I would prepare a feast and be host to the great High King,
with all the company of heaven.
The sustenance of pure love be in my house,
the roots of repentance in my house.
Baskets of love be mine to give,
with cups of mercy for all the company.
Sweet Jesus, be there with us, with all the company of heaven.
May cheerfulness abound in the feast,
the feast of the great High King,
my host for all eternity.*
ATTRIBUTED TO BRIGID

JUNE 30 ✢ A Lesson in Providence

Psalm 65; Genesis 22; Matthew 6

*Abraham named that place "The Lord Provides,"
and even today people say,
"On the Lord's mountain the Lord provides."*
GENESIS 22:14 GNT

Cuthbert was traveling south along the River Teviot, teaching and baptizing the country folk in the hill areas. He had a boy with him, whom he sought to train to understand God's providence, so he asked the boy, "Do you think anyone has prepared your midday meal today?" When the boy answered that he knew of no friends or relatives on their route and did not expect provision from anyone, Cuthbert said, "Don't worry, but seek first the kingdom of God, and the Lord will provide for all your needs." He added, "I have been young; now I am old, but I have never seen God forsake those who do what is right."

A little while later, Cuthbert pointed to an eagle in the sky. "This is the eagle the Lord has instructed to provide us with food today." The eagle settled on the river bank, and, at Cuthbert's bidding, the boy walked over to it and removed a large fish from the eagle's talons. Cuthbert said, "Why did you not leave half of this for our fisherman to eat?" The boy returned half the fish to the eagle, and then Cuthbert and the boy broiled their half of the fish over the fire of some men they came across. They shared the fish with the men, and then they thanked the Lord and worshiped him.

We can learn three lessons from this incident: to expect God to meet our daily needs, to share what we have with others, and to allow others to help us when we are in need. In short: we can let God into our everyday affairs.

There is as much in our Lord's pantry as will satisfy all his bairns,
and as much wine in his cellar as will quench all their thirst.
SAMUEL RUTHERFORD

Where God guides God provides.
FRANK BUCHMAN

Give us this day our daily bread.

SUMMER

RECONCILING ALL

*People and creation are woven together,
revealing the importance of wholeness and community,
with Christ at the center.*

JULY 1 ✢ GARDENERS

Psalm 68:1-10; Genesis 2:4-20; Mark 12:1-12

*Jesus described the Kingdom of God with parables:
"Once there was a man who planted a vineyard...."*
MARK 12:1

When Cuthbert first went to live on the desolate Farne Island, the ground was hard, there was no water, and the birds ate the first seeds he planted. So he made up his mind to dig and plow the hard land.

Guests came to see him, but since he didn't have enough water to offer them to drink, Cuthbert invited them to help dig down into the ground where he had built his cell, and he prayed over them as they dug. Soon, water flowed out: they had dug down to a well.

Next, friends brought wheat seeds for him to sow, but by midsummer, nothing had grown. So Cuthbert concluded it was not God's will for wheat to grow on the island, and he asked his friends to bring over some barley seed instead. The barley seed arrived long after the proper time for sowing it, but Cuthbert persevered—and the barley sprang up quickly and produced an excellent crop. But then there was another setback. The birds began to devour the barley. So Cuthbert talked to the birds along these lines, which was also his way of sorting out things with God: "Why do you touch my crops? If it is because you have greater need of them than I and it is God's will for you, then go ahead. But if not, be off, and no longer damage what belongs to someone else." The birds desisted and Cuthbert was able to live off his barley.

> Be a gardener.
> Dig a ditch, toil and sweat,
> and turn the earth upside down
> and seek the deepness
> and water the plants in time.
> Continue this labor, and make sweet floods to run
> and noble and abundant fruits to spring.
> Take this food and drink
> and carry it to God as your true worship.
> JULIAN OF NORWICH

*Lord, I give to you the "seeds" you have given me at this moment.
Help me to do my very best with them
that a good crop may ensue.*

JULY 2 ✢ SOLDIER OF CHRIST

Psalm 64; 2 Samuel 16:1-14; 2 Timothy 1:15-2:13

*Take your part in suffering as a loyal soldier of Jesus Christ.
A soldier on active service wants to please his commanding officer
and so does not get mixed up in the affairs of civilian life.*
2 TIMOTHY 2:3-4 GNT

Two great Celtic saints, Samson and David (the patron saint of Wales), were pupils in the famous monastery of Illtyd. Illtyd is regarded as the founder of the Welsh church, though holy hermits had prepared the way. He was a well-educated soldier who had come to Wales from Brittany, and, according to one medieval record, he had fought in the army of King Arthur. While Illtyd was serving the King of Clamorgan, he became a Christian. According to the story, his conversion happened like this.

One day, Illtyd took a party of knights hunting and became separated from them. When the knights stumbled on the hut of the hermit Cadoc, they treated him disgracefully, shouting obscenities at him. Illtyd arrived on the scene and was shocked by his men's behavior—and riveted by Cadoc's. The old man refused to retaliate and simply smiled at the knights. Illtyd dismissed his men and fell on his knees, asking Cadoc to forgive their behavior. Cadoc lifted up Illtyd and warmly embraced him.

That night, as Illtyd lay awake, his heart was filled with love for the old hermit. The life of such a man, who was victorious in the battle with Satan, seemed so much finer to him than that of a soldier, whose only battles were with other soldiers. When Illtyd fell asleep, he dreamed an angel spoke to him these words: "Until now you have been a knight serving mortal kings. From now on you are to be in the service of the King of kings."

At dawn, Illtyd crept out of the royal palace, leaving behind his sword and his armor. He set out, clothed only in a rough woolen cloak, to be a soldier of Christ.

*Teach me, my God and King,
to fight with all of my being
for the things that are good and true and peaceable
as a faithful servant and soldier of our Lord Jesus Christ.*

July 3 ❖ A School for Christ

Psalm 66; Micah 4:1-14; 2 Timothy 2:14-26

*The teachings of the wise are a fountain of life;
they will help you escape when your life is in danger.*
PROVERBS 13:14 GNT

Illtyd had been living the life of a hermit for some three months when a stag burst into the clearing where he was meditating. A pack of hounds was hot on its heels, followed by the king and his hunt. When the king realized who Illtyd was, he erupted in fury and accused Illtyd of betraying him. Illtyd, like Cadoc, simply smiled and invited the king and his men into his hut for a meal. Meanwhile, the stag lay down peacefully outside . . . along with the hounds! At the end of the meal, it was the king's turn to have his heart changed, and he asked Illtyd's forgiveness. Then the king asked if he could send his son to Illtyd to be educated. That marked the beginning of a miracle in Christian education. Soon Illtyd's place in the valley by the sea became the largest school in the whole of Britain, a school for Christ—and Illtyd became known as the wisest teacher in Britain.

Illtyd believed that hard physical labor should always be combined with intellectual study, a body-mind balance. Everyone at his school had to spend four hours a day working outside, and soon the entire valley had been farmed. Illtyd even invented a new plough that doubled the speed at which land could be prepared.

After many years, King Paulinus, whose son had died, was succeeded by a malicious man who tried to destroy Illtyd's work. The king's henchmen, who secretly honored Illtyd, warned the wise old man that the king planned to murder him. Illtyd took this as God guiding him to go back to being an anonymous hermit. He secretly trekked to a cave further along the coast, and he grew a beard and long hair so no one would recognize him. However, a year later, a monk was traveling to a new monastery David had founded, with a brass bell that was a gift for David. The monk took a wrong turn and passed near Illtyd's cave. Illtyd heard the bell, came out, and struck it three times. The monk did not recognize his former leader, but strangely, when the bell was delivered to David, it was silent and would no longer ring. When the monk told David about his meeting with the hermit, David said, "God has told us where our dear Illtyd is hiding." He sent the monk to invite Illtyd to join them. Illtyd declined the invitation to go back into a large community, but three of David's monks went to support him and care for him until he died.

*Lord, unlock the treasures of wisdom to me—
but first give me a heart for humble learning.*

JULY 4 ❖ TRUE TO YOURSELF

Psalm 112; Deuteronomy 32:1-18; 2 Timothy 3

Your God is faithful and true.
DEUTERONOMY 32:4 GNT

To thine own self be true.
WILLIAM SHAKESPEARE

We are meant to be faithful and true, just as God is. However, since we all want and need to be affirmed—though many of us are not—we instinctively seek illicit affirmation, by tailoring our actions in order to gain the approval of others. In a subtle way, this means that we are no longer being true to ourselves. We perhaps unconsciously say to ourselves, "If I behave in this or that way, I will not get the affirmation I need—so I will adjust my behavior accordingly."

Once, when Columba visited the brothers on Hinba Island, he felt they needed to learn to enjoy life, to loosen up and relax their strict diet for a while. He wanted this relaxation to include people who were doing penance for some past sin. One of these, Nemen, refused to relax his diet, however. Nemen sounded very pious, but Columba realized that Nemen was not really being true to himself. Columba predicted that, because of this, the time would come when Nemen would end up with a gang of thieves in a forest and would eat a horse that had been stolen. Later, Nemen was found out to be doing just that. He refused legitimate pleasure in order to impress others—only to succumb to a secret and less healthy indulgence.

How can we cure our dependence on others' affirmation? Here is a prescription from the desert: Abba Macarios told a monk to go to a cemetery and shout his anger at the dead. This he did. Then Macarios told the monk to go there again and this time to praise the dead. He did this, too. In both cases, of course, the graves lay silent. Macarios concluded, "I want you to be like those dead, giving no response to praise or blame."

Help me to be true to myself,
true to you, true to others,
true to the call, true to all,
true to heaven.

JULY 5 ⁘ THE JOURNEY TO TRUE CONTENTMENT

Psalm 7; Isaiah 57; 2 Timothy 4

Whether I am full or hungry, I am always contented.
PHILIPPIANS 4:12

Holy voyages were popular during the days of the Celtic saints, but of course, not everyone could leave home for God's sake, nor is everyone called to do so now. Many of the Celtic Christ-followers, however, longed to experience what life was like as a pilgrim exiled from life's comforts. If we share this longing, we too can walk to holy places surrounded by God's creation—or undertake an inner journey of vigil, fasting, and prayer. The point of these holy journeys is to discard along the way, even temporarily, life's excess baggage, all those material things we cannot take with us into eternity. When we let these things drop, we find we can more clearly perceive our inner compass. We sense the calling of God's spirit to ours.

In our daily lives, however, many of us often run away from this call, filling our ears with other sounds. We fear that if we are stripped naked of this world's securities, we will have nothing left. The thought of being so vulnerable and fool-hardy—so dependent on grace alone—scares us. We think we will be miserable and uncomfortable if we follow the Divine call into unfamiliar places. In reality, if we are open to God's direction, we will find our deepest contentment.

The Celts understood this tension between comfort and courage. In this ancient Irish poem, a warrior king asks his brother Marvan why he has given up his position and his feather quilt in order to live as a hermit. This is Marvan's answer:

> Beautiful are the pines which make music for me unhindered.
> Through Christ I am no worse off at any time than you.
> Though you relish that which you enjoy exceeding all wealth,
> I am content with that which is given me by my gentle Christ.
> With no moment of strife, no din of combat such as disturbs you,
> thankful to the Prince who gives every good to me in my hut.

All that I have I offer to you.
All that you wish me to leave behind, I surrender.
Wherever you lead, I will follow you, so help me God.
Lead me on my journey
to places of resurrection, to dwellings of peace,
to healings of wounds, to joys of discovery.

JULY 6 ✥ I BELIEVE

Psalm 68:11-35; Nehemiah 8; Titus 1

*I have total confidence in the gospel;
it is God's power to save all who believe,
first the Jews but also all the other people of the world.*
ROMANS 1:16

I believe, O God of all gods, that you are the eternal Father of life.
I believe, O God of all gods, that you are the eternal Father of love.
I believe, O God of all gods, that you are the eternal Father of the saints
I believe, O God of all gods that you are the eternal Father of each person.
I believe, O God of all gods, that you are the eternal Father of humanity
I believe, O God of all gods, that you are the eternal Father of the world.
I believe, O God of the peoples, that you are the Creator of the high heavens,
that you are the Creator of the skies above,
that you are the Creator of the oceans below.
I believe, O God of the peoples,
that you are the One who created my soul and set its warp,
who created my body from dust and from ashes,
who gave to my body breath, and to my soul its endowment.
Father eternal and Lord of the peoples,
I believe that you have put right my soul in the Spirit of healing,
that you gave your loved Son in covenant for me,
that you have purchased my soul with the precious blood of your Son.
Father eternal and Lord of life, I believe that you poured on me
the Spirit of grace at my baptism.
CARMINA GADELICA

*Praise to the Father,
praise to the Son,
praise to the Spirit,
the Three in One.*
CARMINA GADELICA

JULY 7 ✢ PROPHECY

Psalm 75; 1 Samuel 3; 1 Corinthians 14:1-26

Long for spiritual gifts, especially the gift of prophecy.
1 CORINTHIANS 14:1

When Cuthbert made up his mind to join a monastery, he decided to go to Melrose; he had heard that the abbot there, Boisil, had powerful prophetic gifts. When Cuthbert arrived at Melrose, Boisil watched him dismount from his horse and give his sword and spear to his servant to take away. Boisil turned to those who were with him and said, "Mark this, here is a servant of the Lord." Bede comments that in saying this, Boisil was echoing Jesus' words when he first saw Nathaniel: "Here is a true man of the people, in whom there is nothing false."

Years later, Cuthbert returned to Melrose monastery, where he fell ill with the plague. Boisil prophesied, "You will not get the plague again, nor will you die at the present time. However, I will die of this plague—so let me use the seven days left to me to teach you." They spent each of those days studying John's Gospel, and then Boisil died.

Three years earlier, Boisil had already predicted to Abbot Eata that the plague would carry him off. He declared that the abbot, however, would not die of the plague, but at a later date from dysentery. Events proved that this prophecy was also true. Cuthbert often told people, "I have known many who far exceed me in their prophetic powers. Foremost among these is Boisil, who trained me up and foretold accurately all the things that were to happen to me. Of all these things only one remains to be fulfilled." Eventually, this last prophecy—that Cuthbert would become a bishop—also became reality.

Cuthbert might have refused the pressures on him to become a bishop had it not been for Boisil's prophecy. In this way, the power of Boisil's prophetic insights continued to shape the world, even after his death. Boisil also appeared to others in prophetic dreams, and these also helped shape the future of the kingdom. We may never experience the powerful insights Boisil did, but we too can learn to listen to the Spirit's speaking.

God of the thunder, God of the sap,.
God of the future, God of the map,
God of the silence, God of the gap,
I make room for your spirit, like a child in my lap.

July 8 ❖ A Quiet Place

Psalm 84; 2 Kings 4:8–17; Matthew 6:1–18

*When you pray, go to your room, close the door,
and pray to your Father, who is unseen.
Your Father, who sees what you do in private, will reward you.*
MATTHEW 6:6 GNT

Grant me, sweet Christ, the grace to find, Son of the Living God,
small hut in a lonesome spot to make it my abode.
A little pool but very clear, to stand beside the place
where every sin is washed away by sanctifying grace.
A pleasant woodland all about, and make a home for singing birds
before it and behind.
A southern aspect for the heat, a stream along its foot,
a smooth green lawn with rich topsoil propitious to all fruit
My choice of those to live with me and pray to God as well;
quiet friends of humble mind their number I shall tell.
A lovely church, a home for God, bedecked with linen fine,
where o'er the whitened Gospel page the Gospel candles shine.
A little house where all may dwell, and body's care be sought,
where none shows lust or arrogance, none thinks an evil thought.
And all I ask for housekeeping I get and pay no fees,
leeks from the garden, poultry, game, salmon, fruit and bees.
My share of clothing and of food from the King of fairest face,
and I to sit at times alone and pray in every place,
ABBOT MUNTEITH, THE HERMIT'S PRAYER, *SIXTH CENTURY*

God of the secret, quiet place, I hide myself in you.

JULY 9 ✢ STUDY

Psalm 119:1-24; Ezra 7:1-16; Acts 17:1-15

Every day they studied the Scriptures.
ACTS 17:11 GNT

Samson's longing to understand Scripture's deeper meanings was so intense that he wanted to dig even deeper than what Illtyd, his teacher, could offer him. Once when he and Illtyd came across a doubtful area of interpretation and were unable to find a satisfactory answer—though they carefully studied all the books of both the Hebrew and Greek scriptures—Samson decided to fast and keep vigil until God's understanding broke through his confusion. He was praying in the night when light appeared in his room and a voice spoke from it: "Do not trouble yourself any further on this, God's chosen one, for in the future whatever you ask of God in prayer and fasting you will obtain!" With a happy heart, Samson returned to his cell and went to sleep.

> Urged by devoted Christians and my own inmost heart, I have made as penetrating a study as possible of the entire character, body and mind, of Christians who by their active and their contemplative life shine like stars of heaven to help us.
> THE LIFE OF SAMSON OF DOL

Daily Bible reading is at the heart of this way of life. In addition, we study the history of the Celtic church, becoming familiar with such saints as Aidan, Brigid, Caedmon, Columba, Cuthbert, David, Hilda, Illtyd, Ninian, Oswald, and Patrick. We remember their feast days and consider them as companions on our journeys of faith. We also bear in mind their strong link with the Desert Fathers and the Eastern Church, and wish to draw them too into our field of studies. It is essential that study is not understood merely as an academic exercise. All that we learn is not for the sake of study itself, but in order that what we learn should be lived. We encourage the Celtic practice of memorizing scriptures, and learning through the use of creative arts.
THE WAY OF LIFE OF THE COMMUNITY OF AIDAN AND HILDA

> *O Lord, may it be your wisdom, not my folly*
> *which passes through my arm and hand.*
> *May your words take shape upon the page,*
> *For when I am truly faithful to your dictation*
> *my hand is firm and strong.*
> A SCRIBE IN A CELTIC MONASTERY

July 10 ❖ Abandonment to God

Psalm 86; 1 Kings 8:22-53; Luke 15:71-32

*Lord God . . . you keep your covenant with your people
and show them your love
when they live in wholehearted obedience to you.*
2 Chronicles 6:14 GNT

*Four things by which the Kingdom of heaven may be pursued:
stability and detachment from the world,
devotion and constancy.*
Colmán mac Béognae, The Alphabet of Devotion

O God, manage me because I can't manage myself.
A SCHOOLBOY

Selwyn Hughes, the Welsh author of the devotional readings titled *Every Day with Jesus*, was asked by a television interviewer, "What is the most important lesson you have learned?"

"Dependency," Selwyn replied. "Life works better when you throw all your weight on Christ. Not part of your weight, not even a lot of your weight. All of your weight."

*I am giving you worship with my whole life.
I am giving you assent with my whole power.
I am giving you praise with my whole tongue.
I am giving you honor with my whole speech.
I am giving you reverence with my whole understanding.
I am giving you dedication with my whole thought.
I am giving you praise with my whole fervor.
I am giving you humility in the blood of the Lamb.
I am giving you love with my whole devotion.
I am giving you kneeling with my whole desire.
I am giving you love with my whole heart.
I am giving you affection with my whole sense.
I am giving you existence with my whole mind.
I am giving you my soul, O God of all gods.
My thought, my deed, my word, my will,
my understanding, my intellect, my way, my state.*
Carmina Gadelica

JULY 11 ❖ PRAYER CHANGES THINGS

Psalm 71; 1 Kings 17; Luke 17:5, 6

She answered, ". . . We will starve to death. . . ."
The widow went and did as Elijah told her,
and all of them had enough food for many days.
1 KINGS 17:12, 15 GNT

Christ's followers believe that prayer can change anything. But experience shows that God is not in the business of the "quick fix." Frequently, we go away from prayer disappointed. The following story from the life of Mungo reminds us that prayer, like life itself, is a process. Prayer aligns our hearts and minds with the Divine will—so when our prayers seem ineffective, if we reevaluate and pray from a different perspective, we find that the good God, who is full of surprises, will not fail us.

Morcant, the local ruler at Craigmaddie Moor, was a bitter enemy of Mungo's. His mercenaries looted the local crops and then stored them in Morcant's barn.

That winter, when hunger struck Mungo's people, he walked to Craigmaddie Moor and confronted Morcant. "My people are hungry!"

Morcant laughed. "You Christians teach that God will provide for those who serve him. Well, I don't serve him and I have plenty. You serve him and have nothing. So your teaching must be false!"

Mungo returned empty handed to his base at Clathures, but he did not give up. Instead, he gathered the people to pray.

After they prayed, it began to rain. The rain came down in deluge after deluge until the rivers flooded their banks. Morcant's barn was washed away into the River Clyde, and then it floated downriver like an ark on a wild cruise. On the banks of the Molindar, it went hard aground . . . right beside Mungo's church!

The next morning, Mungo gathered his flock to thank God and eat a good breakfast. Morcant probably did not find it at all funny—but Mungo must have!

Some have meat and cannot eat;
some cannot eat that want it:
but we have meat and we can eat
sae let the Lord be thankit!
ROBERT BURNS

JULY 12 ✢ SERENITY

Psalm 131; Proverbs 16; Philippians 4:1–9

I am content and at peace.
As a child lies quietly in its mother's arms, so my heart is quiet within me.
PSALM 131:2 GNT

Cuthbert was known for always wearing the same peaceful countenance.

> At all hours he was happy and joyful, neither wearing a sad expression at the remembrance of a sin nor being elated by the loud praises of those who marveled at his manner of life. . . . After two years he resigned the bishopric and returned to the solitary way of life on the island. . . . He remained alone, satisfied with the converse and ministry of angels, full of hope and putting his trust wholly in God, though his body was now infirm and afflicted with a certain sickness.
> LIFE OF CUTHBERT *BY AN ANONYMOUS MONK OF LINDISFARNE*

> [Following the imposition of Roman regulations at the Council of Whitby,] there were certain brothers at the Lindisfarne monastery who preferred to conform to their old usage rather than to the monastic rule. Nevertheless, Cuthbert overcame these by his modest virtue and his patience, and by daily effort he gradually converted them into a better state of mind. In fact very often during debates in the chapter concerning the rule, when he was assailed by the bitter insults of his opponents, he would rise up suddenly and with calm mind and countenance would go out, thus dissolving the chapter, but none the less, on the following day, as if he had suffered no repulse the day before, he would give the same instruction as before to the brothers. . . . For he was a man remarkable for the strength of his patience and unsurpassed in bravely bearing every burden whether of mind or body.
> *BEDE*, LIFE OF CUTHBERT

> *The serenity of Christ, the serenity of kindly Cuthbert,*
> *the serenity of mild and loving Mary,*
> *the serenity of Christ, King of tenderness,*
> *be upon each thing my eye takes in;*
> *upon each thing my mouth takes in,*
> *upon my body that is of the earth,*
> *upon my spirit that came from on high.*
> CARMINA GADELICA (ADAPTED)

JULY 13 ❖ ABANDONMENT OF POWER

Psalm 69:1–18; Isaiah 42:1–7; 2 Corinthians 7

*We have wronged no one; we have ruined no one,
nor tried to take advantage of anyone.*
2 CORINTHIANS 7:2 GNT

A group of English people went on a week's prayer walk along the length of the River Thames. The walk began with Celtic prayers in a church dedicated to Saint Samson, near the Thames' source. It ended near a statue of Neptune, a symbol of the power of the City of London and the British Empire, epitomized by the song "Rule, Britannia!" The prayer walk led these followers of Christ to repent the English people's lust for power.

If you ask Irish, Scots, or Welsh folk what they most dislike about the English, they will tell you it is the lust for power that neither notices nor cherishes the other person or nation. Americans must recognize that they too bear something of Mother England's less lovely qualities in their nation's character. And yet the true birthright of all who speak the English language comes from the gentle apostle Aidan who gave up his right to ride a horse in order to be one with the ordinary people, armed only with the defenselessness of love.

Aidan, like the other Celtic saints, truly followed Jesus. Their churches were small, provisional buildings rather than ornate, expensive edifices. For them, the church was built from living stones: the people who grew together in relationships of love, building churches without walls. The Celtic clerics dressed simply, without ostentation. Many bishops were monks, which meant they renounced material possessions and did not take collections "for the church."

At the end of the sixth century, after Pope Gregory had sent Augustine of Canterbury to Britain, Archbishop Augustine met with the Celtic church leaders to ask that they give up their own practices and conform to the Roman church. After their meeting at what came to be known as Augustine's Oak—perhaps very near the same site where that Thames prayer walk began centuries later—the Celtic clergy sought advice from a holy hermit, whose authority lay in his having renounced all power. The hermit's advice was this: "If Augustine is a holy man, you should take his advice. You will know if he is holy if he is humble enough at your next meeting to stand up to greet you. If he does not, you need not take his advice." Augustine did not stand up—and an opportunity for coordinated evangelism of the English people was lost. At the same time, the Celtic church "lost out" in terms of status and power—and yet it kept firm hold of its identity as Christ's followers. This same witness still speaks today to all those who reject any method of being church that is built upon power or status.

Strip from us everything except integrity.

JULY 14 ❖ A BROAD MIND

Psalm 70; Isaiah 55; 1 Corinthians 14:13-25

I will pray with my spirit, but I will pray also with my mind.
1 CORINTHIANS 14:15 GNT

For eagerness of the truth, it is fitting that its proper nature should be reckoned: zeal without anger, humility without neglect. . . . What is best for the mind? Breadth and humility, for every good thing finds room in a broad, humble mind. What is worst for the mind? Narrowness and closedness and constrictedness, for nothing good finds room in a narrow, closed, restricted mind.
COLMÁN MAC BÉOGNAE, THE ALPHABET OF DEVOTION

Pray attentively and you will soon straighten out your thoughts.
DESERT SAYINGS

Always make a practice of provoking your mind to think out what it accepts easily. Our position is not ours until we make it ours by suffering. If you cannot express yourself on any subject, struggle until you can. If you do not, someone will be the poorer all the days of their life.
OSWALD CHAMBERS

Jesus, Son of Mary, consecrate us—
all that we inherit, all that we acquire,
consecrate each mind and body, each thought and action
to yourself, King of kings, God of all.
ADAPTED FROM *THE CARMINA GADELICA*

JULY 15 ✣ DELIVER US FROM EVIL

Psalm 73; 2 Kings 15:1-12; Mark 1:21-34

Rescue us from evil things.
MATTHEW 6:13

A dear friend of Cuthbert's named Hildmer was responsible for the administration of the law in his locality. When his wife became mentally ill—writhing, shrieking, and salivating—Hildmer was not only deeply upset for her, he was also embarrassed. He came to tell Cuthbert she was ill and to ask him to send a priest from the Lindisfarne monastery to administer the prayers for the sick and dying . . . but he could not bring himself to tell Cuthbert the nature of her illness. After all, his wife was a good Christian woman; he didn't want folks thinking she was possessed by demons!

Cuthbert agreed to send a priest, but as Hildmer was leaving, the Holy Spirit stirred Cuthbert to call him back. "It is my duty to come with you," Cuthbert said, "not another's." So Cuthbert, with a group from the monastery, went with Hildmer back to his home. Without having to be told, Cuthbert had sensed the true condition of Hildmer's wife, and during the journey, he reassured his friend.

"It is not only the wicked who are tormented like this," Cuthbert said, "but sometimes God also allows the innocent to be taken over, not only in body but also in the mind. But don't worry, for when we come to your house, your wife whom you think is dying will come to meet me. When she takes these reins of the horse which I have in my hand, she will be restored to full health, and the demon will be driven away."

And that is exactly what happened.

Lord, save us from making judgments about people who are ill.
Make us eager to encircle them with the prayer of loving friends.
Help us discern what you wish to do in each situation,
that a step towards wholeness may always be taken,
not in our way, but in yours.

JULY 16 ✢ SIGNS AND WONDERS

Psalm 74; 1 Kings 18:15-39; Acts 5:1-16

The apostles performed many miracles and wonders.
ACTS 5:12

Let him who will, laugh and insult, I will not be silent, nor will I hide the signs and wonders which were ministered to me by the Lord, many years before they came to pass, as he who knew all things before the world began.
PATRICK OF IRELAND

God who judges the heart showed by signs and wonders what Aidan's merits were.
BEDE

Cuthbert became famous for his miracles. Through his persistent prayers he restored to health many who were sick, he cured some that were afflicted by unclean spirits, not only when present . . . praying, touching, commanding, and exorcising, but also when absent either by prayer alone or even indeed by predicting their cure. . . . Signs and wonders whereby he shone outwardly gave witness to the inward virtues of his mind.
BEDE, LIFE OF CUTHBERT

And after raising of dead men, healing lepers, blind, deaf, lame, and all kinds of sick folk . . . after expelling demons and vices . . . after performance of mighty works and miracles too numerous to mention, St. Brendan drew near to the day of his death.
LIFE OF ST. BRENDAN

Great Father of the blood-red moon
and of the falling stars;
Great Savior of the miraculous birth
and of the rising from death;
Great Spirit of the creators and the seers;
come in sovereign power into our dreams,
into our thoughts, into our mouths,
into our bodies, into our actions,
till we become your sign, and presence, and wonder.

JULY 17 ✣ ORDINARY PEOPLE

Psalm 76; 1 Kings 19:1-18; 1 Corinthians 1:18-31

Now remember what you were when God called you.
From the human point of view
few of you were wise or powerful or of high social standing.
God purposely chose ... what the world considers weak
in order to shame the powerful.
1 CORINTHIANS 1:26-27 GNT

The Lord prefers common-looking people.
That is why he made so many of them.
ABRAHAM LINCOLN

We should never forget that although the words and deeds of the most notable Christians get handed down to us, Christianity was first spread by slaves, working soldiers, and traders. In Celtic times, Christianity was the religion of the people; it took root in ordinary hearts and homes. This fact is reflected in the prayers of the Scottish highlanders and islanders that Alexander Carmichael recorded so many centuries later. In these we have a glimpse of an army of ordinary people whose prayers were like arrows, shot from the midst of their everyday lives.

The following "arrow prayers" for ordinary days are inspired by the *Carmina Gadelica*:

As I wash, the love of Christ be in my breast.
God protect the household,
God consecrate the children,
God encompass our assets.

May I do my rounds under the shield of Michael, chief of angels.

May the ingredients for the meal be mixed together
in the name of God's Son who gives growth.

Circle all my business dealings,
keep out what is false, keep within what is good.

In everything my hands do today, I will keep my fingers as a cross.
In my exercise, may thankfulness pulse through my body.
As I sleep, may your right hand be under my head.

Fair Lord, be in the daily warp and weft of ordinary days.

JULY 18 ✣ MOTHER CHURCH

Psalm 77; 1 Kings 19:19–21; Galatians 4:17–33

*My dear children . . . just like a mother in childbirth,
I feel the same kind of pain for you
until Christ's nature is formed in you. . . .
The heavenly Jerusalem is free and she is our mother.*
GALATIANS 4:19, 26

One Sunday, when Mungo was ailing, he felt a keen desire for a hot bath. With loving care, his friends lowered him into the water. After a time in the soothing warmth, he rallied and gave these, his final words, to his friends: "My children . . . love one another . . . be hospitable . . . beware of heresy . . . keep the laws of the Church . . . she is the Mother of us all." His jaw dropped. This dear soul, known as the Beloved by so many, was dead, but his final words still touch us: "She is the Mother of us all."

The church is Divine, though its members are all too human. Wheat and weeds grow together. Those who pay most attention to the weeds become cynical about the church. Those who focus on the wheat become part of the church's Divine work of fostering and mothering.

Problems within the church are nothing new. According to Rhigyfarch, Saint David's biographer, before Illtyd and Samson brought renewal to the church in Wales, most clergy were drunk. By the end of David's life, "everywhere are heard evidences of churches, everywhere voices are raised to heaven in prayers; everywhere the virtues are unweariedly brought back to the bosom of the church; everywhere charitable offerings are distributed to the needy with open arms."

*Nurture us in the tender mercies of our mother the church.
May we grow in her wisdom. May we be enriched in her heritage.
May we be cherished by her mothers.
May we be stretched by her teachers.
May we be corrected by her shepherds.
May we be illumined by her seers. May we be inspired by her saints.
May we be spurred by her innovators.
May we be made to feel at ease by her little ones.
May we be humbled by her holy ones.
May we be uplifted by her musicians.
May we be warned by her erring ones.
May we be blessed by her givers.
May we be warmed by her welcomers.*

JULY 19 ⁂ CHEER UP!

Psalm 78:1-16; 1 Kings 18:41-46; Romans 14:13-23

To the pure, all things are pure.
TITUS 1:15 NIV

Some years after the death of Kevin at Glendalough, a very pious monk there named Moling often missed meals in order to pray. Not only did he despise food, he never allowed himself the pleasure of listening to music. Then God sent someone to cheer him up.

One day a young man arrived and asked if he could play his harp to the brothers while they were in the refectory. They welcomed him, but Moling was praying in the church and missed hearing the music. The young man then went to the church to play. Moling, who was kneeling in prayer, did not even lift his head but took from his pocket two balls of wax and stuffed them in his ears. The young man smiled and continued playing. To Moling's amazement, the wax in his ears began to melt. Try as he might to push it back into his ears, it just trickled down his neck and under his habit.

At that moment, the young man took a stone and started to scrape the harp. Moling found the sound unbearable. Then the young man threw the stone away and played music so sweet that Moling was filled with a joy greater than he had ever known. When the harpist had finished playing, Moling asked him, "Are you a devil sent to tempt me or an angel sent to bless me?"

"You must make your own judgment," the young man replied. "When I scraped the harp, it made the noise of the devil, and when I played it with my fingers, it made the sound of an angel. Music, like food and drink, can be an agent of evil or a source of goodness."

Then the young man went on his way. But from that day on, Moling welcomed all musicians to play at the monastery, and he gave up undue fasting, abstaining from food only on those days when everyone else fasted. His brothers could not help noticing that he became more gentle and kind. He even acquired a sense of humor!

O Son of God, change my heart.
Your spirit composes the songs of the birds and the buzz of the bees.
Your creation is a million wondrous miracles, beautiful to look upon.
I ask of you just one more miracle: beautify my soul.
FROM A TRADITIONAL CELTIC PRAYER

JULY 20 ✣ THE MIDDLE PATH

Psalm 78:17-39; Ecclesiastes 7:1-19; 2 Timothy 4:1-8

*Enjoy life—and also be willing to sacrifice.
In either case, avoid extremes.*
ECCLESIASTES 7:18

Some people wear out their bodies by denying them food or rest;
but because they have no discretion they are far from God.
ANTONY, SAYINGS OF THE DESERT FATHERS

And so for several years he continued to live a solitary life cut off from the sight of people; and alone in all conditions he bore himself with unshaken balance.... His conversation, seasoned with salt, consoled the sad, instructed the ignorant, appeased the angry, for he persuaded them all to put nothing before the love of Christ. And he placed before the eyes of all the greatness of future benefits and the mercy of God, and revealed the favors already bestowed, namely that God spared not his own Son but delivered him up for the salvation of us all.
LIFE OF CUTHBERT *BY AN ANONYMOUS MONK OF LINDISFARNE*

In accordance with the example of Samson the strong, who was once a Nazarite, Cuthbert carefully abstained from all intoxicants; but he could not submit to this kind of abstinence in food, lest he became unfit for necessary hard labor.

Cuthbert wore ordinary garments and, keeping the middle path, he was not noteworthy either for their elegance or for their slovenliness. Hence his example is followed in the same monastery [Lindisfarne] even to this day, but they are fully satisfied with that kind of garment which the natural wool of the sheep provides.
BEDE, LIFE OF CUTHBERT

*Lord, today may the needs of my body
and the needs of my mind,
the practical needs of work and my social needs,
each be given their rightful place and kept in balance.
May the needs for rest and fun, study and sleep,
household order and justifiable work,
all be completed.*

JULY 21 ⁘ EXTREMITY

Psalm 78:40-72; 1 Kings 20:1-22; 2 Timothy 4:9-22

We are often troubled but not crushed;
we sometimes doubt but we never despair;
we have many enemies, but we are never without a friend;
and though we're badly hurt at times, we are not destroyed.
2 CORINTHIANS 4:8–9

Did Jesus' mother Mary feel she had lost everything when she watched her son die on the Cross? But at his conception, she had surrendered everything to God . . . even to the utmost extremity.

Did Aiden feel he had lost everything as his dear friend in Christ, Oswine (the king who opened the door to Aidan's mission), was killed? Aidan died only eleven days later, and some think he died of a broken heart.

"I'm broken," confessed Columbanus . . . but God used him to the end.

Mungo's great mission partners, Cadoc, Asaph, and Deiniol, all died. Then his royal Christian friends, Aidan, King of the Scots, and Rhydderch, King of Strathclyde, also died, both under the shadow of failure. The Britons were routed and would never act as a united force again. Then, in 603, it was Mungo's time to depart, also under the shadow of failure. What Mungo did not know was that his story had only just begun. The greatest period of evangelization of his people would soon be underway.

Never forget that before the brightest dawn comes the darkest night. Our extremity is God's opportunity.

I know perfectly well that poverty and misfortune
suit me better than riches and pleasure.
Christ the Lord, himself, was poor for our sakes.
PATRICK

God of heaven,
do not leave me in the path
where there is screaming from the weight of oppression.
Great God, protect me from the fiery wall,
the long trench of tears.
DALLAN MAC FORGAILL, THE ELEGY OF COLUM CILLE

JULY 22 ✢ DISCIPLINE

Psalm 81; 1 Kings 20:35-43; 1 Corinthians 14:26-40

Everything should be done in a fitting and orderly way.
1 CORINTHIANS 14:40 NIV

Wise discipline is meant to free us rather than restrict us. These selections from Columba's Rule are good examples:

Do not give room to a person who is full of idle chatter and tittle-tattle; just give them your blessing and send them on their way.

Go along with any rule that evokes devotion.

Divide your work into three parts: first, your personal needs; second, the needs of your community; third, work that meets the needs of your neighbors.

Give to people in need.

Do not eat until you are hungry. Do not sleep until you are ready for it.

Do not converse with people except for a good cause.

Every time you receive something, give something away to a friend or a poor person.

Love God with all your heart and strength.

Love your neighbor as yourself.

Make the Old and New Testaments your home at all times.

Work at your devotion until tears come— or at least until perspiration comes.

Lord, temper with tranquility our manifold activity that we may do our work for thee with very great simplicity.
A SIXTEENTH-CENTURY PRAYER

JULY 23 ✥ ANIMALS

Psalm 96; Hosea 2:2-23; Mark 1:1-12

*I will make a covenant with all the wild animals
and the birds of the sky and the animals that scurry along the ground.*
HOSEA 2:18 NLT

When Jesus commands us to love our neighbors, he does not only mean our human neighbors; he also means the animals and birds, insects and plants, all the creatures among whom we live. Just as we should not be cruel to other human beings, so we should not be cruel to any species of creature. Just as we should love and cherish other human beings, so we should love and cherish all God's creation.

We learn to love other human beings by discerning their pleasure and pain, their joy and sorrow, and by sympathizing with them. We need only poke a horse with a sharp stick to discern the pain it can suffer; and when we stroke and slap that same horse on the neck, we can feel its pleasure. Thus we can love a horse in the same way we can love another human being. Of course, our love for other species is less full and less intense than our love for humans, because the range and depth of their feelings are less than our own. Yet we should remember that all love comes from God, so when our love is directed towards an animal or even a tree, we are participating in the fullness of God's love.
PELAGIUS TO AN ELDERLY FRIEND

Encompass each goat, sheep and lamb,
each cow and horse and store.
Surround the flocks and herds
and look after them in a kindly fold.
CARMINA GADELICA

*Father, bless the pet, and also bless the vet.
Savior, bless the flock, and also bless the cock.
Spirit, bless the horse as much as my own course.*

JULY 24 ✧ HAIL TO YOU, GLORIOUS LORD

Psalm 79; 1 Chronicles 16:8-36; Revelation 15

*Let everyone praise the name of the Lord,
whose name is greater than all others.
The Lord's shining splendor is above heaven and earth.
The Lord made the people strong
so that everyone should give the Lord praise.*
PSALM 148:13-14

Hail to you, glorious Lord.
May chancel and church praise you.
May plain and hillside praise you.
May the three springs praise you,
two higher than the wind and one above the earth.
May darkness and light praise you.
May the cedar and sweet fruit tree praise you.
Abraham praised you, the founder of faith.
May life everlasting praise you,
may the birds and the bees praise you,
may the stubble and the grass praise you.
Aaron and Moses praised you.
May male and female praise you,
may the seven days and the stars praise you,
may the lower and the upper air praise you,
may books and letters praise you,
may the fish in the river praise you,
may thought and action praise you,
may the sand and the earth praise you.
May all the good things created praise you
and I, too, shall praise you, Lord, of glory.
Hail to you, glorious Lord!
EARLY MIDDLE WELSH

*O Being of life! O Being of peace!
O Being of time, and time without cease!
O Being, infinite eternity!
O Being, infinite eternity!*
CARMINA GADELICA

July 25 ✥ Jealousy

Psalm 80; 1 Samuel 18:6-16; Galatians 5:16-26

> *Don't be conceited.*
> *Don't irritate each other.*
> *Don't be jealous of each other.*
> GALATIANS 5:16

> *Whoever made you to envy*
> *swarthy man or fair woman,*
> *I will send three to overcome it*
> *Holy Spirit, Father, Son.*
> CARMINA GADELICA

Jealousy can cripple, whether we find it inside ourselves or we are the victims of others' jealousy.

First, we need to guard against it in ourselves. The worship book of the Celtic Monastery at Cerne, Ireland, contained this petition: "Guard my eyes for me, Jesus, Son of Mary, lest seeing another's wealth make me covetous."

Second, when we encounter jealousy in others, we can stand back from it rather than being swept up in it. We can choose to quietly do the essential things that have to be done, while not aggravating the situation by pushing the boundaries. We place the situation into the hands of God and ask God to deal with it as God chooses, when God chooses. Only time will tell us whether we need to break away from this situation—or whether love can replace jealousy.

Jealousy thrives where affirming love is lacking. Prayer works the cure. The Three who can overcome jealousy are the affirming Creator, Spirit, Christ.

> *I will start this day in the presence of the holy angels of heaven*
> *without malice, without jealousy, without envy.*
> *Without fear of anyone under the sun,*
> *the holy Son of God to shield me.*
>
> *God, kindle in my heart within*
> *a flame of love to my neighbor and to my foe, to my friend, to all.*
> *To the winner, to the loser, O Son of the loveliest Mary.*
>
> *Without malice, without jealousy, without envy.*
> *Without fear of anyone under the sun, the holy Son of God to shield me.*
> CARMINA GADELICA (ADAPTED)

JULY 26 ✢ GOD'S ARMOR

Psalm 83; 1 Kings 22:1-28; Ephesians 6:10-24

*Stand your ground, putting on the belt of truth
and the body armor of God's righteousness....
Hold up the shield of faith.... Put on salvation as your helmet,
and take the sword of the Spirit, which is the word of God.*
EPHESIANS 6:14, 15, 17 NLT

[When Cuthbert arrived on Fame Island], our soldier of Christ entered armed with "the helmet of salvation, the shield of faith, and the sword of the spirit which is the word of God," all the fiery darts of the wicked one were quenched, and the foe was driven far away together with the whole crowd of his assistants. This soldier of Christ, as soon as he had become monarch of the land he had entered and had overcome the many usurpers, built a city fitted for his rule, and in it houses equally suited to the city....

Moreover not only the creatures of the air but also of the sea, yes, and even the sea itself, as well as air and fire did honor to the honored man. For if a person faithfully and wholeheartedly serves the Maker of all created things, it is no wonder that all creation should minister to their directions. For the most part, we lose dominion over the creation because we neglect to serve the Creator of all things....

Many came to the man of God.... No one went away without enjoying his consolation.... He had learned how to lay bare before those who were tempted the many tricks of the ancient foe, by which the person who lacks human or divine love may easily be trapped. But whoever goes strengthened by unwavering faith passes, with God's help, through the enemy snares as if they were spiders' webs. "How many times," Cuthbert said, "have they tried to kill me. But though they tried to frighten me away by one phantasmal temptation after another, they were unable to mar my body or my mind by fear."
BEDE

*As I put on the belt of truth, may I be open to your word
which is truth however it may come to me today.
As I put on the helmet of salvation, may your law
be my guide and delight this day.
As I take up the shield of faith, may I hold on to your
promises and know them in my life.
As I put on the sword of the Spirit may I be open
to the promptings of your Spirit this day.*
MICHAEL HALLIWELL

JULY 27 ❖ BEYOND NATIONALISM

Psalm 82; 1 Kings 22:29-50; Revelation 21:9-27

In Christ there is no difference between people of different nationalities, between citizens and alien workers.
GALATIANS 3:28

Brian Keenan, the Belfast journalist who became a hostage in Beirut, wrote that in his home city there was an unseen and uncontrollable malevolence: "Out of a sense of frustration, of fear, of a raging thirst for identity and purpose. It seemed that people were drinking in this poison. Some unconsciously, and some by choice until they became intoxicated with rage and despair and helplessness."

Keenan wrote in *An Evil Cradling* that he had himself made "the mythic leap and crossed the Jordan. . . . There are those who cross the Jordan and seek out truth through a different experience from the one they are born to, and theirs is the greatest struggle. To move from one cultural ethos into another, as I did, and emerge embracing them both demands more of a man than any armed struggle. For here is the real conflict by which we move into manhood and maturity. For unless we know how to embrace the other we are not men and our nationhood is willful and adolescent."

David Gwenalt Jones, a modern Welsh poet, describes Saint David, Wales's national saint, as God's Gypsy who "brought the church to our homes, and took bread from the pantry and bad wine from the cellar, and stood behind the table like a tramp so as not to hide the wonder of the Sacrifice from us. After the Communion we chatted by the fireside, and he talked to us about God's natural order, the person, the family, the nation and the society of nations, and the Cross, keeping us from turning any one of them into a god."

God of all peoples,
help us to find our deepest identity in you, not in our nation.
Christ incarnate in my people,
help us to forgive what has been done to us.
Spirit between peoples,
help us to be like you, by giving and receiving from others.
May you be our only god.

JULY 28 ✢ SAMSON

Psalm 92; Judges 13; Mark 1:14-20

The woman gave birth to a boy and named him Samson.
He grew and the Lord blessed him.
And the Spirit of the Lord began to stir him.
JUDGES 13:24–25 NIV

Like the Samson of the Bible, Samson of Dol was strong with Divine power from the time he was a child. He was born about 486 in South Wales, and when he was five, his parents took him to Illtyd's famous school at Llanilltud Fawr, near Cowbridge. There, while he was still in his twenties, he was ordained as deacon and priest. God then directed him to join the monastery of Piro, and from there, somewhat reluctantly, he visited his sick father. As a result of Samson's prayer, his father recovered, and the entire family (with the exception of his youngest sister), devoted themselves to God's service and planted churches. Eventually, Samson succeeded Piro as abbot. He went on a mission to Ireland, and on his return, sent his brother Umbraphel back to be abbot of a monastery in Ireland. While resting with his parents near the River Severn, he was summoned to a synod and ordained a bishop. This (unlike present ecclesiastical practice) freed him to evangelize and travel widely. He longed to go over to Brittany, but when a British Christian prophesied that Samson was first to evangelize Cornwall, he went to Cornwall. Once he did go to Brittany, an amazing number of people became followers of Christ and formed Christian communities. Then Samson traveled as far away as Romania, carrying the Gospel to those who lived there. He returned to Brittany, where he died on July 28, and his remains were kept at the great monastery he had built at Dol.

> In truth his humility, courtesy, and gentleness, and above all his wonderful love, beyond human measure, so to speak, was such that he was regarded by all the brothers with wonderful affection.
> THE LIFE OF SAMSON

We thank you, Lord, that Samson's birth,
schooling, and calling were the fruit of prophecy.
We thank you that his prayer, his heroic acts of witness,
his courtesy and wonderful love toward all
showed so many the way of Christ
and patterned a new way of being the church.
As we contemplate his life, give us a holy renewal.

JULY 29 ✢ GOD IS RELATIONSHIP

Psalm 89:1-18; 2 Kings 1; 1 Timothy 3:14-16

No one can deny how great is the secret of our religion:
Christ was made visible in human form;
was given authority by the Spirit; was perceived by angels.
He was announced to all peoples,
who believed in him throughout the world,
and then he was taken up into the substance of God.
1 TIMOTHY 3:16

Anyone who rejects God's will
is like a leaking ship on a stormy sea,
is like an eagle caught in a trap,
is like an apple tree which never blossoms.
Anyone who obeys God's will
is like the golden rays of the summer sun,
is like a silver chalice overflowing with wine,
is like a beautiful bride ready for love.
TRADITIONAL CELTIC SAYING

Loving Savior, show yourself to us
that knowing you we may love you as warmly in return;
may love you alone, desire you alone,
contemplate you alone by day and night and keep you always in our thoughts.
May affection for you pervade our hearts.
May attachment to you take possession of us all.
May love of you fill all our senses.
May we know no other love except you who are eternal;
a love so great that the many waters of land and sea will fail to quench it.
COLUMBANUS

I believe that God is One.
I believe that God is eternal.
I believe that God is Love.
Therefore I believe that God is relationship.
Therefore I believe that God is community.
Therefore I believe that God is Three.
Each of the Three Persons is God.
Without this God could not be the Highest.
Without this God could not be Eternally Love.

JULY 30 ❖ ALL THINGS THROUGH CHRIST

Psalm 89:19-45; 2 Kings 4:1-7; Mark 1:29-45

*I can do anything and everything
through Christ who gives me strength.*
PHILIPPIANS 4:13

Sometimes, perhaps especially during vacation times when things we normally depend on may not be at hand, we slide into the "anything goes" mentality when we run into difficulties. Learn from a convert of Patrick's named Attracta how to overcome a catalog of woes.

Attracta wanted to build a Christian community in a particular location, but Patrick insisted she establish it somewhere else. This proved to be a place where one disaster after another faced her. She could easily have left in a sulk, telling him, "I told you so," but Attracta was made of sterner stuff. When everyone in the area was terrified of a wild animal that was attacking people left and right, Attracta killed it herself, using her metal cross to do so. When a local bard drowned in the nearby lake, Attracta prayed over him and brought him back to life. When her community had no horses to transport the timber they needed to build the monastery, Attracta used deer instead. When she and her companions realized they had no ropes with which to tie the timber to the wagons, she used everything that was at hand, including strands of her own hair, to create strong cords.

Nothing ventured, nothing gained.
TRADITIONAL BRITISH SAYING

*May the cross of Christ be over this face and this ear.
May the cross of Christ be over this mouth and this throat.
May the cross of Christ be over my arms,
from my shoulders to my hands.
May the cross of Christ be with me, before me.
May the cross of Christ be above me, behind me.
With the cross of Christ may I meet every
difficulty in the heights and in the depths.
From the top of my head to the nail of my foot
I trust in the protection of your cross, O Christ.*
ATTRIBUTED TO MUGRON, ABBOT OF IONA FROM 965

JULY 31 ✣ GLEAMS FROM GLASTONBURY

Psalm 87; Isaiah 12:1-10; Acts 9:26-31

Pray for the peace of Jerusalem.
PSALM 122:6 NIV

The exact details of how Christianity first came to the Britons are shrouded in legend. We cannot know for certain whether it was Joseph of Arimathea who actually brought the faith to England, but scholars do think that Glastonbury, which became known as "England's Jerusalem," probably had the earliest church on the island.

> After Jerusalem's Christians were scattered, the entomber of Christ, the noble commander Joseph, the enlightener of Britain, planted here the Tree of salvation. Gildas the Wise, first writer of the Britons, recounted for us in Tiberius' last year, the coming of the Light. In these islands, . . . the Sun's rays shone. With Aristobulos, first Bishop of Britain, fanning the bright flame of Joseph's kindling, Fagan and Dyfan, for King Lucius the Glorious, restored here the church built by Christ's apostles' hands. Set in the jewel of Avalon, a church of wattles was made by holy hands dedicated by command of Christ to the dearest Mother of God; that in these northern lands this first of churches should honor her who brought humanity's fullness to birth. We give thanks for this cradle place of faith, which drew to it, so 'tis said, holy Irish hermits, David and his fiery zeal which draws still a multitude—saints, sinners, strangers, seekers all.
> . . . Better any number of quests, even if some are illusory, than the arid pretence that there is no quest at all.
> GEOFFREY ASHE, AVALONIAN QUEST

As we enter a new millennium
we pray for the withering of gods that fail us.
May the Christ of the cosmos be to those who quest
also the Christ of the womb, the workshop and the wounds.
May the Christ of the resurrection live in our bodies
now and forever.

AUGUST 1 ✢ LAMMAS

Psalm 85; 2 Kings 2:19-25; Mark 4:26-34

God created everything,
And everything exists through God and for God.
To God be the glory for ever!
ROMANS 11:36

The season of Lammas begins on August 1. In the Celtic year, this marks the first of several harvests. By Samhain, November 1, all the fruits and berries had to be gathered in, but Lammas was the wheat harvest.

Giraldus Cambrensis, Archdeacon of Brecon, described how the people of a locality would come together at harvest to do a circle dance around the churchyard. With mime and movements, they reenacted the occupations connected with the fields—the plowing and reaping. They knew that all life is interconnected, and that all life depends upon God.

Few readers will engage in harvesting in the way the following poem depicts from nineteenth-century western Scotland. Yet as we read these words, God may speak to us of the ways in which the Holy Spirit encompasses the manifold activities of our daily lives—the stores, our offices, our homes, and our neighborhoods; and the chain of people, beasts, and plants that brings food to our tables.

God bless thou thyself my reaping,
each ridge, each plain, each field;
each sickle curved, shapely, hard,
each ear and handful in the sheaf.
Bless each maiden and youth,
each woman and tender youngling.
Safeguard them beneath thy shield of strength
and guard them in the house of the saints;
guard them in the house of the saints.
Encompass each goat, sheep and lamb,
each cow and horse and store.
Surround thou the flocks and herds
and tend them to a kindly fold;
CARMINA GADELICA

AUGUST 2 ❖ WANDERING THOUGHTS

Psalm 90; Job 6:1-24; James 1:16-27

I will be quiet and listen to you.
JOB 6:24 GNT

We should always seek to give our utmost attention to the words of whomever is speaking to us, whether in a conversation, a class, or a church service. Unfortunately, most of us often suffer from wandering thoughts. If you pay attention to why your thoughts wander, however, you can learn from them.

You may be too busy. As you sit back, unattended business comes crowding into your mind. This tells you that you need to do less and make your lifestyle simpler.

Or your thoughts may wander because you have repressed "primal inner material"; when you sit quietly, this pops up to the surface. Take hold of whatever comes into your mind asking for attention, and get to know the thing that has been repressed or unacknowledged. Let Jesus pray with you for it.

Your wandering thoughts may be also caused by a flood of creativity pouring through you. If so, write down the thoughts and the inspirations that are coming to you, so that you can do something with them as soon as you have opportunity. Then set them aside for now.

Last, your wandering thoughts may simply be caused by the fact that the human brain is made like that—in which case there is not much you can do about it! Bless whatever thought has wandered into your mind . . . and bless it as it wanders on its way. Then bless God for the present moment, and return to being fully attentive to it.

God help my thoughts!
They stray from me, setting off on the wildest journeys.
They run off like naughty children,
quarrelling, making trouble.
When I read the Bible, they fly to a distant city,
filled with beautiful women.
They slip from my grasp like tails of eels;
they swoop hither and thither like swallows in flight.
Dear, chaste Christ,
who can see into every heart and read every mind,
take hold of my thoughts.
Bring my thoughts back to me and clasp me to yourself.
PRAYER OF A CELTIC MONK

AUGUST 3 ✣ TAMING THE WILD BEASTS

Psalm 91; 2 Samuel 21; Mark 11:1-13

Jesus said: You will find an untamed colt.
Untie it and bring it here.
If someone asks you why you are untying it,
tell him the Master needs it.
LUKE 19:30–31

Tame pigs and goats and baby pigs
at home all round it.
And wild pigs also, tall deer and their does,
badgers and their brood.
In peaceful parties,
crowds from the country visit my home.
FROM A POEM OF MARBAN THE HERMIT

Kevin's desire for solitude was realized when he made his home in the cave near the two lakes of Glendalough. There he developed close relationships with even the wildest animals.

It was said that when he prayed for an hour every night in the cold lake water, a monster distracted and annoyed him by curling itself around his body, biting and stinging him. Another story tells of a monster in the Lower Lake that brought terror to the people who lived there. Kevin did not banish this creature as an enemy, but instead, he took it with him to the Upper Lake. There, his prayers, his patience, and the warmth of God's love in him made the monster feel it no longer had any need to be hostile.

This story can also be understood as a picture of our inner life. We all have dark or wild monsters lurking within us, things we dare not face. Kevin teaches us to embrace the shadow side of our lives without fear. As we accept all that lives within our depths, even that which seems terrifying or hostile, we can be at peace.

Lord, help me to understand my own story,
to fear nothing except fear itself
and to live at peace
with myself, the creatures, and the world.

AUGUST 4 ✢ GENTLE PERSUASION

Psalm 89:46-52; Proverbs 15:1-18; Mark 10:13-16

A gentle answer turns away wrath, but a harsh word stirs up anger.
PROVERBS 15:1 NIV

Saint Molua, who died in Ireland on August 4 in the seventh century, was known for using gentle persuasion rather than strictly imposed rules. When a bard named Conan, who was unaccustomed to manual labor, joined Molua's monastery in the Slieve mountains, Molua personally accompanied him on his first day to a thicket of thistles that needed to be cut down. That day they cut down only one thistle. On the second day, they cut down two, and so it went on, until Conan became used to the labor.

Molua was not afraid to reprove a person when necessary, but he always tried to do it with gentleness, and in God's way, knowing that God always has the last word. When the king of Leinster arrived at Molua's monastery with four hundred of his men and demanded that they be instantly fed, Molua patiently explained why that would be difficult. The king, however, insisted, and food was brought as quickly as was possible, no doubt causing considerable disruption to the life of the community. The very first morsel the king tasted, however, stuck in his gullet for twenty-four hours, preventing him from either eating or sleeping. The king learned his lesson without anything more having to be said. From that time on, he became thoughtful and generous toward Molua's community.

Lord, help me
to take the time to sit in the shoes of the other person.
To start from where they are.
To listen to what they feel.
To refrain from the too hasty judgment
or the too ready answer.
To smile and be gentle
and yet not to collude with the slipshod
but to prayerfully see each thing through.

AUGUST 5 ❖ KINGLY QUALITIES

Psalm 72; 2 Kings 9:1-13; Mark 2:35-39

The Lord has sought out a man after the Lord's own heart to be the leader of God's people.
1 SAMUEL 13:14

When the ambitious King Cadwallon slew the two kings of Northumbria, Oswald, the brother of one of them and a man beloved of God, arrived with a small army to oppose the invader. He placed a large cross in the ground, and as he held the cross, he addressed the whole army. "Let us all kneel, and together pray the true and ever-living God to defend us from a proud and cruel enemy. For God knows that this is a just war we fight in order to liberate our people." They won the victory against huge odds, and the place of battle is called Heavenfield to this day. Heaven's standard was set up there, Heaven's victory won, and Heaven's miracles continued. Many people were healed when splinters from this cross mingled with water were brought to them.

Oswald initiated a mission to his kingdom from Iona, and cared for the poor. He was deeply devout and rose early each day to pray. Under his rule, the previously warring kingdoms of Bernicia and Deira became one peaceful people, although ethnic cleansing was normal in those days in other parts. When Oswald died, still young, on the battlefield, his dying prayer was for the souls of his soldiers, not for himself. In succeeding centuries, peoples throughout Europe longed for examples of Christian kingship, and Oswald became a model far and wide. Many churches in the European Union are still dedicated to St. Oswald.

King Baudouin of the Belgians once told a friend that his purpose in being king was this: to love his country; to pray for his country; to suffer for his country. At Baudouin's funeral in 1993, Cardinal Suenens said, "We were in the presence of one who was more than a king; one who was a shepherd of his people."

Few of us are kings—but nevertheless we each have our own small realms of authority. Do we seek to shepherd those realms?

High King of heaven and earth,
from whom all authority flows,
may the diverse authorities of our times
acknowledge you as the Source of life,
emulate you as the Servant King
and fear you as the Judge of truth.

AUGUST 6 ✢ TRANSFIGURATION

Psalm 93; 2 Kings 2:1-18; Mark 9:2-13

*Jesus was transfigured before them,
and his face shone like the sun,
and his clothes became white as light.*
MATTHEW 17:2 NIV

The Feast of the Transfiguration is August 6. That is also the day we happened to drop the bomb on Hiroshima. We took Christ's Body and we took his Blood, and we enacted a Cosmic Golgotha. We took the key to love and we used it for bloody hell.

Suppose the material order is indeed the garment of Christ, the temple of the Holy Spirit. Suppose the bread and wine, symbols of all creation, are indeed capable of redemption awaiting its Christification. Then what is the atom but the emergent body of Christ?
GEORGE MACCLEOD

On the Feast of the Transfiguration may we be able to pray together for the redemption of the whole creation and a speedy end to the suffering of animals through human exploitation.
MARJORIE MILNE OF GLASTONBURY

The poet Waldo Williams treasured the moment which like a shooting star makes us wonderfully conscious of the mystery and vastness and glory of the universe, the moment which suddenly reveals a presence and suddenly enchants the heart, the second which makes true acquaintance shine.
PENNAR DAVIES

*When the Savior of this globe
was stretched out on the Tree of death,
the elements erupted and the earth gave up its dead.
His blood, spilled on the soil, transfigured earth and heaven.
May his body and blood change us and transfigure this earth.
Transfigure this earth: may your kingdom come on it.
Transfigure this earth: may flowers bloom on it.
Transfigure this earth: may people and animals be friends on it.
Transfigure this earth: may the scarred places be healed on it.
Transfigure this earth: may peace reign on it.
Transfigure this earth: may our bodies be changed into bodies of resurrection.*
FROM A CELTIC EUCHARIST, THE COMMUNITY OF AIDAN AND HILDA

AUGUST 7 ✥ GOD TOOK THE EARTH

Psalm 95; Genesis 1:1–25; John 9:1–11

God commanded "Let the earth produce all kinds of plants. . . .
Let the earth produce all kinds of animals. . . ."
God took of the earth and created a human.
GENESIS 1:11, 24; 2:7 GNT

The earth where King Oswald died was said to have been soaked in his sanctity so that it became a fertile seedbed. The soil from that spot seemed to have power to make the grass grow greener, to resist fire, and to heal all sorts of people. A sick horse and a sick girl were cured by touching the soil.

Soil and sanctity, humus and human, earth and healing growth—we separate these connections at our peril.

The earth is at the same time mother.
She is the mother of all that is natural,
mother of all that is human.
She is the mother of all for contained in her are the seeds of all.
In me be the truth of stream-lover willow, soil-giving alder,
hazel of sweet nuts, wisdom-branching oak.
In me be the joy of crab apple, great maple, vine maple,
cleansing cascara and lovely dogwood.
And the gracious truth of the copper-branched arbutus,
bright with color and fragrance,
be with me on the Earth.
CHINOOK PSALTER

The earth of humankind contains all moisture,
all verdancy, all germinating power.
It is in so many ways fruitful.
All creation comes from it
yet it forms not only the basic raw materials for humankind
but also the substance of the incarnation of God's son.
HILDEGAARD OF BINGEN

God of the earth,
forgive us for becoming proud and disconnected
from your seedbed of wisdom, nourishment, and life.
Help us always to know and feel that we are of the earth.
May we live this day as your humus.

AUGUST 8 ❖ THE EARTH IS THE LORD'S

Psalm 98; Genesis 2:4-14; Mark 4:1-9

*Then the Lord God took some soil from the ground
and formed a man out of it;
he breathed life-giving breath into his nostrils and the man began to live.*
GENESIS 2:7 GNT

Teach your children what we have taught our children:
that the earth is our mother.
Whatever befalls the earth
befalls the sons and daughters of the earth.
If men spit upon the ground, they spit upon themselves.
This we know.
The earth does not belong to us; we belong to the earth.
This we know.
All things are connected
like the blood which unites one family.
All things are connected.
We did not weave the web of life.
We are merely a strand in it.
Whatever we do to the web, we do to ourselves.
CHIEF SEATTLE

Holy persons draw to themselves all that is earthly.
HILDEGAARD OF BINGEN

May all I say and all I think
be in harmony with you,
God within me, God beyond me, maker of the trees.
CHINOOK PSALTER

*The food which we are to eat is earth, water, and sun
coming to us through pleasing plants.
The food which we are to eat
is fruit of the labor of many creatures.
We are thankful for it.
May it give us health, strength, joy,
and may it increase our love.*
A UNITARIAN PRAYER BEFORE A MEAL

AUGUST 9 ✢ SOARING LIKE EAGLES

Psalm 104:1-18; Isaiah 40:21-31; Luke 10:17-24

Those whose hope is in the Lord shall soar like eagles.
ISAIAH 40:31

If you want to know the Creator, understand created things.
COLUMBANUS

The beauty of the trees,
the softness of the air,
the fragrance of the grass
speak to me.

The summit of the mountain,
the thunder of the sky,
the rhythm of the sea
speak to me.

The faintness of the stars,
the freshness of the morning,
the dewdrops on the flower
speak to me.

The strength of fire,
the taste of salmon,
the trail of the sun
and the life that never goes away,
they speak to me.
And my heart soars.
CHIEF DAN GEORGE

My dear King, my own King, without pride, without sin,
you created the whole world, eternal, victorious King.
King above the elements, King above the sun, King beneath the ocean,
King of the north and south, the east and west,
against you no enemy can prevail.
And you created us to be your stewards of the earth,
and we praise you for your boundless love.
THE CELTIC PSALTER

AUGUST 10 ✥ JAWS

Psalm 114; 2 Kings 6:1-7; Mark 4:35-41

*No one helped God spread out the heavens
or trample the sea monster's back....
We cannot understand the great things God does;
there is no end to the miracles God can do.*
JOB 9:8, 10 GNT

When Berach was planning to sail the always-risky journey from Iona to Tiree, he asked Columba to bless his journey. Columba looked at him long and hard. "Take special care not to cross the open sea today in a straight course. Otherwise you will meet an enormous monster who will terrify you—and well nigh overwhelm you. Go in a zigzag around the smaller islands."

Berach set off, but, since everything looked fine and it seemed so much easier to go the direct route, he disregarded Columba's advice. A few hours later, however, an immense whale rose up like a mountain in front of the crew and opened its gaping jaws. The sailors let down the sail in terror and rowed for their lives. In the future, Berach weighed God's prophetic words more carefully!

Baithene had to make a similar journey, but unlike Berach, his impulses were in harmony with God's. On the morning of Baithene's departure, Columba told him and his crew about the whale.

"That beast and I are both under God's power," said Baithene.

"Go in peace," said Columba. "Your faith in Christ will defend you from this peril."

Later, those on the ship did in fact see the whale. The crew was terrified, but Baithene himself was without fear. He raised his hands and blessed both the sea and the whale. At that precise moment, the whale plunged under the waves, and they did not see it again.

*God aid me,
God succor me
when near the reefs.
The Son of God shield me from harm.
The Son of God shield me from ill.
The Son of God shield me from mishap.
The Son of God shield me with power.
The Son of God shield me with might.*
CARMINA GADELICA

AUGUST 11 ✥ KEVIN AND THE BLACKBIRD

Psalm 101; 1 Kings 17; Luke 12:1–7

God hasn't forgotten a single one of these sparrows...
yet you are worth more to God than a whole flock of sparrows.
LUKE 12:6–7

And then there was St. Kevin and the blackbird.
The saint is kneeling, arms stretched out, inside
his cell, but the cell is so narrow, so
one turned–up palm is out the window, stiff
as a cross–beam, when a blackbird lands
and lays in it and settles down to rest.
Kevin feels the warm eggs, the small breast, the tucked
neat head and claws and, finding himself linked
into the network of eternal life,
is moved to pity: Now he must hold his hand
like a branch out in the sun and rain for weeks
until the young are hatched and fledged and flown.
SEAMUS HEANEY

O, King of the Tree of Life,
the blossoms on the branches are your people,
the singing birds are your angels,
the whispering breeze is your Spirit.
O, King of the Tree of Life,
may the blossoms bring forth the sweetest fruit,
may the birds sing out the highest praise.
May your Spirit cover all with gentle breath.
TRADITIONAL CELTIC PRAYER

AUGUST 12 ✣ JEROME AND THE LION

Psalm 104:19-35; Isaiah 65:17-25; Luke 19:1-10

*Cows and bears will eat together,
and their calves and cubs will lie down in peace.*
ISAIAH 11:7 GNT

Saint Jerome, the fourth-century Roman Christian, shared the Celtic saints' understanding of animals as fellow creatures in God's kingdom. One night when he was saying the evening prayer with his brothers in the monastery at Bethlehem, a large lion limped into the cloisters with an injured paw. Jerome took the paw in his hand, turned it over, and found a festering wound.

The brothers bathed the cuts and tended the lion—and the lion made himself at home! This caused considerable discussion among the brothers. Jerome's conclusion was this: "God has sent us this lion to show that the Lord wants to look after us. So instead of worrying about having a lion here, let us give it something useful to do."

The brothers came up with a good idea: each day their donkey would take the lion with him to pasture, and the lion would guard the donkey from any who might steal or harm it. This arrangement worked well until one day the lion fell asleep and some traveling merchants stole the donkey. After this, the lion took to pacing back and forth, roaring, and at night it would hang around outside the monastery, sighing and groaning.

Meanwhile, some of the brothers assumed the lion had eaten the donkey, and they insisted he should be banished. Jerome, however, thought that Christians should not judge others, even lions, without evidence. So the monks continued to give the lion care and food, and they gave him a new job: to go every day with a harness to fetch branches from the wood. The lion did this faithfully, but he still longed for the donkey.

One day, from miles away, he saw the same traders who had stolen the donkey coming toward the monastery, with the donkey leading the way. With a great roar, the lion bounded toward them. The men fled in terror, and the lion brought the donkey, as well as the laden camels, back to the monastery.

Soon, the shamefaced traders arrived to ask for their goods and camels. They begged forgiveness and offered the brothers expensive gifts. Jerome refused the gifts and gently explained that the best way they could show their appreciation was always to thank God for his provisions . . . and never to take what belongs to others.

*Lord, give me gentleness toward all creatures,
integrity in my dealings,
and the wisdom to handle unsettling situations.*

AUGUST 13 ✥ BRYNACH AND HIS STAGS

Psalm 117; Deuteronomy 31:30-32:14; Matthew 6:24-34

> *Swear by the swift deer and the gazelles*
> *that you will not interrupt our love.*
> SONG OF SONGS 3:5 GNT

Brynach, a hermit in sixth-century Pembrokeshire, now and then would feel God leading him to move on and make another little hermitage, which he would furnish with his meager belongings. Each time he changed his hermitage, Brynach would have to transport his furniture, books, and kitchenware. Moving is always a chore, even for hermits!

Brynach had no human or worldly support, but he had developed such a harmony with creation that he felt the wild animals were his support network. So when the time came for a move, he would invite two of the friendliest stags from the nearby herd to help him. With his furniture tied on their backs, the stags went ahead of Brynach to his new abode. When he took the yoke off them, they returned to their herd.

Brynach also selected an especially productive cow and introduced her to a wolf who was a friend of his. Each day, the wolf would lead this one cow to a particularly lush patch of pasture, and then he would bring it back in the evening. In this way, Brynach always had ample milk, and a good security system.

This Pembrokeshire hermit emerges from the mists of legend as a person at peace with both the natural and the supernatural world. He was also said to frequently meet with angels on the mountain between Nevern and Newport, which became known as the Mount of Angels (*Carn Ingli*).

> *Almighty Creator, you have made all creatures.*
> *The world cannot express,*
> *even though the grasses and trees should sing,*
> *all your glories, provisions, and riches.*
> *O Lord, how glorious you are.*

AUGUST 14 ✣ MELANGELL AND THE HARE

Psalm 94; Numbers 35:9-34; Mark 5:21-43

*The Lord said to Moses, "Choose six cities of refuge
for Israelites and for foreigners."*
NUMBERS 35:13, 15

Melangell, the daughter of an Irish king, fled to Wales in order to escape a forced marriage. She settled as a hermit for Christ at Pennant in Powys.

In 604, the prince of Powys went hunting at Pennant, and his hounds chased a hare into the thicket of thorns where Melangell had built her hermit's hut. When he followed the hounds, he discovered Melangell, sheltering the hare under the folds of her cloak as she prayed. The prince shouted to his hounds to catch the hare, but they must have sensed a presence more powerful than their instincts, for they gradually went further and further away, despite all their owner's shouting.

The prince was astonished. He asked the young woman who she was, and Melangell told him her story. He was so impressed that he said to her, "Because Almighty God was pleased to protect this little hare through you, I will give you land you may use for the service of God, and also as an animal sanctuary."

This, according to tradition, is the reason why Pennant Melangell became a place of sanctuary for humans as well as for animals. Melangell remained a hermit there for another thirty-seven years. Her biographer states, "And the hares, wild little animals, just the same as tame animals, were in a state of familiarity with her every day throughout her whole life."

*Lord, you look after even the smallest of your creatures
and even the least of your children.
You are our refuge. With you we are safe.
I pray for all people suffering abuse in their homes,
for all animals who are mistreated
and for myself.
Protect us from all that would harm
either body or soul today.*

AUGUST 15 ✢ PIRAN'S ANIMAL MONASTERY

Psalm 99; 2 Kings 4:8-37; Luke 12:22-34

*Wolves and sheep will live together in peace,
and leopards will lie down with young goats.*
ISAIAH 11:6 GNT

When Piran arrived in Cornwall, he lay down to sleep under a tree where a wild boar was accustomed to rest. At first, the wild boar was frightened and kept away, but soon it sensed the childlike love in Piran, and they became friends. Piran thought of the boar as his first monk, and the boar did, indeed, become a servant of the community. It tore branches and grass with its teeth with which to make a simple cell. Soon, other forest animals—a fox, a badger, a wolf, and a doe—came along to join Piran and the boar. Piran regarded them all as his monks.

However, as you might expect, the fox was more crafty than the others. He abandoned the "monastery," stealing Piran's shoes as he left, and chewed the shoes back at his old lair. Piran talked to the badger about this, and the badger went to the fox, sank his teeth into his fur, and pulled him back to Piran's cell.

"Why have you done this, my brother, which is something a monk should never do?" Piran asked the fox. "We all share the same water and the same food—and if you were hungry, God would have turned the bark of this tree into food for you." The fox repented, and he showed his penitence by refraining from eating until Piran gave permission. From then on, all the animals lived at peace with Piran as their "abbot."

*Deep harmony of the forest be mine.
Child-like love for God's creatures be mine.
Growing trust in God's providence be mine.*

AUGUST 16 ⁜ THE MONK AND HIS PET CAT

Psalm 100; Genesis 7; Mark 2:1–12

Noah and his wife went into the boat with their three sons. . . .
With them went every kind of animal,
domestic and wild, large and small.
GENESIS 7:13–14 GNT

I and my white Pangur
have each his special art:
his mind is set on hunting mice,
mine is upon my special craft.
When in our house we two are all alone—
a tale without tedium!
We have sport never-ending!
Something to exercise our wit.
At times by feats of derring-do
a mouse sticks in his net,
while into my net there drops
a difficult problem of hard meaning.
He points his full shining eye
against the fence of the wall:
I point my clear though feeble eye
against the keenness of science.
He rejoices with quick leaps
when in his sharp claw sticks a mouse:
I too rejoice when I have grasped
a problem difficult and dearly loved.
Though we are thus at all times,
neither hinders the other,
each of us pleased with his own art
amuses himself alone.
He is a master of the work
which every day he does:
while I am at my own work
to bring difficulty to clearness.
KUNO MEYER (TRANS.), THESAURUS PALAEOHIBERNUS

Creator God, may I share creation's fun with you.

AUGUST 17 ✢ SAMSON AND THE SERPENT

Psalm 121:2 Kings 4:38-44; Mark 16:9-20

Believers will be given the power to perform miracles...
if they pick up snakes or drink any poison, they will not be harmed.
MARK 16:17-18 GNT

After Samson's father had been healed of a serious illness, he, his wife, his brother, and his brother's three sons all turned to the Lord. Samson and his family then set out on a journey to tell others about Christ. One day, according to legend, they came to a point in their track that bore signs of burning and destruction from a notorious serpent. Full of apprehension, the family discussed what to do. Samson reminded them of Jesus' promise: "If you have faith even as small as a mustard seed you can tell this mountain to move and it will."

"Wait here, calmly," he told them, "while I go off and try to hear from God on this matter." Fearing for his safety, Samson's uncle tried to go with him, but Samson told him, "Stay with the others until I return in triumph."

Samson saw the fire-spitting serpent in a far-off valley. He went toward it, reciting scriptures such as, "The Lord is my light and my salvation." With great swishings and hissings, the serpent twisted and grabbed its own tail in its teeth. A lump of earth flew past Samson's face, but he made a Circle Prayer around the creature for protection and placed a cross in the ground. Now the serpent reared up with a terrible hiss, as if it had been pierced with a sword, and then gathered itself into a ball, once more savagely biting its own tail with its teeth. Samson continued quietly to sing psalms, holding his staff firmly in the ground.

The others arrived and stood watching from a distance. "Come nearer," Samson told them, "so that you may develop faith in faith." They crept closer and witnessed an uncanny sight: the serpent slowly uncoiled and slithered along the ground until it came to Samson's staff. Over and over again it did the same thing, but never could it raise its head or go beyond the staff. This went on all through the day, while Samson used the time to teach his family, building up their faith with advice such as, "Those who believe in the Creator ought not to fear the creature."

Eventually, as twilight came, Samson said to the serpent, "We have a long journey, but you have no longer to live. In Jesus' name, I command you to die now!" At once the serpent raised its head, as if making a final bow, cast forth all its venom, and lay down dead.

Lord, may I grow more valiant, day by day, starting today.

AUGUST 18 ✢ MALO, A WREN, AND PIGLETS

Psalm 128; 2 Kings 3:1–20; Luke 6:37–45

Give to others, and God will give to you.
Indeed, you will receive a full measure,
a generous helping, poured into your hands—all that you can hold.
LUKE 6:38 GNT

Malo's travels through Brittany to spread the Word of God to humans kept him busy, but he had time for birds and animals too. Far from detracting from his mission, this helped it along.

Malo earned his keep by doing seasonal work in the vineyards. Once, when he came to pick up his coat after he had finished work, he found a wren had laid an egg in it. He decided to leave the coat just where it was until the egg hatched, along with the subsequent eggs that were laid there. No rain fell during the whole time the coat was in the open. The vineyard workers were touched both by Malo's care for the wrens and by Heaven's care of his coat.

On another occasion during Malo's travels, he came across a farm laborer weeping in grief in a meadow, surrounded by piglets and fearful to return to his boss. The mother of the piglets had run amok, trampling down the corn in a neighboring farmer's field. The well-meaning swineherd tried to chase it out of the field by throwing a large stone at it. Unfortunately, the stone hit the pig in just the wrong place, and it died. Now the piglets were trying in vain to find milk from their dead mother. Malo's heart went out to the swineherd, and his prayer went up to God. Malo stretched out his staff and laid it on the ear of the dead sow. The sow was restored to life and got up on its four legs. The emotions of the swineherd went from one extreme to the other: now he was almost delirious with joy, and he hurried to tell his employer and everyone he possibly could all about Malo and what had happened. The farmer personally came to thank Malo and offered him one of his farms as a place to build a new Christian community.

Lord, take away all penny-pinching from me.
Give me a generous heart and a helping hand
for every person and every creature I meet.
And thank you that this will bring blessing.

AUGUST 19 ❖ A COCK, A MOUSE, AND A FLY

Psalm 113; 2 Kings 8:1-6; Matthew 6:16-23

Do not store up riches for yourselves here on earth, where moths and rust destroy, and robbers break in and steal. Instead, store up riches for yourselves in heaven, where moths and rust cannot destroy, and robbers cannot break in and steal. For your heart will always be where your riches are.
MATTHEW 6:19–21 GNT

A friend of Columba's, Mo Chua, had a hermitage in the wilderness. Although he was on his own, he did his best to say the divine prayers at set times throughout the day and night. He had no worldly wealth, but he did have a rooster, a mouse, and a fly, each of which performed a most useful work for him.

All alone as he was, it could have been difficult for him to keep track of the time. But the rooster woke him in time to say early morning prayer. Mo Chua might well have slept through the night vigils, but the mouse always nibbled his ear every five hours, which made sure his master got up! Then the fly, not to be outdone, would walk along every line of the psalm book as Mo Chua read it, so he would not lose his place. Whenever Mo had paused, the fly rested in the same place until Mo began to sing the psalm again.

The time came when these three small treasures died. Mo wrote a letter to Columba, sharing these little bereavements with his friend, and Columba did not brush off his sorrow as trifling or ridiculous. He replied: "Brother, you must not be too taken aback by the death of this flock that has been taken from you, for misfortune only comes where there are riches."

Thank you, Lord, for the little messengers of blessing that you send
(If only I have eyes to see)
from all around me.
When I lose these little comforts and familiar supports,
help me to turn my eyes to you,
who is the Source of all true blessings
and my true and lasting Treasure.

AUGUST 20 ✢ OSWIN AND THE HORSE

Psalm 138; 2 Kings 6:8-23: Mark 6:30-44

*As believers in our glorious Lord Jesus Christ
don't show favoritism.*
JAMES 2:1 NIV

Oswin, who was king of Deira for seven years of great prosperity, was tall, handsome, and courteous, a man of pleasant conversation who treated people from all backgrounds in an open manner. As a result, everyone loved him. He was especially graced with the virtues that spring from self-denial, and in particular, with humility, as the following episode illustrates.

King Oswin had given a well-bred horse to Bishop Aidan so that, although it was Aidan's custom to walk, he could ride it across rivers or for urgent missions. Not long afterward, however, Aidan met a poor beggar and gave him the horse with all its expensive trappings, for Aidan was always like a father to those in need.

Oswin heard the story that evening while he was warming himself by the fire before dinner. He turned to Aidan and demanded, "Why did you give the royal horse to a beggar? We have other things and less valuable horses that can be given to the poor without giving away the horse that I specially chose for your own use."

"What are you saying?" Aidan replied. "Surely that son of a mare is not more precious to you than that son of God?"

Aidan's words smote Oswin's heart; he threw down his sword, fell at Aidan's feet, and asked his forgiveness. "Never again," he said, "will I speak of this or pass judgment on what wealth of mine you should give to God's children."

Aidan was moved to tears by these words. When a priest asked him why he was weeping, Aidan answered, "I know that the king has not long to live. I have never seen a humble king before, and I therefore expect he will soon be taken from this life. This nation does not deserve to have such a ruler." This grim prophecy was, indeed, shortly fulfilled, on August 20. Eleven days later, Aidan himself died, perhaps in part from a broken heart.

*Lord, help me to look upon each person I meet
as a child of God.
To treat each person as a royal soul
and to share with each person in the way you desire.*

AUGUST 21 ✧ CUTHBERT AND THE OTTERS

Psalm 141; 2 Kings 5:1-19; Revelation 4

Human beings have been able to tame wild animals and birds,
reptiles and fish, but no human being can tame the tongue.
JAMES 3:7-8

Ebba, who was King Oswy's sister, kept inviting Cuthbert to stay at her monastery at Coldingham, and eventually he came for a few days. While there, however, he continued his lifestyle exactly as usual. This included going out alone at night to pray while the other members of the community slept, returning just before the community's early morning prayer.

One night, one of the brothers saw him slip out, and curiosity got the better of him. He wanted to know where Cuthbert was going and what he was doing, so he secretly followed him. This benevolent spy saw Cuthbert walk to the shore below the monastery and wade into the sea until the waves lapped at his neck and outstretched arms. Cuthbert spent all the hours of darkness like this, either in silent vigil or singing God's praises, accompanied by the sound of the waves.

When dawn approached, the brother spied Cuthbert go onto the beach and kneel in prayer. Two sea otters came out of the sea at the same time. They stretched themselves out on the sand in front of Cuthbert, and then they began to warm his feet with their breath. They rubbed against him and dried him with their fur. Once he had received the otter's services, Cuthbert blessed them, and they slid back into the sea. Cuthbert returned to the monastery and sang the morning prayer on time with everyone else.

However, the brother who had watched all this from the cliff top was stricken with panic that he had behaved with such slyness toward a holy man. Knowing that God's Word teaches Christ's followers to walk in the light with one another, the next morning the monk flung himself down before Cuthbert and asked him to forgive him for what he had done. Although the brother didn't say what it was that he had done, Cuthbert guessed. He assured the other man that he would forgive him on one condition: that he tell no one what he had seen until after Cuthbert's death. The brother kept his promise not to tell anyone while Cuthbert was alive—but once Cuthbert died, he told absolutely everybody!

Holy are you, O Lord.
When we are one with you, your creatures become one with us.
Help me to be so truly at one with you
that even my most unruly member, the tongue,
becomes at one too.

AUGUST 22 ❖ BRIGID AND THE FOX

Psalm 116; 2 Kings 6:24-7:7; Mark 6:14-29

My servant... will set free those who sit in dark prisons.
ISAIAH 42:1, 7 GNT

A local Irish king loved to show off a tame fox whenever he had a special occasion. It was a favorite court mascot that had learned all sorts of tricks.

One day, a simple man who knew nothing of this, saw the fox and killed it. He neither realized whose was the fox nor why such a large crowd gathered round to watch him kill it. Some of the crowd, of course, immediately reported him to the king, who was furious beyond measure. The king ordered the man's wife and children to be sold as slaves, their home to be taken, and the man to be executed—unless the king received a replacement fox just as skilled, which seemed an impossible condition.

When Brigid heard of this, her heart bled for the man and his family. She took her carriage and did a "prayer ride" along the road to the king's court, pouring forth prayers for the poor family, asking God to turn around the situation. As she was praying, a fox appeared, jumped into her carriage, and sat quietly beside Brigid under her cloak.

Brigid arrived at the king's castle and implored him to revoke his sentence and release the whole family. The king was adamant that he would only release them if he got a fox that was as clever and tame as the one he had lost. That was Brigid's cue; to the amazement of everyone, she brought her fox to the center of the court. The fox entertained everyone with just the same sort of tricks the other fox had. The king was so pleased that he ordered the man and his family to be released.

But who had the last word? According to the story, once the object of Brigid's prayers had been achieved, the wily fox slunk away, never to be seen again!

Father, so many people walk through life
with their feet in fetters, weighed down with unjust burdens,
captives in prisons of body or spirit.
Pour out your compassion,
through your creatures and through us,
that we may be instruments to set others free.

AUGUST 23 ✣ POETRY

Psalm 118:1-18; 2 Kings 12:1-23; Mark 6:7-13

Beautiful words fill my mind, as I compose this song for the king.
Like the pen of a good writer my tongue is ready with a poem.
PSALM 45:1 GNT

He is my king, in my heart he's hid,
he is my joy all joys amid.
I am a drop in his ocean lost,
his coracle I, on his wide sea tossed.
A leaf in his storm.
The book of his praise in my wallet slung,
the cloak of his friendship round me flung.
Hither and thither about I'm blown,
my way an eddy my rest a stone
and he my fire.
My meat his work and my drink his will.
He is my song, my strength, my skill,
and all folk my lovers in good and ill
through him my desire.
In the track of the wind I trace his feet
and none of his coming was e'er so fleet,
so sweet.
Often my heart is a heavy stone,
mocked, trodden under and spat upon.
My way a murk, and I alone, alone.
Then in my heart flames a climbing star
as his pilgrim feet come flashing far
to bring me where the blessed are.
He is the cleft in the dark sky riven
whereby I may leap to the bending heaven
through the storm.
MARJORIE MILNE, RHYMES FROM A LINDISFARNE MONK

King, you created heaven according to your delight,
a place that is safe and pure,
its air filled with the songs of angels.
THE CELTIC PSALTER

AUGUST 24 ❖ Rhythms

Psalm 118:19-29; 2 Kings 18:1-19; Mark 8:1-13

Praise the Lord, you servants of the Lord,
... from the rising of the sun to its going down.
PSALM 113:1, 3

Christ's Celtic followers were in touch with the rhythms of each day of the week and of the seasons, both of nature and of the church. Saturday was a day of Sabbath rest and Sunday a day of resurrection and renewal; the seasons of planting and harvest, Christmas and Easter all gave meaning to their lives. They also understood the rhythms of advance in active mission and retreat into contemplation. This same sense of rhythm filled both their worship and their poetry.

The focus of the following poem is Lindisfarne, the tidal island on Britain's coast that reflects the ebb and flow of the sea, but God can inspire each of us to discover such a rhythm wherever we are today.

> Ebb tide, full tide, praise the Lord of land and sea.
> Barren rocks, darting birds, praise his holy name!
> Poor folk, ruling folk, praise the Lord of land and sea.
> Pilgrimed sands, sea-shelled strands, praise his holy name!
> Fierce lions, gentle lambs, praise the Lord of land and sea.
> Noble women, mission priests, praise his holy name!
> Chanting boys, slaves set free, praise the Lord of land and sea.
> Old and young and all the land, praise his holy name!
>
> Ebb tide, full tide,
> let life's rhythms flow.
> Full tide, ebb tide,
> how life's beat must go.
> DAVID ADAM

Here be the peace of those who do your will;
here be the peace of brother serving other;
here be the peace of holy ones obeying;
here be the peace of praise by dark and day.
ST AIDAN'S PRAYER FOR HOLY ISLAND (ADAPTED)

AUGUST 25 ✢ How Do We Know God's Laws?

Psalm 19; 2 Kings 22; Romans 1:18–32

Ever since God created the world, God's invisible qualities,
divine nature, and eternal power have been clearly seen;
they are perceived in the things God has made.
ROMANS 1:20 GNT

Question: What is best in this world?
Answer: To do the will of our Maker.
Question: What is his will?
Answer: That we should live according to the laws of his creation.
Question: How do we know those laws?
Answer: By study—studying the Scriptures with devotion.
Question: What tool has our Maker provided for this study?
Answer: The intellect which can probe everything.
Question: And what is the fruit of study?
Answer: To perceive the eternal Word of God reflected in every plant and insect, every bird and animal, and every man and woman.
NINIAN'S CATECHISM

Apprehend God in all things
for God is in all things.
Every single creature is full of God and is a book about God.
Every creature is a word of God.
If I spent enough time with the tiniest creature—
even a caterpillar—
I would never have to prepare a sermon.
So full of God is every creature.
MEISTER ECKHART

Teach me my God and King
in all things thee to see,
And what I do, in anything
I'll do it as for thee.
GEORGE HERBERT

AUGUST 26 ✣ SHINING LIKE A STAR

Psalm 119:25-40; 2 Kings 23:21-30; Mark 3:13-35

Those who lead many to righteousness will shine like the stars for ever.
DANIEL 12:3 NLT

God omnipotent, who had scattered shining lights upon the world, gave many bright stars to his people in Britain. Brilliant among these was Ninian. He was outstanding in strength derived from heaven, in miracles, eloquence, and reliance on the gift of God. People came together in vast crowds and opened their hearts to believe in Christ and to follow his teachings.

On his way back to his native Galloway in 398, after training and ordination in Rome, Ninian stayed at the "fellowship of service" established by St. Martin of Tours, and this became his abiding inspiration.

He became a revered teacher and won multitudes of Picts to Christ. They worshipped graven images in the shadow of death until he converted them through his holy living. They all vied with each other to be bathed in the baptismal water and to be cleansed from the stain of their sin in the everlasting fountain.

Ninian established many new churches and monasteries, and instructed these "kingdoms at the ends of the earth" with his teaching.

After a time he left the Pictish nations and came to his own people, the Britons. To them he was a good shepherd, tending his sheepfold with mind and hand, eager to protect from the enemy the flocks entrusted to his care. He built "the Shining House," with its foundation of burnt bricks and lofty walls, in the midst of which he sparkled and shone forth like a star. This is the house which many are eager to visit, for many who have long been afflicted with disease hurry there, eager to accept the ready gifts of health-giving healing.

FROM THE EIGHTH-CENTURY MIRACLES OF BISHOP NINIAN BY AN ANONYMOUS MONK OF WHITHORN

*I pray for modern Ninians who will establish
communities of light in slum places;
sanctuaries of prayer in unvisited places;
links of faith and love with our spiritual home.
And, Lord, begin with me.*

AUGUST 27 ✢ The Blind Can See

Psalm 119:41–56; 2 Kings 24; Mark 10:46–52

A blind man named Bartimaeus shouted, "Jesus, Son of David, have mercy upon me!" Jesus stopped and said, "Tell him to come here." . . . The blind man said "Rabbi, I want to see." "Go," said Jesus, "your faith has healed you." Immediately he received his sight and followed Jesus along the road.
MARK 10:46–47, 49, 51–52

There was a local king named Tudvael, under whom Ninian cared for his flock, who was as cruel as he was ungodly. Tudvael saw Ninian as a threat to his authority, and one day he expelled Ninian from his territories. Immediately, God's judgment came upon Tudvael in the form of sudden blindness.

The king repented and sent his servant to Ninian to ask him to suggest some penances. The servant flung himself at Ninian's feet with loud lamentations and begged, "Dispel the black night, you who are the glory and chief part of our fame. The offence is great, but one that is open to pardon."

Ninian told him to tell the king his sins were forgiven, and he sent the king gifts to express his friendship. Later, he himself arrived to lay healing hands upon the king's face. Tudvael's eyesight was restored, he gave praise to God, and from that time on, he supported Ninian's work.

Lord of my heart,
give me vision to inspire me
that, working or resting,
I may always think of you.
Lord of my heart,
give me light to guide me
that, at home or abroad
I may always walk in your way.
Lord of my heart, give me wisdom to direct me
that, thinking or acting,
I may always discern right from wrong.
Heart of my own heart, whatever befall me,
rule over my thoughts and feelings,
my words and actions.
ANCIENT IRISH

AUGUST 28 ✛ SPEAK UP FOR THE TRUTH

Psalm 119:57-64; 2 Kings 25:1-21; Mark 7:1-13

Then Peter said, "Ananias, how is it that Satan has so filled your heart
that you have lied to the Holy Spirit...?
You have not lied to human beings, but to God."
ACTS 5:3-4

Ninian was refreshing ever more people with Christ's teachings, but he faced pitfalls within the church. Once when he was in a crowded church, a single mother with emotional and guilt problems brought her newborn baby to be baptized by one of Ninian's ministers—and then loudly accused the priest of being the baby's father. Ninian knew the priest had never slept with this woman, but he needed to clear this matter up in the minds of everybody in a way that had the stamp of Christ's authority.

A bold inspiration came to him, and he called for silence. "I believe this man is innocent, but now I ask you, my child"—he pointed to the baby—"to point out to us who is the man who is your father. I command you to do this in the name of the Thunderer."

To the amazement of everyone, the day-old child pointed its finger at a man in the congregation, and then the baby made sounds everyone could understand: "That man is my father and the priest is innocent." The people were convinced this amazing event came from God, and they praised God.

We too should refuse to listen to hearsay and speak out for those who are innocent of wrong-doing. Are there situations over which we need to take authority in the name of the Lord? Remember, the God of Thunder can show us what to do in any situation.

In Ninian there was nothing of fear, all was love.
Forgive us for the places in our lives where fear has driven out love.
In Ninian truth and holiness shone out.
Forgive us for the places in our lives that are false or frozen.
Help us to take authority in your name
over every confused or unsavory situation.

AUGUST 29 ❖ BELIEVE AND SEE

Psalm 119:65-72; Nehemiah 1; Mark 7:24-37

Jesus said: Whoever has faith in me
will do the works that I do also.
JOHN 14:12

Many important people sent their sons to be educated at Ninian's center at the place now known as Whithorn. It was a center that educated them for a whole life. As the following story illustrates, everything that happened was used to help build character.

One youth at the school committed such a serious offence that the instructor turned to the "last-resort" form of discipline—the cane. The boy ran away before he could receive his caning, taking with him Ninian's pastoral staff. He stumbled upon a curragh by the shore; not realizing that it was not properly covered with waterproof leather, he jumped into it and was carried out to sea. Soon, the boat began to leak, and the young man was in terror of his life.

However, our extremity is God's opportunity: he confessed to God his wrongful rebellion and truly repented of it. Then he started to talk to Ninian, as if he were present, asking Ninian to save him. The young man took Ninian's staff and stuck it in the largest leaking hole, and the boat stayed afloat. An easterly wind arose, and took the boat back to the shore.

A crowd of people had gathered there, waiting for him. The young man, now filled with faith, told them what had happened and planted Ninian's staff in the ground, a sign that the miracle-working God will come to the aid of all who truly believe. It was said that the staff took root and sprouted into a tree that became a constant reminder of God's answer to prayer.

Lord, I have rebelled; forgive my proud heart.
Lord, I reach out to you.
I yield myself to whatever you want me to do today.

AUGUST 30 ✣ HAPPY BEYOND MEASURE

Psalm 119:73-80; Nehemiah 2; Mark 10:30-37

*Happy are those whose greatest desire is to do what God requires;
God will satisfy them fully!*
MATTHEW 5:6 GNT

Ninian was always happy beyond measure. He respected all people and was secure in his holiness, with no need to prove his worth to others. Often, he would go to a cave to study and meditate on heavenly wisdom; he could understand books in different languages; and he was a powerful teacher and preacher. Through his eloquence, the hearts of the faithful grew strong as he spoke of the true joys of eternal life.

Ninian offered to all ethnic groups the consolations of life and generously invited them to share food. He gave beautiful clothes to those who had none. He visited people in prison. He personally took food and drink to those who were hungry and thirsty during times of famine. He was like a father to the orphan and a protective judge to the widow. He exercised an authority to be feared by wrongdoers, but those who did good loved him. Ninian was a humble and wise man, and he closed his journey in joy.

Today, many people walk from Whithorn to Ninian's cave. There, innumerable prayers of today's pilgrims are scratched on the rocks.

*Lord, give us happiness, true happiness:
the happiness of knowing we are called by you,
the happiness of knowing we are cleansed people,
the happiness of knowing we are Christ's instruments,
the happiness of knowing we are set free from addiction to created things,
the happiness of cherishing others and being cherished by them,
the happiness of being on a journey toward joy overflowing.*

AUGUST 31 ✢ HERE AM I, SEND ME

Psalm 119:89–96; Nehemiah 3:1–16; Mark 9:38–41

*I heard the voice of the Lord say, "Whom shall I send?
And who will go for us?" Then I said, "Here am I, send me."*
ISAIAH 6:8 NIV

When the Christian King Oswald came to Northumbria's throne, he asked the leaders of the Iona Community, where he had been brought up in the faith, to send a mission to his kingdom, so that the English people might be taught the blessings of the faith and receive the sacraments. The first to go was Corman, a man of stern temperament. He stayed for some time, but the people were unwilling to listen to him, and he returned to Iona.

At a post-mortem meeting of the Iona Community, Corman blamed the Northumbrian people, who, he said, were stubborn and uncivilized. The leaders discussed this matter for a long time, for they were eager to share the Gospel with new peoples.

Then Aidan, who was present, said to Corman, "It seems to me, brother, that you have been unduly severe with the people. You should have followed the guidance of the apostle Paul and offered them the milk of simpler teaching until, as they gradually grew strong in God's Word, they were able to take in a fuller statement of doctrine and carry out the higher commands."

As Aidan spoke, everyone turned and looked at him, and they carefully considered his words. The meeting finally resolved that Aidan should be made a bishop, and they sent him to lead a second mission to Northumbria. Aidan had shown the gift of discretion, which is the mother of all virtues.

So they consecrated him and sent him to preach. Time proved that Aidan was not only endowed with discretion and good sense but with the other Christian virtues also. Above all, he was a willing messenger of the Gospel.

*Here am I Lord,
I have heard you calling in the night.
I will go Lord where you lead me.
I will hold your people in my heart.*
DAN SCHUTTE, SJ

SEPTEMBER 1 ✤ GENTLE AIDEN

Psalm 119:97-112; Nehemiah 3:17-31; Mark 10:35-45

My teaching will fall . . . like gentle rain on tender grass.
DEUTERONOMY 32:2 GNT

Gentleness includes soothing qualities such as politeness, kindness, and courtesy—and yet can also be a firestorm of indignation, kindled by the wrongs suffered by others. In no one does this quality shine forth more clearly than in Aidan.

Among the lessons that Aidan gave the clergy about their lifestyle, none was more salutary than his own example of fasting and self-discipline. His teaching won the hearts of everyone because he taught what he and his followers lived. He neither sought nor cared for the possessions of this world, and he loved to give away to the poor the gifts he received from the rich.

In those days, poor people traveled by foot, while only the rich and influential went on horseback. Aidan insisted on traveling by foot in country as well as town, unless some urgent necessity forced him to do otherwise. Wherever he walked, he was able to have face-to-face contact with people, both rich and poor, and engage them in conversations. If they were not Christ's followers, he would talk to them about the mystery of the Faith; if they already believed, he would encourage them with both his words and his example. He put into practice the generosity, kindness, and mercy of Christ.

> I have described . . . his love at peace and charity, temperance and humility; his soul which triumphed over anger and greed, and at the same time despised pride and vainglory . . . and his tenderness in comforting the weak, in relieving and protecting the poor.
> *BEDE*

May the raindrops fall lightly on your brow.
May the soft winds freshen your spirit.
May the sunshine brighten your heart.
May the burdens of the day rest lightly upon you,
and may God enfold you in love.
AN OLD IRISH PRAYER

SEPTEMBER 2 ✢ Live What You Say

Psalm 119:113-128; Nehemiah 4; Mark 10:17-31

Jesus answered: "How terrible for you teachers of God's Law!
You put on people's backs loads which are hard to carry,
but you yourselves will not stretch out a finger
to help them carry those loads."
LUKE 11:46 GNT

Aidan's way of life contrasted with the slothfulness of later times. All who traveled with him, monks or others, were required to use their time to study the Scriptures and memorize the psalms. This was the daily task of Aidan and his disciples wherever they went. If, as occasionally happened, he had to dine with the king, he attended with one or two of his followers, and then, after eating lightly, they would leave the table in order to read the Bible or pray. Inspired by his example, many men and women undertook to fast on Wednesdays and Fridays until evening, except for the periods of celebration after Easter and Pentecost.

If wealthy people did wrong, Aidan did not keep silence out of fear or favor, but would sternly correct them. He never gave money to influential people, only the hospitality of his table. He used money rich people gave him to buy the freedom of people who had been unjustly sold as slaves. Many of these later became disciples; after training and instructing them, he ordained them.
BASED ON BEDE

> Celtic monks lived in conspicuous poverty; Roman monks lived well.
> Celtic monks were unworldly; Roman monks were worldly.
> Celtic bishops practiced humility; Roman bishops paraded pomp.
> Celtic bishops were shepherds of their flocks; Roman bishops were monarchs of their dioceses.
> Celtic clergymen said, "Do as I do" and hoped to be followed;
> Roman clergyman said, "Do as I say" and expected to be obeyed.
> MAGNUS MAGNUSSAN

Father, whose gentle apostle Aidan
befriended everyone he met with Jesus Christ,
give me his humble, Spirit-filled zeal
that I may inspire others to learn your ways
and to pass on the torch of faith.

SEPTEMBER 3 ✢ OIL ON TROUBLED WATERS

Psalm 119:145-160; Nehemiah 5; Mark 6:45-56

The wind died down and there was a great calm.
MARK 4:39 GNT

We know nothing of Aidan's childhood, but we can assume his faith was nourished by stories of fellow Irish people who had wrought great things by prayer. One of these was Mac Nissi of Connor, who passed into heaven on September 3 about 510. As a result of his intercessions, a woman who had been infertile for fifteen years was able to give birth to a child. Nurtured by these rich traditions, Aidan learned to have faith for all sorts of situations.

When a delegation from Lindisfarne set off on a boat journey far to the south to bring back Princess Eanflaed, who was to become queen to Northumbria's king, Utta, the leader of the delegation, begged Aidan to pray for their safe keeping. As Aidan was praying for them, God revealed something to him, and so he gave them a jar of blessed oil to take with them. He told them they would encounter storms, but that the winds would drop as soon as they poured the oil on the troubled waters.

The men forgot about this—until a storm blew up, so fierce that the boat began to sink, and they thought they would perish. Only then did someone remember Aidan's words and the oil. They poured the oil over the waves, and the wind immediately receded.

This is an example of prophetic prayer, whereby a person foresees trouble for others and is guided by God to give them direction. We too can pray for people we know who seem about to be engulfed in a sea of troubles. You never know—God may give you a word to pass on to them that proves to be as calming as Aidan's oil.

Protecting Father, stalwart Steersman, guiding Spirit,
I pray for friends in a sea of troubles.
I pray for households in a sea of troubles.
I pray for workplaces in a sea of troubles.
I pray for communities in a sea of troubles.
May your inspiration flow to them
and come to them like oil on troubled waters.

SEPTEMBER 4 ✤ CHRIST'S HANDS

Psalm 119:129-144; Nehemiah 6; Mark 8:31–9:1

*There are different ways of serving, but the same Lord is served. . . .
Now you together constitute the body of the Messiah,
and individually you are parts of it.*
ROMANS 12:5, 27 CJB

The Celtic saints were known for their practical kindness to others. Ultari, a friend of Brigid, is said to have fed with his own hands every child in Erin who had no support, and he provided particular care for the children whose mothers had died of the plague. King Oswald used to pray with his hands open, the easier to receive good things from God—and he would then raise his hands to bless people with good things. His prayers moved from the spiritual realm to the physical.

For evil to triumph it is only necessary for good people to do nothing.
EDMUND BURKE

Christ has no body on earth but yours.
No hands but yours, no feet but yours.
Yours are the eyes through which Christ's compassion
is to look out for the world.
Yours are the feet with which he is to go about doing good.
Yours are the hands with which he is to bless us now.
TERESA OF AVILA

Forgive us for the good we ought to have done
which we have left undone,
and for the things we have left undone
which we ought to have done.
BOOK OF COMMON PRAYER (ADAPTED)

*With these hands I bless the lonely,
the forgotten and the lost;
with these hands I shield your messengers
from attacks within, without;
with these hands I dispel darkness
and rebuke the evil forces;
with these hands I pray your victory
for those who fight for right.*

SEPTEMBER 5 ✥ WHERE GOD GUIDES GOD PROVIDES

Psalm 119:161-176; Nehemiah 7:1-7; Mark 9:14-29

Jesus answered, "...If you believe...
you will even be able to say to this hill,
'Get up and throw yourself in the sea,' and it will.
If you believe, you will receive whatever you ask in prayer."
MATTHEW 21:21-22 GNT

Do you sometimes feel that something is unsatisfactory about the path you are on, but since everyone around you assumes there is nothing you can do about it, you "make the best of a bad job" with a resigned spirit? The following story of a little-known Irish saint reminds us that there is nothing about which we cannot pray.

A wandering Irish monk named Molaise was on a difficult journey in a remote part of Ireland. His way was difficult and dangerous, and he easily lost his path. Then he met a group of monks who had a rare possession—a good map. Molaise would have given his right arm to make a copy of this, but no one had the necessary instruments with them with which to do this. Molaise could have shrugged his shoulders and continued his unsatisfactory journey—but he decided to make this a matter of prayer. Before long, a loose feather from a goose that was flying overhead fluttered down from the sky. Molaise caught it and was able to use his new quill as a pen with which to copy the map!

May the hills lie low, may the sloughs fill up in your way.
May all evil sleep, may all good awake in your way.
COLLECTED BY KENNETH MACLEOD

Dear Jesus, you guide your straying sheep
along lush and fragrant valleys,
where the grass is rich and deep.
You guard them from the attacks of wolves,
and from the bites of snakes.
You heal their diseases,
and teach them always to walk in the ways of God.
When we stray, lead us back;
when temptation besets us, give us strength;
when our souls are sick, pour upon us your love.
ANCIENT CELTIC SONG

September 6 ❖ Lust

Psalm 120; Nehemiah 8; Mark 9:42–10:12

Live by the Spirit and you will not give in to the desires of the sinful nature. For the sinful nature desires what is contrary to the Spirit, and the Spirit what is contrary to the sinful nature . . . so that you do not do what you want. The acts of the sinful nature are obvious: sexual immorality, impurity and debauchery.
GALATIANS 5:16–17, 19 NIV

Most of us have times when waves of inappropriate sexual desire threaten to overwhelm us. At those times, everything else in our lives, however fruitful and healthy it may be, often seems faint and faraway compared with this flood of desire. We justify the idea of indulging our lust on the grounds that we will never have lived if we do not experience what we desire. This is a delusion, and the experience is always that of letdown, new barriers, disappointment, guilt. Is there anything we can do to avoid such a defeat? Celtic Christians offer us a drastic remedy: they stood in a cold bath or river in order to cool their passions! And from the Desert Christians comes this intriguing example of a remedy.

A young disciple was so constantly tempted that he eventually announced to his soul friend, "I cannot go on unless I actually commit the deed."

The wise old abba replied, "I want to do it too, so let me come with you to the prostitute's house and then we'll return together to our cell."

The abba took the money with which to pay the prostitute. When they got to her house, he asked that he should have the first session, while the younger man stayed outside. The old man won the trust of the prostitute, explained that his friend was at heart a holy monk, and that what he needed was not a one-night stand, but for his fantasy to dissolve. The woman agreed to cooperate.

When the young man came in for sexual intercourse, she told him, "I too have a Rule. It requires my clients to make repeated obscene oaths with me before we lie together." The young man started to do this, but became so sickened by all the filth, that he realized he wanted to live a life of prayer more than anything else, and left the room. The two men returned, chaste in body and heart, to continue their desert calling.

*Lord, when waves of unhealthy lust roll over me,
remind me that my deepest destiny lies
in being true in body and mind.
Cool me, calm me, and protect me, I pray.*

SEPTEMBER 7 ✢ WASHING FEET

Psalm 123; Nehemiah 9:1–39; John 13:1–20

[Jesus] got up from the meal, took off his outer clothing,
and wrapped a towel around his waist.
After that, he poured water into a basin
and began to wash his disciples' feet,
drying them with the towel that was wrapped around him.
JOHN 13:4–5 NIV

The tradition of washing others' feet was not only followed in hot and dusty lands; folks in Celtic lands did it, too. One of the Desert Fathers used to say, "There are three things we honor—the fellowship of holy communion, the hospitality of meals, and the washing of one another's feet." And it was said that when Cuthbert was put in charge of guests at Ripon Monastery, God sent him a visitor to test just how Christ-like was Cuthbert's hospitality.

One day, Cuthbert found a youth waiting in the guest room and gave him his usual kindly welcome. He fetched water so his guest could wash his hands, and then Cuthbert washed his feet himself, tenderly dried them, and held them against his chest while he gave them a warm massage. Just as a hot evening meal was brought to the young man, he apparently vanished into thin air. Not a footprint could be seen in the snowy ground outside. People wondered if Cuthbert had welcomed an angel!

In a society that has heated bathrooms and running water, washing feet may be an artificial way to reflect Jesus' example, but there are other ways to show the same humble consideration for another. Can you think of any? The next person you meet may be a test case from heaven!

Lord, take my hands.
May your compassion always flow though them.
May they offer tender touch
to people who are deprived of touch or tenderness.
May they offer human warmth
to people who are cold or dispirited.
May they offer practical care
to people who are weary and overworked.

SEPTEMBER 8 ✥ BITTER INTO SWEET

Psalm 122; Nehemiah 9:38–10:39; Mark 10:32–34

When they came to the oasis, the water there was too bitter to drink. So they called the place Marah (which means "bitter"), and the people complained to Moses, "What are we going to drink?" So Moses asked the Lord for help, and the Lord showed him a piece of wood. Moses threw the wood into the water, and the water became sweet.
EXODUS 15:22–25

On the grounds of the monastery at Durrow, a tree grew that provided local people with a prolific supply of apples—but they tasted so bitter that the people complained. One autumn day, Columba went up to it, and seeing it laden with fruit that was going to give more displeasure than pleasure to the people, he raised his hand and spoke to the tree: "In the name of almighty God, bitter tree, may all your bitterness depart from you, and from now on may your apples be sweet." Columba's biographer commented: "Wonderful to tell, more swift than words, all the apples on that tree lost their bitterness and became wonderfully sweet."

> For the one who has left behind the pleasures of Egypt which he served before crossing the sea, life removed from these pleasures seems at first difficult and disagreeable. But if the wood be thrown into the water, that is, if one receives the mystery of the resurrection which had its beginning with the wood (you of course understand "the cross" when you hear "wood") then the virtuous life, being sweetened by the hope of things to come, becomes sweeter and more pleasant than all the sweetness that tickles the senses with pleasure.
> GREGORY OF NYSSA, THE LIFE OF MOSES, BOOK 2

Sweet Jesus, I lay before you now
things that are needlessly bitter—relationships, circumstances.
May your sweetness turn anger into pleasure,
tragedy into triumph, and ugliness into beauty.

SEPTEMBER 9 ❖ FOUNDATION WORK

Psalm 124; Nehemiah 12:24-43; Mark 6:1-6

> *"He's just a carpenter, the son of Mary,*
> *and the brother of James, Joseph, Judas, and Simon.*
> *And his sisters live right here among us.*
> MARK 6:3 NLT

Ciaran, unlike most leaders of the early Irish churches who came from ruling families, was the son of a carpenter. Yet he became such an influential leader that he was known as one of the Twelve Apostles of Ireland. Like the David we read about in the Bible, Ciaran was brought up the hard way, looking after the cattle—yet out in the fields he had God-guided encounters that built up his character.

Whenever his tutor said the divine services some distance away, Ciaran always knew when these began, and he would join in wherever he was. A fox befriended him and fetched his tutor's lesson notes to him each day. So Ciaran grew in wisdom and stature, and in favor of God and beast. The time came for Ciaran to study under the famous Abbot Finnian at Clonard Monastery. Overcoming his mother's disapproval, Ciaran took a cow with him that proved so fertile it provided milk for many more students than himself.

Ciaran was so attractive, both physically and spiritually, that many people gave him land and treasures, which he used for God's glory. He concluded that, having received the best training in scholarship at Clonard, he now needed to receive the best training in prayer, so he decided to go to Aran and be discipled by Enda. There, God gave the two men a vision of a great and fruitful tree growing beside a stream in the middle of Ireland. This tree protected the entire island, its fruit crossed the sea, and birds of the world came to carry off some of the fruit. Enda told Ciaran that he himself was the tree, and that God was calling him to establish a church in the center of Ireland by the banks of a stream.

So step by step, Ciaran was led to establish the community at Clonmacnoise. He died of the plague only seven months after arriving there, and yet Clonmacnoise remained a great community for a thousand years, proving how deeply dug was Ciaran's foundation.

> *Jesus, Master Carpenter of Nazareth,*
> *wield well your tools in this your workshop*
> *that we who come to you rough-hewn*
> *may here be fashioned to a truer beauty by your hand.*
> TRADITIONAL

SEPTEMBER 10 ✣ PURITY

Psalm 15; Nehemiah 12:44-13:3; Mark 7:14-23

Blest are the pure in heart; for they shall see our God.
HYMN BY JOHN KEBEL (MATTHEW 5:8)

It is not only that these [Celtic] scribes and anchorites lived by the destiny of their dedication in an environment of wood and sea; it was because they brought into that environment an eye washed miraculously clear by continuous spiritual exercise that they, the first in Europe, had that strange vision of natural things in an almost unnatural purity.
ROBIN FLOWER IN IRISH TRADITION

As the eye is a sense faculty of the body, so is the healthy imagination a sense organ of the spiritual mind. It can receive spiritual truths from the material world but purity of heart is required for such a healthy functioning of the imagination. Without this purity, the ever-active mind and imagination construct disjointed thoughts and representations that bear little resemblance to reality. Such images debase rather than dignify.
BROTHER AIDAN, AN ORTHODOX MONK AND ICONOGRAPHER

Alas that no stream reaching every part
flows over my breast to be a cleansing tonight for my body and heart.
EARLY IRISH LYRICS

Mary beloved! Mother of the White Lamb,
pure Virgin of nobleness.
CARMINA GADELICA

My strength is as the strength of ten because my heart is pure.
ALFRED LORD TENNYSON

Make and keep me pure within.
CHARLES WESLEY

From the unreal, lead me to the real,
from the impure, lead me to the pure,
from darkness, lead me to light
and from what passes away,
lead me to what is eternal.

SEPTEMBER 11 ✧ REST

Psalm 125; Nehemiah 13:4–31; Hebrews 3

*It is all too plain that it was refusal to trust God
that prevented these people from entering into God's Rest.*
HEBREWS 3:19 JBP

Those who followed the rule of Columba would keep the Jewish Sabbath and rest from work on Saturday as well as on Sunday. The emphasis of Sunday would be renewal and resurrection.

The hours of rest and recreation are as valuable as the hours of prayer and work. The Lord Jesus reminds us that "the Sabbath was made for humankind, and not humankind for the Sabbath" (Mark 2:27). In the Scriptures, even the land was given a Sabbath in the seventh year (Leviticus 15:3–5). The need for rest was built into creation (Genesis 2:1–3). A provision for this kind of rest, which is both holy and creative, should be part of each member's personal Way of Life.
THE WAY OF LIFE OF THE COMMUNITY OF AIDAN AND HILDA

Use the Rest.
NOTICE IN A BILLIARDS ROOM

We who have lost our sense and our senses—our touch, our smell, our vision of who we are; we who frantically force and press all things, without rest for body or spirit, hurting our earth and injuring ourselves: we call a halt.

We want to rest. We need to rest and allow the earth to rest. We need to reflect and to rediscover the mystery that lives in us, that is the ground of every unique expression of life, the source of the fascination that calls all things to communion.

We declare a Sabbath, a space of quiet: for simply being and letting be; for recovering the great, forgotten truths; for learning how to live again.
UN, ENVIRONMENTAL SABBATH PROGRAMME

God is the one quiet unhurried Worker in the universe.
He has eternity in which to do things.
J. PATERSON SMYTH

*I cast off the works that spring from a restless spirit.
I rest in you, my Maker and Redeemer.
Help me to order my life according to your rhythms.*

SEPTEMBER 12 ⁘ LAUGHTER

Psalm 126; 1 Samuel 2:1-11; Romans 15:1-13

> *Being cheerful keeps you healthy.*
> *It is slow death to be gloomy all the time.*
> PROVERBS 17:22 GNT

A frail old Desert Christian had reached about ninety years of age, and he acutely felt the devils tempting him to fall into despair. So he used the weapon of humor to get rid of them.

"What will you do, old man, for you might live like this for another fifty years?" the tempters asked him.

In reply he said to them, "You have distressed me greatly, for I had been prepared to live for two hundred years!"

That did it! With great cries, the devils left him.

> At all hours Cuthbert was happy and joyful, neither wearing a sad expression at the memory of a sin nor being elated by the loud acclaim of those who were impressed by his way of life.
> LIFE OF CUTHBERT *BY AN ANONYMOUS MONK OF LINDISFARNE*

> Caedmon, who lived at Whitby monastery, moved into the house for those who were dying. He and his nurse talked and joked in good spirits with each of the other occupants in turn until after midnight. Caedmon asked if they had the Sacrament in the house. "Why do you need Holy Communion now?" they asked. "You are not due to die yet for you talk with us as cheerfully as if you were in good health." He died with a smile on his face.
> BEDE

> It is the heart that is not yet sure of God
> that is afraid to laugh in God's presence.
> GEORGE MACDONALD

> *Teach us, good Lord,*
> *to enjoy the fun of your creation;*
> *not to take ourselves too seriously;*
> *and to allow the sense of humor,*
> *which is your gift to us,*
> *to bubble over as it should.*

SEPTEMBER 13 ✥ BE CONTENT

Psalm 127; 1 Samuel 2:12-27; Philippians 4:10-23

Godliness with contentment is great gain.
1 TIMOTHY 6:6 NIV

So I must accept with equanimity whatever befalls me, whether it be good or bad, and always give thanks to God, who taught me to trust in him always without hesitation. God must have heard my prayer. . . Daily I expect murder, fraud, or captivity, or whatever it may be; but I fear none of these things because of the promises of heaven. I have cast myself into the hands of God Almighty, who rules everywhere. As the prophet says, "Cast your cares upon the Lord, and the Lord will care for you."

And if I have done any good for my God whom I love, I beg him that I may shed blood with those exiles and captives for his name, even though I should be denied a grave, or my body be torn to pieces. I am convinced that if this should happen to me, I would have gained my soul together with my body, because on that day we shall rise in the brightness of the sun, that is, in the glory of Christ Jesus our Redeemer, as children of the living God and joint heirs with Christ, to be conformed to his image; for of him, and by him, and in him we shall reign.
PATRICK OF IRELAND

> To live content with small means,
> to seek elegance rather than luxury
> and refinement rather than fashion;
> to be worthy, not respectable
> and wealthy, not rich;
> to study hard, think quietly, talk gently, act frankly,
> to listen to stars and birds, babes and sages, with open heart;
> to bear all cheerfully, do all bravely,
> await occasions, hurry never;
> in a word, to let the spiritual, unbidden and unconscious
> grow up through the common.
> This is to be my symphony.
> WILLIAM ELLERY CHANNING

Grant me, Lord, the serenity of knowing that I do your will
and contentment with my lot.
Grant me the courage to change what I can change,
the grace to accept what I cannot change,
and the wisdom to know the difference.
ADAPTED FROM REINHOLD NIEBUHR

SEPTEMBER 14 ❖ THE TRUE CROSS

Psalm 129; 1 Samuel 9; Philippians 2:1–11

*God forbid that I should glory in anything
except the cross of our Lord Jesus Christ.*
GALATIANS 6:14

After Constantine became Emperor of the Roman Empire, he had a vision of a cross in the sky, above it written the words "In this sign conquer." Ever afterward, Constantine encouraged the church as an ally of a united Empire, and the Cross became a popular symbol, though it is doubtful whether Constantine truly knew what the Cross meant. For him, it was a political symbol.

His mother Helena, however, became ever more devoted to Christ. Christians had as yet no written Gospels, and they no longer had the test of persecution as a focus for their devotion—so Helena went on journeys to the Holy Land to find, as a focus for devotion, a fragment of the Cross on which Christ had been crucified. The fragment she believed she found did indeed excite the devotion of many. The story of Helena and her discovery of the "true Cross" became the subject of an epic medieval English poem. Some have attributed this to Cynewulf, the eighth-century Bishop of Lindisfarne.

Celtic Christians realized that the true Cross does not consist in the externals, but in the experience of total self-giving and sacrifice: that is the way those who follow Christ must adopt as their own. Millions are confused about this, and the meaning of the Cross has become corrupted as a result. During the Crusades, Christians slaughtered Muslims in order to capture the site of "the true Cross"; no wonder then that today many Muslims connect the Cross with the sword.

The Celts loved *The Dream of the Rood*. In this poem (attributed to Cynewulf), the cross-beam on which Christ was nailed (the Rood) speaks to us:

> The young hero stripped himself—he, God Almighty—
> strong and stout-minded. He mounted high gallows,
> bold before many, when he would loose mankind. . . .
> May he be friend to me. . . .
> He loosed us and life gave, a heavenly home. Hope was renewed
> with glory and gladness to those who there burning endured.
> That Son was victory-fast in that great venture,
> with might and good-speed, when he with many,
> vast host of souls, came to God's kingdom. . . .

*Lord, may I see your true Cross
and follow always its way of love, self-sacrifice, and hope.*

SEPTEMBER 15 ✤ THE APPLE OF GOD'S EYE

Psalm 130; 1 Samuel 10:17-27; Philippians 3:1-11

The Lord said to his people, "I scattered you in all directions. . . .
But now anyone who strikes you injures the apple of my eye."
ZECHARIAH 2:6, 8

I did not go to Ireland of my own accord; not, that is, until I had nearly perished. This was for my good, for in this way the Lord purged me, and made me fit to be what I am now, but which once I was far from being—someone who cares and labors for the salvation of others. I did not care for anyone, not even for myself.

On the occasion when several of my seniors rejected me God spoke to me personally. He did not say "you have seen" but "we have seen," as if he included himself. It was as if God was saying, "Whoever touches you touches the apple of my eye."

Therefore I thank God who has strengthened me in everything. . . . After this experience I felt not a little strength, and my trust was proved right before God and people.

And so I say boldly, my conscience does not blame me now or in the future: God is my witness that I have not lied in the account I have given you.

Enough of this. I must not, however, hide the gift God gave me in the land of my captivity, because there I earnestly sought him, and there I found him, and he saved me from all evil because—so I believe—of his Spirit who lives in me.

PATRICK OF IRELAND

Father, you affirmed your Son at his baptism
before he entered a time of testing.
Father, you affirmed your servant Patrick
in the midst of his time of trial.
Father, affirm me in my time of need.
May I rest in the assurance
that I am the apple of your eye.

SEPTEMBER 16 ✢ PERSEVERE

Psalm 132; 1 Samuel 11; Revelation 3:1–6

I have done my best in the race,
I have run the full distance, I have kept the faith.
And now there is waiting for me the victory prize.
2 TIMOTHY 4:7–8 GNT

Wales' saint David is a fine example of somebody who persevered in and out of season. The wife of the local chief tried to get rid of his monastery and then to corrupt his monks. His monks then pressured David to move their home elsewhere, even though God had clearly led them to that site. David stood firm, and in the end, the woman herself had to flee. David's biographer observed that David's purpose "was neither dissolved nor softened by prosperity, nor terrified when weakened by adversity."

> Why were the saints, saints? Because they were cheerful when it was difficult to be cheerful, patient when it was difficult to be patient; and because they pushed on when they wanted to stand still, and kept silent when they wanted to talk, and were agreeable when they wanted to be disagreeable. That was all. It was quite simple and always will be.
> ANONYMOUS

> The four securities of the children of Life: the wearing away of the passions, fear of the pains, love of the sufferings, belief in the rewards. If the passions were not worn away, they would not be left behind. If the pains were not feared, they would not be guarded against. If the sufferings were not loved, they would not be endured. If the rewards were not believed in, they would not be attained.
> COLMÁN MAC BÉOGNAE, THE ALPHABET OF DEVOTION

> Never give up. Never, never give up. Never, never, never give up.
> THE ENTIRE SPEECH WINSTON CHURCHILL GAVE AT A SCHOOL PRIZE–GIVING

O God, when we, your servants,
are called upon to undertake any task,
whether it be small or great, help us to know that
it is not the beginning of the task
but the continuing of it to the end
which yields the true glory.
INSPIRED BY WORDS OF SIR FRANCIS DRAKE

SEPTEMBER 17 ❖ HUMANS AND CREATION

Psalm 135; 1 Samuel 12; Revelation 11:15-19

Because of what you did, the Earth shall be cursed.
GENESIS 3:17

The person who tramples the world tramples themself.
COLUMBANUS

The high, the low, all of creation
God gives to humankind to use.
If this privilege is misused
God's justice permits creation to punish humanity.
HILDEGAARD OF BINGEN

I am Eve, great Adam's wife.
It is I that outraged Jesus of old.
It is I that stole heaven from my children.
By rights it is I that should have gone upon the Tree,
it is I that plucked the apple.
It overcame the control of my greed.
For that, women will not cease from folly
as long as I live in the light of day.
There would be no ice in any place.
There would be no glistening windy winter.
There would be no hell, there would be no sorrow.
There would be no fear were it not for me.
EARLY IRISH LYRICS

Since the beginning of time our task has been to harmonize the spiritual and material realms. We were intended to be mediators between God and creation, but have been disobedient. In our failure, God, in human form, fulfils this task by uniting to himself his creation in the closest possible way, taking the form of that which he created.
TIM COOPER, GREEN CHRISTIANITY

There is enough in the world for everyone's need
but not for everyone's greed.
MAHATMA GANDHI

O one God, O true God, O chief God, O God of one substance,
O God only mighty in three Persons, truly pitiful, forgive.
ATTRIBUTED TO SAINT CIARAN

SEPTEMBER 18 ✥ GROWING IN GOODNESS

Psalm 134:2 Chronicles 7:11-22; Revelation 2:18-29

*We are like mirrors reflecting the glory of the Lord,
and we are being changed into the Divine image,
from one degree of splendor to another.*
2 CORINTHIANS 3:18

Whenever I give moral instruction, I first try to demonstrate the inherent power and quality of human nature, I try to show the wonderful virtues which all human beings can acquire. Most people look at the virtues in others, and imagine that such virtues are far beyond their reach. Yet God has implanted in every person the capacity to attain the very highest level of virtue.

But people cannot grow in virtue on their own. We each need companions to guide and direct us on the way of righteousness; without such companions we are liable to stray from the firm path, and then sink into the mud of despair. At first a companion who has achieved a high level of virtue can seem utterly different from oneself. But as friendship grows, one begins to see in the companion a mirror of oneself. The reason is that, in moral capacities, God has created us all the same: we are each capable of achieving the same degree of moral goodness. Once people perceive this truth, they are filled with hope, knowing that in the fullness of time they can share the moral virtue of Christ himself.
PELAGIUS IN A LETTER TO DEMETRIUS

The best thing we can do is to prepare for the five encounters we shall all have: an encounter with disappointments, an encounter with death, an encounter with God's people, an encounter with devils, an encounter with resurrection on Judgment Day.
COLMÁN MAC BÉOGNAE, THE ALPHABET OF DEVOTION

*God, I am bathing my face in the sun, in the nine rays of the sun
as Mary bathed her Son in generous milk fermented.
Love be in my countenance, benevolence in my mind,
dew of honey in my tongue, my breath as the incense.*
CARMINA GADELICA

SEPTEMBER 19 ✣ INTEGRITY

Psalm 137; Ezra 8:21-23; Revelation 2:1-7

We have given up underhanded ways;
we refuse to manipulate or to misconstrue God's word,
and instead we speak the truth openly,
leaving our message to every person's conscience.
2 CORINTHIANS 4:2

When Christianity became the official religion of the Roman Empire, many Christians fell into the temptation to adopt double standards. Aidan's example, however, was different from the model of Christianity that was being expressed in the church elsewhere. Integrity was a hallmark of Aidan and the Celtic saints.

> The highest recommendation of (Aidan's) teaching to all was that he and his followers lived as they taught. . . .
> Such was Aidan's industry in carrying out and teaching the divine commandment, his diligence in study and keeping vigil, his authority, such as became a priest, in reproving the proud and the mighty. . . . To put it briefly, so far as one can learn from those who knew him, he made it his business to omit none of the commands of the evangelists, the apostles, and the prophets, but he set himself to carry them out in his deeds, so far as he was able. All these things I greatly admire and love in this bishop and I have no doubt that all this was pleasing to God.
> BEDE

> I would be true, for there are those who trust me.
> I would be pure, for there are those who care,
> I would be strong, for there is much to suffer.
> I would be brave, for there is much to dare.
> HOWARD ARNOLD WALTER

Sift me, O Lord,
Bring all that is false in me into the light
and take it away.
Give me strength to be true
in all I say and think and do.

SEPTEMBER 20 ❖ CONSISTENCY

Psalm 136; Job 2; Revelation 2:8–11

The father asked his elder son to work in his vineyard that day. "I don't want to," he said—but later he changed his mind and went. The father said the same thing to his second son, who replied, "Yes, I'll go"—but he did not in fact go. Which of the two sons did what his father wanted?
MATTHEW 21:28–31

After Cuthbert reluctantly agreed to become a bishop, he continued with the utmost constancy to be what he had been before. He showed the same humility of heart, the same poverty of dress, and, being full of authority and grace, he maintained the dignity of a bishop without abandoning the ideal of a monk or the virtue of the hermit. . . .

His discourse was pure and frank, full of gravity and probity, full of sweetness and grace, dealing with the ministry of the law, the teaching of the faith, the virtue of temperance, and the practice of righteousness. . . . He followed the example of the saints, fulfilling the duty of peace among the brothers; he held fast to humility also and the excellent gift of love without which every other virtue is worth nothing. He cared for the poor, fed the hungry, clothed the naked, took in strangers, redeemed captives, and protected widows and orphans."
THE LIFE OF CUTHBERT *BY AN ANONYMOUS MONK OF LINDISFARNE*

The silent power of a consistent life.
FLORENCE NIGHTINGALE

Long obedience in the same direction.
FREDERICK NIETZSCHE

I make Christ's Cross over my face.
Each day and each night
that I place myself under his keeping
I shall not be overwhelmed, I shall not be destroyed,
I shall not be imprisoned, I shall not be cast down.
Black thoughts shall not lie on me.
Confusion shall not lie on me.
No ill-will of enemy shall lie on me.

SEPTEMBER 21 ❖ WEANED FROM IDOLS

Psalm 139; Amos 5; Revelation 2:12-17

Do not abandon me and turn to idols.
LEVITICUS 9:4

An idol is any thing I put before God. It might be a computer or a career, a person or a passion, a habit or a house. In Cuthbert's day, an idol was often considered to be a power of nature that allowed people to manipulate circumstances to suit their selfish desires.

After Boisil died, Cuthbert was made prior of the Melrose monastery. Bede writes:

> He not only taught those in the monastery how to live . . . he also sought to convert the neighboring people far and wide from a life of foolish customs to a love of heavenly joys. For many of them profaned the creed they held by wicked deeds and some of them, too, in times of plague, would forget the sacred mysteries of the faith into which they had been initiated and take to the false remedies of idolatry, as though they could ward off a blow inflicted by God the Creator by means of incantations or amulets or any other mysteries of devilish art. So he frequently went forth from the monastery to correct the errors of those who had sinned in both these ways, sometimes on horseback but more often on foot; he came to the neighboring villages and preached the way of truth to those who had gone astray. . . .
>
> None of those present would presume to hide from him the secrets of their hearts, but they all made open confession of their sins because they realized that these things could never be hidden from him; and they cleansed themselves from the sins they had confessed by fruits of repentance. He used especially to make for those places that were far away in steep and rugged mountains, which others dreaded to visit and whose poverty and ignorance kept other teachers away. Giving himself up gladly to this devoted labor, he instructed them with such devotion that he would often leave the monastery for a week, and sometimes for up to a month.

Now robed in stillness in this quiet place,
emptied of all I was, I bring all that I am
your gift of shepherding to use and bless.
CUTHBERT'S PRAYER, ST. AIDAN'S CHAPEL, BRADFORD CATHEDRAL

SEPTEMBER 22 ✢ A SENSE OF PROPORTION

Psalm 142; 2 Chronicles 8; Revelation 3:7-13

Keep your head in all situations, endure hardship...
discharge all the duties of your ministry.
2 TIMOTHY 4:5 NLT

Today is the autumnal equinox, when the hours of light and dark are in equal balance. This is a good day to take stock to make sure that we have a God-given equilibrium in our lives. This may seem a forlorn and frustrating task, until we realize that Christ, who is the perfect specimen of a balanced human being, can calm our agitated or overworked parts, heal our sick parts, and strengthen our weak parts.

Gildas, who has been nicknamed the Jeremiah of the early British church because he was so critical of its lax members, believed in fasting and prayer—yet he was equally aware of the danger of going overboard and losing a sense of proportion. He wrote:

> There is no point in abstaining from bodily food if you do not have love in your heart. Those who do not fast much but who take great care to keep their heart pure (on which, as they know, their life ultimately depends) are better off than those who are vegetarian, or travel in carriages, and think they are therefore superior to everyone else. To these people death has entered through the window of their pride.

Grant me the serenity—
that comes from placing the different parts of my being
under your harmonizing sway.
Today may I grow in balance.

SEPTEMBER 23 ✤ A CIVILIZATION OF LOVE

Psalm 144; Isaiah 58; Revelation 3:14-22

*The Sovereign Lord has filled me with his Spirit.
He has chosen me and sent me to...
announce release to hostages and to set the prisoners free.*
ISAIAH 61:1

Adamnan, who died in September 704 as Abbot of Iona, first proved himself in Ireland, where he helped secure the release of sixty hostages with the help of the Caim, the Celtic Circling Prayer.

When Saxon raiders took the hostages from Meath, in Ireland, Adamnan and his companions sailed to Britain to try to negotiate their release with King Aldfrith. After the Irish company had hauled their boats onto the shore, they walked in a circle round them, saying protective prayers out loud. Soon, the sea surrounded the boats, but a dry circle of sand was left upon which the boats were beached. This created a healthy respect for the negotiators among the Saxons. By the close of the negotiations, the Saxons had not only agreed to the release of the hostages, but also to cease raids altogether.

> People in a religious habit were held in great respect, so that whenever a priest or a monk went anywhere he was gladly received by all as God's servant. If they chanced to meet him by the roadside, they ran towards him and, bowing their heads, were eager either to be signed with the cross by his hand or to receive a blessing. Great attention was paid to his exhortations, and on Sundays the people flocked eagerly to the church or the monastery, not to get food for the body but to hear the Word of God. . . . They were so free from all taint of avarice that none of them would accept lands or possessions to build monasteries, unless compelled to by the secular authorities. This practice was observed universally by the Northumbrian churches for some time afterwards.
> BEDE

*Lord, help us to be peacemakers.
Give us the statesmanship of the prayerful heart,
the willingness to move out toward others.
Give us the faith to do our bit
that we may contribute toward building a civilization of love.*

SEPTEMBER 24 ✣ IN A HARD PLACE

Psalm 140; Esther 3; 2 Corinthians 6

O Lord, don't stay away from me! Come quickly to my rescue!
PSALM 22:19 GNT

I am hated. What shall I do, Lord? I am most despised. Look, your sheep around me are torn to pieces and driven away by those robbers on the orders of the hostile Coroticus. Ravening wolves have devoured the flock of the Lord which, in Ireland, was indeed growing splendidly with the greatest care—I cannot count their number.

They have filled their houses with the spoils of dead Christians, they live on plunder. They do not know, the wretches, that what they offer their friends and sons as food is deadly poison, just as Eve did not understand that it was death she gave her husband. So are all that do evil: they work death as their eternal punishment.
PATRICK OF IRELAND IN A LETTER TO COROTICUS

I stand in the troughs of life's hard seas,
the Savior from ill stands up to his knees.
I stand and look at the wrecks of my time,
the Father of Time puts his hand in mine.
I stand and behold a heart that is grim,
the gentle Spirit puts a smile within.
I kneel before the fates above
and I find the One whose name is Love.
We weep for the hungry without any bread,
for children who need to be fed.
We weep for mistreated ones, strangers to love
the oppressed by force from above.
We pray against cruelty hatred and pain,
inhumanity and greed for gain.
We pray for hostages, may they go free.
And forgive the sinners, starting with me.
ANDREW DICK

SEPTEMBER 25 ✧ ADVICE TO A YOUNG MAN

Psalm 146; Esther 4; 2 Corinthians 8

Be happy with those who are happy, weep with those who weep.
Have the same concern for everyone.
Do not be proud but accept humble duties.
ROMANS 12:15–16 GNT

Be helpful when you are at the bottom of the ladder and be the lowest when you are in authority. Be simple in faith but well trained in manners; demanding in your own affairs but unconcerned in those of others. Be guileless in friendship, astute in the face of deceit, tough in time of ease, tender in hard times. Keep your options open when there's no problem, but dig in when you must choose. Be pleasant when things are unpleasant, and sorrowful when they are pleasant. Disagree where necessary, but be in agreement about the truth. Be serious in pleasures but kindly when things are bitter. Be strong in trials, weak in dissensions. . . .

Be friendly with people of honor, stiff with rascals, gentle to the weak, firm to the stubborn, steadfast to the proud, humble to the lowly. Always be sober, chaste, modest. Be discreet in duty, persistent in study, unshaken in turmoil, valiant in the cause of truth, cautious in time of strife. Be submissive to good, unbending to evil, gentle in curiosity, untiring in love, just in all things. Be respectful to the worthy, merciful to the poor. Be mindful of favors, unmindful of wrongs. Love ordinary people, and don't crave for riches, but cool down excitement and speak your mind.

Obey your seniors, keep up with your juniors, equal your equals, emulate the perfect. Don't envy your betters, or grieve at those who surpass you, or censure those who fall behind, but agree with those who urge you on. Though weary, don't give up. Weep and rejoice at the same time out of zeal and hope. Advance with determination, but always fear for the end.
COLUMBANUS IN A LETTER TO A YOUNG DISCIPLE

For my shield this day I call heaven's might,
Son's brightness, moon's whiteness, fire's glory,
lightning's swiftness, wind's wildness,
ocean's depth, earth's solidity, rock's immobility.
FROM PATRICK'S BREASTPLATE

SEPTEMBER 26 ⁜ FOILING A PLOT TO KILL

Psalm 143; Esther 6; 2 Corinthians 11:16-33

Haman, the enemy of the Jewish people, had cast lots (or "purim" as they are called) to determine the best day to destroy the Jews; he had planned to wipe them out. But Queen Esther went to the king, and the king sent orders, so that in the end, Haman suffered the fate he had planned for the Jews. . . .
ESTHER 9:24, 25

Have you ever had that awful feeling that somebody has got it in for you . . . and that there is nothing you can do about it? If so, take heart from the experiences of Queen Esther, in the Bible, and of Samson of Dol.

Samson had learned that a region of Brittany was in dire distress because an alien king, urged on by his evil wife, had killed the hereditary head of the estates, put his son Judual under sentence of death, and alienated the fearful population. Samson stayed at the palace in order to negotiate Judual's release, to the fury of the queen, who tried one ploy after another to kill him. First, she pressed him to eat a meal before departing, and instructed her servant to take him a poisoned drink. As the servant gave him the glass, Samson made the sign of the cross over it and spilt it, saying calmly, "This is not an appropriate cup for someone to drink."

When the king, softening after Samson had healed one of his staff, arranged for Samson to visit Judual, the queen had an unbroken, angry horse brought for Samson's use. Samson made the sign of the cross again, this time on the horse, and calmly sat astride it. The horse, perhaps sensing the deep peace within Samson, became calm and gentle. But the queen was still determined that Samson should never return, so even when he was leaving to journey on by boat, she arranged for a hungry lion to be let loose at the port. Samson's biographer observed that the indomitable man of God invoked the name of Christ and discharged on the beast "his customary missiles as if from a catapult," saying, "I charge you in the name of Jesus Christ who has given us power to tread under foot you and things like you, that your terrible power against the human race may from this day never rise again, but that you die quickly in the presence of all these people so that the people of this region may know that God has sent me here as a servant of Christ." The lion died that hour, and everyone present, even the queen herself, pledged to support both Judual's release and Samson's mission.

*Lord, help me always to believe
that all things work together for good
to those who love you.*

SEPTEMBER 27 ✣ BORDERLANDS

Psalm 147; Esther 7; 2 Corinthians 12:1-10

The kingdom of heaven is right here.
MARK 1:15

The safety-first mentality that pervades most organized life today is stifling the frontier mentality that is part of the nature God gave human beings. As David Adam reminds us in his book *Borderlands*, we are in danger of becoming "safe people" who have never been all at sea or experienced "the cliffs of fall" (as the poet Gerard Manley Hopkins described the mind's mountain of grief). We avoid crossing frontiers in case we face danger there. Yet in reality, life is ever bringing us to the edge of things, despite all our efforts to hang back.

Frontiers are exciting places, however, and everyone should be encouraged to explore them. Jesus was often in the borderlands: between countries, between heaven and earth; and on the fringes of society, with lepers, tax collectors, prostitutes, as well as with prominent people.

Columbanus described his fellow Irish people as "inhabitants of the world's edge." Celtic Christians were good at crossing borders, by foot or by coracle. Like Saint Brendan, some ventured into the great unknown and possibly reached America. Others, like Patrick and Aidan, went out to a foreign people and became one with them in the love of God. Missionaries such as Columbanus founded Christian communities in the most unlikely locations, and hermits found their place of resurrection in the wildest of places.

Celtic Christians have also been able to keep an awareness of the "other," that which lies outside life's familiar boundaries. This was expressed in a beautifully simple way by a woman from Kerry in the southwest of Ireland; when she was asked where heaven was, she replied, "about a foot and a half above a person." If we can share such an awareness, we will realize that we too live in the borderlands, places of mystery and possibility.

Great Spirit, Wild Goose of the Almighty,
be my eye in the dark places,
be my flight in the trapped places,
be my host in the wild places,
be my brood in the barren places,
be my formation in the lost places.

SEPTEMBER 28 ✢ A WORLD OF ANGELS

Psalm 103; Exodus 23:20-26; Revelation 5

*Then I looked, and I heard the voice of many angels
around the throne and the living creatures and the elders;
and the number of them was myriads of myriads,
and thousands of thousands.*
REVELATION 5:11 NASB

I am weary and forlorn,
lead me to the land of angels.
I think it is time I went for a space
to the court of Christ,
to the peace of heaven.
CARMINA GADELICA

In the Celtic understanding of life—as in the Orthodox—God likes company. We are never alone, and God is never alone either. God filled the world we know with people and creatures, and God has peopled the unseen world with the beings we know as angels. They always delight to do God's will, and they are not weighed down with worldly baggage.

Unlike the fanciful portrayals of angels in medieval times, biblical angel encounters have a more earthy tone. Six roles for these bodiless servants of God can be discerned in the scriptures. They shield (for example, Daniel 3:28, 12:1); they reveal God's message of salvation (Matthew 1:20); they heal (Tobit 3:17); they carry out God's judgments (Revelation 15:7–8); they escort souls at death (Luke 16:22); and they praise God (Luke 2:13).

On this eve of St. Michael and All Angels Day, it is good to turn our thoughts toward angels. Michaelmas should be a significant time for us as it was for Celtic Christians, who offer us a feast of angel stories. Bede's writings brim with stories of encounters with angels, and a third of Adamnan's *Life of Columba* consists of angel experiences. The Celts believed that heaven and earth lay side by side, and angels walk often among us.

*Have mercy on little ones abused,
may tender angels draw them to your presence.
Have mercy on those in black trial,
may healing angels lift them into your presence.
Have mercy on souls at death's door,
may holy angels escort them to your presence.
Have mercy on we who remain,
may smiling angels radiate to us your presence.*

SEPTEMBER 29 ✢ MICHAEL: ANGEL LEADER

Psalm 35; David 10:4-11:1; Revelation 12:7-12

*Then Michael, one of the chief angels, came to help me,
because I had been left there alone.*
DANIEL 10:13 GNT

In the New Testament, Michael is named as the chief of the angels (Jude 9). The Book of Revelation depicts him throwing down the dragon, a symbol for Satan, who can come in the form of anti-Christ in any age.

The first Celtic evangelists introduced Christianity to a society that was under the spell of many kinds of magical and unseen powers. They often built places of Christian worship on high places that had previously been dedicated to such powers; and these churches were often dedicated to Michael. Two well-known examples of such Celtic foundations, built as a result of God giving direction to a Christian leader in the area, are Mont St. Michel in Brittany and St. Michael's Mount in Cornwall. Michael was God's warrior, capable of dispelling all the powers of evil.

*Thou Michael the victorious,
I make my circuit under thy shield.
Thou Michael of the white steed
and of the brilliant blades,
conqueror of the dragon, be thou at my back,
thou Ranger of the heavens,
thou Warrior of the King of all.
O Michael victorious, my pride and my guide;
O Michael the victorious, the glory of mine eye.
I make my circuit in the fellowship of the saint,
on the grass sward, on the meadow,
on the cold leathery hill.
Though I should travel ocean
and the hard globe of the world,
no harm can ever befall me
'neath the shelter of thy shield.
O Michael victorious, the jewel of my heart;
O Michael the victorious, God's shepherd thou art.*
CARMINA GADELICA

SEPTEMBER 30 ✣ ANGELS' HELP

Psalm 34; Zechariah 3; Acts 12:1-10

*Jesus said: Be careful to never look down
on a single one of these little ones—
for I tell you they have angels
who see my Father's face continually in heaven.*
MATTHEW 18:10

As Columba sat transcribing the Scriptures in his little cell at Iona, two brothers who were outside his open door were alarmed when they saw his countenance suddenly change. "Help! help!" he shouted.

"What's the matter?" they asked.

Columba told them, "A brother at our monastery at Oakwood Plain in Derry was working at the very top of the large house they are building there, and he slipped and began to fall. I ordered the angel of the Lord who was standing just there among you two to go immediately to save this brother."

Later, the monks learned that a man had indeed fallen from that great height, but nothing was broken, and he did not even feel any bruise. As the brothers at Iona discussed this, Columba said, "How wonderful beyond words is the swift motion of an angel! It is as swift as lightning. For the heavenly spirit who flew from us when that man began to fall was there to support him in a twinkling of an eye before his body reached the ground. How wonderful that God gives such help through his angels, even when much land and sea lies between."

*O angel guardian of my right hand
attend to me this night.
Rescue me in the battling floods,
array me in your linen, for I am naked;
succor me, for I am feeble and forlorn.
Steer my coracle in the crooked eddies,
guide my step in gap and in pit,
guard me in the treacherous turnings
and save me from the harm of the wicked;
save me from the harm this night.
Drive me from the taint of pollution,
encompass me till Doom from evil.
O kindly angel of my right hand,
deliver me from the wicked this night,
O deliver me this night.*
CARMINA GADELICA (ADAPTED)

AUTUMN

Looking forward

*We are looking to the promise of glory
that is set before us.
It is a time of waiting and praying
and we are encouraged to keep true to the path
by the saints that have died in faith.*

OCTOBER 1 ✣ ANGELIC GUIDANCE

Psalm 149; Daniel 11:2-20; Luke 1:5-25

The angel told Daniel,
"Three more kings will appear in Persia, and then a fourth."
DANIEL 11:2

Perhaps you have been—or will be, later this fall—involved in selecting or voting for someone to fill a vacant post. The Bible warns us against automatically choosing the person with the most charm. The story of the prophet Samuel choosing the future King David, who was regarded as the least of his large and talented family (see 1 Samuel 16), is a timely warning. And the Celtic account of Columba's choice of Aidan mac Gabran to fill the vacant throne of Dalriada not only warns us against presumption, it also encourages us to believe that God always has ways of guiding us to the right person.

When the king of Dalriada died in 574, the question of the succession involved Columba, who was both related to the royal household and also the leader of the now dominant religion. Columba went into retreat on the Island of Hinba to seek God's guidance. He felt that, since there were no sons, the eldest nephew of the deceased king should be chosen.

One night, however, Columba had a vision of an angel carrying a book that contained a list of the kings. Columba's candidate did not appear in it, but his younger brother, Aidan, did. Although Columba read in the book that he was to install Aidan as king, he refused. Suddenly, the angel stretched out its hand and gave Columba a mighty slap on his side, which left a mark for the rest of his life. The angel told him, "You must know for certain that I have been sent to you by God, and if you continue to refuse to install Aidan as king, I shall hit you again."

Columba was not amused by this vision, but it recurred three nights in succession. After the third time, Columba got the point. He sailed to Iona, consecrated Aidan as king, gave him a heartfelt blessing, and prophesied as to the future of his dynasty. Aidan's reign proved to be a period of sound government and of peace between previously warring regions.

O Michael militant, king of the angels,
shield your people with the power of your sword.
Spread your wing over sea and land
and bring us to our goal.

OCTOBER 2 ❖ ANGELS DEFLECT AN EPIDEMIC

Psalm 91; Exodus 12:21-28, Revelation 7:1-8

After this I saw four angels standing at the four corners of the earth holding back the four winds... and I saw another angel coming up from the east with the seal of the living God. The angel shouted to the four angels to whom God had given power to hurt the earth and the sea, "Do not harm them until we mark the servants of our God with a seal on their foreheads."
REVELATION 7:1-3

Despite the advances of medicine, many people still live in fear of a sudden catastrophe or an epidemic such as AIDS. In the era of the Celtic saints, the deadly plague swept through and decimated whole populations. In such situations, human beings easily lose sight of the fact that God is still in overall control. We feel so powerless.

Columba had set aside a day in the Iona woods for sustained prayer. As he began to pray, he saw a wave of black creatures relentlessly attacking Iona with iron darts. Columba linked this experience with the threat of oncoming plague. His biographer, Adamnan, writes:

> But he, singlehanded, against innumerable foes of such a nature, fought with the utmost bravery, having received the armor of the apostle Paul. The contest was maintained on both sides during the greater part of the day, nor could the demons, countless though they were, vanquish him, nor was he able, by himself, to drive them out from his island, until the angels of God, as the saint afterwards told certain persons, came to his aid, when the demons in terror gave way.

After his time of prayer, Columba informed some brothers that Iona would now be spared the plague, but it would invade the monasteries in the region of Tiree. This came only too true. Two days later, Columba also foresaw that Baithen, the leader of one monastery in the Tiree region, had called his community to all-out fasting and prayer, and as a result only one brother there would die of the plague. This, too, came to pass exactly as Columba had foreseen.

Good angels, messengers of God,
protect us from all that would plague our bodies,
protect us from all that would plague our souls.

OCTOBER 3 ✢ SING WITH THE ANGELS

Psalm 150; Daniel 8:1-14; Revelation 7:9-12

Praise the Lord from heaven, you who live in the heights.
Praise the Lord, all you angels and heavenly forces of the Lord.
PSALM 148:1-2

If you pray truly, you will feel within yourself a great assurance, and the angels will be your companions. Know this, that as we pray, the holy angels encourage us and stand at our sides, full of joy, and at the same time interceding on our behalf.
EVAGRIUS OF PONTUS

He created good angels and archangels, the orders of Principalities and Thrones of Powers and Virtues so that the goodness and majesty of the Trinity might not be unproductive in all works of bounty but might have heavenly beings in which he might greatly show forth his favors by a word of power. From the summit of the kingdom of heaven, where angels stand, from his radiant brightness, from the loneliness of his own form through being proud Lucifer had fallen, whom he had formed and the apostate angels also, by the same sad fall of the author of vainglory and obstinate envy, the rest continuing in their dominions. At once, when the stars were made, lights of the firmament the angels praised for his wonderful creating the Lord of this immense mass, the Craftsman of the Heavens, with a praiseworthy proclamation, fitting and unchanging in an excellent symphony they gave thanks to the Lord not by any endowment of nature, but out of love and choice.
ALTUS PROSATOR, *ATTRIBUTED TO* COLUMBA

May the seven angels of the Holy Spirit
and the two guardian angels
shield us this and every night
till light and dawn shall come.
CARMINA GADELICA

OCTOBER 4 ✣ SING WITH THE SUN

Psalm 148; Daniel 8:15–27; 1 John 1

Praise the Lord, sun, moon, and shining stars.
Praise the Lord, highest heavens and the waters. . . .
Praise the Lord, strong winds, all animals and peoples.
Psalm 148:3–4, 8, 10–11

Praised be you, my Lord, with all your creatures,
especially Sir Brother Sun
who is the day, and through whom you give us light.
He is beautiful and radiant, with great splendor
and bears a likeness of you, Most High One.
Praised be you, my Lord, through Brother Wind
and through the air, cloudy and serene, and every kind of weather
through which you give sustenance to your creatures.
Praised be you, my Lord, through Sister Water,
who is very useful and humble, precious and pure.
Praised be you, my Lord, through Brother Fire,
through whom you light the night.
He is beautiful and playful, robust and strong.
Praised be you, my Lord, through our sister, Mother Earth,
who sustains and governs us
and who produces varied fruits with colored flowers and herbs.
Francis of Assisi (translation based on that of Armstrong and Brady)

Blessed Lord,
as Francis found joy in creation, in beauty and simplicity,
but perfect joy in sharing the sufferings of the world,
so may we, abiding in your love, receive your gift of perfect joy,
and by the power of your Spirit radiate your joy
and find, even in suffering, the glory at God.
A Prayer at the Franciscan Priory, Almouth

OCTOBER 5 ❖ CIRCLING

Psalm 20; Job 26; 1 John 2:1-17

God divided light from darkness by a circle.
JOB 26:10 GNT

On Michaelmas Day at Iona, all the humans and even the animals walked sunwise (turning from east to west in the direction of the sun) around the Angels Hill to seek God's blessing on the island for the coming year. Abbots of Iona such as Columba and Adamnan practiced the circling prayer. Adamnan tells us that when Columba sailed from Loch Foyle, he blessed a stone by the water's edge and made a circuit round it sunwise, and it was from that stone that he went into the boat. Columba taught that anybody going on a journey who did the circling prayer round the stone would most likely arrive in safety.

Why did they use the circling prayer? Celtic Christians carried on the Druids' understanding that the Devil was frustrated by anything that had no end, no break, no entrance, because they knew that God is never ending both in time and in love, and the Three Selves within God form an ever encircling Presence. One of the chief rites of the sun-worship of pagan Celts was to turn sunwise in order to entice the sun to bless their crops. The Christians said, in effect, "The Creator of the sun is now among us. We will continue to circle our crops, but now we do it in the name of the Sun of Suns."

This is not magic: it is an expression of the reality of the encircling Presence of God. To say the Caim or Circling prayer, stretch out your arm and index finger and turn sunwise, calling for the Presence to encircle the person or thing you pray for.

Circle me, Lord.
Keep love within, keep strife without,
keep hope within, keep despair without,
keep peace within, keep harm without.

OCTOBER 6 ❖ WHY IS THERE EVIL?

Psalm 44; Deuteronomy 30; 1 John 2:18-29

I have given you the choice between a blessing or a curse.
DEUTERONOMY 30:1

By granting us the wonderful gift of freedom, God gave us the capacity to do evil as well as good. Indeed, we would not be free unless God had given us this ability: there is no freedom for the person who does good by instinct and not by choice. In this sense, the capacity to do evil is itself good; evil actions, although God does not want them, are themselves signs of the goodness of God in allowing them.

Some Christians developed the idea that "original sin," which affects us all, means that people who do not listen to God in nature or in human beings, and who therefore damage them, are not responsible, because only "born-again" Christians can be expected to know God's ways. The holy British monk Pelagius, however, taught that each person is capable of both good and evil, and is responsible for their choices.

> A person might say that the world would be a better place if everyone within it were always good and never evil. But such a world would be flawed because it would lack one essential ingredient of goodness, namely freedom. When God created the world he was acting freely; no other force compelled God to create the world. Thus by creating humans in his image, God had to give them freedom. A person who could only do good and never do evil would be in chains; a person who can choose good or evil shares the freedom of God.
> PELAGIUS IN A LETTER TO DEMETRIUS

In the strength of the Warrior of God,
I oppose all that pollutes.
In the eye of the Face of God,
I expose all that deceives.
In the energy of the Servant of God,
I bind up all that is broken.

OCTOBER 7 ✢ WHY DO GOOD PEOPLE SUFFER?

Psalm 102; Job 1; Romans 2

Count it as joy when all kinds of trials come your way,
for . . . in the end, you will become complete.
JAMES 1:2, 3–4

> There is no follower of Christ who is not at times perplexed by the suffering of good men and women. . . . If an evil person contracts a painful and fatal illness while still young, if their house burns to the ground, if they lose their wealth in some dishonest transaction, we feel that justice is being done. But if a good person falls fatally ill in their youth, if an honest and hardworking person becomes destitute, we are indignant. We cannot understand how God can permit such injustice.
>
> Our indignation arises from superficial knowledge. We look at pain and pleasure, sorrow and joy, in shallow, material terms. Yet a good person, even if undergoing great physical distress, still senses the serene peace of God deep within their soul. The loyal disciple of Christ who is compelled to live in poverty knows that they are sharing the poverty of Christ. And the Scriptures assure us that in poverty and in agony the soul of Christ knew the heavenly joy of God.
> PELAGIUS

No one likes to see a person who is both good and young struck down. This was what happened to the Northumbrian King Oswald—and yet, a generation after his death, when new Christians in the south of England were devastated by plague, God used his example to transform a dying boy and bring faith to the problem of innocent suffering.

The onset of plague had prompted a monastery to begin a vigil of fasting and prayer. On the second day of the vigil, two apostles appeared in a vision to a small boy who lived at the monastery and told him, "Do not let the fear of death trouble you. We are going to take you to the heavenly kingdom. . . . Call the priest and tell him the Lord has heard your prayers and not one more person from the monastery or the estates linked to it will die of this plague; all sufferers will be restored. God has granted this in response to the prayers of the saintly King Oswald. It was on this very day that he was slain in battle and taken to heaven." All this came to pass. The boy died, peacefully and joyfully, and the faith of the people grew stronger.

Lord, help me offer to you the gift of deep but not bitter suffering.

OCTOBER 8 ✥ CHOOSE GOOD OR EVIL

Psalm 7; Genesis 42; Romans 3

If you give heed to the terms I give you today
you will receive gifts of peace.
If you turn away from the way I have laid out for you,
to go after false gods,
you will receive a curse.
DEUTERONOMY 11:27–28

God created all human beings in God's image, to be like God. God has made many animals more physically powerful than human beings, but we have been given intelligence and freedom. We alone are able to recognize God as our maker, and therefore to understand the goodness of God's creation. We alone have the capacity to distinguish between good and evil, right and wrong. This means that our actions need not be compulsions; we do not have to be swayed by our immediate wants and desires, as are the animals. Instead, we can make choices. Day by day, hour by hour, we have to make decisions. In each decision we can choose either good or evil. This freedom to choose makes us like God. If we choose evil, that freedom becomes a curse. If we choose good, it becomes our greatest blessing.
PELAGIUS

There is no evil in anything created by God, nor can anything of his become an obstacle to our union with him. The obstacle is in our "self," that is to say in the tenacious need to maintain our separate, external, egotistic will.
THOMAS MERTON

> Toothache starts in a rotten tooth,
> then the pain spreads through the jaw
> until one's whole head starts to throb.
> Every thought is filled with toothache.
> Sin starts with a rotten action,
> then the pleasure spreads through the body
> until the soul itself becomes enslaved.
> Every feeling is filled with sinful desire.
> Pull out the aching tooth.
> Root out the sinful action.
> ROBERT VAN DE WEYER, CELTIC PARABLES

I open my mouth, Lord, trusting you
to pull out all the aching teeth.

OCTOBER 9 ✥ BLIND SPOTS

Psalm 4; Genesis 43; Romans 5

*Why do you point out the speck in the other person's eye
and pay no attention to the log in your own eye?
...First, take the log out of your own eye,
and then you will be able to see clearly
to take the speck out of the other person's eye.*
MATTHEW 7:3, 5

Even the best and holiest of people have stubborn areas in their lives. Perhaps a person eats or drinks to excess and refuses to restrain his appetite; perhaps a person has a quick and harsh temper and refuses to restrain her anger; perhaps a person needs to be the leader in every situation, and cannot take advice or criticism, nor defer to the better judgment of others. Compared with the other areas in which a person is good and holy, these stubborn areas may seem quite trivial. Yet if they remain unchecked they can corrode a person's soul and blot their record.
PELAGIUS TO A MATURE CHRISTIAN

*O Savior of the human race,
O true physician of every disease,
O heart-pitier and assister of all misery,
O fount of true purity and true knowledge,
forgive.*

*O star-like sun, O guiding light,
O home of the planets,
O fiery-maned and marvelous one,
forgive.*

*O holy scholar of holy strength,
O overflowing, loving, silent one,
O generous and thunderous giver of gifts,
O rock-like warrior of a hundred hosts,
forgive.*
ATTRIBUTED TO ST. CIARAN (ADAPTED)

OCTOBER 10 ❖ CRITICAL SPIRITS

Psalm 12; Genesis 44; Romans 6

*My servant will not crush a bruised reed
or quench a smoldering flame.*
MATTHEW 12:20

In a world of right and wrong, in which we are free spirits, it would be foolish to expect people never to criticize. But think of the occasions when Jesus criticized; they were very few, always timely, and he never crushed a bruised reed. He always affirmed the people who needed affirmation. If we follow his example, criticism should only be made on rare occasions, as a last resort, in a kindly spirit, after prayer and thought, directly to the person concerned, and only if it is both true and necessary.

> The easiest sin to commit is to criticize a brother; calling him a fool. We are usually cautious about accusing a brother of a major sin; we feel we must have sufficient evidence before making such an accusation. But to accuse a brother of doing something stupid hardly seems to matter. So we lightly toss off such critical remarks.
> Yet such criticism can wound deeply. It can stay with a person for years after the person who uttered it has forgotten about it. This is because so many people lack a sense of self–worth, and fear failure. So a critical remark can destroy their confidence completely, discouraging them so much that they may never again attempt the task that was criticized.
> So we must be far more vigilant against committing this easy sin than against the more obvious and serious sins.
> PELAGIUS TO AN ELDERLY FRIEND

*Lord,
let our memory provide no shelter
for grievance against another.
Lord,
let our heart provide no harbor
for hatred of another.
Lord,
let our tongue be no accomplice
in the judgment of a brother.*
NORTHUMBRIAN OFFICE

OCTOBER 11 ✢ AVOID PRESUMPTION

Psalm 14; Genesis 45; Romans 8

Pride comes before a fall.
PROVERBS 16:18

A brother began to pester Abba Theodore with all sorts of questions and opinions about aspects of God's work, none of which he had seriously engaged in himself. The old abba said to him, "You have not yet found the ship you are to sail, or put your baggage in it, so how is it that you seem to be already in the city you plan to sail to? When you have first worked hard in the thing you talk about, then you can speak from the experience of the thing itself."

Three brothers came to an abba in Scete. The first proudly told him, "I have committed the Old and New Testaments to memory."

"You have filled the air with words," the abba told him.

The second informed him, "I have transcribed the Old and New Testaments with my own hands."

"And you have filled your windows with manuscripts," was the reply.

The third, who felt he had devoted so much time to prayer and study that he had no time to spare for household jobs announced, "The grass grows on my hearthstone."

The abba said, "And you have driven hospitality from you."
SAYINGS OF THE DESERT FATHERS

Fools rush in where angels fear to tread.
BRITISH PROVERB

Speak up to but not beyond your experience.
FRANK BUCHMAN

Almighty, I'm steeped in the "I know best" mentality.
I invite your Holy Spirit to convict me of presumption,
to expose every lingering bit of it in any corner of my life
and to winkle it all out of me.
Give to me the wisdom of humility.

OCTOBER 12 ⁘ OLD AND YOUNG

Psalm 26; Genesis 46; 1 Peter 5

You elders ... should not try and dominate those who have been put in your care, but you should be examples for them to follow.... In the same way you younger people should give yourselves to the older ones. And all of you must clothe yourselves with humility, to serve one another.
1 PETER 5:1, 3, 5

Old people often envy the vigor and good health of the young, their greater capacity to enjoy physical pleasures, and the length of years they have ahead of them. The truth is, however, young people should envy the old!

Although old people have less physical and mental energy, they have greater spiritual reserves. Although they can enjoy fewer physical pleasures, they have greater capacity for spiritual enjoyment. Thus the old are better prepared for death, and for life beyond death. So the fewer years that are ahead of them should be a reason to celebrate, not to indulge self-pity.

Although a young person like yourself may assume that you have many years ahead of you, you cannot be sure. The soul is attached to the body by a fragile thread which can snap at any moment. So although you are younger than I am, you may die before me. Do not, therefore, merely envy old age: imitate its virtues. Direct your physical energies into spiritual matters, let these become your major source of pleasure. In this way you will be ready for death whenever it comes.
PELAGIUS TO A YOUNG FRIEND

O God, to whom to love and to be are one,
hear my faith-cry for those who are more yours than mine.
Give each of them what is best for each.
I cannot tell what it is.
But you know.
I only ask that you love them and keep them
with the loving and keeping
you showed to Mary's son and yours.
COLLECTED BY ALISTAIR MACLEAN IN HEBRIDEAN ALTARS

OCTOBER 13 ✥ A RULE OF LIFE

Psalm 51; Genesis 47; 1 Peter 4

*I chose some of your people to be prophets,
and some to be Nazirites...
but you made the Nazirites drink wine,
and ordered the prophets not to speak my message.*
AMOS 2:11–12 GNT

Certain Christians, not just monks and nuns, follow what they call a Rule or a Way of Life. This sets out the values and goals they choose to make their priority, and a checklist, suited to their circumstances, of practices that help them to live these. Other Christians argue that they want to be rid of rules and regulations, and, since no two situations are alike, all they need is the Holy Spirit to guide them.

Here is some advice to consider: In a single day we make so many decisions, we cannot possibly weigh up the good and evil consequences of each decision. We are liable to make foolish and wrong decisions. For this reason we need a rule, a simple set of moral principles we can apply to each decision we make. This will not be foolproof, but with a good rule, our decision will far more often be right than wrong.

Another reason for a rule is this: Jesus tells us to pray always; yet sometimes we love to devote much time to prayer, whereas at other times we are dry or feel far too busy to pray. A rule prevents us from making excuses; it spurs us to pray at a particular time even when our heart is cold towards God.

The teaching of Jesus must be the primary general guide for any disciple, but Jesus himself did not give rules. The source of a rule is inside your own heart. What we call conscience is a kind of rule God has written in your heart. If you wish to formulate a rule, you must listen to your conscience and write down on paper what God has written on the heart.
FROM PELAGIUS

*Eternal God,
our beginning and our end
accompany us through the rest of our journey.
Open our eyes to praise you for your creation,
and to see the work you set before us.*
BASED ON THE MIDDAY PRAYER, ST. FINBARR'S CATHEDRAL, CORK

OCTOBER 14 ✢ PASSING ON WISDOM

Psalm 49; Proverbs 1; James 1:1-15

*Always be prepared to give an answer to everyone
who asks you to give the reason for the hope you have.
But do this with gentleness and respect.*
1 PETER 3:15 NIV

You have a deep desire to appear wise, but you have no confidence in yourself: you do not regard yourself as wise. So in the company of others you remain silent; even when the conversation turns to spiritual matters, where words of wisdom are most necessary; you remain silent. You hope that people will interpret your silence as a sign of the depth of your wisdom—so deep that mere words cannot communicate it. Some people try to deceive others with dishonest words; you are trying to deceive others with dishonest silence.

If you possess wisdom on particular matters, it is your duty under God to express this wisdom to others, so they can benefit from it. If you do not possess wisdom on matters of importance, it is your duty under God to ask questions of those who do possess wisdom so you can learn from it. In either case you must speak.

This does not mean that words must flow ceaselessly from your mouth like a river. Use words sparingly, so that they express exactly what you mean. But without words you will remain ignorant and stupid.
PELAGIUS TO A YOUNG FRIEND

In Sophia, the highest wisdom-principle, all the greatness and majesty of the unknown that is in God and all that is rich and maternal in his creation are united inseparably, as paternal and maternal principles, the uncreated Father and created Mother-Wisdom.
THOMAS MERTON

*Lord help me never to pretend
to know more than I do know,
always to be ready to speak out of my experience,
up to my experience
but not to speak beyond it.*

OCTOBER 15 ✧ GO WITH THE FLOW

Psalm 16; Proverbs 2; 1 Corinthians 9

*When working with the Jews
I live like a Jew in order to win them . . .
when working with Gentiles,
I live like a Gentile . . . in order to win Gentiles. . . .
Among the weak in faith I become weak like one of them,
in order to win them.*
1 CORINTHIANS 9:20–22 GNT

Someone asks, "Surely a Christian should stand against current trends in order to uphold the values of the Gospel rather than to go with the flow?" Wherever contemporary values conflict with those of Jesus, that is certainly true. But have we examined how much in our church ethos is a matter, not of values, but of cultural taste? Saint Paul confronted evil boldly, yet it was also he who gave a mission model of becoming one with different groups and cultures (in all things except sin) in order to win them to a relationship with Christ.

Celtic Christians, too, were clear about sin, but unlike Christians in other parts, they kept a loose hold on churchy culture if it was alien to their people. They had their meetings at the places where the people normally met; they built their places of worship on the places where people had previously worshipped as non-Christians; they carried on customs such as circling farms and homes, but now they did this in the name of the One True God. In the years following Patrick in Ireland, the shape of church organization reflected that of the clan. Instead of organization being imposed from outside, it was like a wheel, in which the clan welcomed a Christian community as its hub. Celtic Christians also resisted the idea that Christians should cut off the long, flowing hair that Celts felt was their glory; Celtic Christians could give glory to God with their long hair. Evangelists such as Aidan and Chad resisted pressure to use the form of transport that important people used but which would have distanced them from ordinary people; they used their feet, not a horse, to make visits. Aidan also resisted pressure to impose all the Christian laws on unchurched people before they had come to know and love Jesus and the milk of his teaching. When groups of Christians gathered at natural meeting places, they would often play traditional music and would join in with other singers, whether they were Christian or not.

*Creator of diverse cultures,
Brother to all peoples, flowing Spirit,
help me to go with the flow of all that is good and human around me.*

OCTOBER 16 ✣ PRIDE BEFORE A FALL

Psalm 36; Proverbs 3:1–20; James 2

"Master," Simon answered, "we worked hard all night long and caught no fish. Nevertheless, if you say so, I will let down the nets." Simon let them down and caught such a large number of fish that the nets were about to break.
LUKE 5:5–6

Simon Peter knew more about fishing than did Jesus, since Jesus had a background in carpentry instead. Peter knew where the fish were, and he knew that night was the right time to catch them. So it must have seemed daft when Jesus told him that if Peter pushed the boat out in the morning, he would make a catch. But Simon Peter was learning that Jesus was a channel of a wisdom higher than his own know-how. Each of us has to learn this lesson in our own way. This is how Saint Gall learned it.

Gall was the best known of Columbanus's followers, and he accompanied him to Annegray and Luxeuil, where they founded some of the first Celtic Christian communities on the continent of Europe. Gall was very bright, but he was also hot-headed, and needed to learn lessons in humility.

One day at Luxeuil, Columbanus, who was the abbot, asked Gall to go to a particular river to catch fish. Gall, who was a keen fisherman, took this as an opportunity to show his independence and his better knowledge of fishing; he went to a different river where he knew there were more fish. And it was true the fish were plentiful; he could see them swimming all around his net. But for some reason, though he tried all day, not a single one would swim into the net! Rather sheepishly, Gall returned to Columbanus. Columbanus said mildly, "Why not try doing what I told you?"

Next day, Gall swallowed his pride and followed Columbanus's instruction. Sure enough, the moment he threw his net into the river, the fish came in so fast that he could hardly pull them out. Gall got the point that although he was more clever than others, he was also more conceited. Humility succeeds where pride fails.

Lord, take pride and false independence from my spirit.

OCTOBER 17 ✤ DEPENDENCY

Psalm 5; Proverbs 6:1-19; James 4

*It is better to trust in the Lord
than to depend upon human leaders.*
PSALM 118:9 GNT

One of the curses of our society is a condition that has been described as "the cycle of dependency." Proud and false independence is wrong, but dependency (which is different from mutual interdependence) and failure to take responsibility is also wrong; it is a subtle form of idolatry. We can so easily put leaders on pedestals, and expect them to do for us what we can only do for ourselves. Certainly, we can only do these things in the strength God gives, but God is as available to us as much as God is to them. In fact, there should never be a "them" in our minds!

Celtic Christianity nurtured close fellowships and delightful friendships, but it did not spawn dependency. If someone wanted to enter a monastery (and sometimes these were the only safe and decent places around), they had to wait outside for days, proving that they could take responsibility for their food, sleep, and time; that they could make their own decisions; and that they could work hard.

Maedoc and Molaise were bosom friends—but they were open to the possibility that they might be called to travel independent paths. "Ah Jesus," they prayed one day at the foot of two trees, "is it your will that we should part, or that we should remain together to the end?" Then one of the trees fell to the south, and the other to the north. They knew then that it had been revealed to them that they must part. Maedoc went south and built a monastery at Ferns; Molaise went north and built a monastery in Devenish.

Recently, during a gathering of a large religious movement, someone begged the leader, "Our children are being murdered in the streets. Come and help us."

The leader was silent for a moment, and then he said, "Brother, you are hurting, and I feel for you. Let me give you my address and phone number. I'll do what I can to help you. But please—do not look to me as a leader. I may be dead tomorrow. God wants to raise up a leader in you."

*Moment by moment you give me choices, O Lord.
Help me to make the right choices.*

OCTOBER 18 ✢ MUTUAL DEPENDENCE

Psalm 2; Proverbs 9; James 5

*When you please the Lord
you can turn your enemies into friends.*
PROVERBS 16:7

Gall learned the hard way that he needed other people. When a hostile ruler came to power, the monks had to leave the region. But Gall became too ill to travel with Columbanus, who left him behind, believing that his illness was in some way connected with a weakness in his character. After the others had left, Gall managed to get his fishing nets and his few possessions onto a boat and get himself to a priest, who nursed him back to health.

Gall now realized he had made many mistakes in the way he related both to the brothers and to local people. He had destroyed their objects of worship before he had made friends with them. Now he decided the best thing he could do was to serve God alone in a life of prayer and prepare for heaven. Gall asked the priest to recommend a place where he could live as a hermit. The priest replied that the mountains and valleys were too full of wild beasts for this to be viable. "If God be for us, who shall be against us?" Gall replied.

So they came to a place by a river where Gall settled, and the wild beasts became his friends. Other hermits joined him, for he had now learned to be humble—to be like the humus, the earth. Columbanus may have sensed this and wanted to heal the divide that had come between them, for before he died, he sent Gall his abbot's staff as a sign that the past was over and that he believed in Gall's God-given calling.

Gall was in fact pressed to become abbot of the monastery at Luxeuil, but he had now no worldly ambitions, and he refused. However, the world flocked to his cell. The monastery that took the place of his hermit's settlement became a center of life and learning for Europe. The town that grew up around, St. Gallen, is now one of the great industrial cities of Switzerland.

*Humble me, Lord.
May I be sensitive to other people
whatever their background.
May I be led, not by my self-opinionated will,
but by you alone.
And may this result in friendships.*

OCTOBER 19 ⁜ THIS AUTUMN DAY

Psalm 65; Ezekiel 17:22-24; Luke 12:13-21

You crown the year with Your goodness.
PSALM 65:11 NKJV

O sacred season of autumn, be my teacher
for I wish to learn the virtue of contentment.
As I gaze upon your full-colored beauty
I sense all about you an at-home-ness with your amber riches.
You are the season of retirement
of full barns and harvested fields.
The cycle of growth has ceased
and the busy work of giving life is now completed.
I sense in you no regrets; you've lived a full life.
I live in a society that is ever restless,
always eager for more mountains to climb,
seeking happiness through more and more possessions.
As a child of my culture
I am seldom truly at peace with what I have.
Teach me to take stock of what I have given and received;
may I know that it's enough, that my striving can cease
in the abundance of God's grace.
May I know the contentment
that allows the totality of my energies
to come to full flower.
May I know that like you I am rich beyond measure.
EDWARD HAYS

*I thank you for the wind
that clears the fog and clog of life,
for chimneys that allow warmth to move through our lives,
for the texture of the bricks and tiles.
I thank you for housetops and streetlights
and for the sound of traffic moving.
I thank you for TV and satellite dishes.
These open the world up to people in their little dwellings.
So much energy, so much enterprise—
the friendly smiles of Sister Earth.*

OCTOBER 20 ✢ APPROPRIATE

Psalm 25; Proverbs 10; 2 Timothy 3

You know who your teachers were, and you remember that ever since you were a child you have known the Holy Scriptures.... All Scripture is inspired by God and is useful for teaching the truth, rebuking error, correcting faults, and giving instruction for right living so that a person who serves God may be fully qualified and equipped to do every kind of good work.
2 TIMOTHY 3:14–17 GNT

When we are young, a thousand little ways of behaving seem like second nature to the adults we know, while we ourselves are unsure and self-conscious about how to react in different situations: how to converse, how to eat things, when and how to arrive and leave. We need the freedom not to have to prove we know things, that it is okay to ask what is the appropriate thing to do, to take time to observe how others behave, to gradually get a sense of what is appropriate, yet to remain open to inspirations that are unique to us.

Once a group of brothers were enjoying a picnic with Columba by a riverside in Ireland, when a bard strolled by. The bard joined the brothers, and they talked for a while until he went on his way. After he was gone, the brothers asked Columba why he hadn't invited the bard to sing some of his songs, composed by himself, before he left them. This would have been the appropriate thing to do at the time.

"Because," answered Columba, "that poor man has been killed; and since I sensed that this would happen, how could I have requested a happy song from someone who is about to meet such an unhappy end?"

Lord of the shadows, Lord of the day,
Lord of the elements, Lord of the grey,
Lord of creation, Lord of the journey,
I am unsure, weak, and frail.
Grant me sureness in the nearness of your clasp.
Father, keep me in every steep,
Savior, reach me in every slip,
Spirit, teach me in every fall.

OCTOBER 21 ✧ IDOLS

Psalm 24; Jeremiah 10; Titus

Dear children, keep yourselves from idols.
1 JOHN 5:21 NIV

The first things that come to mind when idols are mentioned are the carved figures of other faiths. When we relegate the word "idols" to other faiths than our own, we can avoid facing the fact that an idol is an expression of a universal tendency to substitute something in the place of God. Behind all idolatry is the desire to control, to make God in our own image, to chase after illusions.

As Samson passed through the Hundred of Twigg, in Cornwall, he heard a group of people acting out a ritual in honor of a god. He stilled the brothers as he silently watched. In order not to appear threatening, Samson took just two brothers with him and greeted their leader, Guedianus. Gently, he explained that it was not good to forsake the one God who created all things in order to worship one created thing. This brought varied reactions. Some jeered, some were angry, some argued that since it was tradition it surely could not be wrong, others simply told him to go away.

Circumstances, however, intervened, and Samson believed that God, unlike the idol, could use these circumstances. A lad, who had been driving some horses far too fast, fell headlong from his horse and hit his head as he fell. He lay on the ground like a lifeless corpse; everyone gathered round, and as they realized they could do nothing, they began to weep. Samson took the initiative. "You can see that your idol can do nothing for this fellow," he said. "If you promise you will destroy and cease to worship this idol, I, with God's assistance, will restore him to life." The people agreed. Samson asked them to withdraw and prayed over the boy for two hours. At the end of that time, he delivered the boy safe and sound. The people destroyed their idol, and gave their allegiance to Samson, and he instructed and baptized them as Christ's followers. On the hill, in place of the idol, Samson carved a cross on a standing stone with his own hand.

The dearest idol I have known
whate'er that idol be,
help me to tear it from thy throne
and worship only thee.
WILLIAM COWPER

OCTOBER 22 ✣ FAR APART, YET CLOSE

Psalm 3; Proverbs 18; Philemon

*I always thank my God when I pray for you . . .
because I keep hearing about your faith in the Lord Jesus
and your love for all of God's people. . . .
Your love has given me much joy and comfort, my brother,
for your kindness has often refreshed the hearts of God's people.*
PHILEMON 4, 5, 7 NLT

Brendan of Birr was known as the chief of the prophets of Ireland, and he was a lifelong friend of Columba. When a church synod at Meltown, in Meath, excommunicated Columba because he belonged to a hostile clan, only one person rose to greet Columba as he arrived at the synod—Brendan. This took courage. Brendan told everyone, "I dare not slight the man chosen by God to lead nations into life."

The two men remained close even when they were far apart geographically. Not only did Brendan have prophetic foresight of Columba's future ministry; Columba, on Iona, was aware of Brendan's death in the west of Ireland on November 29, and saw angels carrying his soul to heaven.

Have you taken the time to become aware of the souls with whom you have great affinity? Does God want you to move with that awareness? To be in touch through means of new technology—or just by carrying each other in prayer?

Friends are a little bit of heaven here on earth.
ANONYMOUS

*Father, I offer you these friends.
Jesus, I thank you for these bonds.
Spirit, I look to you to maintain this rapport.*

OCTOBER 23 ✢ HONORING GOD

Psalm 21; Isaiah 19:16-25; Romans 1:1-12

Righteousness exalts a nation.
PROVERBS 13:34 NIV

Though the Celtic church and culture was wrecked by Viking invasions, the Gaels triumphed in the end. They converted the Norsemen to Christianity, and even the kings of Norway craved the honor of burial on holy Iona. The kings of Alban continued to be buried there, for it had become home for the hearts of Pict and Scot alike. Kenneth MacAlpin, the half-Pictish Scot who in 845 welded the two people together . . . also was laid in the soil of Iona.

Columba's legacy was something more abiding than relics or buildings. He left his people a vision of what God can do in and through a person, if they were willing to go the whole way. As a prince and an adviser to kings he was inevitably concerned with politics and his work resulted in vast social, political, and economic consequences. . . . But how did he do it? Not by political means but by spiritual...His politics were to change the hearts of politicians.

The founding of Iona stands out like a divine intervention in history. It was the decisive stroke in the war of Faith and it let loose the spirit of the Peregrini (the wanderers for the love of God) which was to transform Europe.
REGINALD B. HALE

People must choose to be governed by God
or they condemn themselves to be ruled by tyrants.
WILLIAM PENN, 1644–1718

May our nation find your will as her destiny.
May our nation find God-guided representatives
at home and abroad.
May our nation find peace within itself
and become a peacemaker in the international family.

OCTOBER 24 ✢ AS I AM SO IS MY PEOPLE

Psalm 18:1-27; Proverbs 31:1-9; Romans 4

O Lord, ... here we are before you in our guilt.
EZRA 9:15 NIV (THE PRAYER OF EZRA ON BEHALF OF HIS PEOPLE)

A romantic idea has gained credence that Celtic saints such as Cuthbert prayed in the sea all night and every night. If they sought out extreme cold purely for the sake of causing themselves discomfort, they would have been masochists. It is true, however, that Celtic Christians at times prayed in cold water as a form of penance. And there is no doubt, as we have learned, that Cuthbert was once seen praying in the sea at night during a visit to the monastery at Coldingham.

In this case, there may have been a particular reason for Cuthbert taking a dip in the cold sea. This is how I see it: The men and women in this mixed monastery had slid into immoral sexual practices. Their abbess, Ebba, though a good person, was ineffective. So she invited Cuthbert to visit the monastery, and no doubt she poured into his ears all the sleaze she had been unable to handle. Cuthbert, within himself, took authority over the situation. He made himself one with his brothers and sisters in the monastery. Then, acting as their representative, he went down into the pure, salt sea. The sharp cold of the water cooled their passions; the size of the ocean put their sins into perspective compared to the love and power of God. The immersion of their representative in the sea was a way of immersing this community in God. The chanting of God's praise in the psalms was an offering on behalf of the community, as well as a weapon that made its enemies—lust, lies, laziness—flee away.

It may be that your attention is drawn to a situation where immorality or dishonesty have taken a hold; it seems like a barrel of apples in which every apple threatens to become rotten. You ask, "What can I do?" Perhaps the example of people in the Bible such as Ezra, or of forebears in the Faith such as Cuthbert, will give us the resolve to take authority in prayer, to make confession, petition, and praise on others' behalf. For, as the saying has it: As I am, so is my people.

Lord Jesus Christ,
who became the representative of the whole human race,
in your name I represent these people
who are in such a mess.
I bring them now to you.

OCTOBER 25 ✣ SLEEP

Psalm 127; Proverbs 3:21-35; Matthew 8:18-27

The Lord gives sleep to those he loves.
PSALM 127:2

Celtic Christians allow God to permeate every area of life, even the hidden or unconscious areas. Since one-third of our lives is likely to be spent in sleep, we need to invite God into our sleeping hours, just as the ancient Celts did.

> I lie down this night with God
> and God will lie down with me.
> I lie down this night with Christ
> and Christ will lie down with me.
> I lie down this night with the Spirit
> and the Spirit will lie down with me.
> The Three of my love will be lying down with me.
> I shall not lie down with sin
> nor shall sin or sin's shadow lie down with me.
> I lie down this night with God
> and God will lie down with me.
> CARMINA GADELICA

> Sleep, sleep, and away with sorrow.
> Sleep in the arms of Jesus,
> sleep in the breast of virgin mother,
> sleep in the calm of all calm,
> sleep in the love of all loves,
> sleep in the Lord of life eternal.
> CARMINA GADELICA (ADAPTED)

> *May the blessing of the Son*
> *help you do what must be done.*
> *May the Spirit stroke your brow*
> *as weary down to sleep you go.*
> *May the Father mark your rest,*
> *empower you for tomorrow's test.*
> *May the Trinity rekindle*
> *the pure flames of your life's candle.*
> RAMON BEECHING

OCTOBER 26 ❖ DESIRING ONLY GOD

Psalm 63; 1 Samuel 1; John 1:35-50

O God, you are my God, and I long for you from early morning; my whole being desires you. Like a dry, worn-out, and waterless land, my soul is thirsty for you. Let me see you in the house of prayer... for your constant love is better than life itself.
PSALM 63:1-3

How happy are those who will be found on the lookout when the Lord comes. O happy lookout, in which they look for God the Creator of the universe, who fills and transcends all things.

I, too, though I am frail, desire to rise up from the sleep of idleness, to kindle the flame of divine love, the longing that is at the heart of divine compassion, and to rise above the stars, so that God's love ever burns within me. O that my life might be like a living flame that burns throughout the dark night in the house of God, giving light to all who come in from the cold.

Lord, give me that love which does not fail people; make my life like an open fire that you are always kindling, which nothing can quench. O Savior most sweet, may I receive perpetual light from you, so that the world's darkness may be driven from us. O eternal Priest, may I see you, observe you, desire you, and love you alone as you shine in your eternal temple.

O loving Savior, reveal yourself to us, so that knowing you we may love you, loving you we may desire you, desiring you we may contemplate you, you alone, by day and by night, and ever hold you in our thoughts.

Inspire us with your love, that it may possess all our inward parts, and all the different parts of our bodies, till this love is so huge that even the many waves of the world, the currents of air, sea, or land cannot quench it.
COLUMBANUS

Awesome lord of earth and heaven,
rule my heart.
My faith, my love, to you be given,
my every part.
EARLY IRISH

OCTOBER 27 ✥ ALL THINGS LIVE IN GOD

Psalm 33; 1 Samuel 2:1-11; John 3

All things that exist were made by God the Word...
and the Word is life.
JOHN 1:3-4

As we approach the close of the three-month harvest period, an important occasion in the Celtic year, we dwell on the theme of creation once again. Let us meditate on these reflections by the Celts' great mystical theologian, John Scotus Eriugena:

> All things, even what seems to us to be without vital movement, live in the Word. If you want to know how all things subsist in God-the-Word, choose some examples from created nature and think about them. . . . Consider the infinite, multiple power of the seed—how many grasses, fruits, and animals are contained in each kind of seed; and how there surges forth from each a beautiful, innumerable multiplicity of forms. Contemplate with your inner eye how in a master the many laws of an art or science are one; how they live in the spirit that disposes them. Contemplate how an infinite number of lines may subsist in a single point, and other similar examples drawn from nature. "For in him," as the Scripture says, "we live and move and have our being."
>
> But . . . human nature, even if it had not sinned, would not have been able to shine by its own strength. Although human nature is capable of wisdom, it is not itself wisdom. Just as the air does not shine by itself, yet is able to receive the light of the sun, so the Word wishes to teach us, "It is not you who shine; but the Spirit of our Father shines in you." You are not a light in yourselves, you are only able to participate in the divine light.
> JOHN SCOTUS ERIUGENA, HOMILY ON THE PROLOGUE TO THE GOSPEL OF ST. JOHN *(ABRIDGED)*

Creator, we are contained in you,
and we are connected to all else that is contained in you.
Help us not to rebel against our connectedness.
Light-giver, we are reflectors for you,
and, as we connect with others, we become rays of light.
Help us not to shut out your light.
Shine, Jesus, shine in us today.

OCTOBER 28 ✢ SUNSET

Psalm 30; Genesis 28:10–22; John 6:1–21

*At sunset [Jacob] came to a holy place and camped there.
He lay down to sleep... and dreamed.*
GENESIS 28:11–12 GNT

A sunset speaks of an ordinary day's work completed well, of a year moving toward its climax, transfigured by glory. It is a gift. It cannot be won by restless striving. It is a glory; it makes the body tingle and the spirit soar. The tiresome or clashing features of the day become silhouettes—beautiful, harmonious. Their darkness speaks of a mysterious but deep meaning.

The evening of our years is meant to be lived in such a dimension. Hear God saying to us, "Let me have my way among you. Do not strive, and I will crown your life with glory."

> On that night when Saint Columba, by a happy and blessed death passed from earth to heaven, while I and others with me were fishing in the valley of the river Find, we saw the whole vault of heaven become suddenly illuminated. Towards the east there appeared something like an immense pillar of fire, which seemed to illuminate the whole earth like the summer sun at noon. After that the column penetrated the heavens, darkness followed, as if the sun had just set.
> ADAMNAN

*We welcome the Sun of suns who dispels the shades of sin.
The sun rises daily only because you command it;
its splendor will not last, created things all perish.
Christ, the true Sun, nothing can destroy;
the Splendor of God, he shall reign forever!
I praise you for the sun, the face of the God of life.
As the sun sets in peace, may I settle in with you.*

OCTOBER 29 ✧ FREED FROM FATE

Psalm 58: Zechariah 4; 1 Corinthians 15:1-34

You are set free from the ruling spirits of the universe.
COLOSSIANS 2:20

The belief was common in country areas that some people could cast an evil eye on anything they pleased; for example, if they cast an evil eye on you, you might either miscarry a baby or have a miscarriage of justice. Modern forms of this belief have an almost universal and equally malign influence.

Many of us go through life conditioned by what someone has said about us. Perhaps a parent told us that we would never be any good at something; maybe our friends and family have a certain image of who we are. Teachers or employers assume we are not capable of certain things because of our background or education. We accept an identity that is distorted by other people's perceptions; we act out the false information that has been fed to us. We live a lie. We are not free to rise to our God-given destiny.

Those who follow Christ discover that no one need be the prisoner of fate. The eyes of Jesus' mother Mary were able to look upon the awful agony of her son and share something of his sacrificial love. This spurs us to believe that we can ask Jesus to cast his eyes, with those of his mother, upon us. Their eyes of love, which want only what is true and best for us, have power to override any spell that a lesser and evil eye has cast on us.

When Mary saw him, as she stood,
high on the cross, all torn and rent,
rained from her eyes three showers of blood
and at its foot she made lament.
An Evil eye has me undone, paling my face in dule and dree;
I cry to Mary and her Son
take the ill eye away from me.
FROM RELIGIOUS SONGS OF CONNACHT *COLLECTED BY* DOUGLAS HYDE

Lord, I want to name those of my reflex actions
that spring from what others have put upon me
through their looks or their words.
I give these to you.
Help me to see myself as you see me.
Set me free to be your child, your adult,
moving freely as a person under the influence of your Spirit.

OCTOBER 30 ❖ The Fear of Death

Psalm 64; Genesis 49:29–50:14, John 6:25–71

Victory has swallowed death.
1 CORINTHIANS 15:54

Soon you and I will die. We do not know the day or the hour of death; God alone has such knowledge. But we can be certain that many more years have elapsed since birth than will pass between now and death. You say that you have no fear of death. I fear death because I fear having to account for my evil deeds before God. You say that you fear the process of dying. I do not fear dying because I know that God will not force me to suffer pain beyond my capacity to endure it. Elderly people like ourselves frequently make attempts to amend their behavior, hoping that God will forgive them past sins and judge them on present goodness. God will not be swayed by that kind of calculation. It is the heart, not the mind, that needs to change: we must learn to love God more fully. And love coming from the heart makes no calculation. If a person loves God with his whole heart, he will entrust himself to God's love, without seeking to sway God's judgment by displays of good behavior. If my heart could change in such a way, my fear of death would disappear.
PELAGIUS IN A LETTER TO AN ELDERLY FRIEND

Alone with none but you, my God,
I journey on my way.
What need I fear, when you are near,
O King of night and day?
More safe am I within your hand
than if a host did round me stand.
My life I yield to your command,
and bow to your control
in peaceful calm, for from your arm
no power can snatch my soul.
Could earthly foes ever appall
a soul that heeds the heavenly call!
ATTRIBUTED TO COLUMBA

OCTOBER 31 ✢ HALLOWEEN

Psalm 97; 1 Samuel 16:14-23; John 14

The Lord Almighty says, "[My people] are oppressed ... but the One who will rescue them is strong—his name is the Lord Almighty. He will take up their cause but will bring trouble to Babylon. ... Babylon will be haunted by demons and evil spirits."
JEREMIAH 50:33-34, 39 GNT

Winter draws near, nights draw in, and something within us draws back and is afraid. Halloween (that is, the evening of All Hallows, meaning all the holy ones or saints of God) is a day when, in the past and today, people focus on the darkness that is encroaching, and on the spirits, fears, and powers that seem to hover around us at this time. The idea of wearing masks and witches hats was not to imitate evil spirits; it was to frighten them off! Today many older people are frightened to go out after dark, or to open the door, not because of evil spirits, but because of youngsters taking "trick or treat" too far.

The Celtic followers of Christ understood that our world is like a good land that is temporarily under occupation by malign forces. Their responsibility was to expel evil forces in the name of the Owner, and to claim back the land for God. In order to do this, they used protective prayers like a coat of armor. Today, we can still focus on Christ's victory over evil and circle in prayer the places that attract fears or forces of darkness; we can light a candle to symbolize Christ, the Light of the world, whom no darkness can quench.

Compassionate God of heaven's powers,
screen me from people with evil intentions.
Compassionate God of freedom,
screen me from curses and spells.
Compassionate God of the saints,
screen me from bad deeds, bad words, bad thoughts.
Compassionate God of eternity,
screen me from bad influences here and in the past.
May your cross be between me
and all things coming darkly toward me.

NOVEMBER 1 ✣ ALL SAINTS

Psalm 93; Deuteronomy 26:1-15; Hebrews 12:1-11

*Therefore, since we are surrounded by such a great cloud of witnesses,
let us throw off everything that hinders and the sin that so easily entangles,
and let us run with perseverance the race marked out for us.*
HEBREWS 12:1 NIV

Christ's Celtic followers observed Samhain, the Celtic New Year that marked the coming of darkness, as All Saints' Day, the glorious celebration of believers who had gone into the dazzling light of God's presence.

> O most dear ones, I can see you, beginning the journey to the land where there is no night nor sorrow nor death. . . . You shall reign with the apostles and prophets and martyrs. You shall seize the everlasting kingdoms, as Christ promised, when he said: "They shall come from the east and the west and shall sit down with Abraham and Isaac and Jacob in the kingdom of heaven."
> SAINT PATRICK'S LETTER TO COROTICUS

> When in the Acts of the Apostles the apostles came together in one place, Solomon's Porch, which became a focus of peace and unity, crowds came who were made whole from diseases even by the shadow cast by the apostles. And truly, up to this day, wherever Christians gather together for the yearly festival of an individual, the Lord never ceases to perform mighty works.
> On this splendid festal day of St. Samson, at God's inspiration, mighty works of God that are just as great have without doubt been witnessed. For this reason we recognize that God has endowed Samson with an everlasting quality and an unhampered freedom. As we celebrate the heavenly kingdom on his day we perceive the next life with a clear, keen insight. For we firmly believe that he is engaged in another, better, unending life among the saints of God, whom we see shining forth among us, strong and mighty in the Land.
> FROM THE LIFE OF SAMSON OF DOL

*Eternal Friend, I thank you
for your cloud of witnesses who shine so brightly.
Help me to grow strong and holy like them
that I may live more fully and boldly for you
and keep my eyes on the eternal kingdom.*

NOVEMBER 2 ✢ ALL SOULS ARE LOVED

Psalm 107:17-43; Daniel 4; Luke 15

They are yours, O Lord, you lover of souls.
WISDOM 11:26 NAB

God has put within us a need to recollect, from time to time, those people who, though now dead, have loved or influenced us: to remember them, to savor them, to talk to God about them, and perhaps to complete a grieving process. Today, All Souls Day, is a good time to remember these individuals in a few moments of silence, thank God for them, and keep them in mind throughout the day.

Celtic Christians believed, as the Bible teaches, that God's attitude toward all people is like the love an earthly mother has for all her children: she longs to draw them close to her. This still leaves the individual the decision whether to reject or respond to that love—but when we remember the dead in our prayers, we can picture God endlessly wooing them with a love that will never end.

Hail, sister! May you live in God.
ON A FOURTH-CENTURY TOMBSTONE AT YORK

Since it was you, O Christ, who bought this soul—
at the time it gave up its life,
at the time of pouring sweat,
at the time of returning to clay,
at the time of the shedding of blood,
at the time of severing the breath,
at the time you delivered judgment—
may your peace be on your ingathering of souls,
Jesus Christ, Son of gentle Mary,
your peace be upon your own ingathering.
High king of the holy angels,
take possession of the beloved soul
and guide it home to the Three of limitless love.
Yes, to the Three of limitless love.
CARMINA GADELICA (ADAPTED)

NOVEMBER 3 ✣ LIFE AFTER DEATH

Psalm 99; Job 42; John 8:31-59

I know a man who was snatched up to Paradise
(I do not know whether this actually happened or whether it was a vision),
and there he heard things he couldn't put into words.
2 CORINTHIANS 12:2-4

In 696, Drithelm died one evening in Northumbria—but he came back to life early the next morning, causing panic among his grieving family. He proceeded to give away his estate and joined a monastery at Melrose. When people asked him what had caused him to make such a dramatic change of lifestyle, this is what he told them: "A shining figure led me northeast to a valley. On one side there was a gale, and on the other a great fire. Both sides were full of souls that seemed to be tossed from one side to the other. The wretches could never find rest. I began to believe this must be hell. But my guide told me it was not that. He took me slowly to the farther end of the valley, which was gradually filled with thick darkness. Huge black flames suddenly arose and subsided into a pit. Each time this happened, I noticed that the flames were filled with human souls, and there was a revolting stench. Then a gang of spirits dragged these howling souls laughingly first into the darkness, and then into the burning pit. Some of them threatened to drag me there too. I was certain this must be hell, but my guide said it was not. In my extremity, a bright star drew near behind me, which caused these spirits to run away. The bright star turned out to be my heavenly guide, who brought me back into the light. However, in front of us was a seemingly infinite wall. I wondered why we approached it, since there was no way through, but somehow, we found ourselves inside it, in a large and fragrant garden. Here were innumerable souls in white, all rejoicing. I wondered if this was the kingdom of heaven, but my guide said that it was not. We passed on toward a place of exquisite scents and singing and brightness. I was eager to enter, but just then my guide led me back the way we had come. The guide explained that we had been to the place of trial and discipline. Though their purging was terrible, they were to repent before their final death and heaven was to be opened to them. Many people are spared their torment through the prayers of God's people. The delightful place is where souls who have led lives full of good works go, though they are not yet ready to see Christ face to face. At the day of judgment they shall all see Christ."

The guide then told Drithelm, "As for you who are about to go back to the earth, if you live a life that is simple and right with God, you will be able to join those joyful troops of the Lord."

BASED ON BEDE

Lord, have mercy upon me.

NOVEMBER 4 ✢ PRAISE IN ICY CONDITIONS

Psalm 56; Daniel 6; John 11:1–44

*Lord, you brought me out from the gates of death
so that I may sing your praises to your people
and tell them of your deliverance.*
PSALM 9:13–14

The radical new lifestyle that Drithelm adopted after his near-death experience had twin peaks.

The first peak was voluntary poverty. Following a day of prayer after his recovery, he divided his estate into three portions. The first third he gave to his wife, the second third to his children, and the last third he kept for himself. That third he promptly distributed to people in the neighborhood who were in greatest need. Is that a model worth considering when we make our wills?

The second peak consisted of singing God's praises. The hut where he went to live as a hermit was on the edge of the monastery grounds, by the River Tweed, and he frequently, as a penance, stood in the water, sometimes up to his waist and at other times up to his neck, reciting Scriptures or singing psalms for as long as he could endure it. He did this even in winter, standing in the river with bits of ice floating about him! Bystanders would say, "It's wonderful that you can stand such cold," and Drithelm would reply, "I have seen it colder." And when they asked, "How can you endure such austerity?" Drithelm dryly replied, "I have seen more austerity."

This man of Melrose became a topic of conversation in the region, and many people were influenced by his example.

> November is a "no" month. It is easy to allow ourselves to be pulled down. So I decided to make it a "yes" month. Each day I make sure there is something for which I can say "yes" to God.
> MARGARET BURNS OF NORTHUMBERLAND

*Champion, save me from being a fair-weather Christian.
When I get cold feet,
remind me of the example of people such as Drithelm.
May the praises of God be in my mouth
whatever I feel like today
and every day.*

NOVEMBER 5 ❖ BONFIRES

Psalm 88; Isaiah 1:1-17; John 11:45-57

Build houses and settle down.
JEREMIAH 29:5 NIV

This is the time of year when the cold and the dark seem set to take over, a time when our instinct is to withdraw. It is the Celtic season of Samhain, when cattle that had to be brought down from the hills and could not be accommodated in the barns were slaughtered. The bonfires we associate with this season get their name from the "bone fires," in which the inedible parts of the carcasses were destroyed. The fires are also associated with the idea of clearing the land for winter; the leaves and summer's leftovers are swept up and burned. Something in the human psyche, too, needs to clear away what is excess, accepting a reduction in the number of choices that are available to us. We need to settle down in the darkness.

But our egos resist the idea of accepting limits. Some people feel depressed at this time of year. Others flout what God is saying through nature by indulging in a reckless lifestyle throughout the winter. Yet think of the animals who hibernate. Think of the wonders of spring flowers—they would not be able to burst forth if they had not first lain still in the wintry earth.

So how should we respond to this time of year? In two ways. First, by fighting against the darkness of fear, despair, self-concern, and evil spirits. We expel these in the name of Christ and receive his strength, faith, and selfless love. Second, by not fighting against the God-given rhythm of the season, but by going with its flow. November's grey days, dark nights, cold rains, and thick fog help me to accept that I am mortal. This means that I will take more time to be inside, alone, still with God; I will take more time for study and the inner life. I will spend less time dashing around, purchasing, planning, starting new enterprises.

Father, Savior, Sustainer,
as this cold, dark month encroaches,
give to us the stability of the deep earth
and the hope of heaven.

NOVEMBER 6 ✥ A DOOR IN PARADISE

Psalm 55; 2 Chronicles 32:24-33; John 12:1-11

*Jesus said to the robber:
"Today you will be with me in paradise."*
LUKE 23:43

Limited by their earthly perspectives, people often pray mutually exclusive things. This happened with Columba when he lay near to death.

Columba had prayed that the Lord would release him into heaven on the thirtieth anniversary of his ministry in Britain. On that day, he saw two shining beings approach, en route to escort him to heaven, and his face was wreathed with smiles. Two monks then observed Columba's expression suddenly darken. They drew out of him the reason: although these angels had come in answer to his prayers, folks in other places had been praying too—that God would spare Columba more years yet. Columba told the monks that, though he was disappointed, God would grant him four more years in answer to the prayers of the churches. The result was that Columba saw these angels withdraw beyond Iona.

Four years later, Columba knew the time of his departure had surely now come, and he carefully prepared his farewells. He went round the island on a cart, blessing the people and crops. He issued this statement from the store barn: "I heartily congratulate the monks of my community because although I have to depart from you, you have enough bread for the year."

When he returned to the monastery, he lowered himself into a seat, and his packhorse, sensing he was to leave earth, laid its head on Columba's lap and began to weep like a human being. Columba told an attendant who wanted to shoo it away: "No. My fellow humans would have known nothing about my dying if I had not revealed this to them, yet God has clearly revealed to this animal that its master is about to depart."

Later, in a final spurt of energy, Columba ran into the church. His attendant lifted his arm, and Columba left this world blessing his brothers with the sign of the cross.

*Almighty God, Father, Son, and Holy Spirit,
to me, the least of saints,
allow that I may keep a door in Paradise.
That I may keep even the small door
that is least used, the stiffest door.
If it be in your house, O God,
that I can see the glory even afar, and hear your voice,
and know that I am with you, O God.*
COLUMBA

NOVEMBER 7 ✥ SOUL FRIENDS AT DEATH

Psalm 133; 2 Samuel 1; John 18:1–11

Saul and Jonathan—in life they were loved and gracious,
and in death they were not parted.
They were swifter than eagles,
they were stronger than lions.
2 SAMUEL 1:23 NIV

Ciaran was young, handsome, and God had used him to establish many churches in Ireland, when suddenly he was struck down with the plague. Knowing he was soon to die, Ciaran asked to be carried to a small mound where he looked at the vast open sky. His monks then carried him to the little church where he blessed them; he then asked that he should be shut in and left there alone until his soul friend, Kevin, arrived from Glendalough.

Ciaran, however, died before Kevin arrived, though the brothers kept his corpse in the church until Kevin arrived. As soon as Kevin entered the church, however, Ciaran's spirit reentered his body, so that he could have fellowship with Kevin.

After a day together, Ciaran blessed Kevin, and Kevin blessed water and gave Holy Communion to Ciaran. Ciaran gave his bell to Kevin as a sign of their lasting unity; and then finally, he went to heaven.

When the soul separates from the perverse body
and goes in bursts of light up from out its human frame,
O holy God of eternity, come to seek me and to find me.
May God and Jesus aid me, may God and Jesus protect me,
may God and Jesus eternally seek and find me.
CARMINA GADELICA

NOVEMBER 8 ✢ A HOME IN HEAVEN

Psalm 131; 1 Kings 2:1-12; John 10

*We know that if the earthly tent we live in is destroyed,
we have a building from God,
an eternal house in heaven, not built by human hands.*
2 CORINTHIANS 5:1 NIV

I have not many friends of influence upon earth;
they have journeyed on
from the joys of this world to find the King of Glory;
they live in heaven with the High Father,
they dwell in splendor.
Now I look day by day for that time
when the cross of the Lord
which once I saw in a dream here on earth
will fetch me away from this fleeting life
and lift me to the home of joy and happiness
where the people of God are seated at the feast in eternal bliss,
and set me down where I may live in glory unending
and share the joy of the saints.
May the Lord be a friend to me,
he who suffered once for the sins of all
here on earth on the gallows tree.
He has redeemed us;
he has given life to us and a home in heaven.
FROM THE DREAM OF THE ROOD, TRANS. KEVIN CROSSLEY-HOLLAND

Savior and Friend, how wonderful art thou,
my companion upon the changeful way,
the comforter of its weariness,
my guide to the Eternal Town,
the welcome at its gate.
HEBRIDEAN ALTARS

*I am going home with you, to your home, to your home;
I am going home with you, to your home of mercy.
I am going home with you, to your home, to your home;
I am going home with you, to the place of all the blessings.*
CARMINA GADELICA (ADAPTED)

NOVEMBER 9 ✣ DEATH SONG

Psalm 54; 2 Kings 13:14-21; John 12:27-36

Since we believe that Jesus died and rose again,
so will it be for those who have died:
God will bring them back to life with Jesus.
1 THESSALONIANS 4:14

A certain brother one night, hearing that Fintan was keeping vigil in prayer, wanted to know where he was praying. The monk searched for him on this side and that, until at last he came to the Christian burial ground. It was a dark night, but as the brother gazed at Fintan face-to-face, he witnessed an extraordinary light, spreading far and wide. This light was so bright that his eyes were almost blinded, but God preserved him through that same grace that was upon Fintan.

Before he leaves on his fated journey
no one will be so wise that he need not
reflect while time still remains
whether his soul will win delight
or darkness after his death-day.
BEDE'S DEATH SONG

Lord of the sunrise, source and ground of my being,
you know me in my mother's womb.
As my first day begins, heal me of the pain and hurt I receive.
Lord of the dawn, you see me grow strong
as I learn to walk and talk;
heal me of tears of separation and loss.
Lord of the high noon, you accompany me along life's journey;
guide me in choice and strengthen me in adversity.
Lord of the dusk, as my life declines,
help me to surrender all that I have
and all that I am into your hand.
Lord of the sunset, as I go to my eternal home,
strengthen me on my last journey with you
that I may entrust my soul into your hands in faith and hope.
MICHAEL HALLIWELL

NOVEMBER 10 ✥ CARRIED IN ANGEL ARMS

Psalm 99; Daniel 12; Hebrews 12:12–29

*You have come to Mount Zion,
to the city of the living God, the heavenly Jerusalem,
and to countless thousands of angels in a joyful gathering.
You have come to the assembly of God's firstborn children,
whose names are written in heaven.*
HEBREWS 11:22–23 NLT

The day came when Ninian, full of years, was stricken with a wasting disease and racked by pain. Yet even while he was beset with illness, his mind soared above the sky. The revered lover of justice spoke these words: "The potter's kiln shakes the pots with the force of the flame, but cruel burdens are the trials of just people. I should like to suffer dissolution and see Christ face-to-face." When he had uttered these words, his spirit departed his pure body and passed through the clear heights of the star-studded heavens.

Then when the breath of life had left his dying limbs, he was immediately surrounded by the shining host, and now blazing bright in snow-white vestment, like Phosphorus in the sky, he was carried in angel arms beyond the stars of heaven. Passing through the companies of the saints and the everlasting hosts, he rejoiced to visit the innermost shrine of the King throned on high. He clearly perceived, united as he was with the celestial hosts in the halls of heaven, the glory of the Trinity, the hymns of gladness, together with the supreme denizens of the Holy City on high.

FROM THE MIRACLES OF BISHOP NYNIA TRANSLATED BY WINIFRED MACQUEEN

*O being of brightness, friend of light,
from the blessed realms of grace
gently encircle me, sweetly enclosing me,
guarding my soul-shrine from harm this day.
Keep me from anguish. Keep me from danger.
Encircle my voyage over the seas.
A light will you lend me to keep and defend me,
O beautiful being, O guardian this night.
Be a guiding star above me;
illuminate each rock and tide;
guide my ship across the waters
to the waveless harbor side.*
COLLECTED BY CAITLIN MATTHEWS

NOVEMBER 11 ✣ REMEMBRANCE

Psalm 20; Isaiah 2:1-5; Luke 6:27-36

Your pride and joy ... lies dead on the hills!
Oh, how the mighty heroes have fallen!
2 SAMUEL 1:19 NLT

Today we remember those untold millions who have lost their lives in war. We mourn for the goodness and the wisdom, the life and the laughter, the potential and the passion that perished with them.

This is also a day when we rededicate ourselves to build a world of peace. How can we do this? How can our remembering our veterans be more than a wistful evaporation of hopes? Perhaps the life of Saint Martin of Tours can encourage us.

In the early church, only those who had shed their blood for the faith were formally pronounced saints—until Martin of Tours. He, who gave up being a soldier in order to create the peace of the kingdom of heaven on earth, was the first non-martyr to be recognized as a saint. His feast day is in three days' time.

His father, a senior Roman army officer, named him Martin, which means warrior, and trained him to become a soldier. While Martin was playing as a boy, in Italy, a thunderstorm struck. He ran for shelter and found himself in a church service. He listened to the stories of Jesus and was captivated. He accepted a new kind of training, to become a soldier of Christ. Before Martin had completed his instruction in the Christian faith and been baptized, however, his father presented him to the Emperor. Although he was only fifteen years old, he was tall and strong, and he was sent to begin military service in France.

On his arrival at Amiens, he met a beggar. Moved with compassion, Martin took off his own fine cloak, cut it in half, and gave one half to the beggar. That night he had a dream. Jesus stood by his bed and said, "Martin, you have done a great act of love for me. I was cold and you gave me half your cloak." Martin dressed, went to the nearest church, woke the priest, and asked to be baptized. After two more years in the army, Martin went to the Emperor, and braving the Emperor's anger, persuaded him to release him from the army, so that he could serve God without any pay and begin to build a Christian community of peace.

Peace between victor and vanquished.
Peace between old and young. Peace between rich and poor.
The peace of Christ above all peace.

NOVEMBER 12 ✥ The Shadow

Psalm 23; Ecclesiastes 1; Luke 11:37-54

*Even though I walk through the valley of shadows,
I will fear no evil, for you are with me.*
PSALM 23:4

November is a time of advancing shadows. Celtic Christians did not run away from these; instead, they went alone into places of shadow, and there they faced the shadows inside themselves. They learned the importance of doing this from the desert Christians.

> Just as it is impossible for a person to see their reflection in a pool whose water is disturbed, so, too, the soul, unless it is cleansed from alien thoughts, cannot pray to God in contemplation.
> SAYINGS OF THE DESERT FATHERS

The psychiatrist Carl Jung called that part of our inner life that is unacceptable to us our "shadow." Jesus drew the distinction between the surface life and the shadow life when he likened some proud church people to sepulchers that were painted white outside but full of rot inside. In his book *Why Do Christians Break Down?* William Miller admits, "I break down because I am afraid to admit that evil, unacceptable, inappropriate tendencies still exist within me, even though I have committed myself to the way of Christ, and I cannot accept them as being truly part of me."

The qualities that we bring to the surface when we interact with the outer world are subtly adapted to get the approval of others. The less attractive qualities get buried in our subconscious and lie there unattended. Subconsciously, we don't want to know these parts of ourselves for fear that they will damage ourselves or others.

Take time to get in touch with your shadow. Make a list of the things that most often make you angry with other people. This may give you clues as to your shadow's feelings. Once you have been honest about your vices, make a conscious effort to replace each vice with its opposite virtue; that was how Celtic Christians approached this matter. And then invite God's light to shine even in your shadowy places.

*Holy Three, help me to stay with you
while I stay with the darkness in myself.
Throw your light upon this darkness.
Give me strength to journey through into a greater wholeness.*

NOVEMBER 13 ✧ ONE VAST FAMILY

Psalm 67; Isaiah 16:1-8; Acts 17:16-23

*Brothers—all the people of the world
who ultimately come from one stock—
the message of safety and deliverance has been sent to us all.*
Acts 13:26

I am sure that the exploration of this Celtic world will be prophetic for the future as we try to break down the barriers so that we may reach out to one another. This discovery of my own Celtic roots has meant that I have also become more aware of the riches of many other traditional peoples. Here, instead of the highly individualistic, competitive, inward-looking approach common in today's society . . . everyone sees themself in relation to one another.
Esther de Waal, The Celtic Way of Prayer

At the root of all war is fear.
Thomas Merton

Only love—which means humility—
can cast out the fear that is the root of all war.

All humankind are one vast family,
this world our home.
We sleep beneath one roof, the starry sky.
We warm ourselves before one hearth,
the blazing sun.
Upon one floor of soil we stand
and breathe one air
and drink one water and walk the night
beneath one luminescent moon.
The children of one God, we are
brothers and sisters of one blood
and members in one worldwide family of God.
From The Book of Remembrance
Cathedral of St. Paul the Apostle, Los Angeles, California

*Christ, victim of barriers,
Christ, vanquisher of barriers,
Christ, linking us across the shores of treachery and time,
be with us all this day.*

NOVEMBER 14 ✧ DULL DAYS

Psalm 89; Ecclesiastes 3; Luke 21:29-32

*For everything there is a season,
and a time for everything that happens in this world....*
ECCLESIASTES 3:1

Do not too easily escape from a dull day.
It is natural to turn from the cold to the heat of indoors.
It is natural to turn from the dusk to the electric light.
It is natural to turn from the damp to a dry house.
There is a time to do these things,
but there is also a time to shake the hand of a November day.
November days are a necessary part of life.
They correspond to something in the "shadow" side of my being.
Part of me is damp, or wet, or grey.
Learn to accept this.
Accept that life is a journey that passes through the seasons.
Do not renege on the journey.
Drabness in nature is not boring; it is merely different.
It is a post-mortem on a fruitful season,
a prelude to a spring-time,
a pause for taking stock, a time to reflect.
It also has its special charisms.
For example, the rows of bare trees become a salute
once they are uncluttered by green foliage.

God before me, God behind me,
God above me, God below me.
I on the path of God, God upon my track.
Who is there on land?
Who is there on wave? Who is there on billow?
Who is there by door-post? Who is along with us?
God and Lord.

*I am here abroad, I am here in need,
I am here in pain, I am here in straits,
I am here alone. O God, aid me.*
CARMINA GADELICA

NOVEMBER 15 ❖ MARTIN OF TOURS

Psalm 27; Deuteronomy 15:1–11; Matthew 25:31–46

*Who through faith conquered kingdoms, administered justice,
and gained what was promised; . . .
whose weakness was turned to strength.*
HEBREWS 11:33–34 NIV

When the Emperor released Martin from the army, he had to walk all the way home. It took him weeks. When he arrived, his mother joyfully became a Christian, but his father, whose pride was hurt, turned him out. So Martin walked all the way back to France. There, he offered his help to Hilary, Bishop of Poitiers, who ordained him as a deacon.

Martin wanted to live in solitude, so after a time, he went to the quiet village of Liguge and built himself a little cell, the first in Europe. He was not alone for long, however.

Each day, he would rise from prayer to respond to the needs of others. One day he tended a leper; another day he prayed for hours over a man who had hanged himself, whose life then returned; on another occasion, he cured a man with mental illness. God's power was at work in him, so when the local Bishop of Tours died in 572, all the people thereabouts were determined to make Martin their next bishop.

As bishop, Martin visited the surrounding villages. One pagan priest challenged Martin to be bound to a tree as it was felled, to test whether his God could save him. The tree turned away from Martin as it fell, and the whole population turned to Christ. When Martin was a guest at the Emperor's table, before he ate anything, he asked for the release of innocent prisoners in Tours. The Emperor deeply respected Martin's example for Christ.

Martin has an honored place in the Celtic calendar for two reasons. First, he pioneered an informal monasticism that, following the Eastern model, combined individual freedom of movement with a framework of common fellowship. The second reason is that Martin did not stay in the towns only; he healed and evangelized even in moors and mountains all over France until he died at the age of eighty.

*Great God, thank you for Martin, soldier, servant, and soul-winner.
Inspire us by his example
to live lives of discipline and compassion.*

NOVEMBER 16 ❖ CONTEMPLATE YOUR DEATH

Psalm 28; Isaiah 28:14-29; 1 Timothy 6:2-21

> *We brought nothing into the world,*
> *and we can take nothing out of it.*
> 1 TIMOTHY 6:7 NIV

Remembrance of the dead is emphasized in the *Sayings of the Desert Christians*:

> If there are graves in the area where you live, go to them constantly and meditate on those lying there. . . . And when you hear that a brother or sister is about to leave this world to go to the Lord, go and stay with them in order to contemplate how a soul leaves the body.
> A truly philosophical works (says an abba to visiting philosophers) is to meditate constantly on death.

The Desert Christians referred to death as "the Great Passage." Like the Celtic Christians after them, they knew that death was, in some cases, very painful; yet even then, they experienced it fundamentally as a celebration, as the following story illustrates:

> The brothers said to Abba Moses (the former brigand), "Let us escape since the barbarians are coming.'"
> "I'll stay here," Moses replied, "I have been waiting so long for this day so that the word of my Lord Jesus Christ may be fulfilled, 'All those who have used the sword will die by the sword.'" There were seven brothers there. Before any of them could escape, the barbarians arrived and slew them all.
> However, a brother who was not with them in that hut hid under some palm fronds and saw everything. He saw seven crowns coming down to rest on the heads of Abba Moses and the six brothers killed with him.

> *Lord of the Great Passage,*
> *you hold a crown ready in your hand.*
> *If I trust in my own will,*
> *I cannot receive it.*
> *I trust in you alone,*
> *and I am eager to come to you.*

NOVEMBER 17 ✥ HILDA OF WHITBY

Psalm 119:97–112; Proverbs 8; Matthew 13:31–35

Wisdom is calling out at the crossroads:
"Take my instruction, for wisdom is better than wealth,
and all that you desire cannot compare with her.
I hate pride and arrogance. I have good advice.
By me, rulers rule, and all who govern with justice."
PROVERBS 8:1, 10–11, 13–15

Hilda was born in 614, and in 627, she was baptized by Paulinus, a missionary sent from Rome. She nobly served God for the first half of her life as a laywoman within a large royal household. Aidan and his friends "visited her frequently, instructed her assiduously, and loved her heartily for her innate wisdom and her devotion to the service of God."

In 635, she decided to enter a monastery in France. Aidan acted swiftly, however, and persuaded her to use her gifts in Britain instead. After a trial period at a small community house by the river Wear, Hilda ruled over the monastery at Hartlepool for some years, where she established the Rule of Life that Aidan had taught her, no doubt based upon the Rule Columba had introduced at Iona. Here she showed such qualities of leadership that she was called upon to either establish or reform a community at Whitby.

The community at Whitby lived by the same Rule. These Christ-like qualities particularly made an impression upon people: peace, love, respect for every person, purity, and devotion.

> After the example of the primitive church, no one was rich, no one was in need, for they had all things in common and none had any private property. So great was her prudence that not only ordinary people, but kings and princes sometimes sought and received her counsel when in difficulties.
> BEDE

Wisdom on High, help me to learn from the likes of Hilda:
to be reliable, to grow in prudence,
to study, work, and pray hard, but not too hard;
to treat every person with courtesy and none with contempt;
to maintain resolute faith,
balanced judgment, and outgoing friendships.

NOVEMBER 18 ✧ HOMILY OF ST HILDA

Psalm 131; Isaiah 61:10-62:5; 1 Corinthians 13

Like the jewels of a crown, they shall shine on his land.
ZECHARIAH 9:16

All who knew Hilda used to call her Mother because of her outstanding devotion and grace. She was not only an example of holy life to all who were in the monastery but she also provided an opportunity for salvation and repentance to many who lived far away and who heard the happy story of her industry and virtue. This was bound to happen in fulfillment of the dream which her mother had when Hilda was an infant. She dreamed that her husband was taken away and, though she searched, no trace of him could be found [he was, in fact killed by poisoning]. Suddenly, in the midst of her search, she found a most precious necklace under her garment and, as she gazed closely at it, it seemed to spread such a blaze of light that it filled all Britain with its gracious splendor. This dream was truly fulfilled in her daughter Hilda; for her life was an example of the words of light, blessed not only to herself, but to many who desired to live uprightly.
BEDE

Hilda trained a stream of leaders who went out to establish Christ's way in places far and near; five of these became bishops.

> Trade with the gifts God has given you.
> Bend your minds to holy learning that you may escape
> the fretting moth of littleness of mind
> that would wear out your souls.
> Brace your will to action
> that they may not be the spoils of weak desires.
> Train your hearts and lips to song
> that gives courage to the soul
> Being buffeted by trials, learn to laugh.
> Being reproved, give thanks.
> Having failed, determine to succeed.
> HOMILY OF ST. HILDA, ANONYMOUS

Sacred Three, as we thank you for the life of Hilda,
a jewel in your church who lit up a dark land,
release the hidden treasures in the lives of women,
and in the lives of all your people today,
that we too may come to shine for you.

NOVEMBER 19 ✢ RECONCILIATION

Psalm 87; Isaiah 26:1-11; Matthew 5:17-26

*If you remember that you have a bone of contention
with your brother or sister,
first make peace with them.*
MATTHEW 5:23-24

Hilda stands as a symbol of reconciliation: she was host to the deeply divided Roman and Celtic parties who gathered at Whitby for the Synod of 664. After the synod agreed to impose Roman regulations upon the Celtic churches, some of the Irish monks resigned from their monastery and departed to Ireland, devastated. Other Celtic monks stayed but were hostile. Hilda, however, maintained friendships with people on both sides. Even on her deathbed, she urged her sisters and brothers to maintain peace and unity with all people, not just with those of their own party.

> This is not an easy peace I would give you, my children. It cost me the cross to reconcile you to my Father. You must humble yourselves before each other, listen to each other's pain, share your brother's burden, seek his forgiveness, if you would really be reconciled in my love and my way.
> A PROPHECY RECEIVED BY MYRTLE KERR OF ROSTREVOR CHRISTIAN RENEWAL CENTRE, NORTHERN ISLAND

> God give to me by grace what you give to my dog by nature.
> MECHTHILD OF MAGDEBURG

> It is not our differences that really matter;
> it is the meanness behind that is ugly.
> MAHATMA GANDHI

*Peace between parties, peace between neighbors,
peace between lovers, in the love of the King of life.
Peace between peoples, peace between traditions,
peace between generations, in the love of the Lord of all.*

NOVEMBER 20 ✥ GOD FIRST

Psalm 119:57-72; Hosea 13:4-14:3; Matthew 10:26-39

Jesus said, "Whoever loves father or mother more than me is not ready to be my disciple."
MATTHEW 10:37

Columbanus was born in the south of Ireland, where he grew to be tall, fair, and handsome, the darling of a close and loving family. He received a superb education, and he dressed, like others of his rank, in a fine silk tunic bordered with gold. He had, in fact, everything the world could offer. But Columbanus wanted something more than the world could offer; he wanted to give his whole life to God. Since he did not know how to do this, he consulted a wise old hermit. She told him there was only one way for him: he had to leave all forms of human security behind—even his beloved family—and make life-long vows of service to God.

In those days that meant becoming a monk. His mother was against this, so much so, that on the day Columbanus was due to leave home, she lay down across the doorway to keep him from leaving. But Columbanus was clear about what he needed to do; perhaps he had reflected upon the words of Jesus quoted above. He knew that, though we are to honor our mothers and fathers, we are never to put them first, for that place belongs to Jesus alone. So Columbanus joined the monastery at Bangor, and he went on to become its most famous pupil.

A friend of mine once returned to live with her mother in order to help her recover from alcoholism. My friend did this because she felt God had told her to do so. But after a time, she realized that her mother was becoming as dependent upon her as once she had been dependent upon alcohol. As my friend prayed about this, she felt God was telling her it was time to move on, though she was to maintain caring contact. Mature Christian friends agreed this was right. However, on the day she was to leave, her mother went berserk and threatened to commit suicide if her daughter left. The younger woman wondered if she should stay after all and went aside to pray. God clearly said to her: "Go now, I will look after your mother." So she did leave, and God did look after her mother, who became creative, at times vigorous, and even radiant.

O Mighty One, may I put no one on a pedestal.
Help me to honor my parents
but never to put them in the place
that only you should have.

NOVEMBER 21 ✥ OPPOSITION IS NOT THE END

Psalm 31:1-14; Micah 1; 1 Peter 1:1-12

He will not give up until he has made justice victorious.
MATTHEW 12:20 ERV

Columbanus trained at the Irish monastery at Bangor, which was rich in its enterprises. Yet he felt impelled to go out to the great continent, where so much of the Christian heritage was being swept away, and eventually he was given permission to leave with twelve other monks. They traveled across what is now France, through the ruins of former Roman cities. The poor people who lived in the shadow of these ruins welcomed the brothers, and their faith was transplanted.

When they reached northern Gaul, several local kings welcomed them, since, whatever their personal lifestyle, they held men of God in respect. Columbanus told King Sigebert, "He who seeks nothing has need of nothing. My sole ambition is to follow Christ." The king was so struck by this that he offered Columbanus land; Columbanus, however, was shrewd enough to realize that the kings often slaughtered one another, so he chose some land for a monastery on neutral territory in the Vosges Mountains. Although winter was approaching, the monks set aside their own needs for comfort and built a place of prayer before they built their own beehive-shaped cells.

Starvation threatened them, but a man whose wife had been cured in response to their prayers gave them food supplies. Crowds began to flock to them, and guest accommodations had to be built. The number of monks increased, so another monastery was built at Luxeuil, and then a third.

Once a service to the people of the kingdom had been established, Columbanus turned his attention to the king, Theodoric. Columbanus did his best to wean the king away from his many mistresses and persuade him to marry, which he did. The power behind the throne, however, was the king's grandmother, Brunhilda, and she soon sent the new queen packing and declared unofficial war on Columbanus's monasteries. Eventually, Columbanus was ordered out of Theodoric's territory, but on the monks' way to the port, crowds flocked to seem them. Moreover, the boat on which they were to be transported back to Ireland struck a sandbank, and the captain discharged his passengers. So the monks became free again.

Faithful God, teach me that defeat, if given to you,
is your opportunity for a new advance.
Help me to remain faithful in every setback today.

NOVEMBER 22 ❖ STAND FIRM

Psalm 10; Micah 2; 1 Peter 1:13-25

People will stumble and fall, but we will rise and stand firm.
PSALM 20:8 GNT

Columbanus and his monks made their weary way to the courts of several kings as they traveled north, stopping for a time by the shores of Lake Zurich, which was under the jurisdiction of their friend, King Theodobert. There they established a community that would grow into the Swiss town of Bregenz.

Columbanus then made a long journey south to pass on some prophetic words to King Theodobert: "You will lose your life and your soul unless you become a monk now. If you do not do this voluntarily, you will be made to do it against your will." Sadly, Theodobert disregarded Columbanus's advice. The king's army was completely destroyed in battle; he was taken captive and forced to wear a monk's habit as a sign of submission. This defeat meant that Theodobert's lands returned to the jurisdiction of relatives who were hostile to Columbanus, so he said farewell to his monks and moved on to Italy, accompanied by just a small band of brothers, one of whom, Gall, they left behind on the way. The Lombard king and queen welcomed him, and they built their last monastery at Bobbio. There Columbanus died on November 23, 615.

After his death, the sternness of Columbanus's original Rule gave way to the gentler system of Benedict. This may have been what was needed over the long term, but tough times call for tough measures, and the Celtic monks had been called to a task tougher even than breaking virgin ground—they had to win back lost territory. Only people with an overpowering faith could have seen why it was worth doing. Only men who trained their bodies to stand up to unbelievable physical hardships, and their souls to battle through seemingly impossible situations, could have survived.

We can learn this lesson from Columbanus: he trained his followers to depend upon God alone. They were not put off from their calling by the way other people treated them, however harsh. They used the spiritual armory of prophetic direction and faith-directed mission to overcome all things in Christ's power and stand firm in all circumstances.

Toughen me, Lord.
Give me a heart of love
but a backbone of steel.

NOVEMBER 23 ❖ RESPECT FOR ALL

Psalm 5; Micah 3:8–4:5; 1 Peter 2:11-25

Respect everyone.
1 PETER 2:17

Adamnan, whom we remember today, was born into the same royal family as Columba. Abbot of Iona, diplomat, writer, peacemaker, he was respected for his wisdom and knowledge of the Scriptures, and near the end of his life he achieved a major advance in social justice on the plains of Birr. Leaders from Scotland, England, and Ireland assembled at a great convention on the plains of Birr in 697 and accepted the Law of Adamnan, which guaranteed the protection of women, children, and other civilians.

Adamnan's mother Ronnat had first turned his thoughts toward the plight of women. Then he received divine guidance to make, "a law in Ireland and Britain for the sake of the mother of each one, because a mother has borne each one, and for the sake of Mary, the mother of Jesus Christ." This law protected women from offences ranging from murder and rape to impugning the good name of a married woman. Penalties were exacted and fines had to be paid to the communities established by Columba, which were known for their honesty. This law came to be known as Cain Adamnain or the Law of the Innocents. The attitude that inspired this legislation was this: "Great is the sin when anyone kills the one who is mother and sister to Christ's mother."

What a contrast to this horrific description of women in war in those days: "On one side of her she would carry her bag of provisions, on the other her babe . . . her husband behind her flogging her on to battle . . . for at that time it was the head of a woman or her two breasts which were taken as trophies."

High King, Creator of all,
remind us that every human life is sacred
whether it belongs to a woman in a war-torn land
or to a person with disabilities who lives next door;
to an unborn infant or a terminally ill patient.
Remind us that whatever a person's age, race, or creed,
each individual has been made in your likeness
and Christ has given his all for each one.
This makes each precious in your sight.

NOVEMBER 24 ❖ HOSPITALITY

Psalm 9; Exodus 2:11-25; Hebrews 13:1-3

*Do not neglect to show hospitality to strangers,
for by this some have entertained angels
without knowing it.*
HEBREWS 13:2 NASB

We came from Palestine to one of the Abbas in Egypt, who gave us generous hospitality. So we asked him, "When the monks in Palestine give hospitality to visitors they keep to their own Rule of fasting; why don't you do that?" The Abba gave us this reply: "I am always fasting, but I can't keep you here always. Although fasting is useful and necessary, it is a matter of my personal choice. But whether I show love to you is not a question of choice, it is the law of God. So, to receive Christ in you, I must be fully present to you, and be sharing with you. When I have sent you on your way, I can take up fasting again." The Abba also quoted the words of Jesus: "The friends and family of a bridegroom do not fast while he is with them; they wait until he has left before they fast."
CASSIAN

*We saw a stranger yesterday.
We put food in the eating place,
drink in the drinking place,
music in the listening place
and with the sacred name of the triune God
he blessed us and our house,
our cattle and our dear ones.
As the lark says in her song:
Often, often, often goes the Christ
in the stranger's guise.*
A CELTIC RUNE OF HOSPITALITY

*Bless, O Lord, the food we eat,
and if there be any poor creature
hungry or thirsty walking along the road,
send them into us that we can share the food with them
just as you share your gifts with all of us.*
FROM AN IRISH GRACE
COLLECTED BY MOUNT MELLERAY MONASTERY, IRELAND

NOVEMBER 25 ✣ PRAYER FROM HEAVEN

Psalm 68:17-35; 2 Kings 20:1-11; Matthew 19:16-30

*The Lord told Isaiah to go back to King Hezekiah and tell him,
"I have heard your prayer and seen your tears,
and I will let you live fifteen years longer."*
2 KINGS 20:4-6

God extended Hezekiah's life as a result of his prayers. Some early Irish Christians asked their beloved Saint Moninna to pray that her life would be extended, too. But in her case, God had something else in mind.

Moninna was one of the earliest saints of Ireland about whom we have reliable information. She was a contemplative linked to a community, and she was much loved by her own people throughout the region. When they learned that she was on her deathbed, the local rulers and many others gathered round and appealed to the local bishop to give this message to her: "We ask you as those who are linked to you by blood and by the spirit, that you will give just one more year of your earthly presence with us. For we know that God will give you whatever you ask. In fact any of us who has a slave girl will set her free to the Lord, and every man employed as a fighting man will give away a cow in its prime in exchange for your life."

Moninna gave these good folk the following reply through the bishop: "May God bless you for bothering yourselves with my weak self. If you had asked before yesterday I would have granted your request. But from today I cannot do so. You see, the apostles Peter and Paul have been sent to guide my soul to heaven and they are here with me now. I see them holding a kind of cloth with marvelous gold and artwork. I must go with them to my Lord who sent them. God hears your prayers. He will give a life to one of you. I pray God's blessing on your wives, children, and homes; I leave you my badger skin coat and my garden tools. I have no doubt that if you carry these with you when enemies attack, God will deliver you. Do not be sad at my leaving you. For I truly believe that Christ, with whom I now go to stay, will give you whatever I ask of Him in heaven no less than when I prayed to Him on earth."

*Savior and Friend,
may I leave this life with my loved ones around me.
May I leave this life united with your dear ones in heaven.
May I leave this life with oil and with gladness.
May I leave this life in order to give more blessings.*

NOVEMBER 26 ✣ DEPRESSION

Psalm 42; Isaiah 40:12-20; 1 Thessalonians 5:16-26

*Why are you cast down, O my soul, and why are you in turmoil within me?
Hope in God; for I shall again praise him, my salvation and my God.*
PSALM 42:11 ESV

As nights draw in earlier and earlier, dark depression sometimes settles on many of us. In some cases, it is clinical depression. Treatment may include prescribing the right chemicals, vitamins, and so on. For others, the depression, though not clinical, is still bad enough. Our lives have less sun, less exercise, less fresh air, less stimulus, less relaxation, less fun, less travel—and we become stale and cast down.

What can we do about this? We can't help a slump in our spirit, but we can choose not to yield to self-pity and selfishness, and we can choose not to hide from depression in hyperactivity that only builds up future trouble. We can follow the example of the Celts and tell stories of the heroes. Then we can raise our downcast spirits in two ways.

First, through constant praise. Some people do this by singing hymns or speaking in tongues. As we have seen, Columba linked our praise with the angels' eternal praise being offered to the Trinity:

> By the singing of hymns eagerly ringing out
> by thousands of angels rejoicing in holy dances
> and by the four living creatures full of eyes
> with the twenty-four elders
> casting their crowns under the feet of the Lamb of God,
> the Trinity is praised in eternal threefold exchanges.
> COLUMBA, ALTUS PROSATOR

Second, we can respond to depression by praying over the depressed person within us. Talk to it and cherish it, be gentle to it and give it a treat. Let the love of Jesus come to your depressed inner being. Put oil or water on your face and repeat this prayer from the *Carmina Gadelica*: "I will bathe my face in the nine rays of the sun as Mary washed her Son in the rich fermented milk."

Now place your hand over your heart and pray these words;

*The love that Mary gave to her one Son may all the world give me.
The love that Jesus gave to John the Baptist grant that I give to whoever meets me.*
CARMINA GADELICA

NOVEMBER 27 ✥ HEAVEN IS AMAZING!

Psalm 110; Ecclesiastes 12:1-8; Luke 16:1-11

*Make the best of what you have here on earth
and you will be given other opportunities
in the eternal homeland.*
Luke 16:9

Have you sometimes wondered what heaven is like? Some people project onto it inadequate, boring, fading images from human life. The opposite is the truth. The unknown author of this fourteenth-century account of the death of Saint David knew that heaven was amazing!

> After David had given his parting blessing to everyone who had gathered, he spoke to them, saying, "Take care that you guard your faith and do the little things which I have taught and shown you. Goodbye. Be good. For we shall never meet again." The people broke out in a great crying. From the Sunday to the Wednesday after David's death, they ate and drank nothing; they just prayed. On Tuesday night the whole town and the sky were filled with singing and joy of angels. In the morning, Jesus Christ came, accompanied by nine orders of angels, and the sun shone with brilliance. That day, the first day of March, Jesus Christ bore David's soul away in great triumph and gladness and honor.
>
> The angels bore his soul to a place where there is rest without labor, joy without sadness, an abundance of good things, victory, brilliance, and beauty; a place where Christ's champions are commended and the undeserving wealthy are ignored, where there is health without sickness, youth without old age, peace without dissension, glory without vain ostentation, songs that do not pall, and rewards without end.
>
> FROM THE BOOK OF THE ANCHORITE OF LLANDDEWIBREFI, 1356 (ADAPTED)

*Faithful vigil ended.
Watching, waiting cease.
Master, grant your servants
their discharge in peace.*
TIMOTHY DUDLEY-SMITH, BASED ON WORDS FROM LUKE 2

NOVEMBER 28 ✥ TIME TO WAKE UP!

Psalm 108; Isaiah 41:1-16; Romans 13:8-14

It's time to wake up!
ROMANS 13:11

Do not consider what you are but what you will be. What you are lasts for a mere moment; what you will be is eternal. Do not be lazy; but acquire in a short time what you will possess forever. Overcome the dislike of exerting yourself now by thinking of the reward to come. Why do you chase after vain things? Remember, life's joys disappear like a dream in the night. So wake up.
COLUMBANUS

We sleep when we think that the world is as it always was.
It is high time to awake to the truth that Jesus has come.
His summons is urgent in our midst.
Nearer than we know he is coming in judgment.
He might come in judgment this Christmas.
We confess that we sleep
when we think that power is still of this world.
It is high time to awake
to the truth that his power alone is working permanently.
All the civilizations built in scorn of his power
are as if they had never been.
And our civilization with them will equally go down.
Nearer than we know, he will be seen coming in power.
He might even come in power this Christmas.
Give us grace to wait in spiritual expectancy his coming again,
to practice true humility, to be exercised in the ways of real power,
to express his glory that we may recognize the kingship of a cradle,
the royalty of being ruled, the seniority of service
so that should he come this Christmas,
his body bloody but his head crowned,
we would be found among those who worshipped
and not among those who would kill.
If these things would be, it is high time to awake out of sleep.
GEORGE MCLEOD, FOUNDER OF THE 20TH-CENTURY IONA COMMUNITY

Wake me up, Lord.

NOVEMBER 29 ✢ A MISSION KICK-START

Psalm 89; Isaiah 42:1-9; Mark 5:1-20

*The man who had had the demons went all through the Ten Towns,
telling what Jesus had done for him.
And all who heard it were amazed.*
MARK 5:20

The Church is the only organization
that exists for those who are not its members.
ARCHBISHOP WILLIAM TEMPLE

The lives of Jesus' first apostles demonstrated their great zeal to spread the Good News to others. We learn of their mission journeys in the Bible, and through tradition, which tells, for example, of Thomas founding a church in India. Britain's own early apostles had a similar zeal.

When Samson first landed on the beaches of Brittany, he brought with him a large crew to help begin the great mission there. But God's first lesson for them was this: no amount of evangelistic organization is a substitute for a prayed-into-being, God-architected, God-timed healing encounter. Such an encounter can have a domino effect that influences a whole region before the organization has even begun to get into gear.

As Samson and his men were mooring their boat, they saw a hut not far from the harbor and a man weeping as he gazed out toward the sea. Samson went to him and asked what was the problem.

"I have now waited here three days and three nights," the man told him, "for someone to come and help me from across the sea." He was a devout man of prayer, who had a wife with leprosy and a daughter with mental illness—but as he had prayed for them, God had given him the assurance that he was to wait at the harbor for such a man who would heal them.

Samson went to the man's home and poured forth prayers over the sick women, who were restored to health. This was the start of a wonderful ministry, and from there Samson established Christian communities throughout the region, one of which, at Dol, became the most famous of all.

*God of healing, God of strategy,
help me pray like that weeping man;
help me act like that heroic apostle.*

NOVEMBER 30 ✢ BE PREPARED!

Psalm 66; Isaiah 40:1–9; Matthew 25:1–13

Prepare the way of the Lord.
MARK 1:3 ESV

In the wasteland may the Glory shine.
In the land of the lost may the King make his home.

For Celtic Christians, the time before Christmas (known as Advent, which means "the Coming") is a period of preparation, as we repent and wait in hope for Christ's arrival. This period used to be known as a second Lent. Fasting was less severe, but people nevertheless carved out time to go apart and wait on God. Can we today make it our aim to dispel the spirit of restlessness and acquisition, and to instill the spirit of wonder, warning, and waiting during this period? What did those Celtic Christians focus their minds on during these weeks . . . and what should we focus our minds on?

God used prophets to prepare people for the birth of Christ. Many of these prophets lived in simplicity as a sign that they were waiting for God to fulfill the Divine promises. As we meditate on the lives and words of these prophets, we, too, hear the call to live lives of simplicity as a sign. Then we think about the witnesses at the time of Christ's birth—Mary and Joseph, Elizabeth and Zechariah, Anna and Simeon—whose waiting was joyful and humble.

This is also a time for thinking about what the universe, humanity, and ourselves are coming to, and about the four last things: death, giving account, eternal bliss, and separation.

At heart, this should be a time of waiting, of contemplating the presence of Christ within us . . . for we are called, like Mary, to be bearers of Christ now and into the future.

In the coming days the readings will focus on all these things.

Calm us to wait for the gift of Christ;
cleanse us to prepare the way for Christ;
teach us to contemplate the wonder of Christ;
touch us to know the presence of Christ;
anoint us to bear the life of Christ.

DECEMBER 1 ✦ WE WAIT IN THE DARKNESS

Psalm 17; Isaiah 42:14-23; Romans 8:31-39

You know my heart. You have come to me at night...
reveal your wonderful love and save me.
PSALM 17:3, 7 GNT

We wait in the darkness, expectantly, longingly, anxiously, thoughtfully.
The darkness is our friend. In the darkness of the womb,
we have all been nurtured and protected.
In the darkness of the womb
the Christ-child was made ready for the journey into light.
It is only in the darkness that we can see
the splendor of the universe—blankets of stars,
the solitary glowing of the planets.
It was the darkness that allowed the Magi to find the star
that guided them to where the Christ-child lay.
In the darkness of the night, desert people find relief
from the cruel relentless heat of the sun.
In the blessed desert darkness, Mary and Joseph were able to flee
with the infant Jesus to safety in Egypt.
In the darkness of sleep, we are soothed and restored,
healed and renewed.
In the darkness of sleep, dreams rise up.
God spoke to Joseph and the wise men through dreams.
God is speaking still.
Sometimes in the solitude of the darkness
our fears and concerns, our hopes and visions rise to the surface.
We come face to face with ourselves and with the road that lies ahead of us.
And in that same darkness, we find companionship for the journey.
In that same darkness, we sometimes allow ourselves to wonder
and worry whether the human race is going to survive.
And then, in the darkness we know that you are with us, O God,
yet still we await your coming.
In the darkness that contains both our hopelessness and our hope,
we watch for a sign of God's hope.
For you are with us, O God, in darkness and in light.
PRESBYTERIAN CHURCH OF AOTEAROA, NEW ZEALAND (ABRIDGED)

O God of life, darken not to me your light, O God of life, close not to me your joy,
O God of life, shut not to me your door,
O God of life, refuse not to me your mercy.
CARMINA GADELICA

DECEMBER 2 ✢ CLEARING THE GROUND

Psalm 53; Isaiah 43:8-21; Ephesians 5:1-20

Clear a way for the Eternal through the waste...
fill every valley, knock down every mountain and hill,
smooth out all the rough places.
ISAIAH 40:3–4

I recall a local person saying, as a team of people cut the hedges and grass verges the day before a royal visit, "A royal visit is the only way we'd have got some of these things done. Without it, we would have waited forever." You too can prepare the way for Christ by drawing up a list of things you would need to clean and clear if Christ were to make a personal royal visit to our area. Then pick one or two things from your list that you can begin to do something about now.

Three most basic ways you can clear the way for Christ is with honesty, reconciliation, and preparing for your own death. *Honesty:* so many shoplifters deceive themselves that they are not thieves, that stores put up signs saying: "Shoplifting Is Theft." Do you deceive yourself that tax evasion—or withholding rightful information from another person—is not also theft? *Reconciliation:* is there someone who is upset with you to whom you can give the gift of love this season? *Preparing for your own death:* are you ready to be "called home" today? Are your affairs in order? Have you done those things that you ought to have done? Can you get rid of clutter that prevents you from fulfilling the heart's desires God has put within you?

Heaven, shed your dew.
Clouds, rain down salvation.
Earth bring forth the Savior.
Praise in all our days.
COMMON PRAYER AT TAIZÉ

Christ, Light of the world,
meet us in our place of darkness,
journey with us,
and bring us to your new dawning.

DECEMBER 3 ❖ FRIENDS OF GOD

Psalm 85; Isaiah 44:21-28; John 15:1-17

You are my friends if you do what I command you.
I do not call you servants any longer,
because a servant does not know what his master is doing.
JOHN 15:14–15 NIV

The Celtic church was composed not only of outstanding individuals such as Patrick, Columba, and Brigid, but also local indigenous movements that shaped and reshaped its life. In the eighth century, a reform movement began within monasticism in southern Ireland, which over time spread to northern Ireland and Scotland, inspiring new bursts of holiness and literature. The monks of this reform were known in Gaelic as *Celi De*, which roughly means "Friends of God."

These Christians, like the prophets who cleared away wrong things so that God could move in, tried to clear up certain abuses that had crept into the monasteries. The leadership of monasteries was often hereditary; as the generations passed, some descendants of founders were far from God. This meant that truly holy monks were sometimes shut out, and corrupt practices flourished. This in turn created feelings of vengeance among the people and among some monks, and there were violent attacks on monasteries and abbots, not all of who deserved it.

The reforms were not brought in by force or rebellion, so much as by example and persuasion. Monks were encouraged to withdraw from worldly affairs in order to concentrate on "the three profitable things:" prayer, work, and study. The anamchara or soul friend played a particularly important role in this renewal.

This concentration on holiness produced many inspired writings: lists of martyrs, accounts of the saints, guidelines for making restitution (known as "Penitentials"), liturgy such as *The Stowe Missal*, and early Irish nature and hermit poetry.

Each generation has to learn that "God has no grandchildren." We each of us have to be born anew of God's spirit, brought to our knees in penitence and wonder at the presence of God. Are you relying on the faith of those who have gone before you . . . or are you flowing in the life of the Holy Spirit that is ever fresh?

Lord, take from me all that is mere human accretion.
Give to me a broken spirit and a humble heart
that I may be intent on you alone.

DECEMBER 4 ✣ LIVING ON THE EDGE

Psalm 7; Isaiah 43:1-7; Luke 5:27-32

*They asked Jesus, "Why do you eat and drink with tax collectors
and other outcasts?" Jesus answered them,
"People who are well do not need a doctor."*
LUKE 5:30–31 GNT

Jesus lived life with the marginalized—the lepers, prostitutes, and tax collectors. Jesus was edged out of the synagogue, out of the temple, out of the city, out of society, and out of life—yet he remained totally in touch with the heart of life.

Celtic Christians have a strong sense of living on "edges" or "boundary places" between the material world and the other world. Dr. George MacLeod, founder of the twentieth-century Iona Community, spoke of Iona as a "thin place" where the membrane between this world and the other world, between the material and the spiritual, was very permeable.

This sense of living in a "between place" enabled Celtic Christians to make connections between the physical and the intangible, the seen and the unseen, this world and a permanent "other" world.
PHILIP SHELDRAKE, LIVING BETWEEN WORLDS

Many ancient Celtic sites are on the edge—Iona, Lindisfarne, Whitby, Jarrow, Burgh, Bradwell, Whithorn. At the edge we see horizons denied to those who stay in the middle. Walking along a cliff-top our bodies and souls face each other and that is how we grow. The edge is in fact always the center of spiritual renewal. We are called to mould the kingdoms of the earth so that they reflect the Kingdom of Heaven. Any Christian movement that becomes respectable risks being brought from the edge to the center—and so risks being given the kiss of death.

How will I keep myself on the spiritual edge?
REFLECTIONS FROM MARTIN WALLACE

*Lead me from that which fades to that which endures.
Lead me from day's dawning to Light eternal.
Lead from tide's turning to heaven's ocean of Love.
Lead me from the shore's edge to eternal life.
Lead me from serving the weakest to finding the Highest.*

DECEMBER 5 ⁖ THE DAY OF THE LORD

Psalm 50:1-15; Isaiah 44:1-9; Revelation 5

I saw the dead, great and small alike, standing before the throne... the dead were judged according to what they had done, as recorded in the books... whoever did not have his name in the book of the living was thrown into the lake of fire.
REVELATION 20:12, 15 NIV

Fierce winter winds are an onslaught to our security. Everything that is not fastened down and in place is swept away: loose tiles fall from the roof, stray items get blown away in the wind.

Yet what seems like an enemy is actually a good thing. Winds remind us that we are mortal, that the things we want to keep must be made secure. This is even truer of eternal things. The idea of God's judgment can seem pitiless: in truth it is all mercy. God longs for us to be right, to be true, for things to be in place in our lives, so that we can endure and live with him in the world that is indestructible.

> The day of the Lord, most righteous King of kings, is at hand:
> a day of anger and vindication, of darkness and of cloud,
> a day of wonderful mighty thunders,
> a day also of distress, of sorrow, and of sadness
> in which the love and desire of women will cease
> and the striving of men and the desire of this world.
> We shall stand trembling before the Lord's judgment seat
> and we shall render an account of all our deeds,
> seeing also our crimes placed before our gaze
> and the books of conscience thrown open before us.
> COLUMBA, ALTUS PROSATOR

Holy God, holy and mighty,
strip from me all that is false and out of place.
Strengthen my roots in you.
Bring me to that place
where I desire you alone.

DECEMBER 6 ✧ CHOICES

Psalm 50:16-23; Isaiah 44:9-20; 1 Corinthians 4:1-5

[When] the Lord comes,
he will bring to light the things now hidden in darkness,
and will disclose the purposes of the heart.
1 CORINTHIANS 4:5 NRSV

Suppose that in the next life you see two doors in front of you. Over one door are the words "What I want." Over the other door are the words "What God wants." Which door will you choose to go through? In this life we may fudge the issue and try (unsuccessfully) to go through both doors. But it is not possible in fact to go through both doors. The time will come when we have to choose one or the other. Suppose you walked through one or the other of these doors. Looking back, the name written over the first door is "hell." The name written over the second door is "heaven."

Christ's wondrous figure, the form of the noble king, will come from the east out of the skies, sweet to the minds of his own folk and bitter to those steeped in sin, strangely diverse and different towards the blessed and the wretched.

To the good he will be gracious in appearance, beautiful and delightsome to that holy throng, attractive in his joy, affectionate and loving; agreeable and sweet it will be for his cherished people to look upon that shining form, to look with pleasure upon the mild coming of the Ruler, the mighty King, for those who had earlier pleased him well in their heart with words and with works.

To the evil he will be fearsome and terrible to see, to those sinful people who come forth there condemned by their crimes. It may serve as a warning of punishment to one who is possessed of the wise realization, that he indeed dreads nothing at all who will not grow terrified in spirit with fear for that figure, when he sees the actual Lord of all created things journeying amid mighty marvels to judgment of the many, and round about him on every side journey squadrons of celestial angels, flocks of radiant beings, armies of saints, teeming in throngs.

CHRIST III, THE JUDGMENT, FROM THE EXETER BOOK, TENTH CENTURY

O Christ, deliver me from the ways of darkness
so that, holding firmly to your Word,
the gate of glory may be opened to me.

DECEMBER 7 ✜ CROOKED THINGS

Psalm 48; Isaiah 48:12-22; Revelation 21:1-8

The crooked shall be made straight.
ISAIAH 40:4 ESV

We talk about crooks and people with sexual perversions as bent people; but the truth is that all of us are bent in some way, and not one of us can move into a state of bliss, into our ultimate fulfillment in God, unless every crooked thing is straightened. We can prepare the way for the Lord by putting straight what is crooked. Crooked things include things that seem big and things that seem little: overeating and gossip; tax evasion and financial dishonesty; emotional and physical abuse, and willful failures to communicate; manipulation of others for our own purposes and sexual immorality.

What things then are good? Those that have remained whole and uncorrupted as they were created, the things that God, according to the apostle, "has prepared that we should walk in, the good works in which we are created in Christ Jesus." These are: goodness, integrity, devotion, fairness, truth, mercy, caring, peace, spiritual joy; all these with their fruits—the things that come into being as a result of these qualities—are good. The opposites of these are things that destroy goodness: malice, irreverence, discrimination, lying, greed, hatred, discord, bitterness, with all the many fruits they bear. For the fruits of both good and evil are innumerable.

True discernment is the inseparable companion of Christian humility and opens the way to perfection to the true soldier of Christ. If we all weigh our actions in the just balance of true discernment we shall not be hijacked into crooked ways. If we walk by the divine light we "shall not go astray either to the right or to the left" but we shall always keep on the straight way, chanting with the conquering psalmist, "O my God, light up my darkness, for through you I shall be delivered from temptation."
BASED ON THE RULE OF COLUMBANUS

Lord Spirit, show me the things
that are crooked in my life.
Lord Judge, spare me from things
that could be crooked in my life.
Lord Christ, straighten out the things
that are crooked in my life.
O my God, light up my darkness
and deliver me this day from temptation.

DECEMBER 8 ✢ FOUR DESTROYING FIRES

Psalm 52; Isaiah 45:20-25; 1 Corinthians 3:9-23

*Go to the Lord and you will live.
If you do not go, he will sweep down like fire on the people....
The fire will burn up the people...
and no one will be able to put it out.*
AMOS 5:6 GNT

When Fursey [in an out-of-the-body vision] had been taken up to a great height, he was told by the angels who were conducting him to look back at the world. As he looked down, he saw some kind of dark valley immediately beneath him and four fires in the air, which were to kindle and consume the world. One of them is falsehood, when we do not fulfill our promise to renounce Satan and all his works as we undertook to do at our baptism. The second is covetousness, when we put the love of riches before the love of heavenly things; the third is discord, when we do not fear to offend our neighbors even in trifling matters; the fourth is injustice, when we think it a small thing to despoil and defraud the weak. Gradually these fires grew together and merged into one vast conflagration. As it approached him, he cried out in fear to the angel, "Look, sir, the fire is coming near me." But the angel answered, "That which you did not kindle will not burn you; for although the conflagration seems great and terrible, it tests each person according to their deserts, and the evil desires of everyone will be burned away in this fire."

...The angel then went on to give helpful advice as to what should be done for the salvation of those who repented in the hour of death. When Fursey had been restored to his body, he bore for the rest of his life the marks of the burns that he had suffered while a disembodied spirit; they were visible to all on his shoulder and his jaw. It is marvelous to think that what he suffered secretly as a disembodied spirit showed openly upon his flesh.

An aged brother who is still living in our monastery relates that a truthful and pious man told him that he had seen Fursey in East Anglia and that, although it was during a time of severe winter weather and a hard frost, and though Fursey sat wearing only a thin garment, yet as he told his story, he sweated as though it were the middle of summer, either because of the terror or else the joy which his recollections aroused.
BEDE

*From deceit, greed, strife, and dishonesty,
Good Lord deliver us.*

DECEMBER 9 ✣ THE THUNDERER

Psalm 29; Isaiah 46; 1 Thessalonians 5:1-11

Then the Lord thundered from the heavens,
and the voice of the Most High was heard.
PSALM 18:13

There was a time when a famous British newspaper was known as "The Thunderer." In those days it was the mouthpiece, not of Money or Power so much as of Moral Truth. When that newspaper thundered, people in high places—or wrong places—shook. This gives us a clue to an aspect of God's nature.

> Chad was greatly filled with the fear of the Lord and was mindful of his last end in all he did. If a high wind arose, he would immediately stop whatever he was doing and pray God to have mercy on the human race. If the wind became a gale, he would lie prostrate in earnest prayer. If there was a violent storm, lightning, or thunder, he would go to the church and devote himself to prayers and psalms until it passed.
>
> When people asked him why he did this, he replied, "Have you not read 'The Lord also thundered in the heavens and the Most High gave voice. Yes, the Most High sent arrows and scattered the people, shot out lightnings and discomforted them?' For the Lord moves the air, raises the winds, hurls the lightnings, and thunders forth from heaven in order to rouse earth's inhabitants to revere him, to remind them of future judgment in order to scatter their pride and confound their presumption. The Lord does this by calling to their minds the time when he will come in clouds in great power and majesty to judge the living and the dead, while the heavens and the earth are aflame."
>
> Chad concluded, "And so we ought to respond to God's heavenly warning with due fear and love, so that as often as he disturbs the sky and raises his hand as if about to strike, yet spares us still, we should implore his mercy, examining our consciences, turning from our sins, and thereafter behaving with such care that we do not deserve to be struck down."
>
> TOLD TO BEDE BY ONE OF CHAD'S FELLOW MONKS, TRUMBERHT

God of the storm, God of the stillness,
of squalls of power and of shimmering calm,
into life's troughs and into life's billows,
come with the reach of your long right arm.

DECEMBER 10 ✣ INTENT ON HEAVEN

Psalm 136; Isaiah 48:1-11; 1 Thessalonians 4:13-18

*Jesus was letting them know the way Peter would die
to bring glory to God.*
JOHN 21:19

Here is an example of the hermit poetry the Culdee renewal inspired. It takes as its theme Death, one of the "four last things" upon which Christians reflect during Advent:

> Alone in my little oratory
> without a single human being in my company,
> dear to me would such a pilgrimage be
> before going to meet death.
> A hidden secret little hut
> for the forgiveness of every fault,
> a conscience upright
> and untroubled, intent on holy heaven.
> Let the place which shelters me
> amid the monastic enclosures
> be a beautiful spot hallowed by holy stones
> and I all alone therein.

Few of us have the opportunity to reach our end in such an untrammeled, untroubled fashion. Peter the apostle had no such opportunity; tradition says he was crucified upside down. Yet his life teaches us that, whatever the circumstances of our death, we may die intent on heaven alone. Here is a prayer to say over our friends, or to pray, in advance, for ourselves:

> *In the name of the all-powerful Father,*
> *in the name of the all-loving Son,*
> *in the name of the pervading Spirit,*
> *I command all spirit of fear to leave you.*
> *I break the power of unforgiven sin in you,*
> *I set you free from dependence upon human ties*
> *that you may be free as the wind,*
> *as soft as sheep's wool,*
> *as straight as an arrow*
> *and that you may journey into the heart of God.*

DECEMBER 11 ✢ MIST

Psalm 135; Isaiah 49:1-7; 2 Peter 3

God will complete his mysterious work.
ISAIAH 28:21

Mist makes my spirit aware that everyday things are only one dimension of life. Another, less static Presence can envelop my world. This is a living presence. It is beautiful, yet not frolicsome like spring. There is something mysterious, something somber about it. December mist is God's outer aura, a prelude to something sharper and nearer God's heart. In it I can be lost in wonder, love, and praise. Behind the mist are treasures waiting to be discovered—a bright month of advent and nativity; the hope that a new year will kindle my heart flame ever anew.

> Now I command you, my loved man,
> to describe your vision to all people:
> tell them with words this is the tree of glory
> on which the Son of God suffered once
> for the many sins committed by humankind,
> and for Adam's wickedness long ago.
> He sipped the drink of death, yet the Lord rose
> with his great strength to deliver humanity.
> Then he ascended into heaven. The Lord himself,
> Almighty God, with his host of angels
> will come to the middle world again
> on Domesday to reckon with each mortal.
> Then he who has the power of judgment
> will judge each one just as they deserve
> for the way in which they lived this fleeting life. . . .
> Then folk will be fearful and give
> scant thought to what they say to Christ.
> But no one need be numbed by fear
> who has carried the best of all things in their breast;
> each soul that has longings to live with the Lord
> must search for a kingdom far beyond the frontiers of this world.
> FROM THE DREAM OF THE ROOD, TRANS. KEVIN CROSSLEY-HOLLAND

O Jesus, Son of David,
you have given us to see the light of day.
May you carry us home with you to the city of grace.
ANONYMOUS, MOUNT MELLERAY MONASTERY, IRELAND

DECEMBER 12 ✢ STARS AND DARK NIGHTS

Psalm 139:1-12; Isaiah 49:8-18; Philippians 2:12-18

> *I could ask the darkness to hide me,*
> *or the light round me to turn into night,*
> *but even darkness is not dark for you.*
> PSALM 139:11-12 GNT

Stars are distinct, fixed points. Navigators steer by them. Yet stars twinkle.

God's standards are like stars. They are distinct, fixed sky marks by which all people can steer their lives. God's standards are absolutes—truth, fairness, love, purity, unselfishness. Yet these are also qualities that bring a sparkle to life. The person with these qualities is transparent and glows.

> Risen Christ we welcome you.
> You are the flowering bough of creation.
> From you cascades music like a million stars,
> truth to cleanse a myriad souls.
> A CELTIC EUCHARIST, THE COMMUNITY OF AIDAN AND HILDA

> *We know that night is not dark with you, O Lord.*
> *But a great deal of me is not yet one with you.*
> *In the night the things I fear come to the surface.*
> *The unacknowledged parts of my personality*
> *poke through the shadows to haunt me.*
> *It helps me to know that the blackness will lift*
> *as surely as the dawn follows night.*
> *But before that there is work to do.*
> *Night has a purpose of its own.*
> *My task is to acknowledge the shadows*
> *and bring them to you who are the Morning Star.*
> *You are author of light and dark.*
> *The morning star would be nothing to us*
> *without its prelude, the night.*
> *So thank you, Lord, for the night.*

DECEMBER 13 ✛ STARS OF WONDER

Psalm 19; Isaiah 45:5–19; Romans 8:33–36

*God hung all the stars in the sky: the Great Bear,
Orion, the Pleiades, and the stars of the south.*
JOB 9:9

"To foster a sense of wonder"—this should be written into the goals of every school and of every home. One of the best ways we can prepare for the coming of the King is to allow a sense of wonder to grow in our hearts.

> My eyes like to see
> the lovely stars in the sky
> shining like diamonds and crystals;
> and the sun above my head,
> and the moon shining and shining.
> Eyes are shiny, too,
> and the golden water shines.
> My eyes like to see candles
> and the light in the sky.
> God will give me a new heart
> that shines with happiness inside me.
> ANGUS, AGE 6

> O star of wonder, star of light,
> star with royal beauty bright,
> westward leading, still proceeding
> guide us to the perfect light.
> J. H. HOPKINS

> Let the flowers close and the stars appear,
> let hearts be glad and minds be calm,
> and let God's people say Amen, Amen.
> CREATION LITURGY OF THE IONA COMMUNITY

*Open my eyes to your beauty,
open my ears to your call,
open my heart to your coming,
Great King, born in a stall.*

DECEMBER 14 ✢ LOVE'S COMMUNICATION

Psalm 142; Isaiah 51:1-16; Luke 1:26-38

Mary had been engaged to Joseph, but before they lived together,
she was found to be pregnant by the Holy Spirit.
Her husband, Joseph, being a good man
and not willing to expose her to public disgrace,
planned to break up with her quietly.
MATTHEW 1:18-19

In our society today, it's hard to grasp the feelings of deep shock that engulfed Joseph when his fiancée, who had committed herself to him as a virgin, informed him that she was pregnant. A poet in ninth-century Mercia, who writes in the style of Caedmon, tried to "get under the skin" of Joseph and Mary.

Mary: O my Joseph, do you mean to divide us who are one, and to disdain my love?
Joseph: All at once I am deeply troubled, robbed of dignity. I have endured hurtful abuses because of you, bitter insults; people mock me with acid words. I must shed tears, full of sorrow. Yet God can easily heal my grieving heart's wounds. Everyone knows that I willingly received an innocent virgin. Now where is her chastity? And which is best, to keep quiet or to confess? If I tell the truth, David's descendant will be stoned to death. Even so, it is worse to conceal her crimes; a perjurer is despised for as long as he lives.

Then the virgin revealed the miracle and spoke thus:

Mary: By the Son of God, savior of souls, I speak the truth when I say that I have not embraced any man. The archangel of heaven appeared to me and said that the heavenly spirit would fill me with radiance, that I should bear the Triumph of Life, the bright Son, the mighty child of God, of the glorious Creator. Now I am made his immaculate temple, the Spirit of Comfort resides in me—now you may set aside your sorrow.
FROM ADVENT LYRICS, NINTH-CENTURY MERCIA

Today, O Lord,
as I contemplate Mary and Joseph,
may I live in the wonder of your divine conceiving,
may I live in the wonder of our divine receiving.

DECEMBER 15 ✤ INCARNATION

Psalm 96; Isaiah 54:1-10; Luke 1:39-45

[Christ] was like God in every way
PHILIPPIANS 2:6 ERV

The Gaelic race see the hand of God in every place,
in every time and in every thing.
DOUGLAS HYDE

He was imprisoned by his Jewish flesh and bones
within the confines of his country
but he gave them as living planks to be nailed
and raised from the grave, despite the guarding,
a catholic body by his Father.
And now Cardiff is as near as Calvary,
Bangor every inch as Bethlehem.
The storms in Cardigan Bay are stilled
and on each street the deranged
can obtain salvation at the edge of his hem.
He did not hide his Gospel among the clouds of Judea,
beyond the eye and tongue of man.
But he gives the life that will last forever
in a drop of wine and a morsel of bread, and the Spirit's gift in drops of water.
GWENALLT, TRANS. C. DAVIES

Those whose faces are turned always towards the sun's rising
see the living light on its path approaching,
as over the glittering sea, where in tide's rising and falling
the sea beasts bask, on the Isles of Farne
Aidan and Cuthbert saw God's feet walking
each day towards all who on world's shores await his coming.
That we too, hand in hand,
have received the unending morning.
KATHLEEN RAINE, LINDISFARNE

Let the rumble of traffic diminish and the song of the birds grow clear,
and may the Son of God come striding towards you walking on these stones.
ST. AIDAN'S CHAPEL, BRADFORD CATHEDRAL

DECEMBER 16 ✣ A PERSONAL SIGN FROM GOD

Psalm 97; Isaiah 57:14-21; Luke 1:46-56

*The law of sin is at work in my body.
What an unhappy person I am!
Who will rescue me from this body
that is taking me with to death?...
Our Lord Jesus Christ!*
ROMANS 7:23-25

The glory of the human race is God; but it is the human race that receives the benefit of God's actions, God's wisdom, and God's power. Just as a doctor proves herself in her patients, so God is revealed in human beings. That is why Paul states, "God has imprisoned all in unbelief, in order to have mercy upon all." God is speaking here of the human race, which was excluded from immortality as a result of disobedience to God, but then obtained mercy by being adopted through the Son of God.

Without pride or boasting, human beings should truly value created things and their creator—that is, God, the all-powerful. We should live in God's love, willingly, thankfully; if we do, we will receive a greater glory from God and will go on to become like the one who died for us.

He, like us, was made of frail human flesh, in order to expel sin from human flesh. He came to invite us to become like himself, commissioning us to imitate God, placing us under obedience to the Father so that we might see and know God. He who did this is the Word of God, who lived in and became Son of humankind in order to accustom humans to live in God and to accustom God to live in humanity.

That is why he is a sign of our salvation, Immanuel, born of the Virgin, a sign given us personally by the Lord.

Isaiah makes the same point as St. Paul, "Be strong, weak hands and feeble knees; pluck up your courage, faint hearts. Be strong, do not be afraid. See, our God is coming with justice and to settle up; God is personally coming to save us." It is not by ourselves but by the help of God that we are saved.
BASED ON IRENAEUS, AGAINST THE HERESIES

*Dear Son of God, change my heart.
You took flesh to redeem me;
dear Son of Mary, change my heart.*

DECEMBER 17 ✥ O COME FROM ON HIGH

Psalm 60; Isaiah 60:1-3; Luke 2:1-7

The one who is holy and true has the key of David,
and when he opens a door, no one can shut it;
when he closes a door, no one can open it. . . .
The great Son of David has triumphed.
REVELATION 3:7; 5:5

As Christians reflected over the centuries on the nature of the coming King, they were given awesome insights. These were expressed in "The Prayer of the Great O's," known as the Advent Antiphons, which were said from December 17. This prayer expresses two great truths about Christ. First, that he was the eternal Son of God, the second person of the Trinity, the eternal Wisdom who had always been guiding God's people. Second, that the great representatives of God's people, such as Moses and King David, prefigured Christ. Jesus was perceived as living to the full what these characters lived in a measure.

In the fourteenth century, a monk from the Durham monastery became a hermit on the island of Farne, just as had their monastery's founding saint, Cuthbert. As this unknown hermit meditated along this train of thought, his imagination ran riot, and he wrote this prayer to Christ:

You are David who scattered with strong arm your foes
and shattered death's barred gates to free your own people;
you slew the giant vaunting
and the sons of Jacob taunting
though you had but a sling.
You like wormwood undermining,
armed and battle not declining victory did nobly gain.
Philistinian ranks were saddened,
Saul and his retainers gladdened
by the trophies of the slain.
Warfare for us waging blithely
to the cross-top leaping lithely,
hell's great might you overthrew.
Wondrous tones from your harp ringing—
your wounds were in painful stringing—
yield a tune folk did not know.
Kindest Jesus then uphold us
when death's darkness does enfold us
be our comfort and our stay.

Give to us Christ's strength blithely to surmount life's ills.

DECEMBER 18 ✢ CHILD OF HUMANITY

Psalm 89:1-14; Isaiah 11:1-5; John 1:1-14

The Word became a human being and,
full of grace and truth, lived among us.
We saw his glory, the glory
which he received as the Father's only Son.
JOHN 1:14 GNT

On the face of the world there was not born his equal.
Three-person God, Trinity's only Son, gentle and strong.
Son of the Godhead, Son of humanity, only Son of wonder.
The Son of God is a refuge, Mary's Son a blessed sanctuary,
a noble child was seen.
Great is his splendor, great Lord and God
in the place of glory.
From the line of Adam we were born.
From David's line the fulfillment of prophecy,
the host was born again.
By his word he saved the blind and the deaf
from all suffering.
The ragged, foolish sinners and those of impure mind.
12TH OR 13TH CENTURY WELSH
(*DAVIES IN* CELTIC CHRISTIAN SPIRITUALITY)

Child of glory, Child of Mary,
born in the stable, King of all.
You came to our wasteland, in our place suffered.
Happy we are counted who to you are near.
Strengthen our hope, enliven our joy,
keep us valiant, faithful and near.
CARMINA GADELICA (ADAPTED)

December 19 ✢ Mary Nurtures a Life

Psalm 89:46–52; Proverbs 23:15–25; Galatians 4:1–7

This was how the birth of Jesus Christ took place.
His mother Mary was engaged to Joseph,
but before they were married,
she found out that she was going to have a baby by the Holy Spirit.
MATTHEW 1:18

Mary nurtures the Son of tenderness,
God, supreme ruler of every nation:
her father, her strengthener, her brother.
Mary nurtures a Son on whom dignity rests:
none can violate his boundaries whose words are beauty,
who is neither young nor grows old.
The unwise can never perceive how Mary is related to God:
her Son, her Father, her Lord.
But I know, though I be but frail and earthly,
how Mary is bonded in the Spirit to the Trinity:
her Son and brother in the flesh,
her Father, her Lord, blessed almighty.
EARLY OR MIDDLE WELSH, TRANS. PAUL QUINN

Medical experts tell us that getting fit to have a baby takes time. If a mother's body is full of addictive substances from smoking, alcohol, or drugs, or if it is lacking in vitamins, three to six clean months are needed before it can provide a healthy womb. Research now also confirms that stress, or lack of harmony, harms the unborn baby. Parents who pray for the child in their womb, who sing to it, feel it, and love it, are following in the path of Mary.

Celtic Christians often imagined that they were present when Mary gave birth to Jesus, and they made beautiful prayers for the children they themselves bore. And if we imagine that we are each called to "birth" the Christ Child into the world anew, how can we prepare our bodies and our minds to nurture him?

Help me to nurture your life in myself.
Help me to nurture your life in others.

DECEMBER 20 ✢ CREATIVE MINORITIES

Psalm 48; Isaiah 17:10–12:5; Luke 13:18–21

The royal line of David is like a tree that has been cut down;
but fresh shoots will sprout from the stump,
and a new king will arise from among these.
ISAIAH 11:1

Big doors swing on little hinges; God's people learned that after their capital city, their temple, and their kings were destroyed. Out of the rubble, prophet voices spoke. These voices said that, like new shoots growing from the stump of a tree that has been cut down, a creative minority would arise to swing history God's way once again.

Jesus' parents were nobodies, but they had slender links with the great King David. God used them to bring into being a new Person, and a new people, that transformed the Roman Empire. The creative minority of Celtic saints did the same in the period of the Dark Ages. Think of cradle places such as Llantwit Major, Iona, and Lindisfarne.

Will you be part of God's creative minority for the third millennium?

> If five percent of any body of people are wholly convinced
> about anything, they can swing the rest.
> J. C. SMUTS

As we, the Romans of the twentieth century, look out across our Earth, we see some signs for hope, many more for despair. Technology proceeds apace, delivering marvels . . . the conquering of diseases . . . revolutions in crop yields . . . the information highway . . . that would dazzle those who built the Roman roads, the first great information system. But that road system became impassable rubble, as the empire was overwhelmed by population explosions beyond its borders. So will ours. . . .

The future may be germinating today not in a boardroom in London or an office in Washington or a bank in Tokyo, but in some antique outpost or other . . . an orphanage in Peru . . . a house for the dying in Calcutta . . . in some unheralded corner where a great-hearted being is committed to loving outcasts in an extraordinary way. . . . If our civilization is to be saved—forget about our civilization which, as Patrick would say, may pass "in a moment like a cloud or smoke that is scattered by the wind"—if we are to be saved, it will not be by Romans but by saints.
THOMAS CAHILL, HOW THE IRISH SAVED CIVILIZATION

Make me one of your dedicated minority, wholly surrendered.

DECEMBER 21 ✛ A THIEF'S LESSON

Psalm 37:1-20; Zechariah 5:7-4:1 Corinthians 6:9-11

The Lord almighty says that he will send this curse out,
and it will enter the house of every thief
and the house of everyone who tells lies under oath.
It will remain in their houses and leave them in ruins.
ZECHARIAH 5:4 GNT

How often after we have been injured by another, have we longed to take things into our own hands to bring justice? An experience of Samson's may fortify us.

A thief stole a beautiful jeweled crosier from the monastery where Samson was based. Within an hour, the thief was so overwhelmed with the enormity of what he had done that he fell prostrate to the ground as if half dead. Nevertheless, he hardened his heart, and continued his life of crime, carrying round his waist a cloth in which he kept the jewels he had extracted from the crosier. On the night of the winter solstice he was crossing an iced-over pond, when the ice cracked under him and he drowned.

The following day a brother from the monastery was going for a stroll. He saw the cloth with its contents lying on the ice, and the stiffened corpse standing rigid in the middle of the ice. The lessons the brothers drew from this incident were that it is not possible to hide anything from God, either good or evil, and that God can work things out for his friends even in traumatic, depressing situations.

Christ at the yearly turning,
Christ at every bend.
Christ at each beginning,
Christ at every end.
Christ in every break-in,
Christ in shades of death,
Christ in icy waters,
Christ in wintry, earth.

Lord, when anyone does something to damage or diminish me,
help me to place them into your hands,
to trust you to deal with them as you will,
and to guide me in my responses.

DECEMBER 22 ✢ WINTER SOLSTICE

Psalm 8; Isaiah 45:8-13; Luke 21:20-38

I will give you treasures from dark, secret places.
ISAIAH 45:3 GNT

The darkest and the coldest time
is also the brightest time:
O Christmas Christ,
the radiance around the moon
is not as fair as the radiance
around your head.
O Holy One
the majesty of the winter sea
is not as glorious as your majesty.
At the departing times,
the coldest times of our lives;
at the times of excitement
and the times of expectancy;
at the times of intersection,
when hard choices have to be made,
be with us, Prince of Peace.
KATE MCLLHAGGA

Now begin the twelve long nights of Yule. One night soon, Jesus will be born, Son of the King of Glory, creation's Joy.

You will gleam to him, moon and furthest star.
You will gleam to him, hills and housetops afar.

Lord of the solstice, on this day of briefest light,
help us to be at home with the treasures of the dark.
As the days have drawn in,
help us to flow with the ebb tides of life.
At the turning of the year,
help us to welcome the Dawn from on high.

DECEMBER 23 ✢ LOVE'S FURNACE

Psalm 138; Isaiah 9:2-7; Matthew 1:1-17

*The angel said to Mary,
"Don't be afraid! God has been kind to you.
You will become pregnant and give birth to a son,
and you will name him Jesus. He will be great,
and he will be called the Son of the Most High God."*
Luke 1:30–32

Forget not, Trinity, holy and glorious
that heaven's bright prince came down to bestow on us
his love, as babe, into Mary's fair womb.
For nine months he who is angels' Lord
was hidden, love's furnace, in a little room
humbler than all, whom all adored.
A pure lamb, he stole down to earth to free us from our sin so blind.
No city home will shield his birth,
his mother a stable for bed must find;
there poorest of the poor she lay,
nor wine nor meat for hunger's sting
in the rude confines of the cattle bay
where God was born, apostles' King.
Cold and exile he did not scorn
in the donkey's manger, that holy morn.
Tadg Gaelach O Suilleabhain, medieval Irish

*May the trust of Mary troubled by her strange call
and Joseph's encouragement beside her through all
be God's gift to us.
May the radiant brightness and light of the Star,
the hope and longing of searchers traveling from afar,
be God's gift to us.
May the wonder of shepherds surprised by God's love,
the joy of the angels who came from above,
be God's gift to us.
May the peace of the Christ-child in carved trough of stone
sounding the word "Savior" fashioned by Grace alone
be God's gift to us.*
Crawford Murrey

DECEMBER 24 ✣ EVE OF THE GREAT NATIVITY

Psalm 47; Isaiah 62:10-12; Matthew 1:18-25

*An angel of the Lord appeared to the shepherds,
and the glory of the Lord shone round about them.*
LUKE 2:9 NIV

This night is the long night.
It will snow and it will drift.
White snow there will be till day,
white moon there will be till morn.
This night is the eve of the Great Nativity,
this night is born Mary Virgin's Son,
this night is born Jesus, Son of the King of Glory,
this night is born to us the root of our joy,
this night gleamed the sun of the mountains high,
this night gleamed sea and shore together,
this night was born Christ the King of greatness.
Ere it was heard that the Glory was come,
heard was the wave upon the strand.
Ere 'twas heard that his foot had reached earth,
heard was the song of the angels glorious;
this night is the long night.

Glowed to him wood and tree,
glowed to him mount and sea,
glowed to him land and plain,
when that his foot was come to earth.
CARMINA GADELICA

*Babe of Heaven, Defenseless Love, in order to come to us
you have to travel far from your home.
Come to strengthen us on our pilgrimage of trust on earth.
Your birth will show us the simplicity of the Father's love,
the wonder of being human.
Help us to live fully human lives for you.*

DECEMBER 25 ✣ BORN FOR US

Psalm 98; Isaiah 62:1-5; Luke 2:1-7

Mary gave birth to her first son ... and laid him in a manger because the inn had no room for them.
LUKE 2:7

The night the star shone
was born the Shepherd of our flock
of the Virgin of the hundred charms,
the Mother Mary.
The Trinity eternal by her side
in the manger cold and lowly.
Come and give tithes of your means
to the Healing Man,
the foam-white breastling beloved
without one home in the world,
the tender holy Babe driven forth,
Immanuel!

The three angels of power,
come you, come you down
to the Christ of the people,
give salutation.
Kiss his hands, dry his feet
with the hair of your heads.
And O! you world-pervading God,
and you, Jesus, Michael, Mary,
do not forsake us.
CARMINA GADELICA

Your gift to us this day
is more than we could ask or think—your very life.
This day may my gift to you be nothing less than my very life.

Hail King! hail King! blessed is he! blessed is he!
Hail King! hail King! blessed is he! blessed is he!
Hail King! hail King! blessed is he
the King of whom we sing. All hail! let there be joy!
CARMINA GADELICA

DECEMBER 26 ✥ KEEP WATCH

Psalm 46; Isaiah 66:22-24; Luke 2:8-20

The shepherds said to one another,
"Let's go to Bethlehem and see this thing
the Lord told us has happened."
So they hurried off and found Mary and Joseph,
with the baby lying in the manger.
LUKE 2:15-16

Once when I was living alone in my island, some of the brothers came to me on the holy day of the Lord's nativity, and asked me to go out of my hut so that I might spend with them this day so sacred, yet so joyful. I yielded, and we sat down to a feast. In the middle of the meal I said, "Let us be careful not to be led into temptation through recklessness." They answered, "Let's be joyful today because it is the Lord's birthday." After a time, while we were still indulging in feasting, rejoicing and story telling, I again began to warn them that we should always be alert to any approaching temptation. They said, "You give us excellent instruction, but let us rejoice, for the angel, when the Lord was born, gave the shepherds glad tidings of the great joy that was to be observed by all the people." I said, "All right: but later, for a third time, while they were still feasting, I gave a warning. This time they understood that I was not making this suggestion lightly, and they responded, "Let's do as you say. We do actually now feel compelled to guard against temptations and the snares of the devil, keeping our minds alert." When I said this, I did not know, nor did they, that any new trial would attack us, I was warned by instinct alone. However, when they got back to Lindisfarne the next morning, they found that the plague had struck and one of their number had died. This pestilence grew worse and worse, and nearly all that great company of spiritual fathers and brothers departed to be with the Lord. So will you, too, please always watch and pray.
CUTHBERT, AS RECORDED IN BEDE'S LIFE

O Savior Christ, you existed before the world began,
You came to save us and we are witnesses of your goodness.
You became a tiny child,
showing us the simplicity of our parents' love.
You chose Mary as your mother
and raised all motherhood to a divine vocation,
May all mothers be bearers of life and grace
to their children and to all who come to their home.

DECEMBER 27 ✢ MOTHER AND CHILD

Psalm 123; Isaiah 66:7-14; Matthew 2:1-12

*The star went ahead of them
until it stopped over the place where the young child was.
They went into the house,
and when they saw the child with his mother Mary,
they knelt down and worshipped him.*
MATTHEW 2:9, 11

The Virgin was beheld approaching
Christ so young on her breast,
angels bowing lowly before them
and the King of life was saying, "'Tis meet."
The Virgin of locks most glorious,
the Jesus more gleaming-white than snow;
seraphs melodious, singing their praise,
and the King of life was saying, "'Tis meet."
O Mary, Mother of wondrous power,
grant us the succor of thy strength,
bless the provision, bless the board,
bless the ear, the corn, the food.
The Virgin of mien most glorious,
the Jesus more gleaming-white than snow;
she like the moon in the hills arising,
he like the sun on the mountain crests.
CARMINA GADELICA

*Cheers, the Gift; clap, the Gift, cheers, the Gift on the living.
Son of the dawn, Son of the clouds, Son of the planet, Son of the star.
Son of the flame, Son of the light, Son of the spheres, Son of the globe.
Son of the elements, Son of the heavens, Son of the moon, Son of the sun.
Son of Mary of the God-mind and the Son of God first of all news.
Cheers, the Gift; clap, the Gift, cheers, the Gift on the living.*
CARMINA GADELICA

Psalm 36; Jeremiah 31:15-18; Matthew 2:13-78

> *King Herod gave orders to kill all the little boys*
> *in and near Bethlehem who were two years old and younger.*
> *This is the way the words of the prophet Jeremiah came true:*
> *A sound of mothers weeping is heard.*
> MATTHEW 2:16–18

Why do you tear from me my darling son,
the fruit of my womb?
It was I who bore him, my breast he drank.
My womb carried him about, my vitals he sucked,
my heart he filled.
He was my life, 'tis death to have him taken from me.
My strength has ebbed, my speech is silenced,
my eyes are blinded.
Then another woman said: . . .Infants you slay,
the fathers you wound, the mothers you kill.
Hell with your deed is full, heaven is shut,
you have spilt the blood of guiltless innocents.
And yet another woman said, O Christ, come to me!
With my son take my soul quickly!
O great Mary, mother of God's Son,
what shall I do without my son?
For your Son my spirit and sense are killed.
I am become a crazy woman for my son.
After the piteous slaughter, my heart is a dot of blood
from this day till Doom.
ELEVENTH CENTURY, ANONYMOUS

The vivid Celtic imagination transposed the agony of the Bethlehem killings into their own breasts. Which situations in our world demand that we do the same? Who are the weak whom we need to defend against the tyranny of the strong?

High King of the universe,
by choosing to be born as a child
you teach us to reverence every human life.
May we never despise, degrade, or destroy it.
Rather, help us sustain and preserve life.

DECEMBER 29 ✢ HOLY FAMILIES

Psalm 146; Proverbs 31:10-31; Luke 2:36-40

*When Joseph and Mary had finished doing
everything they had to do,
they went back home to Nazareth.
The child grew and became strong;
he was full of wisdom, and God blessed him.*
Luke 2:39-40

To come into thy presence,
thou Virgin of the lowly;
to come into thy presence,
thou mother of Jesus Christ;
to come into thy presence,
thou dwelling of meekness;
to come into thy presence,
thou home of peace;
to come into thy presence,
beauteous one of smiles;
to come into thy presence,
beauteous one of women.
Carmina Gadelica

*We pray for people who have no decent house to live in;
for those who provide foster homes;
for parents who think deeply about their child's character and calling.
May our sons grow up strong and straight like young trees.
May our girls have the beauty of inner serenity.
May our farms and industries overflow.
May the voice of complaining cease from our streets.
Happy are the people from whom such blessings flow—
who put their trust in God.*
inspired by Psalm 144

DECEMBER 30 ✣ OUR BRIEF FLIGHT

Psalm 121; Proverbs 30:1-5; John 16:25-28

I came from the Father, and I came into the world;
and now I am leaving the world and going back to the Father. . . .
It is better for you that I go away,
because if I don't go away, the Helper will not come to you.
JOHN 16:28; 16:7

King Edwin informed the missionary Paulinus that he was willing to accept the Christian faith for himself, but he first wished to consult with his pagan advisors; if they agreed, they would together be consecrated in the waters of life. Coifi, the chief of the pagan priests told the king: "I frankly admit that the religion which we have hitherto held has no virtue nor profit in it." Another of the king's advisers added, "This is how the present life of human beings on earth appears to me, King. You are sitting feasting with your staff in a hall warmed by a fire, while outside the wintry storms rage; then a sparrow flies across the hall. It enters at one door and quickly flies out through the other. For the few moments it is inside the wintry storm cannot touch it but after its brief moment of calm it departs from your sight. Out of the wintry storm and into it again—that is what human life is like. We know nothing of what comes after it, or what went before it. If this new teaching brings us more information, it seems right that we should accept it. . . ." So King Edwin, with all the nobles of his race and a vast number of the common people received the faith, and were baptized at York in 627.
BEDE

When the time came for Alexander Carmichael to bid a final farewell to the friends he had made in the western parts of Scotland, Mor MacNeill, who was "poor and old and alone," sent him on his way with this prayer:

And you are now going away
and leaving your people and your country, dear one of my heart!
Well, then, whole may you be and well may it go with you
every way you go and every step you travel.
And my own blessing go with you
and the blessing of God go with you
and the blessing of Mary Mother go with you,
every time you rise up and every time you lie down,
until you lie down in sleep upon the arm of Jesus Christ.
CARMINA GADELICA

DECEMBER 31 ✧ SUPPOSE

Psalm 90; Isaiah 30:19-26; Matthew 17:14-21

All things are possible to the one who believes.
MARK 9:23 ESV

I said to the man who stood at the gate of the year, "Give me a light that I may tread safely into the unknown." And he replied: "Go out into the darkness and put your hand into the hand of God. That shall be better to you than light, and safer than a known way."
M. LOUISE HASKINS, THE DESERT

Suppose we were to find again the faith in God our forbears knew!

The richest year of miracles in our history awaits those who are ready to follow God's leading without checks or conditions.

Journey on with God. What blessings await you!

> *May the blessing of light be on you*
> *light without light and light within.*
> *May the blessed sunlight shine upon you*
> *and warm your heart till it glows like a great peat fire,*
> *so that the stranger may come and warm herself at it, as well as the friend.*
> *And may the light shine out of your eyes,*
> *like a candle set in the windows of a house,*
> *bidding the wanderer to come in out of the storm.*
> *And may the blessing of the rain be on you, the sweet soft rain.*
> *May it fall upon your spirit,*
> *so that all the little flowers may spring up*
> *and shed their sweetness on the air.*
> *And may the blessing of the great rains be upon you,*
> *that they beat upon your spirit and wash it fair and clean*
> *and leave there many a shining pool*
> *where the blue of heaven shines, and sometimes a star.*
> *And may the blessing of the earth be on you, the great round earth.*
> *May you ever have a kindly greeting*
> *for people you pass as you go along the roads.*
> *And now may the Lord bless you and bless you kindly.*
> AN OLD IRISH BLESSING TRANSLATED BY B. O'MALLEY

Who's Who in the Celtic World

Adamnan (627–704): Ninth abbot of Iona and **Columba**'s biographer.

Aelfflaed (654–713): Daughter of King Oswy of Northumbria and Abbess of Whitby, succeeding her kinswoman **Hilda**.

Aidan (died 651): Irishman who became apostle to the English and founder and first bishop of the Monastery of Lindisfarne in Northumbria.

Alexander Carmichael (1832–1912): Scottish folklorist and writer who researched folk traditions of the Scottish highlands and islands resulting in the *Carmina Gadelica*, an important source of information on traditional Celtic prayers and beliefs.

Antony (251–356): One of the most influential figures in all of Christian history, Antony left a life of ease to become a desert ascetic. An account of his life by Bishop Athanasius of Alexandria popularized the monastic movement in both Eastern and Western churches.

Beccan Mac Luigdech (7th century): Irish poet and monk who came to live on the Holy Island of Iona.

Bede (672/673–735): Northumbrian writer known as "the first English historian." His most famous work is *The Ecclesiastical History of the English People*. He favored the customs of the Latin Church against the "errors" of Celtic Christians but nevertheless admired the Celts' holy lives. Much of what we know about many of the Celtic saints we owe to Bede.

Branwalader (6th century): A roving missionary monk, he was born in Cornwall, trained in monastic life in Wales, and traveled extensively, spreading Celtic Christianity in the Channel Islands and Brittany, Northern France.

Brendan of Birr (died 573): Founder and first abbot of the monastery in Birr, Ireland. He was called "Prophet of Ireland" and listed among the Twelve Apostles of Ireland—a set of especially noteworthy 6th-century saints. A close friend of Columba, Brendan swayed a church synod to exile **Columba** rather than excommunicate him—a critical decision that enabled evangelization of the land now known as Scotland.

Brendan the Navigator (484–577): Brendan established several monasteries in Western Ireland, but he is most famous as the hero of the popular medieval *Voyage of Saint Brendan*, which relates his fabulous adventures sailing west from Ireland. This Irish sailor saint may have reached the Americas centuries before Columbus.

Brigid (451–525): She is the most influential Celtic saint (after **Patrick**) and the founder and abbess of a great monastery in Kildare, Ireland. Legends of Saint Brigid have taken on many aspects of the older goddess of the same name. She is intimately connected—as was the goddess—with the feast of Imbolc, the Celtic beginning of spring. She is known as "Mary of the Gaels" for her importance in bringing Christ to the Celtic peoples.

Brynach (6th century): A Welsh saint dwelling in the Pembrokeshire region, he was especially noted for his communion with wildlife.

Cadoc: Born late in the 5th century, Cadoc was a Welsh saint and abbot of the monastery of Llancarfan, who also planted churches in Cornwall, Brittany, and Scotland.

Caedmon: The earliest known English poet, he is mentioned in **Bede**'s *Ecclesiastical History* as being given the miraculous—as it was entirely nonexistent in his life—talent of composing beautiful songs. This took place sometime during the abbacy of Saint **Hilda** at Whitby (657–680).

Chad (died 672): Along with his brother Cedd, Chad trained under Saint **Aidan** at the Monastery on Holy Island Lindisfarne; he eventually became bishop of Northumbria and afterward bishop of Mercia. Along with Cedd, he is credited with bringing the Gospel message to Mercia.

Ciaran (516–546): Founded the important monastery of Clonmacnoise in the center of Ireland on the banks of the river Shannon. Saint **Kevin** of Glendalough was his anamchara (soul friend).

Colmán mac Béognae (555–611): The son of Beogna and Mor—who was the sister of Saint **Columba**—he was founder and first abbot of the Monastery of Muckamore and later Bishop of Connor. His work *The Alphabet of Piety* is the oldest surviving composition written in Old Irish prose.

Columba (521–597): Also known as Colum Cille, he was born to the powerful Irish O'Neil clan. Columba established a number of monasteries in Ireland. Then, according to legend, he became embroiled in a blood feud over a rare copy of the Psalms. Consequently, a church synod exiled him from Ireland. He sailed to the Island of Iona off the Pictish coast (modern-day Scotland), where he founded the famous monastery of Iona and evangelized the Picts.

Columbanus (540–615): Born in County Meath, he was foremost among traveling Irish missionaries, spreading the Gospel and planting monasteries and churches in France, Switzerland, and Germany. A lover of both people and animals, he left the mark of Celtic spirituality in large portions of continental Europe.

Comgall (died either 602 or 597): A proponent of strict Irish monasticism, he was founder and abbot of the monastery in Bangor, Ulster.

Comghan (5th century): An Irishman who founded the monastery at Killeshin.

Cormac (6th century): Irish disciple of Saint **Columba** who succeeded him as abbot of the monastery at Durrow.

Cuthbert (634–687): Patron saint of northern England, he was an Anglo-Saxon monk trained at the Scottish monastery of Melrose who later became Bishop of Lindisfarne. His remains were the most important relic at Holy Island Lindisfarne until their removal—following Viking raids—to Durham Cathedral, where they are enshrined today.

David (500–589): Born in Pembrokeshire Wales—his mother having conceived him as the result of being raped—he became a famous preacher, monk, evangelist, and eventually, the patron saint of Wales. He established a famous monastery at the present site of Saint David's Cathedral in the city of the same name. He was known as "the waterman" due to his ascetic practices of praying while standing in water.

Ddyfnog (6th century): A saint of northeast Wales known for standing in water as a penitential practice.

Drithelm (died 700): A resident of Northumbria, he joined the monastery of Melrose after a near-death experience and a vision of the afterlife. He lived as a hermit at Melrose Abbey.

Ebba (615–683): Daughter of Aelthefrith, the first king of Northumbria, she was exiled after her father's death in battle. She converted to Christianity and founded monasteries at Ebchester and St. Abb's Head. Noted for her teaching skills and political savvy, she converted many Angles to the new faith.

Enddwyn: Patron saint of Llanenddwyn in Gwynneth, Wales. A holy well reputed to do miracles is named after her.

Fechin (died 665): Founder of the monastery of Fore in Westmeath, Ireland.

Finbarr (550–623): Bishop and abbot of the monastery of Cork, Ireland, and patron saint of the city.

Finnian (470–549): Irish saint who founded Clonard Abbey in County Meath. At the high-point of his career, he was instructing 3,000 students in the ways of the monastic life.

Fintan (died 603): A disciple of **Columba**, he was known for miracles, prophecies, and severe asceticism.

Fursey (died 650): A traveling Irish missionary monk, he evangelized throughout Britain and established a monastery in France.

Gall (550–646): He was a companion of **Columbanus** who helped spread Celtic Christianity in Europe. One legend recounts how a bear brought wood to stack a fire for Gall and his companions.

George MacLeod (1895–1991): A minister of the Church of Scotland, he founded the Iona Community, providing work for unemployed Scottish laborers and reestablishing the ruined Iona Abbey as a place of worship. The Iona Community continues its ministry of justice, community, and worship today.

Gildas (500–570): A Briton priest, educated by Saint **Illtyd**, his writings are unique as the sole remaining contemporary record of 6th-century British history.

Hilda (614–680): Born into a royal Anglian family, she grew up to become an influential abbess at monasteries in Hartlepool and Whitby. Noted for her teaching and counsel, kings and commoners sought her advice. **Caedmon** discovered his poetic gift at her monastery.

Illtyd (6th century): Welsh abbot of Llanilltud Fawr in Glamorgan. After a career as a soldier—and perhaps a druid—he converted and educated many of his countrymen in the Christian faith.

Irenaeus (died 202): Bishop of Lyons, France, he is one of the most influential theologians and leaders in the formative years of Christianity. His book *Against Heresies* helped define Christian orthodoxy. One important contribution was his insistence that all four Gospels be included in the New Testament canon.

Ita (died 570 or 577): Known as "the **Brigid** of Munster," she established a monastery at Kileedy in County Limerick, Ireland, that included a school for training children in the Christian faith. **Brendan the Navigator** was one of her students.

Jerome (347–420): Born in Dalmatia, he eventually, after studying in Rome and Antioch, settled in Bethlehem, Israel, where he lived as a hermit and translated the Old Testament from the original Hebrew text. He is the principle translator of the Latin Bible known as the Vulgate, which was used for the next millennium as the Bible of Western Christendom.

Kevin (died 618): Founder and abbot of the monastery in Glendalough, Ireland. Kevin is known as the "Irish Saint Francis" because of his love for wilderness and natural creatures. The most famous tale of his life tells of a blackbird that nested in his hand—while he remained motionless until its chicks hatched.

Kieran the Elder (died 530): He is known as the first saint born in Ireland. A contemporary of **Patrick**, he established a monastery at Saigir and is famous for his love of animals.

Maedoc (6th century): Maedoc studied under Finnian in Clonard, and then David in Wales, and went on to establish monasteries in both Ireland and Wales.

MacCuirb (6th century): The Irish bishop who baptized **Finbarr**.

Mac Nisse (died 514): Irish saint and founder-abbot of Connor Monastery. He lived at Kells as a hermit prior to the establishment of the monastery there.

Malo (6th century): Born near Llancarfan, Wales, he is supposed to have sailed with **Brendan** on his legendary voyage before establishing a monastery in Saint-Malo, Brittany, France.

Melangell (died 590): The daughter of an Irish king, she became a hermit in Cornwall and later established a female monastery, where she served as abbess for 37 years.

Mo Chua (late 5th and early 6th centuries): An Irish Christian who founded a monastery at Balla.

Modomnoc (died 550): An Irishman who became a disciple of David in Wales, he is said to have introduced beekeeping from Wales to Ireland.

Molaise (566–640): Born of Irish and Scottish royalty, Molaise lived as a hermit on Holy Island off Aran, consequently known as Eilean Molaise

(Molaise Island). He later traveled to Rome and then returned to Ireland to become abbot of Leighlin Monastery. There, he introduced Roman liturgical customs to the Celts. St. Molaise's Cave on Holy Island contains ancient Norse pilgrim runes.

Moling (died 697): He was born in Wexford, Ireland, and became a monk at Glendalough under **Saint Kevin**. He later established the monastery that became known as St. Mullins.

Molua (died 609): An Irish monk and abbot, he established his monastery at the site known since as Killaloe (the church of Lua).

Moninna (435 to 518): Saint Patrick baptized her as a child and prophesied that her name would become famous. In adulthood, she became a missionary in both England and Scotland. (Her name is also sometimes spelled Monenna.)

Morcant (6th century): A contemporary of Mungo, Morcant was a northern Brythonic prince who opposed both the Anglo-Saxons and also Christianity. He consistently acted against Mungo's efforts to evangelize the Scottish borderlands.

Mungo (died 612): Also known as Kentigern, he was born in Fife, Scotland. He began evangelizing in that area but the opposition of King **Morcant** forced his withdrawal to Wales, where he founded a monastery. Later, Mungo moved back north and established a Christian community that grew into the city of Glasgow (a name that in Gaelic means "dear family"). He is noted for his gentle but persistent manner of sharing the Christian faith. Mungo is the patron saint of Glasgow.

Noel Dermot O'Donoghue (1920–2006): Born in Killarney, Ireland, he became a priest and then a teacher at a number of theological schools. In 1971, he became the first Roman Catholic priest in a Faculty of Theology in Scotland since the Reformation. He promoted Celtic spirituality in his teaching and his writing.

Ninian (died 432): He is the first known Christian in Scotland. He was born in Britain, studied in Rome, and then established the first Pictish church at Whithorn in Galloway. Archaeology has established the site of his church; that and his nearby hermit cave are places of pilgrimage today.

Oswald (604–642): King of Northumbria, he invited missionaries from Iona to come evangelize his kingdom, leading to Aidan's establishment of the monastery at Lindisfarne and the subsequent conversion of the northern

English people. He ruled as a model of justice and generosity but died in battle the eighth year of his reign.

Pachomius (292–348): Born in Luxor, Egypt, he was converted as a young man by seeing the charity of Christians. He undertook the ascetic life but innovated by creating a community of ascetics—an innovation that led to the flowering of monasticism in Christendom.

Padarn (6th century): A British Abbot-Bishop, he established a monastery near Ceredigion, Wales. Later, he traveled to Brittany and built a monastery at Vannes.

Patrick (387–460): He is the most famous Celtic saint. Born in either Wales or Scotland, he was raised as a Roman citizen and then captured by slavers and sold into captivity in Ireland. A miracle freed Patrick and allowed him to return to his home, but a vision then impelled him to return and evangelize Ireland. His kindness, honoring Irish people and culture, led to the conversion of much of the island.

Paul the Hermit (died 341): He is famous as the model for innumerable Christian hermits who followed his solitary and ascetic way of life. He fled to the Egyptian desert in 250, fleeing imperial persecution. The famous Ruthwell Cross near Dumfries, Scotland, portrays Saint Paul the hermit breaking bread with **Antony**.

Paulinus (6th century): Welsh saint who taught **David** (who later restored Paulinus's vision after he went blind).

Pelagius (354–420): Born in the British Isles, he was the first theologian of the Celts. His teachings on free will conflicted with the beliefs of Augustine of Hippo, and Pelagius' teachings were eventually tried and condemned. However, his ideas remained influential among the Celtic Christians. His Welsh name is Morgan.

Petroc (died 564): He was born in southern Wales and studied in Ireland before embarking on his career as missionary in Devon and Cornwall. He is the patron saint of Cornwall (along with **Piran**).

Piran (6th century): Originally from Ireland, he evangelized Cornwall.

Rhydderch (580–614): King of the Scottish border region, he supported **Mungo** in his attempts to evangelize that part of the country.

Samson (late 5th century): A Welsh saint who was born in Gwent, he later became abbot of the monastery at Caldey Island off the Welsh Coast, then traveled spreading Christian teachings in Cornwall, Sicily, and Brittany.

Samthann (died 793): Irish nun and saint who became abbess of Clonbroney.

Senan (born 488): Born in County Clare, Ireland, he established the influential monastery on the Island of Innishmore off the Galway coast.

Taliesin (6th century): The legendary "Chief of the Welsh bards," his life spanned from pagan times to the adoption of Christianity. Poems allegedly written by him still exist.

Teilo (500–560): A Welsh saint, he was born near Caldey Island, trained under **Paulinus**, and worked with **David** in Pembrokeshire. Later he moved with **Samson** to Brittany.

Tighernach (died 548): Irish saint who was the godson of Saint **Brigid** and founder of the Monastery of Clones.

Index of People

Adam, David Jan 30, May 11, Aug 24, Sept 27
Adamnan Feb 14, Apr 18, May 19, June 19, Sept 23, 28, Oct 2, 5, 28, Nov 23
Aidan Jan 5, Feb 21, Apr 3, June 18, 29, July 13, 21, Aug 20, 31, Sept 1–3, 19, Oct 15, Nov 17
Antony Jan 17–18, 23, Feb 15, 21, Apr 18, July 20
Arthur (King Arthur) Jan 8–9
Ashe, Geoffrey July 31
Attracta July 30

Baudouin, King of the Belgians Aug 5
Bede Jan 22, Feb 14, 21, 27, Mar 19, May 27, June 5, 18, 28–29, July 7, 12, 16, 20, 26, Sept 2, 12, 19, 21, 23, 28, Nov 9, 17, 18, Dec 8, 26, 30
Blake, William July 14
Boisil May 15, July 7, Sept 21
Bradley, Ian Feb 24
Branwalader (Brelade) Jan 19
Brendan Jan 4, May 16–18, July 16, Sept 27
Brendan of Birr Oct 22
Brigid Feb 1, 3–16, Apr 20, Aug 22
Brynach Aug 13
Buchman, Frank Jan 8, Apr 16, June 13, 30, Oct 11, 23
Burns, Robert July 11

Cahill, Thomas May 12
Chambers, Oswald July 14
Churchill, Winston Sept 16
Chad Mar 2, Oct 15, Dec 9

Caedmon Feb 11, Sept 12
Cassian, John Feb 14, Nov 24
Ciaran of Clonmacnoise Sept 9–10, Nov 7
Climacus, John Feb 27
Colmán mac Béognae Apr 26–29, May 26, July 10, 12, Sept 16, 18
Columba Jan 3, 12, 28, Feb 14, 26, Apr 18, 29, May 19, June 2, 7–14, 16, 22–25, 27, 29, July 4, 22, Aug 10, 19, Sept 8, 11, 28, 30, Oct 1–3, 5, 20, 22–23, 28, 30, Nov 6, 26, Dec 5
Columbanus Jan 4, 11, 20, Feb 16, 26, Apr 14–15, 19, 25, May 1, June 19, 29, July 21–29, Aug 9, Sept 17, 25, 27, Oct 16, 18, 26, Nov 20–22, 28, Dec 7
Comgall Jan 11, June 5, 18
Cuthbert Jan 22, Feb 12, 14–15, 17, 19–20, 27, Mar 11, 19–20, 22, 31, Apr 4, 12, 20, 24, May 15, June 5, 30, July 1, 7, 12, 15–16, 20, 26, Aug 21, Sept 7, 12, 20–21, Oct 24, Dec 15, 17, 26

David of Wales Jan 22, Feb 9, 13, 19, 28, Mar 1, 3–4, 6–10, 18, Apr 10–11, May 13, 19, July 2–3, 27, Sept 16, Nov 27
Desert Christians Jan 17–18, 30, Feb 15, 18, 21, 23, 25, Mar 12, Apr 14–15, May 20, July 14, 20, Sept 6–7, 12, Oct 11, Nov 12, 16
Dick, Andrew Sept 24
Drake, Francis Sept 16
Drithelm Nov 3–4

388

Edwin Dec 30

Faustus of Riez Feb 27
Feheily, Tom May 31
Finbarr Apr 10
Francis of Assisi Oct 4
Fursey Jan 16, Dec 8

Gall Jan 11, Oct 16, 18, Nov 22
Gandhi Sept 17, Nov 19
George, Chief Dan Aug 9
Gildas July 31, Sept 22
Gwenallt (David G. Jones) July 27, Dec 15

Hale, Reginald Jan 15, Oct 23
Halliwell, Michael July 26, Nov 9
Helena Sept 14
Hilda Jan 22, Feb 11, June 28, Nov 17–19
Hildegaard of Bingen May 22, Aug 7–8, Sept 17
Hopkins, Gerard Manley Apr 19, Sept 27

Illtyd June 15, July 2–3, 9, 18, 28
Ignatius Loyola Feb 27
Irenaeus May 30, June 17, Dec 16
Ita Jan 11, May 23

Jerome Feb 10, Aug 12
John Scotus Eriugena Oct 27
Julian of Norwich July 1

Kagawa May 15
Kentigern (Mungo) Jan 13, 15, 25–28, July 11, 18, 21
Kevin of Glendalough June 3, July 19, Aug 3, 11, Nov 7

Lawrence, Brother May 13
Lubich, Chiara June 26

Macleod, George June 12, 17, Aug 6, Nov 28, Dec 4
Mellhagga, Kate Mar 18, 20
Malo Aug 18
Marban the Hermit Aug 3
Martin of Tours Feb 10, June 12, Aug 26, Nov 14–15
Mary, Virgin Mar 25, May 14, July 21, Oct 29, Nov 30, Dec 14, 19, 23–27
Melangell Aug 14
Merton, Thomas Jan 22, 24, May 30, June 1, Oct 8, 14, Nov 13
Milne, Marjorie of Glastonbury Aug 6, 24
Mitton, Michael Apr 30, June 13
Modomnoc Feb 13
Molaise Sept 5, Oct 17
Moling July 19
Molua Aug 4
Monk of Fame Dec 17
Moninna Nov 25
Mungo (Kentigern) Jan 13, 15, 25–28, July 11, 18, 21

Ninian Jan 25, Apr 2, 3, 16, Aug 26–30, Oct 5, Nov 10

Oswald Apr 3, June 18, Aug 5, 7, Sept 4, Oct 7
Oswin Aug 20

Patrick Mar 13–18, Apr 8, 11, 23, May 12, 30, July 16, 21, 30, Sept 13, 15, 24, 27, Oct 15, Nov 1, Dec 20
Pelagius Feb 24, May 4, July 23, Sept 18, Oct 6–14, 30
Penn, William Mar 10, Oct 23
Petroc June 4
Polycarp Jan 26
Raine, Kathleen Dec 15

Samson Jan 2, 10, 12, 19, Feb 7, 9,
    22, 29, June 15, July 2, 9, 18, 28,
    Aug 17, Sept 26, Oct 21, Nov 1,
    29, Dec 21
Samthann May 20
Chief Seattle May 8, Aug 11
Sellner, Edward C. Apr 14
Seraphim Apr 22–29
Shakespeare, William May 15, July 4

Taylor, Hudson June 29
Teilo Feb 9, May 19
Teresa, Mother Apr 15
Teresa of Avila Feb 26, Sept 4

Waal, Esther de May 4
Wallace, Martin Dec 4
Wesley, John May 24

Index of Subjects

Advent Nov 30–Dec 9, Dec 17, 20
Angels Sept 28–Oct 3
Anger Feb 18
Animals Jan 15, July 23, Aug 3, 8–22
Art May 12
Authority Mar 9, Oct 24

Balance July 3, 20, Sept 22, Nov 17, Dec 7
Baptism Jan 14, Apr 19, May 9, Aug 26, Dec 8
Beltane May 1
Bible Study July 9, Sept 2
Births Jan 7, 10–11, 13
Blessing Feb 13, Dec 31
Breath May 3

Celi De (Friends of God) Mar 21, Dec 4
Celtic Psalter, The Aug 9
Circling (Cairn) prayer Oct 5
Channel Isles Jan 2, 19
Christmas Dec 22–27
Children Jan 2, Mar 11, Apr 4, June 1, Nov 18
Church Jan 17, 19, 22, 25, 28, Mar 9, Apr 10, May 15, July 13, 18, Nov 29
Community of Aidan and Hilda, The May 10, 16–17, July 9, Aug 6, Dec 12
Confession Feb 25
Creation Jan 14, Feb 1, 11, Mar 10, 23, 26, Apr 1, May 4, 11–12, 22, 28, June 4, July 23, 26, Aug 6, 7, 25, Sept 17, Oct 4, 27
Criticism Feb 23
Cross, the Mar 22–29, Sept 14

Death, Dying Mar 30, Nov 3, 6–10, 13–14, 16, 19, 25, 27
Depression Nov 5, 26
Detachment Jan 14, Feb 26, July 5, 10, Sept 13
Divine plan Jan 12, 25, Apr 16, May 10, 15
Dream of the Rood, The Mar 26–27, Nov 8, Dec 11
Dreams Jan 7, 10, 12, Feb 11, 22–24, 28, May 23, June 15, July 2, 7, Oct 28, Nov 14, Dec 1

Earth Apr 21, May 8, Aug 2, 7–8
Easter Mar 29–Apr 7
Elements Jan 14, Apr 19–21, May 8, 19, Aug 7
Epiphany Jan 6–7, 14
Evangelism Jan 28, Mar 3, 20, Aug 26, 31, Sept 1, Nov 29
Evil Jan 2, 27, Feb 18, 27–28, Mar 6, 23, July 15, 19, 27, Oct 6, 8, 29, 31

Faith Mar 1, May 25, July 11, Oct 21
Families June 10, Dec 28–29
Fathers Jan 10, 12–13, 21, Feb 4, 28, Mar 7, 13, May 6, June 15, July 28, Aug 28, Nov 14–15
Forgiveness Feb 8, 28, June 1, 16, 27, July 2–3, 27, Aug 12, 20–21, 27, Sept 17, Oct 9, Nov 19
Friendship Feb 17, Mar 8, Apr 22, 26, June 23, July 11, 21, Aug 19, Sept 6, Oct 22, Nov 7
Generosity Feb 5, 13, Apr 5, June 11, 25, 29, Aug 18, 30, Nov 24
Gentleness Jan 5, Feb 9, 24, June 18, July 13, 19, 28, Aug 4, Sept 1, Nov 26

Glastonbury July 31
God's plan Apr 16, May 10

Halloween Oct 31
Healing Feb 5–6, Mar 3, June 11, July 15, Aug 27, Oct 2, 21
Heaven Nov 1–4, 6–10, 27
Holy Communion Feb 22, June 5
Holy Spirit Apr 21–May 19, June 7
Hospitality Jan 22, Feb 6, May 27, 29, June 25, Sept 7, Oct 11, Nov 24
Humility Mar 2, 9, July 13
Humor May 25, June 1, July 19, Sept 12

Imbolc Feb 1
Incarnation May 8, Dec 13–19, 24–25
Integrity Jan 26, Mar 2, July 6, Sept 2, 13, 18–20
Iona June 11–12, 16, Oct 23
Iona Community May 26, June 12, December 10, 12
Jesus Prayer, The Feb 12
Journeys Jan 1–7, May 16–18, June 23, July 5
Justice June 12, July 11, Aug 5, 20, 22, Sept 23, Nov 23
Lammas Aug 1
Leadership Jan 5, 8–9, June 14, 24–25, Dec 20
Listening Apr 12–16, May 10–14, 26
Love Jan 2, 11, May 26, 29, 31

Martyrdom Jan 26, Feb 10
Mission Jan 25–28, Mar 3, 17, May 20–31, Sept 4, 21, Oct 14, Nov 29
Moderation Aug 22
Mothers Jan 12, 15, 25–26, Feb 4, Mar 9, Apr 21, July 21, Aug 20, Sept 9, Oct 29, Nov 20, 23, Dec 27–29

Nations Jan 8, May 27, June 13, July 13, 27, Aug 20, Oct 23
New Year Jan 1–4, Dec 31
Northumbria Community Jan 29, Oct 10

Peace Jan 22, Mar 31, Apr 25, May 27, July 12, Aug 24, Oct 1, Nov 14, 19
Penance Feb 10, May 19, June 11, 20, 27, July 4, Oct 24, Nov 4
Pentecost May 18, 27, 29 (See also Holy Spirit)
Prayer Jan 4, 9, Feb 7, 25, Apr 15, May 2, 31, June 8, 15, July 9, 11, 13, Aug 21–22, Sept 3, 5, Oct 2, 5, 7, 13, 24, Nov 26, 29, Dec 9
Prophecy Jan 10–11, Apr 10, June 12, 26, July 28, Aug 20, Nov 19, Dec 18

Rainbow June 26
Reincarnation May 21
Remembrance Nov 14–15
Resurrection Mar 31, Apr 1–7, May 21
Resurrection, place of Apr 7, 10, Sept 27
Rhythm Mar 7, 30, Aug 9, 24, Nov 5

Sanctity of life Dec 28
Samhain Nov 1
Signs and wonders Jan 11, 15, Feb 6, Apr 24, June 14, July 16, Aug 5, 10, 17, 26–29
Silence Feb 14, 23, Apr 13, 15
Simplicity Mar 10, July 5
Sleep Oct 25

Solstice June 21, Dec 21–22
Sorrow Feb 8, 16, 19, Mar 24, 26, 28
Spiritual warfare Feb 17, 27, Mar 6, July 15, 26, 30
St Patrick's Breastplate Feb 3, Mar 17, Sept 25, Nov 29
Stowe Missal, The Dec 3
Suffering Jan 6, Mar 28, July 2, 14, Aug 6, 14, Oct 4, 7

Taize Community Mar 7
Temptation Mar 12, July 26, Sept 6, Dec 26
Trinity May 29–June 2, July 29

Wandering thoughts Aug 2
Water Jan 14, May 9, 19
Work Mar 4, 7, May 1

Young people Mar 13–14, 19

Index of Bible Texts

Genesis
1:1–2 Apr 30
1:11, 24, 2:7 Aug 7
1:26 May 31
2:7 Aug 8
3:17 Sept 17
7:13–14 Aug 16
9:16 June 26
12:1 Jan 3
22:14 June 30
28:11 Oct 28
37:8, 18 Feb 24
49:25–26 May 6

Exodus
3:8 Feb 13
3:14 May 28
15:22–26 Sept 8
32:10 Jan 8
35:31 May 12

Leviticus
9:4 Sept 21
19:18 Feb 9

Numbers
35:13, 15 Aug 14

Deuteronomy
6:5 Mar 19
6:6, 9 Feb 1
11:26–28 Oct 8
30:1 Oct 7
32:2 Jan 5, Sept 1
32:4 July 4
33:26 June 4

Judges
13:24–25 July 28

1 Samuel
13:14 Aug 5

2 Samuel
1:19, 24–25 Nov 14
1:23 Nov 7
21:3 June 27

1 Kings
17:12, 15 July 11
18:21 June 25
19:13, 15 Mar 15

2 Kings
2:8–9 Sept 3, Dec 4
20:4–6 Nov 25

2 Chronicles
6:14 July 10
31:21 May 1

Ezra
9:15 Oct 24

Nehemiah
9:20–21 Mar 16

Esther
9:24–25, 31 Sept 26

Job
6:24 Aug 2
9:8, 10 Aug 10
9:9 Dec 13
25:10 Oct 5
37:1, 5, 21 May 22
38:25–30 Aug 2

Psalms
8:2 Mar 11

9:13-14 Nov 4
17:3, 7 Dec 1
18:13 Dec 9
18:32-34 Jan 30
20:8 Nov 22
22:19 Sept 24
23:4 Nov 12
24:1 May 8, Aug 8
32:8 Apr 16
32:12 Mar 17
33:18-19 Mar 22
39:5, 12 Jan 2
42:11 Nov 26
45:1 Aug 23
46:10 Aug 9
51:17 Feb 16
59:16 June 23
63:1-8 Oct 26
65:11 Oct 19
78:67-70 Mar 4
84:7 Jan 16
97:1 May 18
103:14-15 Apr 21
104: 12-13 May 7
106:4-7 Jan 4
107:22 Feb 11
113:1, 3 Aug 24
18:9 Oct 17
119:9-10 Mar 13
122:6 July 31
127:2 Oct 23
131:2 July 12
133:1 Jan 21
134:10 June 9
139:7, 9-10 May 4
139:11-12 Dec 12
148:1-2 Oct 3
148:3-4, 8, 10-11 Oct 4
148:13-14 July 24
150:6 Mar 21

Proverbs
8:1 Mar 20
8:1, 10-11, 13-15 Nov 17
11:28 June 20
13:14 July 3
13:34 Oct 23
14:22 Mar 5
14:34 June 13
15:1 Aug 4
16:7 Oct 18
16:18 Oct 11
17:17 Mar 8
17:22 Sept 12
24:26 Jan 24

Ecclesiastes
3:1, 22 Nov 11
4:12 May 29
7:18 July 20
7:29 Mar 10
9:10 May 3

Song of Songs
1:3-4 Feb 29
3:5 Aug 13
8:6 May 26

Isaiah
6:8 Aug 31
11:1 Dec 20
11:6 Aug 15
11:7 Aug 12
11:9 Mar 1
28:21 Dec 11
31:6-7 Jan 2
30:15 Jan 9
40:3-4 Dec 2
40:31 Apr 13, Aug 9
42:7 Aug 22
45:3 Dec 22
53:6 Mar 24

53:4–5 Mar 28
61:1 Sept 23
64:5 June 23

Jeremiah
1:4 Jan 13
6:16 Jan 19
29:5 Nov 5
31:33 Apr 29
50:33–34, 39 Oct 31

Lamentations
3:23 Mar 31
3:28 Apr 15

Daniel
10:13 Sept 29
11:2 Oct 1
12:3 Aug 26

Hosea
2:17–18 July 23

Joel
2:12 Feb 19
2:28–29 May 23

Amos
2:11–12 Oct 13
5:6 Dec 8

Zechariah
2:6, 8 Sept 15
5:4 Dec 21
9:16 Nov 18
10:11 May 16

Malachi
3:10 Feb 4

Matthew
1:18–19 Dec 14

2:10–11 Jan 6
2:12 Jan 7
2:10–11 Dec 27
2:16–18 Dec 28
5:5 Sept 20
5:6 Aug 30
5:23–24 Nov 19
6:6 July 8
6:13 July 15
6:19–20 Feb 6, Aug 19
6:22 June 10
7:1 Feb 23
7:3, 5 Oct 9
7:28–29 Mar 9
10:37 Nov 20
10:38–39 June 12
11:5–6 June 6
11:15 Apr 14
11:29 June 18
12:20 Oct 10, Nov 21
16:18–19 Feb 22
17:2 Aug 6
18:10 Sept 30
21:21–22 Sept 5
21:28–31 Sept 20
23:8–9 Apr 22
23:21 Jan 28
23:37, 40 Apr 3
28:19 June 2

Mark
1:3 Nov 30
1:10–11 May 30
1:12 Feb 7
1:15 Sept 27
1:35 Feb 15
5:20 Nov 29
6:2–3 Sept 9
6:46–47 June 3
8:19–21 Apr 2
9:23 Dec 31
9:40 May 20

10:46–47, 52 Feb 8
10:48 Feb 8
12:1 July 1
15:47 Mar 30
16:17–18 Aug 17

Luke
1:26, 31–32 Dec 23
1:30, 35 Mar 25
2:7 Dec 25
2:9 Dec 24
2:15–16 Dec 26
2:76–79 Jan 10
2:39–40 Dec 29
2:40 Jan 15
3:5 Dec 7
3:16 Apr 26
3:21 Jan 14
4:42–43 Mar 3
5:5–6 Oct 16
5:30 Feb 7
6:36 Aug 18
6:38 Feb 5
7:26, 28 June 24
8:49 Apr 9
9:58 Jan 29
10:3 Jan 5
11:46 Sept 2
12:6–7 Aug 11
12:27 May 5
12:49 Apr 20
13:20–21 Feb 2
14:8, 10 Mar 16
16:9 Nov 27
16:10 May 13
18:13 Feb 25
19:31 Aug 3
23:43 Nov 6
25:53, 55–56 Mar 29

John
1:2, 4 Jan 31, Oct 27

1:14 Dec 18
2:8 Apr 18
4:6–7, 14 May 19
5:19; 8:28 Apr 12
7:38–39 Apr 19
10:10 June 21
13:4–5 Sept 7
14:12 Aug 29
15:14–15 Dec 3
16:28; 16:7 Dec 30
17:21 Jan 20
19:17, 19 Mar 26
20:11, 16–17 Apr 10
21:19 Dec 10

Acts
2:1, 7, 10–11 May 27
4:24, 30 Apr 17
5:3–4 Aug 28
5:12 July 16
7:59 Jan 26
8:36, 38 May 9
10:44, 45 June 7
12:7, 10, 12, 14 May 25
13:26 Nov 13
17:11 July 9
20:9–11 Apr 5
20:35 June 29
22:14 Jan 25

Romans
1:16 July 6
1:20 Aug 23
4:16–17 Jan 11
7:23–25 Dec 16
8:26–27 Mar 14
11:36 Aug 1
12:5 Jan 22
12:5, 27 Sept 4
12:7, 10 May 14
12:11 Apr 23
12:15–16 Sept 25

12:21 Mar 6
13:11 Nov 28

1 Corinthians
1:26–27 July 17
4:5 Dec 6
6:15, 20 May 10
9:20, 21–22 Oct 15
11:24 June 5
14:1 July 7
14:15 July 14
14:40 July 22
15:22 Apr 7
15:42–44 May 21
15:54 Oct 30
15:58 June 16

2 Corinthians
3:12 Mar 18
3:18 June 17
4:2 Sept 14
4:8–9 July 21
4:10–11, 14 Apr 8
5:1 Nov 8
6:17 Jan 17
6:10 Feb 26
7:2 July 13
12:2–3, 5 Nov 3
13:7–8 Apr 11
13:14 June 1

Galatians
3:28 July 27
4:19, 26, 31 July 18
5:16–17 Sept 6
5:22 Apr 24, 25
5:29 July 24
6:9–10 June 8
6:14 Sept 14

Ephesians
2:13, 19 May 24
3:17, 18–19 Apr 28

4:6 Feb 18
4:10 May 11
4:29 June 15
5:16 Jan 27
5:18 Apr 27
6:7 May 2
6:13 Feb 27
6:14–17 July 26

Philippians
2:2 Jan 18
2:6–7 Dec 14
3:13–14 Jan 1
4:12–13 July 5, July 30

Colossians
1:27 Jan 12
2:7 June 28
2:20 Oct 29
3:1 Apr 6
2:20, 3:1, 9–10 Apr 1

1 Thessalonians
4:14 Nov 9

2 Thessalonians
3:10 Mar 7

1 Timothy
3:16 July 29
4:8 Feb 20
6:6 Sept 13
6:7 Nov 16

2 Timothy
1:8 Feb 12
2:3–4 July 2
3:14–17 Oct 20
4:5 Sept 22
4:7–8 Sept 16

Titus
1:15 July 19

Philemon
4:7 Oct 22

Hebrews
2:18 Mar 12
3:19 Sept 11
11:33–34 Nov 15
11:37, 39 Feb 10
11:35 Apr 4
12:1 Nov 1
12:23 Sept 28
13:2 Nov 24

James
1:2 Feb 17
1:3–4 June 19
1:26, 3:6 Feb 21
2:1 Aug 20
3:7–8 Aug 21

1 Peter
2:17 Nov 23
2:24 Mar 27
3:15 Oct 14

2 Peter
5:3, 5 Oct 12

1 John
1:5 Feb 2
4:1, 5:19–20 Feb 28, June 11
5:21 Oct 21

Revelation
3:7, 5:5 Dec 17
5:11 Sept 28
7:1–3 Oct 2
13:18 Mar 23
20:12, 15 Dec 5

Sources and Acknowledgements

The publishers wish to express their gratitude to the following for permission to include copyrighted material in this book:

Geoffrey Ashe for the extract from *Avalonian Quest* (Fontana, 1984).

Ramon Beeching, Janet Donaldson, Michael Halliwell and Craig Roberts for their prayers as printed in *Pocket Celtic Prayers* (Church House, 1996).

Juliet Boobbyer and Joanna Sciortino, for extracts from *Columba: the Play with Music* (Fowler Wright Books Ltd., 1981).

Thomas Cahill, for the excerpt from *How the Irish Saved Civilization* (Doubleday, 1995).

Cambridge University Press, for excerpts from *Two Lives of Saint Cuthbert*, trans. Bertram Colgrave, (Cambridge University Press, 1985).

Ted Carr, for an extract of the spoken words to his song "I AM," part of the album *Mystic Prophet* (Red Cliff Sound Studios, 1994).

The Central Board of Finance of the Church of England, for the extract from *The Promise of His Glory* (Church House Publishing and Mowbray, 1991).

T & T Clark Ltd. for the extracts from the translation of St. Patrick's Breastplate in *Introduction to Celtic Christianity*, Mackey (ed.), 1989.

Darton, Longman & Todd Ltd, for the extract taken from *Living Between Worlds* by Philip Sheldrake, (Darton, Longman & Todd Ltd., 1995).

Oliver Davies and Fiona Bowie, for excerpts from *Celtic Christian Spirituality* (SPCK, 1995).

The Dean and Chapter of Durham Cathedral, for prayers from their booklet *The Spirit of the Cathedral*.

Edinburgh University Press for excerpts from *John, the Earliest Poetry of a Celtic Monastery*, Thomas Owen Clancy and Gilbert Markus, 1994.

Msg. Tom Fehily, for an extract from his leaflet on Christian meditation.

Tomas O Fiaich (trans.), *Columbanus, In His Own Words* (Veritas Publications, 1974).

Forest of Peace Publishing, Inc. for an extract from *Prayers for a Planetary Pilgrim* by Edward Hays, 1989.
Brian Frost, for excerpts from *Glastonbury Journey* (Becket Publications, 1986).
Gomer Press, for the excerpt from Eples by David Gwenallt Jones, 1960.
Michael Halliwell, for extracts from his booklet *Thou My Whole Armour*.
HarperCollins Publishers Ltd., for the extract from Mother Teresa, *Spiritual Counsel*, 1982.
Hannah Hopkin, *The Living Legend of St. Patrick* (Grafton Books, 1990).
Stephen Lawhead, for an extract from *Arthur: Book III of The Pendragon Cycle* (Lion Publishing, 1989).
Llanerch Publishers for excerpts from *The Life of Samson of Dol*, Thomas Taylor (trans.), 1991; from *Life of Saint Columba* by Adamnan, 1988; from *The Celtic Saints: The Lives of Ninian and Kentigern* by Joceline Ailred, 1989; and from *Lives of Saints from the Book of Lismore*, Whitley Stokes (trans.), 1995.
John and W. MacQueen, for extracts from *St. Nynia* (Polygon, 1990).
Kate McIlhagga, for prayers from *Seasons and Celebrations* (N.C.E.C., 1996).
The Northumbria Community Trust, for extracts from *A Way of Life, Rule of Life of the Northumbria Community*, 2009; also for a prayer taken from *Celtic Night Prayer*, "Into a Desert Place," (HarperCollins Publishers Ltd, 1996).
Brendan O'Malley, for extracts from *A Pilgrim's Manual: St David's* (Paulinus Press, 1985).
The Very Revd. J. S. Richardson, Bradford Cathedral, for two prayers from the Cathedral's *St Aidan Chapel Booklet*.
Oxford University Press, for excerpts from Bede's *The Ecclesiastical History of the English People*, ed. Bertram Colgrave and R. A.B. Mynors (Oxford University Press, 1969).
Richard Sharpe, for extracts from Adamnan of Iona's *Life of St. Columba* (Penguin Books, 1993).
SPCK, for excerpts from *The Open Gate* (1995) and *Border Lands* (2000), both by David Adam.

The Revd. Dr. Patrick Thomas, for extracts from *Candle in the Darkness* (Gomer Press, 1993).

University of Wales Press, for extracts from *Rhigyfarch's Life of Saint David*, J. W. James (trans.), 1967.

Robert Van de Weyer, for extracts from *Celtic Parables* (DLT, 1997); *Celtic Fire*, (DLT, 1996) and *The Letters of Pelagius: Celtic Soul Friend* (Arthur James, 1995).

Wild Goose Publications, for extracts from *The Whole Earth Shall Cry Glory* by George MacLeod, 2006; *Iona Community Worship Book*, 1991; *The Wee Worship Book* by F. Klemm, 1999.

Valentine Zander, for selections from *St. Seraphim of Sarov* (St. Vladimir Seminary Press, 1975).

Every effort has been made to trace the owners of copyright material, and we hope that no copyright has been infringed. Pardon is sought and apology made if the contrary be the case, and a correction will be made in any reprint of this book.

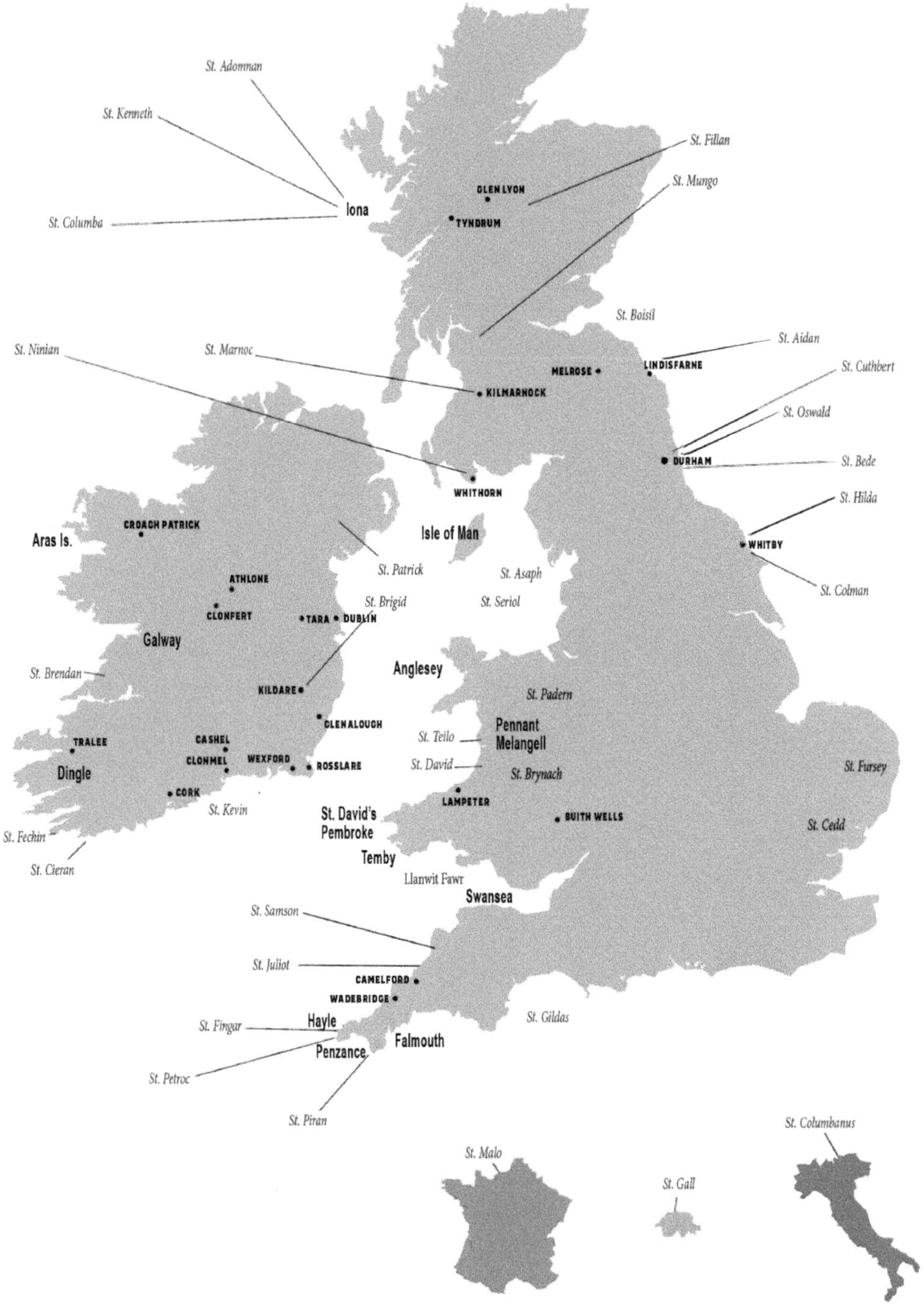
St. Adomnan
St. Kenneth
St. Fillan
St. Mungo
GLEN LYON
Iona
St. Columba
TYNDRUM
St. Boisil
St. Aidan
St. Ninian
St. Marnoc
MELROSE
LINDISFARNE
St. Cuthbert
KILMARNOCK
St. Oswald
DURHAM
St. Bede
WHITHORN
St. Hilda
CROAGH PATRICK
Aras Is.
Isle of Man
WHITBY
St. Patrick
St. Asaph
ATHLONE
St. Colman
St. Brigid
St. Seriol
CLONFERT
TARA
DUBLIN
Galway
St. Brendan
Anglesey
KILDARE
St. Padern
GLENALOUGH
Pennant
Melangell
TRALEE
CASHEL
St. Teilo
CLONMEL
WEXFORD
ROSSLARE
St. David
St. Fursey
Dingle
St. Brynach
CORK
LAMPETER
St. Kevin
St. David's
Pembroke
BUITH WELLS
St. Cedd
St. Fechin
Temby
St. Cieran
Llanwit Fawr
Swansea
St. Samson
St. Juliot
CAMELFORD
WADEBRIDGE
St. Gildas
Hayle
St. Fingar
Falmouth
Penzance
St. Petroc
St. Piran
St. Columbanus
St. Malo
St. Gall

CHECK OUT THESE OTHER TITLES FROM
RAY SIMPSON & ANAMCHARA BOOKS

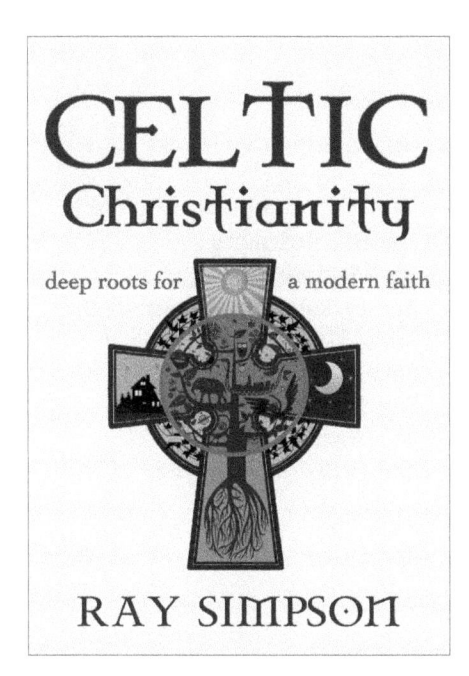

**Celtic Christianity:
Deep Roots
for a Modern Faith**
Author: Ray Simpson
Price: $24.95
Paperback
E-book Available
ISBN: 978-1-62524-058-3

The world of the long-ago Celts appeals to many of us in the twenty-first century. Whether we are looking to find our cultural heritage or are seeking an alternative to worn and restrictive religious forms, the earth-centered, woman-friendly, inclusive faith of the Christian Celts offers us a deep-rooted alternative approach to traditional Christianity. The Celts experienced "thin places," where they sensed the supernatural world; they honored their poets, singers, and artists; and they passionately followed the Christ of the Gospels. Theirs was a church without walls, which lived naturally and comfortably within the community. Ray Simpson, the founder and guardian of the modern-day Community of Aidan and Hilda on the Holy Island of Lindisfarne, has spent his life walking in their footsteps. Now he allows us to experience for ourselves the dynamic spirituality of the Christian Celts.

**Water from an Ancient Well:
Celtic Spirituality
for Modern Life**
Author: Kenneth McIntosh, M.Div.
Price: $24.95
Paperback
E-book Available
352 pages
ISBN: 978-1-933630-98-4

Discover the world of the ancient Celtic Christians and find practical insights for living in the twenty-first century. Using storytelling, careful research, and personal experience, the author invites you to get to know Brendan and Brigid, Columba and Patrick, as well as Myrddin (better known as Merlin) and other lesser-known figures from the great pageant of Celtic history. These stories both entertain and inspire; rooted in legend and history, they offer us here-and-now hope and insight.

"The author writes with humility; he does not prescribe. In the process, he takes us to places made sacred by inspired believers, depicting their lives as a romance that proved itself in everyday things. He invites us to enter into a similar divine love affair that involves the whole of life. This book could become a classic."
—Ray Simpson, author of *The Celtic Book of Days*; Founding Guardian of the International Community of Aidan and Hilda and Principal Tutor of its Celtic Christian Studies program. He lives on Britain's Island of Lindisfarne and writes a weekly blog on www.aidandhilda.org.

**Facing Death Now:
Practical Strategies
for a Good Death**
Author: Ray Simpson
Price: $19.95
Paperback
E-book Available
ISBN: 978-1-62524-274-7

We who live in the modern Western world seldom regard death as a friend. While other books may try to persuade us to think differently about this topic, Ray Simpson's book offers practical exercises that will reshape our thoughts, helping us face the end of life without fear.

An inspiring but practical resource for preparing for your own death, it includes stories from the deaths of both saints and ordinary people, thought-provoking quotations, scripture, and comforting prayers, as well as how to prepare a will and make funeral arrangements.

Like it or not, all of us will die one day. This heartening book suggests a more positive way to face death.

ANAMCHARA BOOKS
BOOKS TO INSPIRE
YOUR SPIRITUAL JOURNEY

In Celtic Christianity, an *anamchara* is a soul friend, a companion and mentor (often across the miles and the years) on the spiritual journey. Soul friendship entails a commitment to both accept and challenge, to reach across all divisions in a search for the wisdom and truth at the heart of our lives.

At Anamchara Books, we are committed to creating a community of soul friends by publishing books that lead us into deeper relationships with God, the Earth, and each other. These books connect us with the great mystics of the past, as well as with more modern spiritual thinkers. They are designed to build bridges, shaping an inclusive spirituality where we all can grow.

ANAMCHARA BOOKS
Vestal, New York 13850
www.AnamcharaBooks.com